Sovereign Fantasies

THE MIDDLE AGES SERIES

Ruth Mazo Karras, Series Editor
Edward Peters, Founding Editor

A complete list of books in the series
is available from the publisher.

Sovereign Fantasies

ARTHURIAN ROMANCE AND
THE MAKING OF BRITAIN

Patricia Clare Ingham

UNIVERSITY OF PENNSYLVANIA PRESS · Philadelphia

10 9 8 7 6 5 4 3 2 1

Published by
University of Pennsylvania Press
Philadelphia, Pennsylvania 19104–4011

Library of Congress Cataloging-in-Publication Data

Ingham, Patricia.
  Sovereign fantasies : Arthurian romance and the making of Britain /
Patricia Clare Ingham.
    p. cm. — (Middle Ages series)
  Includes bibliographical references (p.   ) and index.
  ISBN 0-8122-3600-9 (cloth : alk. paper)
    1. English literature—Middle English, 1100–1500—History and criticism.
2. Arthurian romances—History and criticism.   3. Literature and history—
Great Britain—History—To 1500.   4. Historical fiction, English—History
and criticism.   5. National characteristics, British, in literature.   6. Romances,
English—History and criticism.   7. Kings and rulers in literature.   8. Britons
in literature.   I. Title.   II. Series.
PR328 .I54   2001
809'.93351—dc21

00-066966

In memory of my parents
Dolores Gormley Ingham and Charles Grant Ingham

And for
Louise Aranye Fradenburg

Contents

Introduction

"A HISTORY without the imagination," wrote Jacques Le Goff, "is a mutilated, disembodied history" (5). Imagination, Le Goff implies, has the power to repair historical fragments, turning mutilated details into a coherent whole. Le Goff's striking image of a "disembodied" history without imagination links materiality with the imaginative faculty. History's special claim to the material and embodied comes not merely from facts about the past, but from what an imagination does with those facts. Le Goff thus rearranges what has been until recently the standard opposition between history (the Real, the material, and the embodied) and fiction (the imagined, the literary, and the textual). Our histories need imagination, Le Goff and many medievalists since insist, at least in part because, as Gabrielle Spiegel has suggested, "imaginary dreams" have the power to "motivate human behavior" (86). Such work has helped us see that fantasy and history have had a long acquaintance, and not simply because medieval writers about the past cared less for verisimilitude than did their modern or early modern counterparts. Indeed, as the 1839 text of the Middle English version of the *Travels of Sir John Mandeville* suggests, the imaginative faculty can assist in the very real process of creating empires. Imperial governments use, as that text puts it, "[a]lle here lust and alle here Ymaginacioun . . . for to putten alle Londes undre hire subjeccioun" [all their desire and all their imagination so as to put all lands under their control] (251).[1]

Le Goff emphasizes the unifying and synthetic power of the imagination; imagination, in this view, repairs mutilation, places pieces together, crafts wholeness out of parts. The remarks attributed to "Mandeville," in contrast, emphasize the role of the imagination in processes of conquest, annexation, and subjugation, thus hinting at the sinister side of imaginary unifications. Unity is an imaginary quality valuable to imperial governments and to processes of colonization. And yet processes of conquest, annexation, and subjugation can be said to unify only if we take a conqueror's perspective. As the history of the "Troubles" in Northern Ireland suggests, the value of unity is a matter of perspective: what from one view constitutes a longed-for unification, can also be experienced as a painful separation, a destructive fragmentation. Analyses of the imaginary syntheses of medieval history have had little to say about the colonizing uses of imagination and fantasy; medievalists have not examined as frequently as we might what traumas, losses, imaginary fragments, or contradictions fuel historic medieval legends. We have, as a result, often had less to say about the alternative histories, alternative imaginings also legible in medieval texts; we are often silent about the other dreams and desires sacrificed, often forcibly, to traumatic imperial, or national, unities.

This study takes seriously the role of imagination in making (and contesting) notions of union in late medieval Britain. *Sovereign Fantasies* examines romance narratives of Arthur from the late fourteenth and fifteenth centuries in the context of changing political and cultural identities in late medieval Britain. I argue that late Middle English Arthurian romance offers a fantasy of insular union, an "imagined community" of British sovereignty. Stories of Arthur, King of Britain, rework notions of insular British unity because Arthurian sovereignty can be used to designate an indigenous tradition (based upon its Welsh associations). As "native" folk hero, Arthur offers a royal legend grown on British soil. Yet tales of Arthur also point to the complications of community, the disaffections and aggressions that inhabit, and threaten, union. They thus offer a view of both how unions are crafted and how they break apart. In this way Arthur's court becomes a fiction of historic British sovereignty useful for competing accounts of British identity. Arthur's story can serve both those who wish to praise union and recommend centralization and those who wish to indict centralized power. The ambiguities of Arthurian geography— is his court at Caerlion or Carlisle, at Winchester or Camelot?—allude to historic struggles over the geography of British union, particularly to relations between central England and the regions of its so-called "Celtic Fringe." Tales of Arthur encode utopian hopes for communitarian wholeness; yet they also poignantly narrate the impossibilities, the aggressions, and the traumas, of British insular community.

The question of Arthur's "indigenous" British roots is, of course, a complicated one. Welsh fantasies of Arthurian sovereignty, for example, remind us that the colonized cultures of insular Britain had utopian dreams of their own, dreams pertinent to Arthurian traditions. While focused on Middle English texts from the later period, my study attempts to take seriously such dreams and the political and cultural oppositions they signify. Middle English romances of King Arthur are important in this regard for two reasons: first, they emerge with force at times of insular instability and change; second, they occupy (even in the twelfth century) a shared border between cultural identities of historic importance to British sovereignty: English, Welsh, and French.[2] Because of these specific attributes, Middle English Arthurian traditions offer an important site for viewing the intersections and dialogues between "oppositional" discourses and dominant cultural modes. These texts offer access to the shared dreamings and political contestations between England and Wales in the late medieval period. The historic legend of Arthur's rule over a lost insular wholeness (what Geoffrey of Monmouth terms the *totius insulae* of Britain) is important both to Welsh (and Scots) claims as rightful heirs of Britain's crown and to the ambitions of late medieval English kings in annexing Wales and Scotland. Fantasies of a pastoral, ancient, and united Britain ruled by sovereigns such as Arthur were at play differently, at different historical moments, and deployed by different groups. At stake both in the wide circulation of Arthurian traditions in the late Middle Ages, and in the difficulty in recognizing some of those stories as history, are contestations over the ownership of a British imaginary past, indeed of Britain itself.

To be sure, late Middle English texts emphasize the tragedy of Arthur's loss, only hinting at the glorious possibility of Arthur's return. Malory's *Morte Darthur* moves inexorably toward its tragic culmination; the Alliterative *Morte Arthure* mourns Arthur's fall from Fortune's Wheel; even the delightfully fantastic *Sir Gawain and the Green Knight* opens with a history of British kingship linked to treachery, war, and woe.[3] Late Middle English tales return again and again to the loss of fellowship and the death of Arthur. Because of their repetitive and poignant delectation of this tragic sovereign and his fragile, fractured community, these Middle English tales can help us see that narratives of fragmentation, of sovereign mutability and loss, might be just as culturally useful as stories that emphasize cultural unity, wholeness, or recovery. When romance stories of King Arthur narrate the mutability, failures, and infidelities surrounding the sovereign, they raise doubts about an unwavering united British past. Such doubts allude to a contested history of Britain, to other desires and lost dreams. Arthur's apocalyptic story can also, however, calibrate desire for a sovereign future. The tragic fragility of Arthur's fellowship heightens our longing, since we gain only the briefest glimpse of Arthurian chivalry and justice. Traditions of Arthur as the *Rex quondam, Rexque futurus* answer such longing with the image of a dying sovereign body passing away yet ever poised to recover the throne. This Arthur is already lost, yet still somehow perpetually surviving.

This image of the legendary King Arthur, lost and yet surviving, resonates with Ernst Kantorowicz's description of the influential early modern political theory known as the King's Two Bodies. Stories of Arthur past and future anticipate the combination of sovereign death and survival that will, in the early modern period, structure orthodox notions of sovereign power. Arthurian traditions of the past and future king gesture toward what Kantorowicz will term "sovereign sempiternity," a "plurality" of kingship that, according to Kantorowicz, "did not expand within a given Space but was determined exclusively by Time" (387). Sovereign sempiternity stabilizes the sovereign's right to rule by imagining his place in an unbroken train of rulers stretching out of the distant past. Sempiternity offers an "imagined community" of rulers through the ages, a fiction of sovereignty apparently unharmed by loss, death, or other "natural defects." It imagines a transcendent, sovereign "body politic" untouched by age or disability: "The king's body politic is a Body utterly void of Infancy and Old Age and other natural defects and imbecilities which the body natural is subject to, and for this cause what the king does in his Body politic cannot be invalidated or frustrated by a disability in his natural body." Despite its use of the metaphor of the royal body, the theory of the King's Two Bodies nevertheless disavows all the problems of bodiliness. The physical facts of "Infancy and Old Age and other natural defects and imbecilities" are imagined as utterly unlike the apparent durability of sovereign power. Power vests in a mystical body beyond particular times; it is transcendental power acting upon the material world. The King's Two Bodies thus homogenizes the multiplicity of rule and the fractious moments of state politics into the image of a solitary, united sovereign will, offering a tendentious image of state power as a monolithic unity. When the theory of the King's Two Bodies splits the physical mortality of kings from the "sempiternity" of the line of kingship, it promises state survival despite the vicissitudes, failures, and changeabilities of particular times and particular monarchs. It recasts sovereign death as a transcendental union outside individual sovereign bodies and lives, and thus copes with the poignant problem loss poses to individual agency and to state power. Its success as a political theory is marked in part by the ease with which histories of British sovereignty, despite prodigious "defects and imbecilities," can nonetheless trace a genealogy from Britain's early days.

Yet the political theory of the King's Two Bodies proved culturally powerful precisely because the survival of particular sovereigns was not, historically, so easily assured. Late medieval English aristocrats and royals had cause to fear for their perpetuity. Throughout the late fourteenth and fifteenth centuries, various groups vied for control of large portions of British territory. The fifteenth century is, of course, infamous for its problems of royal succession; it is also a period throughout which the English throne responded to crises of identity which, while "international" in scope, had "national" implications. Between 1380 and 1485 the crown, while at war with its putatively most infamous enemy, France, solidified the annexation of its geographically most intimate Celtic ally, Wales.[4] Welsh soldiers fought variously against the French and against the English during the Hundred Years War; Scottish soldiers more consistently supported the French against their colonizing enemy beyond the Tweed; the exiled English King Richard II fled to Cheshire seeking rebel support for his beleaguered monarchy; not far from Cheshire, Owain Glyn Dŵr organized what would become a very nearly successful home rule rebellion against Henry IV, appealing to the French crown for assistance; the Wars of the Roses fractured aristocratic communities in both London and the North; Henry Tudor, with ties to Wales and to France, killed a crowned Richard III at Bosworth field under the banner of Arthur, king of the Britons. The messianic figure of the Sovereign Returned (or the Welsh *Mab Darogan*), an image variously and repeatedly identified with Arthur Pendragon, appears in the politics of Glyn Dŵr's Cymric home-rule movement, and in the mythology of the apparently "British" Tudor who claims to unite Wales and England in his rule from a London court. This same period, moreover, witnessed a significant increase in the manuscript production of tales of Arthurian romance in England: *Sir Gawain and the Green Knight*; *Arthur*; *The Red Book of Hergest* (containing, among other things, the Welsh tales "Owein," "Peredur," "The Dream of Rhonabwy"); *The Marriage of Sir Gawaine*; the Stanzaic *Morte Arthur*; the Alliterative *Morte Arthure*; *Awntyrs off Arthure*; *Avowynge of King Arthur*; Henry Lovelich's *History of the Holy Grail*; Henry Lovelich's *Merlin*; *Weddyng of Sir Gawen and Dame Ragnall*; the prose *Merlin*; Malory's *Morte Darthur*; *Grene Knight*.[5] This book examines the intersection between this remarkably prolific cultural production and the political disputes over the meaning of Arthur's legendary kingship.

From the late fourteenth to the fifteenth century English sovereigns, the last Plantagenets, lose many of their territorial holdings in France.

Adversarial relations with France (seen in the Hundred Years War) and aristocratic fragmentation in England (as in the Wars of the Roses) will urge the elaboration of a specifically insular set of affairs. Middle English Arthurian traditions become a crucial means to explore England's historic indebtedness to, and intimacies with, insular cultures; yet those same traditions will also, in part, be the means whereby English sovereignty claims Welsh (and eventually Scots) loyalty away from the French. In is in this context that I read Arthurian tales as "sovereign fantasy": these stories allow nobles to repudiate their dynastic ties to their French cousins and (in the wake of the Hundred Years War) to claim an insular heritage. This "imagined community" across time enables the imagination of a parallel community across the space of a realm and united under its "sempiternal" kingship.[6]

A number of scholars have argued the case for linkages between late medieval theories of political sovereignty like that of Kantorowicz and Malory's *Morte Darthur*. Scholars are likewise examining the political import of individual Arthurian tales.[7] Those studies have made important interventions into an earlier opposition of the romance genre to the politics of history itself. The current study, while certainly interested in political readings of particular texts, foregrounds aspects of Arthurian romance thought to compromise the genre's political nature: its link to legend, its delectation of loss, its interest in death, its fascination with prophecy, its incorporation of strangeness and magic. These are the aspects of legend usually thought to be opposite the *realpolitik* of statecraft; yet these same attributes impel the material power of Arthurian fantasy. This is, I argue, because they offer a way of understanding the fascination with loss, trauma, fragmentations, and disaffections—the drives and desires that circulate within group identities, yet which rhetorics of union or enduring sovereign genealogies seek to disavow. I will argue that late-medieval British Arthurian legend has broad and far-reaching cultural ambitions. Those ambitions can be read in the tropes that signal the failures of and resistances to a monolithic community: in the losses that accrue to Arthur, and in the various Arthurs imagined in the contradictory multiplicities of romance and legend.

Middle English Arthurian traditions organize an extended meditation on British ruin, a poignant and abjected sovereignty that fascinates through its representations of pleasure and pain, longing and loss. This "sovereign fantasy" obtains in both senses of the phrase: *sovereign* here means both the King and the power (pretended or legitimate) to hold or

to contest rule; *fantasy* signifies both (as often in the colloquial sense) utopian hopes for imagining a different world and (as often in psychoanalytic
use) the *jouissance* (enjoyment) that surfaces through desire. Psychoanalytic
treatments of fantasy emphasize the limitations fantasy places on pleasure,
structuring an enjoyment that resides "beyond the pleasure principle."
Arthurian romances, especially in their Middle English emphasis upon destruction and death, fascinate through stories of hopeless impossibility.[8] I
am thus interested in a psychoanalytic notion of fantasy for its explication
of enjoyment as, paradoxically, "pleasure in unpleasure"; yet I also deploy
the term *fantasy* to signal more utopian possibilities.

Louise Fradenburg has shown us that the fascinations of romance can
offer subversive pleasures, since both "the transformation and preservation of relations of power depend on the fantastic pleasure of imagining
the world otherwise" ("Fulfild of Faerye" 220). My interest in claiming
Arthur as "sovereign fantasy" registers these fantastic pleasures too: the
imaginative expansiveness and interpretive play of Arthur's rule over archaic Britain signals hope for utopian community, for insular wholeness
as a promise of satisfaction. I explore when and how the Arthurian promise of satisfaction "preserves" the power of English rule, yet I also note
when and how it encodes the desire to transform or to resist such rule. In
its psychoanalytic meaning, moreover, *sovereign fantasies* gains a purchase
upon the material consequences of imaginative texts. It can help us read
the longstanding controversies over the "truths," historical or otherwise,
of Arthur's story. Shared fascinations with Arthur, furthermore, channel
antagonisms across insular space, between (for example) the Welsh and
Anglo-Norman audiences of Geoffrey of Monmouth's *Historia regum Britanniae*, or among England's regions.[9] Early modern Arthurian editors (as
in William Caxton's edition of Malory's *Morte Darthur*) or authors (as in
Edmund Spenser's epic *The Faerie Queene*) view Arthur as the genealogy
necessary for imagining a British national future; those imaginings depend
upon the losses and the antagonisms crucial to this earlier romance tradition. Finally, my use of the term *fantasy* is meant to signal an interest in
how these romances work both subjectively and culturally, that is, both for
exploring the desires of particular subjects and for encoding broad contests
concerning a British "imagined community."

I have, up to now, avoided using the term *nation*, while also repeatedly deploying the phrase that cannot help at the present moment but
evoke it: "imagined community." My phrase, like my thinking, is indebted
to Benedict Anderson's monumentally influential *Imagined Communities:*

Reflections on the Origin and Spread of Nationalism. The present study marks a set of medieval identifications that suggest the need to qualify Anderson's (but not only his) insistence on the "nation's" modernity, on what Anderson calls its "astonishing youth." I do not, however, simply appropriate Anderson's analysis for a late medieval case. It would be difficult to do so since Anderson, as Kathleen Davis has shown in detail, conceptualizes nation precisely through an absolute difference from things medieval. Anderson defines national affiliations as possible only after the *loss* of three "medieval" perceptions: sensibilities having to do with religion (a consciousness of international Christendom), state power (a confidence in dynastic sovereignty), and time (typological notions of history). The importance of these "medieval" sensibilities to his analysis means that Anderson must ignore the particularity and variability of medieval cultures in favor of the familiar caricature of historical difference which "medieval" so often signifies in scholarship of later periods. This has made *Imagined Communities* an account of nation that medievalists love to hate; but Anderson's work has also been useful for medievalists, as Michelle Warren argues, precisely because "imagined community" offers a substantial conceptual flexibility. Deploying this flexibility, medievalists have, sometimes without referencing Anderson explicitly, offered lots of examples that belie Anderson's historicism.[10]

There is, pace Anderson, a tradition within medieval studies suggesting the significance of national formulations to medieval politics. More than fifty years ago, V. H. Galbraith linked medieval concepts of nationality with the content of a people's language and customs. Joseph Strayer stressed the "medieval origins" of the "modern state." Susan Reynolds suggested confluences between the term *gens* and later developments of nation, arguing that "regnal communities" developing around a particular court have similarities to later formulations of nationhood. With Reynolds's work in mind, R. James Goldstein demonstrates the profoundly nationalistic aims of the "regnal communities" in medieval Scotland. And in a recent study of English language and literature for *England, the Nation* in the thirteenth and fourteenth centuries, Thorlac Turville-Petre argues that "the similarities between medieval and modern expressions of national identity [are] fundamental, and the differences [are] peripheral" (v).[11]

Yet my work diverges from these accounts in various ways. In Galbraith's and Strayer's account, for example, nation figures as a relatively organic identity, a modern wholeness that can be traced genealogically back to a point of medieval origin. Interested as they were in tracking stable coherences through time, these studies tend to depend upon a progressive chronology, imagining the history of "a people," as a teleological trajectory from early origins to a fully realized national present. I seek, on the other hand, to analyze the psychic and political instabilities of such fictions of wholeness so as to read the political and cultural disputes over the people's identity. I am not, therefore, arguing for a teleological history, nor am I claiming that Arthurian texts "develop" into later discourses of the nation. This would be a foolish claim since, from the long view of history, Arthurian traditions play out very differently even in the different insular spaces of England, Wales, and Scotland. Welsh prophecies linked to Merlin, for example, will appear in texts of Welsh resistance to English control well into the eighteenth century; but this is not, of course, the case in England, where Arthurian traditions (after Spenser's *Faerie Queene*) nearly vanish altogether until their reemergence in Tennyson's nineteenth-century medievalism.

Sovereign Fantasies argues that medieval community is imagined not through homogeneous stories of a singular "people," but through narratives of sovereignty as a negotiation of differences, of ethnicity, region, language, class, and gender.[12] While I am indebted to Susan Reynolds's suggestion that aristocratic groups identified with a particular king (what she usefully calls "regnal communities") cohere with later ideas of a nation, I also wish to show that such identifications work variously for different groups, often through antagonisms, or in oppositional ways. Reynolds suggests that dynastic formations can produce "imagined communities"; I hope to show that corporate desire for legendary sovereignty suggests not—as Anderson would have it—confidence in a divinely ordained ruler, but controversial and contentious identifications with sovereign power, identifications that channel anxieties about, even critiques of, specific royal genealogies. This also suggests that, unlike many (but not all) modern imaginings, this nation takes the *sovereign* as a primary organizing figure around whom divergent groups build or contest alliance. And while I share Turville-Petre's interest in noting similarities between medieval and modern, especially in response to the claim that "medieval nation" is an oxymoron, I remain wary of assigning differences (whether historical or cultural) to a "periphery," both because the politics of the "periphery" are very much at issue here, and because nation is such a variable, protean concept.

Yet difference is still only half of the story I want to tell. The historic shared sovereignty (not to mention the relative geographic nearness) of

England and Wales demonstrates in a particularly intense way that "difference" here is not absolute, signifying instead a complex of shared spaces, histories, and imaginings. It is the combination of shared imaginings and differential politics embedded in British Arthuriana that I attempt to convey through the concise term *national fantasy*, one that I will employ throughout this study.[13] I hope in what follows it will be clear that while this oppositional "imagined community" shares some attributes with later such imaginings, it is not their teleological ancestor.

Focusing on a particular time of imagining and contesting British identity, I am also surveying broadly, hoping to contribute to an analysis of the similarities and differences that mark this identity across a *longue durée*. The legendary, prophetic return of a British *totam insulam* suggests that the cadence of this insular identity might not be linear and chronological so much as recursive, repeating at times of cultural instability, or during transitional periods.[14] As a lost yet promised figure of insular wholeness, a late medieval imaginary *tota insula* alludes to ancient British days while it also encodes massive political, geographic, and military losses for England, Scotland, and Wales, not the least of which involves the loss of England's long-standing claims to sovereignty in France. Those claims, from one view a lingering consequence of Norman Conquest, suggest the complex dynamics of the insular with the continental, and demand that we frame the history of medieval Britain as a study of the interdependence of cultures, of histories of exchange, violent as well as peaceful, traumatic as well as pleasurable, sexual as well as political.[15] The polyglot culture of late medieval Britain deploys a language and custom forged out of repetitive intercultural encounters. The conquering ambitions of Roman, Viking, Saxon, and Norman follow in succession in an insular history of intercultural exchange, migration, conquest, and coexistence. Scholars of the relations between medieval England and the regions of its insular neighbors continue to disentangle the legacies of conquest from the narratives of "British" history, literature, and culture.[16]

This *longue durée* of Britain's identity is thus embedded in a history of conquest.[17] Of course medieval Britain is also one of the formerly colonized spaces of the Roman Empire. The colonial inheritance of Britain's early years—an imperialism J. S. P. Tatlock nearly fifty years ago described as an "unavoidable" motif in Geoffrey of Monmouth's *Historia regum Britanniae*—haunts the fantasy of British insular wholeness. Arthur's association with Geoffrey of Monmouth's story of imperialism, and with a conquered Welsh "native" tradition, marks this story as a particular scene of such literary and historiographic engagements. Many of the Middle English tales make explicit reference to Britain's colonial past or to Emperor Arthur's imperial ambitions. Admittedly the medieval understanding of the category of emperor, as Felicity Riddy recently put it, "has to do with royal sovereignty and jurisdiction, not territorial expansion." She continues, "it means that the king has the powers of the Roman emperor within his own realm" (69).[18] From the view of the English kings, then, claims to territory they considered part of England (even if the territory was in France or in Wales) amounted to their recovery of a rightful inheritance. The assumption that medieval definitions of sovereignty were therefore non-imperial deserves interrogation, however. For as Riddy also suggests, from the perspective of vanquished peoples, those who disputed England's claim in the first place, English kings were imperialist "in the modern sense [since they] held [territory] by terror" (69). Furthermore, Roman imperial models of sovereignty gesture toward long-standing legacies of Rome's colonization of Britain, indeed, of Europe. Territorial claims of rightful inheritance have a long history of imperial uses; in the twentieth century Afrikaner landowners used such justifications as part of the political mythology of apartheid.[19] Those justifications testify to the complexity and intransigence of relations of conquest and settlement rather than to their absence.

The difference between medieval and modern colonialisms has exerted substantial influence on the growing number of medievalists working on the topic.[20] The list of medievalists analyzing settlement, conquest, linguistic minorities, and crusade is a long and vibrant one, to which much has recently been added. Recent work inspired, implicitly and explicitly, by the rich and powerful insights of postcolonial cultural studies, suggests that medievalists can contribute much to an analysis of the repetitions and patternings of conquest, violence, and desire at different historical moments, and different geographic sites.[21] As is probably clear by now, I am particularly interested here in the relations between dominant European cultures and those groups Felipe Fernandez-Armesto calls Europe's "internal primitives," among whom he numbers the Welsh. Specifically the intimacies of conquest, the complicated interminglings of cultures different from, yet also in proximity with, one another are of crucial importance to me. Recent theorists of postcolonial cultural studies (particularly Homi Bhabha and Sara Suleri, but also, if in a different way, Benita Parry) have addressed just such questions and, as a result, their work will be important to the analysis that follows.

Yet, from the vantage of historical chronology, the premodern period seems far indeed from a postcolonial one. Bill Ashcroft, Gareth Griffiths, and Helen Tiffin, editors of *The Post-Colonial Studies Reader*, offer a definition of postcolonial that moves its signification from a temporal chronology to the spaces of opposition. They write, "post-colonial . . . does not mean 'post-independence,' or 'after colonialism,' for this would be to falsely ascribe an end to the colonial process." They continue, "Post-colonialism, rather, begins from the very first moment of colonial contact. It is the discourse of oppositionality which colonialism brings into being. In this sense, postcolonial writing has a very long history" (117).[22] With this definition in mind one could rightly say that medieval studies has a long history of postcolonial inspirations. Yet other areas of overlap exist between medieval and postcolonial cultural studies. For one thing, postcolonial scholars and medievalists share a common appreciation of the problems that progressivist, or teleological chronologies pose for an understanding of the complicated sophistication of so-called primitive cultures. Medievalists navigate the problem of teleology in various ways, sometimes stressing what has been called the "orientalism" of medieval studies, its historical disciplinary development during the nineteenth-century Age of Empire. Other approaches try to replace a linear temporality from medieval to modern with a sense of time as multiple and overlapping, what Jeffrey J. Cohen has called the "interminable difficult middle" ("Midcolonial," 5).[23] I hope to contribute to the longstanding medievalist concern for oppositional histories of linguistic minorities; yet I will also, if obliquely, address this "difficult middle." In the case of Wales, for example, we can mark no time after colonization (Wales remains a colony of England to the present), nor is it possible to recover a pure space before. I offer no claim about Welsh Arthurian origin, nor would I insist upon pure "Celtic" or "English" texts. I wish instead to take seriously the repetitive temporal returns to Arthur, as well as the oppositions, the heterogeneities, and the overlapping cultures legible in the difficult middle spaces, the shared Arthurian texts produced amidst conquest.

My interest in this approach has developed from a concern for the politics of "imagining community" during transitional times in Britain's insular identity. Scholars increasingly argue that the nation emerges not prior to, but in relation with, the conquering impulse. Their insights gesture toward, but do not adequately develop, the poignant losses produced by unified national identities. By joining a sovereign "imagined community" with an attention to the oppositional imaginings of Britain in the later Middle Ages, I hope to provide a way of registering some of the losses that, in early modern England, silently serve formal discourses of nationhood.

Interested as I am in the multiple and conflictual elements that are (seemingly) surmounted by narrations of cultural unity, my study shows debts to Homi Bhabha's analysis of the slips and misses of apparently un-equivocal national discourses. Bhabha's insights have been helpful, yet the medieval case also registers certain differences. Bhabha reads "the language of culture and community" as "poised on the fissures of the present be-coming the rhetorical figures of a national past" (*Location*, 142). I wish to construct an account of early ruptures and contests frequently deemed inconsequential to later "British" cultural identity. Bhabha argues that national discourses stabilize a culture's present instabilities by imagining those difficulties in the past, surmounted through modernity. My work suggests that those same discourses can, for all their interest in past an-tagonisms, obscure oppositional histories, trivializing the antagonisms and fissures on which they nonetheless depend. The medieval "middle spaces" of a *longue durée* of British identity, thus, encode losses of important material consequence.

A sustained attention to loss and mourning elucidates the dynamics of cultural identities in conquest, helping us to analyze who is served most by the gains and sacrifices of community. The losses produced by national centralization can be seen particularly clearly by scholars of periods be-fore centralization was bureaucratically solidified. What has not often been noted about national imaginings is the extent to which fantasies of unifi-cation encode mournful things even as they try to disavow them. National fictions must imagine a coherent identity that crosses both time and space despite the passings that constitute history, or the aggressions that consti-tute community. They must, to recall Le Goff's formulation with which I began, cope precisely with the mutilations and disembodiments produced by death. Coping which such facts can involve (as it does in the theory of the King's Two Bodies) disavowing the threatening, physical facts of death, "old age and other natural defects and imbecilities," removing these attributes of loss from the fiction of a transcendent, abstract, community outside particular bodies and beyond the reach of the grave. In this fantasy the community both requires particular bodies and can nonetheless outlast them; the sempiternal community apparently remains above the particular desires, disabilities, and lives on which it nonetheless depends.

Gender and sexuality have long been linked—in psychoanalytic, feminist, and anthropological theory—to the power to cope with the psychic and cultural problems of death, loss, and submission. Thus, the work of feminist, psychoanalytic, and anthropological theorists will also be important to my readings. Elisabeth Bronfen reads images of dead or deadly beauties for their ability to translate "an anxiety into a desire," that is, to make the image of death appear desirously irresistible, rather than anxiously so. Julia Kristeva suggests that abject images and the "death-bearing woman" can help the male author cope with fears of individual annihilation. Klaus Theweleit has examined the psychoanalytic logics of such "male fantasies," poignantly arguing that gendered imaginaries like these have material power with tragic consequences for women's lives. Anthropologist Maurice Bloch describes the cultural assignment of physical decay and fragmentation to women. He argues that hierarchically structured "traditional societies" cope with the threats that bodily decay pose to belief in a community's survival by splitting the morbid aspects of physical decay from the notion of death as a spiritual union, a life beyond the grave. Death as transcendent community, Bloch argues, remains linked to men and to brotherhoods. Triumph over "death (in its polluting and sad aspects)," Bloch argues, "is achieved by breaking through, vanquishing the world of women, of sorrow, of death and division" (217–18). Women's cultural relation to the particularity of individual birth means that women come to stand for the individuality of particular dying bodies and particular fragmented lives, an image of division that threatens the fiction of the transcendent, unified clan or community. Fradenburg has noted the extent to which psychoanalytic analyses of loss work to install loss as the condition of individual subjectivity with disastrous consequences for women's lives.[24]

The long-standing cultural identification of women with particularity and with particularly fractured losses can readily be seen in stories of Arthur's death; these texts, moreover, frequently raise questions about women's complicity in the destruction of fellowship. Putatively disordered, even destructive, female desires, rendered through figures like Guinevere, Morgan le Fey, or Bertilak's Lady, prove powerful enough to threaten, if not entirely dismantle, sovereign community. As the previous discussion implies, I will be arguing that the national fantasy emerging in late Middle English Arthurian texts deploys a gendered structure of loss so as to define community as a brotherhood that can accommodate a certain amount of regional and ethnic difference. Women are powerful in these texts, and their desires are important. They constitute repetitive obstacles to communitarian wholeness, disruptions to communitarian desire. These are nonetheless stories of a certain kind of female power, and thus they hint at alternative desires for other kinds of groupings.

Given the sheer volume of late Middle English texts of Arthurian romance, I cannot hope to offer satisfying accounts of the entire Middle English corpus. The study that follows, therefore, makes no claims to be exhaustive. Part I, "The Matter of Britain," makes the case for the subtle cultural relation between Arthurian history and Arthurian fantasy. Chapter 1 begins with the controversies over the historicity of Geoffrey of Monmouth's *Historia regum Britanniae*, and their pertinence to current debates on history and textuality. Emphasizing Geoffrey's ambiguity, I argue that the popularity and cultural usefulness of Monmouth's fantasy of the Britons involves its ability to accommodate diverse uses. The manuscript history of Geoffrey's text suggests, moreover, that representations of insular loss can help consolidate competing claims on insular inheritance, serving both the pleasures of parvenu Anglo-Norman aristocrats and their Welsh resisters. Chapter 2 moves to the uses of Geoffrey's text in the fifteenth century, focusing particularly upon the oppositional politics of the Merlin Prophecies. I examine what it means that such prophecies, based upon Welsh vaticinative poetry, came to fuel diametrically opposed political agendas, and how those contestations led to the increasing identification of certain versions of Britain's past with interpretive "truth." Imaginative ambiguity, as the Merlin Prophecies suggest, is deeply useful to fifteenth-century English sovereigns who wish to imagine themselves, in the wake of losses in France, as Arthur's insular heirs. Yet that same ambiguity is deeply disturbing to those in power, since it can also be used to legitimate the claims of rebel royal pretenders.

Part II, "Romancing the Throne," examines the romance's structure of longing and loss for a cultural imagining. In Chapter 3, I read Arthur's status as both European emperor and British sovereign in the Alliterative *Morte Arthure* for collocations between European international identities and insular British ones. The Alliterative *Morte Arthure* provides a way of renouncing Arthur's Welsh connections without having to jettison all hope for a united insular future. The poem's poignant concern with the slaughter of innocents, moreover, encodes the longing and losses of conquest, losses that nonetheless offer consolation to the male, aristocratic subject. Chapter 4 examines the complicated Welsh geography of a text that makes use of French traditions, *Sir Gawain and the Green Knight*. I make the case for reconsidering the magical elements of the Green Knight and the geography of Gawain's journey as a kind of colonial exoticism, one that nonetheless alludes to alternative (Welsh) claims on Arthurian sovereignty. Situated at a colonial frontier, *Gawain* deploys the intimacies of gender and sexuality to compensate for the limitations that a borderland position places on Gawain's agency. The apparent evil machinations of women work here, moreover, to rescue Arthur's sovereignty (and Gawain's agency) from the implication that it might be unmanly and frivolous. Chapter 5 addresses, through the adultery plot of the Stanzaic *Morte Arthur*, the common identification of women with the romance genre. I reconsider this Middle English version of an originally French story in the context of the militarized culture of the Hundred Years War. Like the previous two texts, the Stanzaic *Morte Arthur* addresses questions of insular community as it raises the issue of female guilt. And it links women with a particularly hopeless kind of loss. This poem thus suggests that medieval Arthurian romance might be a particularly tragic genre for women.

Where Part II focuses attention on a Welsh-French-English cultural triangulation, Part III, "Insular Losses," examines insular and regional collocations in some fifteenth-century texts. In Chapter 6, rivalry and brotherhood take center stage in two shorter romances from the north of the island: *The Avowing of Arthur* and *Awntyrs off Arthure at the Terne Wathelyn*. Both texts offer poignant evidence that chivalric rivalry disciplines knights. Knightly victimization and sacrifice remain crucial to the creation of Arthur's brotherhood. In the context of the Wars of the Roses, moreover, these texts suggest regional critiques of Arthur that can be read as contestations over the geography of insular British union. Female aggression and brotherly heterosexuality function in these texts as means to cope with the losses and deaths required by militarism. My final chapter considers Malory's massive tome, *Le Morte Darthur*. I join those who position this volume in the context of England's territorial losses in France; yet, against the grain of Malory's text, I read the poignant tale of Arthur's loss as a fantasy that can provide hope for historical coherence while accommodating innovation and change, the very things Malory deplores as "newfangleness." *Le Morte Darthur* thus implies the necessity of eschewing old loyalties for new ones; by the early modern period, Welsh and English, Yorkist and Lancastrian have all had to refashion their hearts and memories to a London-based Britain and for an Arthur whose court is at Winchester. The Afterword moves this study into the early modern period, suggesting very briefly the implications of this work would have for a reading of Edmund Spenser's *Faerie Queene*.

In its analysis of legend and its attention to historico-literary fantasies, this study foregrounds the fantasmatic character of communitarian loyalties and loves. The nation is always an illusion, a fantasy of wholeness that threatens again and again to fragment from the inside out. Fantasies of national identity teach peoples to desire union; they help inculcate in a populace the apparent "truth" that unity, regulation, coordination, and wholeness are always better, more satisfying and more fascinating, than the alternatives. Yet in order to promote desires for national unity, the nation, its core identity, must appear to have always already been there, poised to fascinate its people, and ready to be desired.[25] And this too, as we will shortly see, is one of the riches of Arthurian romance. Arthurian tales constitute powerful fantasies because they trace a heritage to the most ancient of British days. Through Arthur an increasingly literate public can learn to desire a unified future by delighting in the imagined glories of a unified past.

PART I
The Matter of Britain

CHAPTER ONE

Arthurian Imagination and the "Makyng" of History

I have not been able to discover anything at all on the kings who lived here before the Incarnation of Christ, or indeed about Arthur and all the other who followed on after the Incarnation. Yet the deeds of these men were such that they deserve to be praised for all time. What is more, these deeds were handed joyfully down in oral tradition, just as if they had been committed to writing, by many peoples who had only their memory to rely on.

—Geoffrey of Monmouth, *Historia regum Britanniae*[1]

This is the Arthur about whom the trifles of the Britons rave even now, one certainly not to be dreamed of in false myths, but proclaimed in truthful histories—indeed, who for a long time held up his tottering fatherland, and kindled the broken spirits of his countrymen to war.

—William of Malmesbury, *Gesta regum Anglorum*

KING Arthur has long been subject to controversy. Even in the twelfth century, as the quotes from William of Malmesbury and Geoffrey of Monmouth suggest, Arthur's relationship to Britain's past was a vexed one. Malmesbury, on one hand, deplores some stories about Arthur as "delirium"; Monmouth, on the other, seems troubled that such Arthurian traditions had not yet influenced the "official" histories of his time.[2] In response Monmouth's *Historia regum Britanniae* offers the fullest (and most influential) account of Arthurian sovereignty of his day, rendering stories of Arthur in the prestigious, and official, language of Latin. But twelfth-century history writers (followed by more than a few of their twentieth-century readers) would vehemently condemn Geoffrey's work as an excessively extravagant fiction.

William of Malmesbury, Gerald of Wales, and William of Newburg all judge Geoffrey's history to be flawed, and unflatteringly contrast his work with the Venerable Bede's sacred history. Their criticisms emphasize the falseness of Geoffrey's popular account, characterizing the distinction between Geoffrey's and other narratives of early Britain in the opposition of fiction to truth. Geoffrey's "false myths" are stacked against the "truthful histories" read in William's work and Bede's, an opposition which recurs even today. Malmesbury's opposition of "false myths" to "truthful histories," moreover, raises an issue important to readers of history and literature both in Monmouth's time and in our own. The relation of historical narrative to imaginative literature has been the subject of rich and persistent analysis for at least a quarter of a century; Arthurian scholars and devotees continue to debate Arthur's historicity, and their discussions frequently complicate the standard opposition of fact to fable. Malmesbury's remarks suggest, however, that there may be other issues at stake in this opposition than a simple search for the truth.

William of Malmesbury alludes to the cultural power of Arthur's image, invoking the historic king as support for a tottering fatherland and praising Arthur's monumental greatness, a hero who can "kindl[e] the broken spirits of his countrymen to war" (*quippe qui labantem patriam diu sustinuerit, infractasque civium mentes ad bellum acuerit*). Truthful histories need figures like Arthur, Malmesbury implies, sovereign icons to inspire and captivate their countrymen. Yet a captivating Arthur, Malmesbury also suggests, has a dangerous relation specifically to the "trifles" of the raving Welsh (*Britonum nugae hodieque delirant*).[3]

Emphasizing Arthur's popular appeal, Malmesbury insists that Arthur's popularity can sponsor his nation's endurance. Though deeply admired, Arthur's popularity is also suspect: Arthur apparently inspires excessive ravings among the Welsh. Malmesbury's condescension toward the "trifles" of the Welsh, the strength of his rhetoric in casting Welsh stories as delirium, intimates disquieting elements to Arthur's power. Arthur's apparently dangerous inspirations, Malmesbury anxiously implies, need to be constrained by historical accounts officially sanctioned as "true."

In this chapter I will argue that this anxiety about popular belief haunts the denigration of Geoffrey of Monmouth's imaginative history as "false." I will suggest, moreover, that accounts of early British history that pit the excesses of Monmouth's extravagant fiction against other, more sober truths implicitly encode fears about the popularity and the cultural power of his text. Such charges work anxiously to disavow the somewhat disturbing fact (one hinted even by Malmesbury) that popular "ravings" can indeed change the world. Yet Malmesbury's assertion that some popular fantasies are advantageous while others are simply false requires a very delicate negotiation of the categories of truth and fiction he deploys. If Malmesbury disavows Welsh fantasies as delirious falsehoods, he also reminds us that fantasy itself (and the widespread inspiration it provides) is useful to governments, offering the stirring of hearts that move a populace to fight a war, or support, at great personal sacrifice, a sovereign's claim to the throne.[4] This paradox of popular fantasy means that governments will work hard to produce and manage, as well as to constrain, the popular power of belief.

The enduring popularity of Monmouth's captivating story indicates the power of Arthur for belief in British sovereignty. What is not often emphasized in accounts of Arthurian romance in England is the extent to which the meaning of British sovereignty in Arthur's story (the cultural uses made of Arthur for various political projects) was contested throughout England, Wales, and Scotland from Monmouth's time well into the late medieval period. Fantasies of Arthur and his return fueled diametrically opposed, as well as intimately related, political agendas: Edward III's imperial pageantry, along with both Owain Glyn Dŵr's rebellion against the English crown, and Henry Tudor's (later Henry VII) battle for it. In the context of that history, efforts to identify some Arthurian sovereign fantasies as "untrue" despite their popularity will obscure, rather than reveal, the histories of political, social, and cultural exchange in medieval Britain. We need instead to consider what medieval "popular" and "official" accounts of Arthur might suggest about the process by which some beliefs about Britain were transformed into national fact, while others were rendered literally outlandish, increasingly unimagined and, thus, unimaginable.

Fantasy's role in processes of cultural identification, and the historical legitimization of some, and not other, fantasies of Arthur can help us understand the importance of myth and legend to the history of British community. I begin with a brief account of the contributions medieval studies has made to our understanding of history's relation to the fantastic. I follow medievalists who argue that psychoanalysis can help us to interpret the desires, the pleasures, and the powers embedded in historico-legendary texts. Unlike approaches to myth that oppose legend to historical realism, and unlike traditionally psychological approaches to Arthuriana that link specific stories or story cycles to transcendental processes of a universal or collective unconscious, I engage psychoanalysis with historical specificity, so as to understand the fascination and popularity of certain tales at particular historical moments. Psychoanalysis can help us see the material consequences of belief, reminding us that fantasies, even in the absence of what could be identified as historical fact, can and do affect the world.

To remark that fantasy does not require fact to have effects upon the world does not mean, of course, that fantasy is the opposite of history. I will suggest below a way to understand the relation between history and popular fantasy. Following this discussion, I turn my attention to Geoffrey of Monmouth's fantasy of a British past. In the second and third sections of this chapter I argue that Geoffrey's deft use of ambiguity and imagination makes the outlandish traditions of a linguistic minority useful–indeed, crucial–to the rulers of Anglo-Norman England. Geoffrey's ingenious history recasts largely ignored Welsh literary-historical traditions into the authoritative form of Latin manuscript culture; in so doing, Geoffrey renders Welsh traditions useful to those in the very centers of power. The consequences of this are multiple and long-standing. Geoffrey's acts of translation, alongside Geoffrey's own historical method, suggest that we might view him as an historical innovator, an intellectual who offers an important intervention into twelfth-century historiography, and crafts an influential fantasy productive for an oppositional history of British identity.

Fantasy, Fact, and Popular Pleasures

The debate between Malmesbury's "truthful history" and Geoffrey's "false myths" no longer dominates conversations among scholars of early Britain; yet the questions implicitly raised by Geoffrey's text are as hotly debated today as they apparently were in the twelfth century.[5] The categories of history and textuality have been important to medieval literary studies, a field itself long associated with an opposition between textual methodologies (New Criticism) and historicist ones (Exegetics). As a result medievalists have had much to say about these questions.

In the last twenty years, medievalists have complicated our understanding of the relation between history and imagination, arguing against a strict opposition between the truth of history and the power of the fictional.[6] Paul Strohm, for example, suggests that fictionality is "no embarrassment to history," since "fabulists and romancers conceive episo within imaginary structures or value systems their audiences embra true, and lies accepted as a basis for actions gain retrospective truthfulness through their influence on events" (3). Stressing a reciprocity between fictionalizing activities and history making, Strohm insightfully insists that "a text can be powerful without being true" (5). Strohm's work reminds us that authors consolidate (and legitimize) the power of their texts through the truth-claims they make. Such truth-claims can obscure the political interests embedded in official versions of the past.

Despite this nuanced approach to history's relation to fiction, however, even Strohm's important reconceptualization of the power of romance links fictionalizing with lying. In the context of Arthurian traditions and given late-medieval disagreements over the meaning of Arthur's sovereignty (evident in Malmesbury's critique of the raving Britons), slippages between "fiction" and the "lie" prove especially disabling. When late medieval English sovereigns, anxious about the stability of their claims to the throne, commission fictional genealogies that trace their lineage back to King Arthur, they are, I would argue, doing something more complicated than lying. They are imagining the possibility of their future rule through a fictionalized identification (hardly itself an innocent act) with an imagined community of British kings. Likewise when fourteenth-century Welsh poets identify Owain Glyn Dŵr with Arthur (and others) as the heir of a specifically Welsh rule from London, they too are doing something other than lying. They are contesting the ownership of British sovereignty through the fantasy of a salvific return of Welsh rule, although these are exactly the kind of Welsh "ravings" William of Malmesbury deplores as "false myths."[7] The evidence of, and the competition between, such sovereign fantasies require a further development of Strohm's important insights. And this is especially the case since one side of this competition has, more persistently and insistently, been thought to be "raving," luxuriating in "false myths," and rejecting the apparently sober truths of history. We thus need a way to understand the power and the differences of official and unofficial fictions of the British Arthurian past as contestations of important material consequence.

R. James Goldstein has suggested the power of such disagreements about the past to materially affect a contested (and colonial) cultural politics. In *The Matter of Scotland: Historical Narrative in Medieval Scotland*, Goldstein analyzes the distinction between romance and history in the historiography of medieval Scotland's engagements with an English crown, reading in this intercultural encounter a moment when the categories of "history" and "fiction" were divested from one another. Goldstein ges-

tures, albeit briefly, toward the power of psychoanalysis to help us understand the material consequences of such disagreements. In an effort to
keep the material consequence of military battles in full view, Goldstein
briefly identifies the category of history with Jacques Lacan's notion of the
"Real." While Goldstein does not take full advantage of the subtle account
of the relation of fantasy to the material world that Lacan's work might
offer, the example he uses can prove informative for us. With reference to
the Battle of Flodden Field, one of Scotland's most famous (and failed)
stands against English aggression, he writes:

The scene of transgression [read in the Battle of Flodden] takes place in the context
of the real, Lacan's problematical third term that lies beyond the dialectic of the
imaginary and the symbolic: "The Real, or what is perceived as such, is what resists
symbolization absolutely," he says. By Fredric Jameson's reckoning, "it is not terribly difficult to say what is meant by the Real in Lacan. It is simply History itself."
As Jameson writes elsewhere: "History is what hurts, it is what refuses desire and
sets inexorable limits to individual as well as collective praxis." This sense of setting
inexorable limits to desire is precisely what the Scottish host led by James IV was
to discover at Flodden Field. (283)[8]

Goldstein identifies the Lacanian "Real" with history as the materiality of
war: the fact of dead bodies on a field of battle. He moves very quickly,
from Lacan's complicated notion of the "Real" to Fredric Jameson's description of "History" to the Scottish host at Flodden Field. His conclusion emphasizes a soldier's death as the ultimate determination, the
irrefutable limit, a tragic constraint that can never be imagined away. Goldstein thus implies that the materiality of dead bodies can grant history its
claim to the Real. To be sure, as Elaine Scarry argues, the bodily pain suffered by soldiers in war offers a touchstone for reality—in Scarry's terms
the lethal physicality of war substantiates a culture's insubstantial "truths";
those abstract "truths" ("liberty," or "democracy," or "freedom") are literally made to matter, to be material, because of the soldier's body in
pain. Abstract ideas, in other words, borrow materiality from the body
of a soldier willing to suffer pain for belief in those abstractions.[9] Yet in
Goldstein's understandable emphasis on the materiality of death in war, he
forgets how pain and imagination *together* structure our belief in history's
truth; in the process, he implies that "history" has little to do with imagination. But "history," I would argue, is as much about the meaning given
for why those soldiers died as it is about the fact of their dead bodies.
    Lacan's psychoanalytic theory of culture is more complicated than
either Fredric Jameson's words or Goldstein's use of them implies, and

a more detailed understanding of it can shed light on the interweaving of materiality with imaginary structures like belief or fantasy. While the Lacanian 'Real' certainly pertains to limitation, it pertains as much to the interior state of the subject (and the limitations prompted by the subject's relation to individual prehistory and to culture) as it does to traumas, like war, that intrude from without. The sentence from Lacan which Goldstein cites, moreover, ("The Real, *or what is perceived as such*," my emphasis) urges upon us the complexity of the relation between the Real and articulations of it. Elsewhere Lacan describes the interweaving of his three domains, the Imaginary, the Symbolic, and the Real, with the mathematical figure of "the borromeanean knot" (*Feminine Sexuality*, 163), a grouping of "three or more interlocked rings which fall apart when one of the links is severed" (Fuss 10). These interlocking relations cannot be separated from one another so neatly as Goldstein implies. Jameson's Lacanian gloss is, in fact, an imprecise rendering of the Lacanian Real, a category that cannot be easily coordinated with events. While Goldstein apparently reads Lacan's predicate ("is what resists symbolization absolutely") to figure the materiality of physical pain (Jameson's "what hurts"), I would read Lacan's phrase to imply that the Real stands not absolutely outside symbolization, but outside absolute symbolization. While the Real can never be symbolized once and for all, it remains bound to the Imaginary and the Symbolic, it exists "in relation both to the imaginary and to language" (*Feminine Sexuality*, 171).

It thus matters a great deal what imaginary structures and what languages are understood to grant special access to the Real and to the "truth" about it. It matters a good deal which languages and narratives are thought to be materially true. So long as some imaginary structures are disavowed as simple "lies" or, in another trope familiar to readers of medieval historical debates, dismissed as excessively immodest imaginings, we are unable to see the extent to which assessments of falsity or fiction can further tendentious definitions of what can count as "real." Those definitions, and the imaginary possibilities they declare "narcissistic," "extravagant," or the mad ravings of an undisciplined people, point to how official cultures use history's special claim to the "real," to establish what postcolonial critic Homi Bhabha calls a "regime of truth" ("Other Question," 19).

Before developing the implications of how this might help us to read the fantasies of Arthurian history, I turn to consider briefly the ways in which charges of "false myths" converge, in medieval rhetorical theory, with charges of an excessive and immodest imagination. Malmesbury's rhetoric which identifies 'false myths" with Welsh delirium is a case in point, but I would also like to note that this rhetoric continues to influence some scholars analyzing medieval historiography today. For example in *Chaucer and the Subject of History*, Lee Patterson insightfully stresses the importance of imagination for the historical subject, yet he nonetheless implies that some imaginings are excessive and need constraint. Describing imagination—in particular Chaucer's creative *makyng*—as a means to display agency in the face of historical limitation, Patterson offers fiction and creative endeavor as a response to the necessities of Chaucer's historical moment.[10] In praise of this historical vision Patterson writes, "The classical poets, and especially Virgil and Statius, were essentially historians; and they provided [Chaucer] with a historical vision that allowed him to step outside the suffocating narcissism of court *makyng* and to recognize the mutual interdependence of subjectivity and history" (61). Patterson helpfully suggests that imagination can constitute a crucial response to limitation. And yet, in a formulation striking in both its forcefulness and in its use of the frequently gendered and ethically charged "narcissism," imagination, specifically non-classicist imagination, liable to dangerous excesses, requires control.[11] Patterson implies that Chaucer's scholarly, classical proclivities protect him from the selfish imaginary fancies to which his aristocratic audience falls victim. One can certainly appreciate this reminder of the difficulties of life at court; and I sympathize with Patterson's implication that poetic imagination offers a means to resist court politics. Nonetheless, charges of narcissism have long been used to castigate the desires and imaginations of the powerless.

Like Chaucer, Welsh writers of vaticinative (prophetic) poetry deployed imagination as a response to historical limitation, although the material they drew upon was not limited to the classical. Late medieval sovereigns, moreover, paid their scribes to imagine British history in ways that supported their effort to solidify their sovereignty through their identification as Arthur's heirs. (This last example would, to be sure, offer exactly the kind of "narcissism" Patterson wishes to critique.) Rather than dismiss one or the other of these as "excessive" in their pleasures, we can learn much more about the cultural function of Arthurian romance in late medieval Britain by analyzing the contested space of the pleasures themselves. Moreover, in light of Malmesbury's influential castigation of the immodest excesses of Welsh traditions, we would do well to remember that rhetorics of excess have served to obscure precisely these contestations over meaning and pleasure. Charges of immodesty and excess prescribe limits; and they have long been used to sanction official desires while disallowing the alternatives.[12]

While medieval rhetorical theory emphasizes modest restraint and not pleasure, the preceding discussion suggests the importance of pleasure to medieval cultural negotiations over history and truth. The links between history and pleasure—the desire prompting those Welsh "ravings" Malmesbury wishes to dismiss from history's "truth"—return us to psychoanalysis and to Lacan's intermingling of the Real, the Symbolic, and the Imaginary. These domains converge in the invocation of a certain kind of pleasure. According to Slavoj Žižek, these three intermingle in Lacan's notion of *le sinthome* (the symptom), "a fragment of the signifier permeated with . . . enjoyment," "the meaningless letter which immediately procures *jouis-sense*, 'enjoyment in meaning,' 'enjoy-ment' " (*Looking*, 129).[13] The fascinations available through historical narration can grant this kind of enjoyment. History, to return to Goldstein's example, satisfies insofar as it produces a fascinating (glorious, tragic, or ignominious) image of the bodies on Flodden Field. Žižek helps us see that the politics and the ideology of claims to historical truth link with the pleasures encoded in tales of the past. Thus, it matters a great deal which fantasies—and whose pleasures—are recorded in officially sanctioned "true" accounts.

Žižek's larger work, moreover, can help us see the pertinence of these structures to questions of group identity. Elsewhere he argues that communities organize their identities not simply around "a point of symbolic identification," but around a bond which always implies pleasure, as he puts it, "enjoyment incarnated" (51). The jouissance gathering around such identities, again with debts to Lacanian psychoanalysis, Žižek calls the "Nation-Thing," a "non-discursive kernel of enjoyment which must be present for the Nation *qua* discursive-entity-effect to achieve its ontological consistency" ("Republics of Gilead" 53). This organization of jouissance surfaces as pleasure in unpleasure, Žižek argues; this means that groups have access to pleasure through a paranoic account of its theft, a paranoid fantasy of the excessive and threatening pleasure of another group. A fantasmatic belief in the "excessive" pleasures of others thus provides a paranoiac index of how those "others" menace our nation, stealing our pleasure and threatening the possession of enjoyments distinctly claimed as "ours."

With Žižek's analysis in mind we are ready to return to Malmesbury's castigation of Welsh "ravings." Malmesbury approaches the pleasures of Arthurian narrative through his displeasure over Welsh "delirium."

This structure of "pleasure in unpleasure" registers through Malmesbury's anxious rhetoric of Welsh "ravings," wherein he argues that the Welsh need the constraint of simple "truth." Such paranoic fantasies, of course, embed material conflicts with material consequence. Malmesbury's insistence on Arthurian "truth" mounts an effort to forbid the Welsh from stealing, through their "trifles" about Arthur, the powers and fascinations of Arthurian history. The pleasure available in stories of Arthurian rule apparently "belong" to "truthful histories" and to official historians—that is, to non-Welsh culture. At stake here is the desire to forbid the pleasures of Welsh creative *makyng*; at stake too may be the fear that enjoyment of Arthur might "kindle the broken spirits" of the Welsh "to war."

Where Žižek's work helps us see how pleasure inhabits the fantasmatic desires implicit in Malmesbury's words, Fredric Jameson's Marxist historiography suggests that one group's pleasures frequently require another group's pain. Jameson's work also reminds us that texts are material in form as much as in content. And when he writes, "history is what hurts; it is what refuses desire and sets inexorable limits to individual as well as collective praxis," that statement applies as well to definitions of what counts as "real" (and the concomitant elimination of possible alternatives) which also "refuse desire and set inexorable limits." Like cautionary tales and words in legal statutes, historical narratives can be employed to give pain; they can punish, prohibit, and constrain desire; they can circumscribe our vision of what might be possible. The generic classification of "history" naturalizes, as it does in Malmesbury's repudiation of Welsh "trifles," what can count as real. History can grant to the Real the air—inexorable, determined—of sober tragedy; it can render loss an act of "nature," "fate," or even the wages of "narcissism," rather than a production of collective cultural desire.[14] Once granted a privileged access to "what actually happened," the genre of history can be used to discount, and to make us forget, alternative stories of the past. And it can lend events (like plague, war, or famine) the aura of unavoidable disaster, obscuring the extent to which such events were themselves culturally produced and, thus, could have been avoided.[15]

Divesting the pleasures of "fiction" from those of "history" has profound implications for an analysis of the contestations over Arthurian "truth" in medieval Britain. The opposition of "realism" to "fiction" can preclude us from seeing fiction making as an activity in which sovereign powers, committed as they are to the "realism" of statecraft, engage. The distinction between "fantasy" and the "real" implies, as it did in Plato's account, that when governments do participate in fiction-making (efforts usually understood to constitute propaganda) such activity is an aberration, or a mark of "bad" government, rather than a fundamental aim of the powerful. When imagined as activities committed to "truth" and "reality"—in a famous phrase "the art of the possible"—politics and statecraft, perhaps even history, are seen to have only accidental relation to the production of fictions. This presupposition obscures how the powerful use fantasy for their ends whether in the medieval period or our own.[16]

Geoffrey of Monmouth's *Historia regum Britanniae*—poised over the breach we have been examining—can elucidate the pleasures and dangers of popular belief for a national fantasy. Beginning with critical assessments of Geoffrey's work, I argue below that his Arthurian account displays a "British" identity fantastically dependent upon Welsh pleasures, popular figures, and poetic forms. It is to Geoffrey's fantasy that we turn.

Geoffrey of Monmouth and the Pleasures of History

The *Historia regum Britanniae* (c. 1135–38) narrates the story of early Britain from its founding by the Trojan Brutus, through Roman and Saxon rule, with special focus on King Arthur's birth, rule, and death. The account offers fabulous tales of giants and monsters, dragons, sovereigns, and soothsayers. Despite the denigration of the imaginative excesses of these stories by historians like Malmesbury, Geoffrey's history would be wildly popular, enormously increasing the renown and influence of King Arthur. Julia Crick counts over 200 extant manuscript redactions of Geoffrey's text, whether complete or partial, in a variety of languages stretching over a significant period [17]; Geoffrey's narrative would inspire chronicle accounts in Latin, English, French, and Welsh, as well as a genre of romances of the "Matter of Britain"; Geoffrey's Merlin prophecies would fuel the dynastic prophecies and genealogies of fifteenth-century political propaganda. According to Crick's now standard account of the dissemination and reception of Geoffrey's text, its popularity continued, perhaps even increasing in England, into the later medieval centuries.[18]

For years the debate over the problems of Geoffrey's historicist project focused attention on his claim to be translating an ancient British (Welsh) book, a claim that was, scholars believed, dubious. Geoffrey's history was compromised by doubts about the existence and authority of this elusive *vetustissimus liber* (old book), and the value of the *Historia* as a historical text was delimited by a longstanding scholarly consensus concerning Geoffrey's fraudulent "British" source. Even this consensus conveyed a cultural bias. Acton Griscom, the editor of what was for many years the standard vulgate text of the *Historia*, implied nearly seventy years ago that the preeminence of Latinists within the medieval scholarly community produced at least a premature rejection of the possibility of Geoffrey's Welsh source.[19] Geoffrey's claims to the contrary were interpreted, moreover, in the most ungenerous terms, with scholars suggesting that his Welsh source was duplicitously invented "to cover the romantic creations of [his] own imaginative genius" (Griscom 102).

Admittedly Geoffrey may have had no written source. But his assertion of the *vetustissimus liber* amounts to his use of a standard rhetorical figure, the "old book" topos. Monmouth's deployment of the "old book" topos locates him firmly within the established tradition of medieval historiography; it does not imply that he perpetrated "one of the best hoaxes of the Middle Ages" (Crick 226). As Julia Crick points out, Geoffrey's use of the imagination in recounting his history is not at all unusual; like his competitors, Geoffrey amplified and elaborated a story within an already existing narrative tradition. Ruth Morse argues that invention and rhetorical embellishment were especial features of medieval and classical histories written about a very distant past. If an account could be demonstrated as authorized, as Morse puts it, "'truth' might be secondary. . . . [The] inescapable but highly exploited interpretative circularity depends upon the variety of authority which authorities had" (102). Given these facts, what is striking about the *Historia* is neither Geoffrey's fondness for invention nor his use of the "old book" topos, but the fact that, despite a tradition of historical invention endorsed by medieval rhetorical theory, his is the only account of early Britain dismissed for its apparently extravagant inventions.[20] When Bede peppers his famous ecclesiastical history with descriptions of miracle cures and visions of heaven and hell, his excursions into the fantastic fail to compromise his appeal for "scholars [who] respect his historical thoroughness and competence" (Gransden 17). Christian tradition and historiography remain legitimate and authoritative sources for fantasy and magic; other fantasy traditions do not. Thus Antonia Gransden declares Bede's "grasp of historical method . . . unique in the middle ages," displaying as evidence of this methodological competence the fact that "he was the first historian to date consistently by the era of the Incarnation—the system of dating AD. and BC. in use today" (25). Here Bede's commitment to marking time in Christian terms testifies to his historical expertise. Monmouth's narrative seems, on the other hand, the only early history held accountable to objectivist standards; his history is, in fact, the very place where the definition of "history" gets made.[21]

Scholarly concern with Geoffrey's extravagant fictions may, in fact, displace anxieties about his extravagant popularity. Scholars have consistently, if implicitly, linked the problem of Geoffrey's authority to his text's popularity. Gransden's (once very influential) account of medieval historiography critiques the apparent problem of Geoffrey's popularity in terms that denigrate the pleasures of his text. Describing Geoffrey as "a romance writer masquerading as a historian" (I, 202), Gransden classifies the *Historia* as romance because it was so delightfully amusing and so remarkably popular (Gransden I, 207; II, 459).[22] More recently Julia Crick has revised this opinion, reminding modern readers of the importance of pleasure and delight for historians writing during the Middle Ages, a time when "history was not a free-standing discipline, but an auxiliary one" (225). Crick continues, "Lacking a niche in the academic world, historians . . . had to catch their audiences in a way that writers of technical literature generally did not. . . . In such a market content, style, and general appeal to the reader were essential to success" (225–26). By such standards, as Crick concludes, Geoffrey of Monmouth "was an exceptional artist fully governing and not governed by his material. His choice of subject was a brilliant success" (226). Crick reminds us that Geoffrey was not writing from a position of textual authority and disciplinary influence. Her remarks imply that critical condescension toward Geoffrey's artistry and brilliance remains linked to his success. Indeed, the *Historia* was far more influential than the authorized "technical literature" of the time.

For his part, Geoffrey of Monmouth evinces his own anxiety about the pleasures of his text. He endeavors to ensure that those pleasures not be identified with himself as a writer. Geoffrey's prefatory remarks (cited as epigraph to this chapter), explicitly link Arthurian pleasures with Welsh culture. The "old British book" drawn from Welsh oral tradition was, Geoffrey insists, invested with enjoyment: stories of Arthur were handed down joyfully ("a multis populis quasi inscripta *iocunde* & memoriter predicarentur," emphasis mine), his source "book" of British traditions was an aesthetic delight ("ex ordine *perpulcris* orationibus proponebat" [Griscom 219, emphasis mine]). In contrast to the joys of the Welsh tradition, Monmouth insists upon his own modest and unpretentious style. The following quotation (from Lewis Thorpe's translation) addresses those issues:

I have taken the trouble at [Archdeacon Walter's] request to translate that [old British] book into Latin, although I have been content with my own expression and my own homely [rustic] style and I have gathered no gaudy flowers of speech in other's gardens. If I had adorned my page with high flown language I should have bored my readers, for they would have been forced to spend more time discovering the meaning of my words than following the story.[23]

Perhaps such a statement amounts to the standard trope of authorial humility; perhaps, too, it offers rhetorical concessions to competing traditions of historiography (like that of the Venerable Bede or William of Malmesbury) narrating the history of the English people or of their church.[24] Monmouth's investment in rhetorical modesty, here again, situates him firmly within the status quo. But what would Monmouth gain by identifying the aesthetic pleasure of his text with the Welsh stories he chose to "translate," rather than with his own imagination? Might his humility signal something more than another standard topos?

To answer these questions we turn to a central section of Geoffrey's text that will serve as an important source for late-medieval political propaganda. In the center of the *Historia*—wedged in between two episodes in the history of Constantine—Geoffrey "translates" "The Prophecies of Merlin." Up to this point, the account of British history has moved forward in chronological progression: beginning with the story of Brutus, continuing through the time before and during Roman colonization of Britain. Geoffrey next tells the story of the dynasty of Constantine, interrupting that narrative immediately after the famous episode of Vortigern's tower, a monumental edifice crumbling (so Merlin advises) because of two dragons, one red and one white, locked in battle beneath it. At this point, in most redactions, Geoffrey's authorial voice intrudes in dedication.[25] In most (but not all) manuscripts his patron is now identified as Alexander Bishop of Lincoln, "a man of the greatest religion and wisdom . . . waited on by so many noblemen" (170).[26] At this point Geoffrey recapitulates his humility, linking himself and Bishop Alexander with Merlin, the prophet:

I [Geoffrey] . . . pressed my rustic reed-pipe to my lips and, modulating on it in all humility, I translated into Latin this work written in a language which is unknown to you. All the same, I am greatly surprised that you should have deigned to commit the task to so poor a pen as mine, when your all-powerful wand could command the service of so many men more learned and more splendid than I . . . Leaving on one side all the wise men of this entire island of Britain, I feel no shame at all in maintaining that it is you and you alone who should . . . declaim it with bold accompaniment, if only the highest honour had not called you away to other preoccupations . . . . [S]ince it has pleased you that Geoffrey of Monmouth should sound his own pipe in this piece of soothsaying, do not hesitate to show favour to his music-makings. If he produces any sound which is wrong or unpleasant, force him back into correct harmony with your own Muses' baton. (Thorpe 170–71; VII, 1)

Alexander's power becomes a magician's wand; Geoffrey maintains proudly that Alexander "alone should declaim [the prophecies] with bold accomplishment," despite the fact that their original language is "unknown" to him. In place of Alexander's "all powerful wand," Geoffrey offers his own more modest "rustic reed pipe," a figuration which marks authorial power with tropes of male virility while simultaneously placing Alexander as an imaginary intermediary between Geoffrey and Merlin. This description compliments Alexander's majesty while distancing Geoffrey's own artistry from Merlin's prophetic authorship. Geoffrey is merely the humble medium; he mediates the creations of a fictional magician and the desires of a powerful bishop. Through this dedication Geoffrey displays the usefulness of imaginative ventures like prophetic soothsaying to those in power. Powerful bishops like Alexander, Geoffrey reminds us, have access to their own muses; it is their aesthetic pleasures—their designations of "correct harmony" and "favorable music-makings"—that determine which sounds will gain a fair hearing and which will fall on deaf ears.

Geoffrey's text displays a crucial fact of patronage.[27] Sovereigns and bishops need aesthetic creation (and linguistic techniques) to display their power. In fact, the story of Merlin that Monmouth tells will link linguistic technologies (the powers of storytelling, translation, and prophecy) to a powerful set of material activities. Merlin's skill in the power of the story, his ability to "foretell the future," is linked with his knowledge of "mechanical contrivances" (195). Skilled in tales and technologies, Merlin's prophecies restore stability to Vortigern's military fortifications: he solves the problem of the crumbling tower by revealing the fighting dragons underneath it. He is able, in explicit contrast to the brute strength of Vortigern's warriors, to dismantle the Giant's Ring in Ireland, reerecting it as Stonehenge. Indeed, Merlin's usefulness to his sovereign is matchless. More important than any army, "his artistry is worth more than any brute strength" (ingenium que uirtuti preualere) (198). And Merlin manages explicitly innovative technologies of sovereign succession, providing the magical means whereby Uther Pendragon and Ygraine beget Arthur. As a prophet and magician, Merlin builds monuments and produces monumental kings.

As Martin Shichtman and Laurie Finke have noted, Merlin's awesome abilities mark him as more than the average court poet. Shichtman and Finke call him "the possessor of intellectual property a monopoly so absolute and valuable that it almost equalizes the relationship between client and patron" (35).[28] And this, as Shichtman and Finke also point out, is one way to read Geoffrey the historian. Geoffrey, like Merlin, mediates influential pleasures to amazing cultural and political effect. In Merlin Geoffrey may well craft a veiled representation of the power of his own *ingenium*, the word Monmouth used repeatedly to describe Merlin's craft, a term which in the Middle Ages could mean both "artistry and genius" and "deviousness, artifice and fraud" (Shichtman and Finke 34). Despite their attention to the ambiguities of *ingenium*, Shichtman and Finke characterize Geoffrey's use of the word as unequivocally enthusiastic: "Geoffrey glosses over the limitations of Merlin's *ingenium*," they argue, "just as he glosses over the limitations of his own" (34). But Geoffrey's efforts to distance himself from the pleasures of the text he "translates," the dedications that identify Merlin's skills with Bishop Alexander's power rather than with Geoffrey's own, all hint at anxieties about his own *ingenium*. When he positions himself as the medium and not the source of the pleasures of his own text, Geoffrey's dedications—read as "fulsome" and "sycophantic in the extreme" by some[29]—suggest an artistic and historiographic agency constrained by pleasures other than his own. He is, in the textual variants that include these dedications, overcome by the wishes of his patrons; their dictates and their pleasures may likewise overwhelm his text.

Such a reading suggests Geoffrey's political canniness; it suggests as well that Geoffrey may have been trying to point out that histories were always written for politicians with political axes to grind. In light of this we can now consider the ambiguities of the Merlin Prophecies, a central, and perhaps the most imaginatively excessive, section of the *Historia*. Geoffrey's representation of Merlin's power for Vortigern may indicate sobering testimony to what massive things sovereigns can do with soothsayers like Merlin at their service. Yet Geoffrey also places in Merlin's mouth radically prophetic words powerful enough to jolt an imperial king like Vortigern out of his sovereign complacency. Merlin's prophecies warn of a horrific British future:

For Britain's mountains and valleys shall be leveled, and the streams in its valleys shall run with blood. . . .
The race that is oppressed shall prevail in the end, for it will resist the savagery of the invaders. . . .

The island shall be called by the name of Brutus and the title given to it by foreigners shall be done away with . . . .

Three generations will witness all that I have mentioned, and then the kings buried in the town of London will be disinterred . . . .

London shall mourn the death of twenty thousand and the Thames will be turned into blood.

The Daneian Forest shall be wakened from its sleep and, bursting into human speech, it shall shout: "Kambria, come here! Bring Cornwall at your side! Say to Winchester: 'The earth will swallow you up. Move the see of your shepherd to where the ships come in to harbour. Then make sure that the limbs which remain follow the head! The day approaches when your citizens will perish for their crimes of perjury. . . . Woe to the perjured people, for their famous city shall come toppling down because of them.'" (Thorpe 171, 175, 176, 178; VII, 3, 4)

The prophecies warn of injury, death, devastation, and a vengeful repayment for "the savagery of invaders." As Rupert Taylor points out, Merlin's prophecies resonate with Biblical indictments from apocalyptic literature of Isaiah, Ezekiel, Jeremiah, and Revelation (27). Those prophetic books, identified by Biblical scholars as "crisis literature," narrate the captivity of a conquered, yet holy, people, and of their messianic hopes for deliverance. Embedded, in the vulgate version, within Monmouth's larger text, Merlin's prophecies launch a sharp critique of conquest, prophesying death to London, a scene of such geological tumult that Wales ("Kambria") and Cornwall shout curses upon Westminster. London shall mourn; the Thames will be turned to blood; the Kings of London will be disinterred after three generations. Statements like these allude to promises of divine wrath meted out upon oppressors.

The prophetic traditions that fueled Merlin's apocalyptic tone, moreover, were borrowed from Welsh vaticinative tradition. The Merlin Prophecies and the story of the Red and White Dragons battling beneath Vortigern's tower were, according to A. O. H. Jarman, "lifted bodily . . . from the ninth-century collection of early British and Welsh saga material and semi-historical traditions known as the *Historia Brittonum*" (131). These prophetic and symbolic Welsh traditions date from "memories of the struggle of the Britons and the English for supremacy in the fifth and sixth centuries," when the figure of the Red Dragon represented the Welsh who "will arise, and valiantly throw the English people across the sea," while the White Dragon represented "the people who have seized many peoples and countries in Britain" (*Historia Brittonum*, as cited by Jarman, 136). The Welsh poem *Armes Prydein Vawr*, dated c. 930, prophesies Welsh efforts to vanquish foreign invaders; it mentions Vortigern and Merlin as well.

Jarman argues through linguistic and textual evidence that Geoffrey was "clearly aware" of Welsh vaticinatory tradition, and used "the [general] nature and purpose of vaticination"—that is, a critique of conquest and invasion—borrowed from Welsh tradition to craft Merlin's prophecies.[30]

Developed from this Welsh tradition, the Merlin Prophecies encode an early version of what postcolonial scholars term "oppositional discourse." Postcolonial cultural studies, a field marked by a commitment to the agency of conquered peoples, has reminded scholars in all disciplines of the importance of acknowledging the historical agency of such groups. In the words of critic Benita Parry, oppositional works attest "to the counter-hegemonic strategies" of a people under siege as they struggle to resist or to accommodate the vicissitudes of their experience. As I noted in the introduction to this study, oppositional discourse has come to define "postcolonial" itself. Bill Ashcroft, Gareth Griffiths, and Helen Tiffin, editors of *The Postcolonial Studies Reader*, define "postcolonial" as "the discourse of oppositionality which colonialism brings into being" (117).[31] Ashcroft, Griffiths, and Tiffin among others imply that the "post" prefix in "postcolonial" signifies "against," rather than "after," colonialism. In this view, the "post" of "postcolonial" becomes, as K. Anthony Appiah puts it, "the post of the space-clearing gesture" (348). Such insights remain specifically resonant for scholars working in early periods. We can, I would argue, deploy "postcolonial" to signal a concern with agency and oppositional texts, even as we appreciate the historical specificity (the similarities and differences) of twentieth-century or medieval scenes of conquest.

The oppositional discourses of Welsh vaticinative poetry could, in this way, be viewed as a "postcolonial" collection. Yet the complicated textual status and linguistic nature of these traditions might also offer a crucial qualification to standard definitions of "opposition." On the one hand, early vaticination, as E. M. Griffiths established, characteristically links the restoration of insular rule to the Britons through figures like Arthur. Yet the texts that survive (as the *Historia Brittonum* to which Jarman refers) are themselves notoriously complicated, combining elements of Latin clerical and Welsh "native" cultures.[32] This difficult situation means that these "oppositional" texts are not romantically "pure." Such complications have sometimes produced scholarly diffidence on questions of Welsh oppositional agency, particularly with regard to Arthur. Yet evidence of oppositional traditions in texts "contaminated" by substantial interlinguistic, cultural, and historical complexity registers, I would argue, not the absolute absence of resistance so much as the absence of resistance as a "pure" process or event. These texts testify to the complexity of "native" culture and resistance in Wales, a locale that combines conquest and difference with a long history of intimate exchange. Viewed as complicated, mixed sets of texts, these "oppositional discourses" themselves emerge as an extraordinary kind of creative agency, to recall Patterson's formulation, an imaginative *makyng* in the face of constraint. Furthermore, I would argue that so long as we understand the "post" of "postcolonial" to refer solely to the time after the withdrawal of colonial rule, we will likely miss that such poignant complications suggest not a complicity with conquest that must be deplored, but the difficulty of oppositional strategies. And this, again I would argue, is exactly the case with the scholarly reception of Geoffrey's *Historia*.

The importance and power—the historical agency—of the oppositional traditions Geoffrey deploys have been traditionally under appreciated in favor of an overemphasis upon the genealogical interests of Geoffrey's Anglo-Norman patrons and audience. As a result many readers have emphasized what they see as Monmouth's collusion with Anglo-Norman colonial desires for things Welsh, arguing that Geoffrey appropriates, even "colonizes," Welsh material for his own uses.[33] Yet arguments that emphasize Anglo-Norman patronage and rule tend to render insignificant, and often ignore altogether, the agency of other audiences and other uses of Geoffrey's text. In these accounts, the *Historia* remains almost exclusively an instrument of hegemonic power, a text that sponsors only the desires of parvenu Anglo-Norman conquerors, despite the fact that the *Historia's* popularity, as the diversity of extant manuscripts suggests, obtained far beyond their concerns.[34] In contrast to this approach, I will argue shortly for a reading of the subtle relation between Monmouth's Anglo-Norman patrons and Welsh resisters of Anglo-Norman rule. For if Monmouth's text aided the Norman conquerors, it also gained important benefits for a linguistic minority and contributed to the further development of Welsh discourses of resistance. Those gains occurred in part because of the evocative (and puzzling) ambiguity of the texts themselves, and of Monmouth's clever use of them. The ambiguity of the Prophecies, and Geoffrey's own political acuity, meant that those resisting the designs of the Anglo-Normans had access to authoritative and popular texts that enabled resistance. The Merlin Prophecies, articulated in the *Historia Brittonum* as texts of Welsh resistance to Saxon conquest, could resonate as well with the later scene of Anglo-Norman Conquest. I argue below, moreover, that these important ambiguities make Geoffrey's text crucial for competing accounts of Britain's future, and that this explains in part the long-lived popularity of Geoffrey's text.

Scholars have already noted that the flexible ambiguity of Geoffrey's *Historia* proved useful in the context of twelfth-century Anglo-Norman aristocratic enmity. Shichtman and Finke remind us of the awkwardness of Geoffrey's multiple dedicatees, a group of enemies, key figures from both sides of the bitter dynastic struggles following Henry I's death.[35] As a result, they describe Geoffrey's *Historia*, following the work of Pierre Bourdieu, as *symbolic capital*, "the creation of a past which could ease the [genealogical] anxieties of a powerful ruling class concerned with discovering family origin" (35). Geoffrey's work was so popular because of its ability to accommodate such a diverse and fractured audience. I am suggesting that there is an even broader and more diverse audience to which we must attend. For Geoffrey's popularity ventured far beyond a court circle interested in the particularities of dynastic politics. And it pertained as well to a set of contestations between the Welsh and Anglo-Normans rooted in divergent interpretations of the Merlin Prophecies.

We thus still need to address the crucial question of these traditions, asking why the history Geoffrey chose to tell was, unlike Malmesbury's *Gesta regum Anglorum* or Bede's *Historiam ecclesiasticam gentis Anglorum*, not the story of an English past, but of a British one.[36] How did this story of British kings help create an insular future, and what might this mean for our understanding of the category of "Britain?" The legacy of Geoffrey's matter of Britain in the later Middle Ages—its appearance in texts of futuristic prophesy and political propaganda, its uses as genealogical data for aristocratic pedigree, its elaboration in regionalist romances of Arthur, or in the plans of English (or Scottish) sovereigns who name their first-born sons after the mythical king—means that Monmouth's fantasy offered an enduring imaginary ground for creating (and contesting) the identity of an historic British community. I turn now to examine how and why Geoffrey's "Britons," and the ambiguity of Merlin's futuristic prophecies of their return, prompt these uses. The Britain Geoffrey describes evokes a doubled history: one specifically linked to a remnant Welsh population, and another linked to an insular return, and to a British *totam insulam*.

Doubled Time and Spaces: The Riches of British History

Francis Ingledew has shown that the genealogical impulse in the *Historia* links with territorial claims to land, arguing that as Geoffrey's text eased Anglo-Norman genealogical disputes, it also came to sponsor

territorial claims for an entire class of aristocrats. This is because, Ingledew argues, Geoffrey advanced the very definition of what constitutes
a "national" history, where "the possession of territory and power came
to correlate distinctively with ownership of time; time came to constitute
space—family and national land—as *home*, an inalienable and permanent,
private and public territory" (669).[37] Ingledew offers a view of time that
is useful for imagining, and then claiming, the unified space of a realm.
Geoffrey's *Historia* imagines a genealogical union (across time) that can
prefigure the imagination of territorial unity, in the united (broadly familial) ownership of a realm. Yet, like so many other insightful analyses
of the *Historia*, Ingledew's work does not consider the significance of
Geoffrey's relation to Welsh traditions, wherein we might find a different account of the broad family descended from Brutus. Instead Ingledew
emphasizes Geoffrey's book as an exclusively Trojan history. Geoffrey of
Monmouth's genealogy of the Britons, while a Trojan story, also depends
upon a view of British territory borrowed from very old popular Welsh
traditions.[38] Indeed Monmouth's genealogical narrative will help sponsor
Welsh claims to London's crown.

At the time Geoffrey wrote, "Briton" was an equivocal category, referring both to the Welsh and to their linguistic kin in Brittany. While
there is the sense that, for modern scholars, the early medieval term is
liable to slippage between these two referents, scholars rarely consider
what that slippage might have meant for Monmouth, or how its doubleness might have been useful to him. Instead scholars imagine Geoffrey's
identity in singular terms—he was, they assert, a Breton. Yet questions
of flexibility and of cultural doubleness remain important to Monmouth
who represents it as an important strategy for dealing with complicated
cultural relations.[39] Ambivalence and doubleness emerge in Geoffrey's representation of the Welsh, a group he describes as both vulnerable and
noble. Geoffrey's Welsh do appear poor and vulnerable (vi, 2), yet it is
their "nobility in bearing" (vi, 4) that gains for them a hearing with Aldroenus' King of Brittany, implying that their fortunes are tarnished but
not bankrupt. An army of the most illustrious Britons conquer Amorica
for Maximianus and Coranus Meriadorus, settling there and leaving their
lower-born kinspeople in Britain. Yet it is through the politicking of what
Brynley Roberts calls the "listless, low-born, and timid remnant" (x) left
behind that the dynasty destined to produce Arthur—the glorious king
and narrative center of Geoffrey's work—returns to the island. Geoffrey's
representation of the conquest of Brittany implies a ruthlessness (rather

than a forthright glory) of the invading Maximianus.[40] Those left behind by Maximianus, moreover, testify to the losses this conquest wrought for his own kin, counting themselves "poverty-stricken" since "Maximianus despoiled [the] island of its soldiers." And when Aldroenus, King of Brittany, refuses to accept the crown of Britain—an episode frequently cited as prime evidence of Geoffrey's Breton, rather than Welsh, loyalties—he nonetheless keeps the crown in the family, offering his brother Constantine in his place, describing an island in "peace and tranquillity" as the most "fertile country in existence" (vi, 5). Finally Arthur, the central figure in Geoffrey's monument to British kings, is descended from both insular and continental ancestors.

According to Monmouth's story the Britons are a doubled people, occupying two places at once: they remain in the western reaches of the island, but have also migrated to the continent. The cultural migrations of the Britons offer a long history of continental and insular interaction. Geoffrey's tale of the conquest of Amorica is, moreover, a direct inversion of Norman Conquest of the island of Britain; Norman migration from continent to island mirrors a previous, and British, migration from island to continent. In light of Geoffrey's story of British conquest throughout all of Gaul, Norman invasion of the island of Britain amounts not to a new conquest so much as a recurrence: Britons left the island, conquering the continent; the Normans leave the continent, conquering the island. This conjunction of interactions implies geographic settlement is fluid; cultural exchange between continent and island has a long, and specifically British, history.

From an Anglo-Norman point of view, this double geography of Britain (as a number of scholars have suggested) marks Briton and Norman as distinct yet related cultures. Insular Britons, by virtue of their affiliation with this continental kin, deserve respect. Yet, as readers repeatedly point out, the Welsh Britons have none of the glory of the Normans, appearing debased and lost by the end of Geoffrey's story. Their history is strikingly glorious, but their present is weak and unsteady. Despite such weakness, it is the Britons in Wales who offer hope for a future recovery: "Living precariously in Wales, in the remote recesses of the wood" Welsh Britons look for "the appointed moment" when "the British people would occupy the island again" (282–83; xxi, 17, 18). In the context of the geographic doubleness of British rule, Geoffrey's text thus ends with the implication— the textual status of which will be clearer in a moment—that the promised British recovery might be displaced through Norman Conquest. The

Anglo-Norman politics of Geoffrey's history lies with the very important implication that the Normans can rightly inherit from the imperial Britons, a race on a par with the Romans who, "were able to conquer the island" (272; xii, 5). By implication—but only by implication—Norman presence on the island represents a British future, while the (Welsh) Britons figure its past. The Normans can, by learning and respecting the history of the isle of Britain, begin to weave their glory with the glory of the land they rule and with the British king Arthur. This history provides a way for a Norman aristocratic audience to capture the richness of a mythic Welsh past while still remaining the conquerors of those whose glorious history they wish to imagine as their own.

If historians since Geoffrey have been as happy to see his implication as the Normans themselves must have been, they have not considered the import of its status as an insinuation rather than a forthright claim. Elsewhere Monmouth emphasizes ambiguity as an important factor both for his own writing and for Merlin's activity: in his self-conscious distancing from his text's pleasures; in the ambiguity of the Merlin Prophecies; in the diversity of his dedications. In fact Geoffrey himself repeatedly notes that the ambiguity of Merlin's prophecies were the source of Merlin's popularity. All were "filled with amazement by the equivocal [*ambiguitate*] meaning of [Merlin's] words" (Thorpe 170). "Ambiguitate" glossed as "inclined to both sides; hybrid" and "wavering, hesitating, uncertain, doubtful, obscure." The *OED* notes the early English meanings taken from Medieval Latin pertain to the second of these connotations, "a wavering of opinion, hesitation, doubt, uncertainty as to one's course." The diversity of manuscript redactions points further to "a wavering of opinion" in the contradictory interests of Geoffrey's multiple and diverse dedicatees. But it also points far beyond Anglo-Norman partisan concerns. The politics of "ambiguitate" explain the *Historia's* diverse and complicated reception. Welsh versions of Geoffrey's text will be important to Welsh nationalist politics at various times throughout the Middle Ages. In that context it is unsurprising that some redactions of Geoffrey's text identify (in prophecies known as the "Breton Hope") British recovery of the *totius insulae* with Welsh claims to the island kingdom while others call such interpretations explicitly into question. The Bern and Harlech manuscripts of the *Historia*, for example, end with a disclaimer that denies any hope for a future Welsh rule: "The Welsh, once they had degenerated from the noble state enjoyed by the Britons, never afterwards recovered the overlordship of the island" (Thorpe 284).

This disclaimer explicitly contests Welsh "oppositional texts," and precludes Welsh hopes that they are the Britons who will return to rule the land. Disclaimers like this one, combined with Geoffrey's equivocation, helped consolidate the power of Geoffrey's patrons. Yet Geoffrey's "ambiguitate" also means that his text will prove useful to Welsh resisters of Anglo-Norman conquest. J. S. P. Tatlock notes the early popularity of the *Historia* in Wales, a fact corroborated by Brynley Roberts's important account of the significance of the *Brut Y Brenhinedd* (the earliest Middle Welsh translation of Geoffrey's text) for Welsh intellectuals in the twelfth century and beyond when it became "a potent element in Welsh national consciousness until the end of the eighteenth century" (*"Historia* and *Brut Y Brenhinedd,"* 113).[41] The ambiguity of Geoffrey's *Historia* — read especially in the final ambiguous implication of British return — meant that subversive "oppositional" Welsh material could gain influence even at court.

Such is a powerful (and effective) display of creative *makyng* in the face of constraint. By some accounts Geoffrey's history gained political prestige for the Welsh Britons into the next generation of Anglo-Norman affairs, a time when the direct conquest of Wales seemed a likely corollary of a Norman colonizing program. According to Welsh historian R. R. Davies, Wales was initially "peripheral" to Norman conquerors concerned with the security of their position in England and Normandy. Yet during the late eleventh and into the twelfth century (and in partial response to Welsh aid to Saxon dissidents) the conquerors turned their attentions westward. A struggle for supremacy over Wales ensued with the map of Norman control of Welsh regions constantly changing. During the period of Geoffrey's initial popularity, Norman control of the area had weakened enough that, according to Welsh chroniclers of the 1160s, "all the Welsh united to throw off the rule of the French" conquerors who desired "to carry into bondage and to destroy all the Britons" (*Brut y Tywysogyon*, 1165, 1167, as cited by Davies, *Conquest* 52–53). Henry II's 1165 campaign to crush Welsh resistance proved a failure; that fact apparently inspired a change in Henry's policy. By 1171, again according to Davies, Henry's policies "toward native Welsh princes . . . had changed radically" and "no English king would again invade Wales for almost forty years" (53–54). If Henry II's failed military campaign inspired in him a desire to change his policy toward Wales, such a desire could find an ideological justification in Geoffrey's book. Furthermore, there is evidence that Henry was well acquainted with Geoffrey's text: interested in literature and history himself, Henry II had been educated at the Bristol residence of his uncle, Robert of Gloucester, Geoffrey of Monmouth's chief patron.[42] Laʒamon's Middle English *Brut*, a verse rendering of Wace's French verse rendering of Geoffrey's *Historia*, links this insular chronicle tradition with Henry II, mentioning a dedication to Eleanor of Aquitaine, Henry's queen.[43] The links between Henry II's policies and his role as patron of legendary histories has been noted by Patterson, who remarks that "much of the court literature of the period shows patterns of interest that are consistent with Henry's political needs" ("Historiography," 3).[44]

Geoffrey's *Historia*, and later versions of its story, could encourage Henry II to appreciate the value of the Welsh as peers and allies rather than as conquered subjects. Representing the once glorious Welsh now debased by their own weaknesses and disgraced by aggressive Saxon conquerors implicitly identify the Saxons as the real Norman enemy. Joined by common enmity toward the Saxons, Norman and Briton become allies rather than rivals. Tatlock retorts that "those who profited most from Geoffrey's work were the Britons; one of [Geoffrey's] motives may well have been to heighten respect for them among his Norman superiors" (428). Modern histories of medieval Wales emphasize the Welsh, in contrast to the Saxons, as successful resisters of Norman invasion. In those accounts, Welsh resistance in the Anglo-Norman period produced Welsh independence from the English until Edwardian days.[45] This image of a Welsh remnant resistant to conquest, maintaining an intact community amid loss, resonates with the image of the Britons from the end of the *Historia*, poised on the western edge of the island. The fantasy of a native British survival in Wales, as I will argue in Chapter 2, grants fifteenth-century sovereigns access to insular native roots resistant to continental aggressions, a resistance through which, by the second half of the fifteenth century, Edward IV will claim himself heir to a continuous native line of kings.

In the decades following Norman Conquest the meaning of such an image remains paradoxically ambiguous.[46] Its popularity with the Anglo-Norman aristocracy and with Welsh resisters alike suggests both contestations over the identity of Brutus's heirs, and the text's ambivalent political uses in that debate. This ambivalence, moreover, links intercultural insular unity to what I am calling a national fantasy. Homi Bhabha's account of "nation and narration" emphasizes both the fantasmatic nature of national narratives and the ways in which such texts always gesture, despite themselves, to the contestations and disunities they earnestly seek to avoid. Bhabha describes "the Janus-faced discourse of the nation," one liable to "subordination, fracturing, diffusing, reproducing, as much as producing, creating, forcing, guiding" (*Nation* 3–4). Bhabha's formulation seems uncannily pertinent to the twelfth century scene we have been examining— despite the fact that Bhabha, like many, identifies national narratives as modern inventions. Thus I turn finally to consider how we might understand this medieval oppositional history as, nonetheless, the history of a national fantasy.

Bhabha describes national narrations as ambivalent texts situated in crisis. This is because the definition of a national "people" evokes both a past (putatively shared) history and a present field of differences. The national "people" signify a crisis of representation and a contestation of meaning. Positioned amid this crisis, the "people" are both "pedagogical historical objects" learning who "they" are and "performative subjects" effecting the identity that "they" are thought to inhabit. In their pedagogical function, the people learn from the past; in their performative function, the people display an identity in the present. And the performative field may disrupt the apparent national "truths" registered in the pedagogical. Contemporary activities of the people may, in other words, trouble the stability of an identity that we have been taught to embrace as "ours."

But Bhabha links the "margins of the nation" with "modernity," and he is interested in explaining how modern national discourses disavow conflicts by positioning such problems as temporally past, surmounted in a "modern" present. Through such temporal limits, according to Bhabha, modern narrations of the nation both deny and imply the antagonistic variety of people claimed by national rule. In this way national narratives mark the limits of community through rhetorical tropes of time and space. They encode what Edward Said has called the "overlapping territories" and "intertwined histories" of an intercultural past, but as the liminal spaces bounding the nation's (present) identity.

In the twelfth century, before the consolidation of any singular nationalist British pedagogy, Geoffrey's *Historia* performs a narrativization with pedagogical and performative pretensions. Yet it also differs in significant ways from the national narration that Bhabha describes. On one hand, the *Historia* crafts a British "people" as its object, and its diverse reception for various political uses contests the identity of which British subjects rightfully follow as Brutus's heirs. The scholarly reception of Monmouth's text seems, moreover, to make something like Bhabha's point. In that tradition, Monmouth's use of Welsh vaticination is read merely as a "colonization" of the Welsh, and Geoffrey's text can thus be said to bound Britain's identity by placing the oppositions of vaticination in the past. If this is the case, then the kinds of disavowals that Bhabha links with modernity emerge even in a premodern account of the past.

Yet Monmouth's *Historia* does not, I would argue, offer any such easy chronology. His interest in the difficult, provocative futurism of the Merlin Prophecies, to my eyes, disrupts a progressivist confidence that the past is forever (or ever) surmounted. Monmouth's ambiguous moments of futurism mean that his readers cannot move back to genealogy or chronology in any triumphant or untroubled way. Furthermore, Monmouth's combination of prophecy with genealogy suggests that future imaginings (and not just disavowals in the present) drive fantasies of community, even as the restoration of insular unity or wholeness remains a sovereign dream. Monmouth's history repetitiously invokes the past and future fiction of an entire kingdom ruled by a sovereign family; in this, as Tatlock and Ingledew both remind us, Geoffrey's history enables annexation. But his history also, and at the same time, contests monolithic rule by disrupting chronological history. His inclusion of the Merlin Prophecies means that the category of 'Britain' gestures to (at least) two futures for the crown. Monmouth thus formally encodes differential futures for Britain while displaying not the march of time but repetition and loss as Britain's fundamental story.

The oppositional "crisis literature" of an insular minority offers a trace history of the material power of those hopes for a different future. Geoffrey's use of Welsh traditions in a history written in Latin seeks to imagine a future for Welsh as well as Norman by narrating a past repetitively fraught with conflict and filled with loss. This history ultimately encodes the losses wrought by conquest and migration and, in the complex rhetorical figure of "the Britons," tentatively promises a future of wholeness and recovery. The popularity of Geoffrey's *Historia* demonstrates the substantial pleasure of such fragile hopes. Geoffrey's fragile "Britons" provide (to recall Žižek's formulation from earlier in this chapter) a captivating "kernel of enjoyment" haunted by devastating losses.

Such a project may also, before certain of audiences, enable the disavowal of twelfth-century Welsh differences from the Anglo-Normans. Desire for a British *totam insulam* will of course be used to impel as well as to justify England's efforts to annex Scotland and Wales. But it will also repeatedly be used in opposition to English hegemony. This flexibility has to do in part with the very term "Britain," a name with a doubled medieval etymology. Traditional etymologies of the word "Britain," trace its roots in two directions: from the classical figure of Brutus (the etymology listed in the *OED*), and from the common Welsh phrase "Ynys Prydein" (Island of Britain). Emphasis upon the first of these linguistic histories has traditionally eclipsed the second.[47] In Monmouth's *Historia* we find both: the story of Brutus and the Merlin's prophecies linked to the *Armes Prydein*. Insofar as the eponymous name for the island came from Brutus and his classical conquering army, "Britain" designates a conquering people, a race of invaders adopting the island as their home. Thus is "Britain" a cultural import from Troy, a legacy of conquest displaced from the heart of the Roman world. With Welsh tradition in mind, the category of Britain also refers to hopes for particular geographic integrity—to wholeness and to a native insular geography. "Britain" signifies a geographic completion lost, a unity gone from a people (and an identity) once imperial in power.

This doubled Britain will prove pliable enough, richly ambivalent enough, to accommodate the desires not just of parvenu Anglo-Norman aristocrats anxious to take part in glorious sovereign fantasies, but of later English kings and conquerors. In the fifteenth century, Monmouth's history, with its representation of a native, British glory, captivates the imagination of English kings who, in the wake of the Hundred Years War, wish to repudiate their dynastic ties to France (resisting their history as the heirs of Norman conquest). Through Arthur they claim an insular, native tradition, and a heritage more ancient than Norman invasion. For these English kings part of the useful doubleness of Geoffrey's story is that it figures an insular wholeness, and a British identity, as both a loss to be mourned and as a rightful inheritance to be regained. Since the Britons "once occupied the land from sea to sea," the category of "Britain" provides the imagination with a new insular hegemony as a very old heritage. Later sovereigns will deploy both native and classical traditions in imagining their sovereignty—English kings and aristocrats will wage war against Welsh, Scots, and Irish, building colonial outposts in the edges of the realm while encouraging court poets to tell of their classical roots. This doubleness will render insular hegemony a rightful legacy of a mystical Welsh past as well as domination forged through military, economic, and political policies.

The cultural doubleness legible in my reading of Geoffrey of Monmouth's *Historia* (and in the important work done by scholars of medieval Wales to whom my work is indebted) disappears from later notions of "Britain" and its empire. This disappearance means that William of Malmesbury's denigration of Welsh "ravings" with which we began successfully located Welsh oppositional fantasies outside the realm of the "real." The trivialization of these alternative versions of "Britain" suggests an interpretive history that favors one portion of Geoffrey's readers. Alternative fantasies have nonetheless left their traces. Those traces remain legible today thanks in part to Monmouth's careful ambiguity, and to his use of the traditions of a linguistic minority in the authoritative genre of a Latin history. In this instance, Latin becomes a vehicle for legitimizing (and rendering massively influential) a popular vernacular tradition.

These remarks again suggest some of the power medievalists can offer to postcolonial cultural studies. A consideration of the *longue durée* of British identity can offer readings of resistance that seem to have disappeared from later discussions of nation or Empire, perhaps precisely because Wales remains a colony of England today. This is not to suggest that the story of Welsh resistance told here replace (or displace) important contemporary efforts at analyzing the racist and imperialist aspects of contemporary British (or American) culture or politics. It does remind us, however, to watch for traces of a variety of resistances already obscured in authoritative accounts of history.

Furthermore, the condensation of resistance and conquering aggression told through Monmouth's *Historia*, and repeated in the history of its reception and dissemination, might offer a useful qualification to recent debates within postcolonial cultural studies. Benita Parry critiques Homi Bhabha's work as overly focused on texts produced in the colonizer's locale. She argues that such an emphasis obscures the agency of the colonized, and she calls for "a cartography of imperialist ideology more extensive than its address in colonialist space, [and] a conception of the native as historical subject and agent of an oppositional discourse" ("Problems," 44). Yet Parry's formulation itself implies that "oppositional discourses" are never found in "colonialist space"; this implies that Europe's conquerors were (ever) the only inhabitants of Europe, a fact that (with regard to the medieval colonial scene at least) overemphasizes the power of dominant cultures at the expense of the conquered. In so doing Parry inadvertently discounts the powerful intimacies of medieval borderlands, and the complicated minglings of medieval textualities. The divergent reception of the *Historia* instead suggests that both desire for and resistance to conquest can be read in a single text. My reading of the *Historia* offers the history of cultural contestation both passionately fraught and deeply intimate.

Colonial histories would, in subsequent centuries, continue to contest and disavow Welsh oppositional sovereign fantasies. They will, in fact, continue to disavow some versions of Arthur's story as fable, fancy, or mad ravings. Such a complicated literary history should, however, give us pause before charges of truth or fable, charges that will recur throughout the Middle English corpus. Through such charges Arthurian traditions, widely known and widely used for centuries, became increasingly tied to the pleasures of Europe's conquerors. Yet oppositional uses of Arthurian traditions will also persist for some time. The interpretive pleasures of Welsh separatists will face repetitive insistence that they are mad, utterly false, and thus unreal.

This history of disputes and contests over interpretive legitimacy, perhaps somewhat paradoxically, also structures what I am calling Arthur's national fantasy. In later chapters of this study I will argue that this contentious narrative history renders Arthur a king for all Britons, and helps explain the diversity, the seeming contradictions, and the impressive expansiveness of the Middle English tradition. A Middle English tradition of political prophecy, propaganda, and genealogy built upon a textual futurism borrowed from Welsh poetry means that Welsh poetic practice becomes a way of encoding England's doubled history as both conquered space and conquering sovereignty (see Chapter 2). Monmouth's tale of Merlin and Arthur offers a set of differential readings of British destiny and how it might be legitimately fulfilled. In the late medieval period, and in a century marked at one end by the Glyn Dŵr rebellion and at the other by Tudor succession, these versions of Arthur constitute a crucial—and crucially contested—account of British sovereignty.

CHAPTER TWO

Arthurian Futurism
and British Destiny

The Cat, the Rat and Lovel our dog,
Rule all England under a hog
 —Quoted by V. J. Scattergood, 211

I N 1484 this couplet, posted on the door to St. Paul's Cathedral
and aimed at deriding Richard III and his intimates, cost its author,
William Collingbourne, his life. Collingbourne was executed for treason, "put to the most cruel deth at the Tower Hylle, where for hym
were made a newe payer of gallowes" (Scattergood 21).[1] In his analysis of
fifteenth-century political poetry, V. J. Scattergood makes clear the political dangers of such poetic license, even when efforts were made (as in
Collingbourne's case) to keep the identity of the poet a secret. Political
poetry borrowed the ambiguity of animal symbolism from prophetic texts;
these kinds of prophetic traditions became, in the words of Rupert Taylor,
a "potent factor in [late medieval] English affairs" (104). Political poetry
that deployed prophetic metaphor would prove a dangerous medium.[2]
    The English crown took Collingbourne's resistant act of writing
very seriously. The textual ambiguity that produced, in Geoffrey of Monmouth's day, state-sanctioned political coalitions was, in the fifteenth century, disconcerting for the crown. The disciplinary prohibition evident in
Collingbourne's execution also obtained in the strained relations between
England and Wales, especially in the years following the Glyn Dŵr rebellion. As early as 1402 Henry IV would decree against Welsh vaticinative
poetry, arguing that Welsh bards were by "divinations and lies . . . the
cause of the insurrection and rebellion in Wales" (*Rotuli Parliamentorum*,
as cited by Taylor 105). English fears about Welsh vaticinatory poetry
were long-standing, and linked to Welsh prophetic accounts of their recovery of rule over a British *totam insulam*, the prophecy known as the

"Breton Hope." The writer of the *Vita Edwardi Secundi*, for example, links Welsh rebellious "madness" with such prophecies. His rhetoric recalls Malmesbury's castigation of the raving Welsh, focusing upon the power of prophecy for armed insurrection: "The Welsh habit of revolt against the English is a long-standing madness . . . And this is the reason. The Welsh formerly called the Britons, were once noble crowned over the whole realm of England; but they were expelled by the Saxons and lost both name and kingdom . . . But from the sayings of the prophet Merlin they still hope to recover England. Hence it is that they frequently rebel."[3] Merlin's prophetic dictums, as Malmesbury might have put it, kindle the spirits of the Welsh to war. The link between "oppositional discourses" and Welsh revolt corroborates Glanmor Williams's assertion that Merlin's texts were widely popular among various groups in Wales throughout the period: like Christian apocalyptic literature, vaticination was not confined to the aristocracy, but spread to the free population (108–10). The Crown's response to politically charged prophetic fictions throughout the century would be swift, if not altogether sure. A charge made against Lollardy in a law of 1406, for example, cites the publication of false prophecies as an explicitly seditious act. Prophetic texts would continue unabated despite such legislation; and interdictions against prophecy would be repeated into the Tudor Period, under Henry VIII, Edward VI, and Elizabeth I; and the punishments in such cases could be quite severe (see Taylor, 105).

Prophetic fantasies of insular recovery were not limited to those in conflict with the realm, however. English sovereigns and aristocrats likewise harnessed Merlin's power to support future claims to sovereignty. Yorkist King Edward IV used genealogical and prophetic texts from Monmouth's *Historia* to bolster his sovereignty, claiming Yorkist rule a legitimate recovery of an originally "British" kingship. Manuscripts replete with diagrams of Edward's "British" genealogical pedigree were commissioned, used as a means to contest rival claims to legitimate rule over England.[4] Yorkist political propaganda worked with the same ancient genealogical traditions and prophecies as did Welsh vaticinative poets, though of course to different effect.

A number of scholars have detailed the importance of Arthurian prophetic material for English historiography and sovereignty in the fourteenth and fifteenth centuries. Allison Allan documents Edward IV's use of fictional genealogies in a series of texts she has named the "Long" and "Short English Pedigrees." Caroline Eckhardt lists chronicles that include "official" versions of Merlin's statements: Robert of Gloucester's *Rhymed Chronicle*, Thomas Castleford's *Chronicle*, Robert Mannyng of Brunne's *Rhymed Story of England*, *The Short Metricle Chronicle of England*, and Nicholas Trevisa's translation of Ranulph Higden's *Polychronicon* (an edition of which would later be published by William Caxton's press).[5] Eckhardt catalogues Yorkist miscellany collections including texts of Merlin's dictums extant in the Bodleian and British Libraries.[6] David Rees shows the utility of prophetic Arthurian symbolism for Henry Tudor's triumph over Richard III. In the decades that followed Henry VII's succession, his heir apparent will be named Arthur. Scotland's James IV will also name his eldest son Arthur at a time when that child stands directly in the line of succession.[7] Finally Sydney Anglo's analysis in *Spectacle, Pageantry and Early Tudor Policy* explores the indebtedness of Tudor dynastic propaganda to the forms and figures of the Arthurian tradition.

The tendentious (and contentious) uses made of the Merlin prophecies during the time suggest the problematic nature of Merlin's claim to "truth." Authors of such ambiguous texts could gain authority for prophecy, however, by emphasizing the durability of a particular text's link to Merlin. During a turbulent political time, moreover, Merlin's value lies precisely in the ambiguity of his statements that, as Allan puts it, "could be applied and re-applied with impunity to fit new and contemporary political situations *ad infinitum* and with ever greater respect for their growing antiquity" (178). With this in mind, it is perhaps unsurprising that by the late fifteenth century, English sovereigns will be increasingly anxious to foreclose subversive accounts of Merlin's words.

Prophetic texts link history's imagination of the past with its claim on the future, a fantasy of what will be as a return to a past now gone. Because of this recursiveness, scholars tend to emphasize the nostalgia of these texts. Yet I would describe them as melancholic. For all their utopian impulses, these prophecies strain toward the apocalyptic, offering little view of a longstanding British golden age; instead they depict loss and devastation as an historical inheritance of Britain. Why, at a turbulent time like that of the later fifteenth century in England, would solemn and fatalistic texts depicting the end of British sovereignty be so popular?

I will argue in this chapter that melancholy prophecies inspire late medieval British fantasies of insular recovery by signaling a melancholy British endurance through loss rather than despite loss. They link cultural recovery to the work of mourning. To demonstrate this, I turn first to a Middle English commentary of the *Prophetia Merlini* dating from the

fifteenth century.[8] Images of a small remnant of conquered Britons cling-
ing to life in the recesses of the island and on the edge of Wales stand
as a synecdoche for a specific insular history: an ancient Britain suffering catastrophic ruin yet nonetheless remaining poised for wholeness. In
its representation of the remnant and surviving Britons, the commentary
on the Merlin prophecies appropriates the survival and endurance of a
conquered insular people for a future of insular stability.

A similar analysis applies to the popular prophecy of the end of British
sovereignty known as the "Last Six Kings" or the "Six Kings to Follow
John." Widely attributed to Merlin, but not found in Geoffrey of Monmouth's *Historia*, versions of the "Six Last Kings" circulated during the
fifteenth century as part of the most popular Middle English history, the
Prose *Brut* or *Chronicles of England*. The text's melancholy refrain, " 'alas'
shall be the common song of fatherless folk," encodes common loss and
mournful longing as unity. Through the figure of Merlin this account of
insular loss nonetheless alludes to the contentious political history that
produced it, and thus to disagreements over its legitimate fulfillment. I
will argue that this commentary and these prophecies deploy what Michael
Taussig has called "the magic of mimesis," borrowing the resources of
recovery and loss from a conquered Welsh in order to imagine a future
English sovereignty. The image of a lost and desolate insular British sovereign past becomes a means for mourning losses to English sovereignty,
and predicting a future beyond dire accounts of England's last days.

Prophetic Historicity and the *Prophetia Merlini*

An English commentary on the *Prophetia Merlini* of Geoffrey of Monmouth constitutes the sole text of a fifteenth-century manuscript held by
the Pattee Library, Pennsylvania State University.[9] As its editor Caroline
Eckhardt notes, the manuscript offers "the longest medieval translation of
[Monmouth's] *Prophetia Merlini* into English prose" and "the sole continuous medieval commentary on the *Prophetia Merlini* in English" (19).
In its special concentration of prophecy and commentary, this text establishes an historical specificity for, and an orthodox interpretation of, Merlin's prophetic words, implicitly challenging the provocative ambiguity so
important to Geoffrey of Monmouth's *Historia*.

The two parts of this text, prophecy and commentary, are framed by
a double formalistic repetition: the prophecies are introduced with the

formula "and Merlyn said"; their respective commentaries begin, "and Merlyn seid sooth." This double structure recurs throughout the text's 490 lines, alternating between Merlin's speech act and its fulfillment, between distant past (written in what seems an eternally imminent future tense), and the more recent (although equally past) corresponding fulfillment. The commentary's doubled structure attempts to foreclose interpretive ambiguity. Claims to Merlin's words and to their truth testify first to the prophet's authenticity and then to the commentator's accuracy. The two parts, prophecy and commentary, are thus mutually defining. The precision of the latter proves the truth of the former.

The historical interpretations cover the period of British history from Saxon conquest through Norman invasion to the period of Norman and Angevin rule. The text omits some prophecies given in Geoffrey's *Historia*, specifically the prophecy of the "Breton Hope" and the prophecies of the Apocalypse. It includes the prophecies of the Red and White Dragons, another group called the Norman Conquest prophecies, the succession of the two dragons, the lion of justice, the eagle, the Sextus, the lynx, all related to Norman and Angevin rule. At the point in Geoffrey's text where the prophecy of the "Breton Hope" begins, the fifteenth-century commentary turns instead to the first prophecy in the series on the "Six Last Kings," material not included in Geoffrey. The text ends abruptly with the first of the last kings and a brief mention of Henry III.

The following excerpt (a version of Merlin's famous twelfth prophecy) details and explicates the battles between red and white dragons. (In Monmouth's text, the dragons fight beneath Vortigern's crumbling tower.)[10] This is an episode, we recall, that A. O. H. Jarman identifies with Welsh vaticination. The excerpt below exemplifies both the repetitious structure of the *Prophetia Merlini* and one of the Commentator's most persistent concerns, British loss and disinheritance:

Merlyn seid . . . that the whight dragon schall [rise] ayen. and he schall calle to him Þe doghter of Saxonie. Than schall oure gardeyns be replenished with straunge seede, and Þe Reede dragon schall langwyssch and moorne in the boordis of a water.

Merlyn seide sooth. For the Englissh peple that were left o lyve aftir the greete derth and deth sent in to saxonie. where thei were boore for men wymmen and childre to stuffe cities and townes with peple a geyn. Than come the saxons and multiplied wondir thik and used the langage of hir oune contree. and chaunged the names of cities and townes and castels and held the countries baronages lordshcippes as bretons had compaced hem be forne. And among hem that come from saxonie to Englond came Þe noble quene sexburga with men and wymmen with ovte nombre. and arrivid in Northumbrelond. and toke the lond from scotland in to Cornewaille for hir and for hir peple. for al that lond was desolate and voide of peple except a fewe powre bretons that were left in mountayns and in woodis. Than began saxons for to reigne. and departed the lond be twix hem and made kinges by dyuerse contries. The first was of westsex. The second of Estsex. The thrid of Estangle called Northfold and Southfold be iiij king of Merchlond with many oÞer as king of Northumbrelond & cetera. And the bretons sum of hem fled into walis. vnto Þe boordis of the see. (ll. 125–35)

The vague symbols of what is to come, in the short space of a few lines, are transformed into a forthright historical narrative: red dragons signify the Britons driven by invaders "into Wales unto the borders of the sea." The strange seeds in "our" gardens are said to signify the progeny of Saxon conquerors who multiply "wondrously thick." The commentary offers an orthodox English interpretation of the two dragons' fate, with the White Dragon standing as a figure for the English, now united with the Saxons, and the Red Dragon as the newly conquered Britons. The dragon symbolism follows the prophecy of insular devastation from famine (told in prophecy ten), the land "desolate and voide of peple": "Þe feeldes shall disceyve the plowman. And the peple schall suffre hungre and greete deeth, and tho Þat be lefft o lif schall forsake Þer natif contre . . . And Þan schall bretayn be nere hand desolat" (ll. 93–95). Queen Sexburga and her people, a Saxon (re)population, come onto British territory at the invitation of the English, usefully repopulating what is here described as a nearly vacant countryside. These Anglo-Saxon bodies quickly move in on British territory ("changing the names of cities and towns and castles and taking ownership of the baronages and lordships"), gesturing in this moment to the links between territorial acquisition and linguistic change.

The image of a new people settling and (re)naming a vacant countryside is a common trope of narratives of migration and conquest. Desolation from conquest is here specifically named British: "Bretayn" was "nere hand desolat"; the vacant land offers only the trace of a "fewe powre bretons" remaining "in mountayns and in woodis." The pleasures of Saxon repopulation contrast with an explicitly British poverty and ruin. While the commentator identifies two insular groups predating Saxon arrival, he links intense devastation only with the "few, poor Britons" left on the land. While the impoverished Britons turn inward, the English, with apparently more foresight, look across the seas for aid. This contrast between English and British will be important, and I will return to it shortly. But I wish first to note the insularity of this image of interior Britain. Hidden in the mountains, the Britons constitute a desolate yet intact interior; they occupy a remote, yet deeply intimate, insular geography, abiding in the heart of the island. A concealed remnant, they apparently do not join in the cultural mixing of Anglo-Saxon days. They constitute an insular population untouched by immigrant rulers. Yet they also signal the trace of conquest; they are the relics of a native history suffused with loss.

Despite their identification with loss, the Britons are also continually imagined as resistant to Saxon invasion. Unlike the English, they remain obdurate before Saxon seductions. Earlier in the *Prophetia* this resistance has been linked to impressive, male rule. Before Queen Sexburga and her people arrive, the British King Cadwall (in prophecies seven and eight) resiliently rebuffs the Saxon threat.[11] Yet even, perhaps especially, at this moment of British victory loss links with resilience:

[7] Merlin seide also that ther schall be so greete tormentrie that Þe childer schall be cut ovt of hir modir wombes. and straunge men schall be restored.
And he seide soth. For king Cadwall was so sore annoyed with saxons that he thought vtterly to distroie hem. and to restore it a yet to bretayns. and he did slee man woman and childe for to performe his entencion and to enhaunce the bretons. (71–72)

Horrific loss, this time perpetrated by a British king, sponsors British restoration. Cadwall's success and British restoration follow the most atrocious devastation. British loss and restoration are gendered here, moreover. "Strange men" are restored; women (and the children in their wombs) suffer catastrophically. The motif of the violent deaths of children ripped from their mothers' wombs, indebted to biblical images of the Slaughter of Innocents, usually stands as testimony to tyranny. This common image of wartime loss gains poignancy through its gender strategies. It acutely expresses the horror of war through gendered images of slaughter. One obvious implication would be that the perpetrator of these deaths must be most excessively tyrannical, the fortunes he wishes to enhance as unjust as the methods used to enhance them.

In contrasting the image of victimized mothers with Cadwall's violence the text emphasizes Cadwall's tyranny as a function of his masculinity. A male sovereign forges restoration through a virile force of arms. Cadwall's violence is imagined as productive for British restoration, but only temporarily and only by engendering catastrophic destruction on female reproductive bodies. This contrast resonates with the contrast between British and English we have just seen, where the English host join

with Queen Sexburga and, in contrast to the insular British, offer the child-
less island a (re)productive future. This gendering of sovereign rule splits
a British violent (male) sovereignty from a Saxon reproductive (female)
one. From the long view, the point seems to be that for all Cadwall's virile potency, British insularity, in contrast to English exogamy, is literally
barren.

Yet if the commentator merely wishes to cast British insularity as
impotent, he misses an opportunity to drive the point home. Indeed, following the description of slaughter in prophecy seven, the commentary
seems unconscionably mild. Prophetic apocalypticism sits uneasily with
the explanation that follows; in fact, the prophecy offers a gripping depth
and texture to wartime loss, a texture that is then flattened out by the
abstract nouns of the commentary. In place of castigations of a tyrannical
victimization of the innocent, or of the uselessness of Cadwall's unchecked
aggression, the commentary forthrightly details Cadwall's success against
the Saxons. The commentary backs away from a castigation of war crimes
in favor of what seems a more dispassionate historicism.

This may be because while the commentator wishes to suggest that
British insularity has no future, he also remains fascinated by Cadwall's
restorative power for his people. Focusing on Cadwall's desire to destroy
the Saxons (mentioning his aggressive ambitions five different times in a
single line), this ambivalent description combines desire and derision: a
fascination with British resistance and a horrific image of British savagery.
To be sure, the author may wish to link Cadwall to charges of tyranny; I
will be arguing shortly that this commentary is not particularly pro-Welsh,
despite a fascination with the fortunes of these "British" ancestors. Taken
together, prophecy and commentary display horrible loss as a means to
British restoration.

King Cadwall remains one of the most vivid images from the *Prophetia*. In prophecy eight, his dead sovereign body provides salvific powers
that persist beyond war, beyond insular barrenness, beyond even his own
treachery:

[8] Merlyn seyde also that he þat schall doo this Rigour schall be come a man of
brasse. And he by a long tyme schall kepe london gatis vppon a brasen hors.
And Merlyn seid soth. For king Cadwal after he had destroied Saxons he died
and was beried in a brasen ymage made after his ovne stature. This ymage was set
vppon a brasen hors. And put vp on the west gate of london in token that he had
discomfited and dryven ovte the Saxons. and the bretons beleved that thei schuld
neuir be put ovt as long as this ymage kepts the portes of london (72).

The massive materiality of a dead sovereign body shelters his people from their enemies. The statue, not unlike those used in Imperial Rome, both resembles the sovereign's body and contains it. Cast in brass, a sovereign *memento mori* raised above the city gate magically grants the British people belief in their safety. Both triumphant and dead, Cadwall offers his people an apotropaic fantasy from beyond the grave; his brass body shields them and keeps them safe. In memorializing their sovereign, the Britons claim the magnificent space of London as theirs. This ancient sovereign artifact, the iconic relic of a dead British king, continues to safeguard belief in a sovereign British community in London—a British body politic—even as Cadwall relinquishes his own prodigious body to physical death.

The encryptment of Cadwall's body in brass above the gates of London, moreover, is structurally similar to the earlier image of lost and surviving Britons encrypted deep in the heart of the island. The encryptment of these vanquished Britons, like the dead body of Cadwall in brass, combines desolation with survival. The future tense of such prophecy, furthermore, gestures toward the power of remembrance for the imagination of a future. I wish to pause here to note that the doubleness of Cadwall's body, decaying and yet encrypted in protection of his people, anticipates the structure of loss and survival in the early-modern political theory of the King's Two Bodies. The death of the sovereign, in both prophecy and in theory, does not mean the death of sovereignty. The fantasy of a people perpetually alive, of a sovereign body defying death, sits at the heart both of eerie visions of royal corpses contained in brass and of later political theories that rationalize sovereign sempiternity. In maintaining Cadwall's special body, the Britons will not lose; they refuse to give up their victorious leader, and by implication, the moment of their victory. Cadwall's victory over the Saxons makes him the token for a belief in insular power despite perils from without.

The ambivalent images of Cadwall (tyrannical yet powerful) mean, however, that Welsh oppositional claims to British restoration (the so-called "Breton Hope") haunt the text of the *Prophetia Merlini*. And this may be why the commentary offers a puzzling (and contradictory) description of insular British history. As "strange men," the Britons are nonetheless "restored" to rule. A restoration of British rule implies, of course, that the Britons are not strangers at all; it implies that they have already ruled; it implies (as well as represses) a prehistory of British claims to London's crown. King Cadwall's successful resistance to Saxon conquest in prophecy seven, furthermore, seems especially paradoxical in light of the text's opening insistence, repeated just two dozen lines earlier, that all the Britons are already gone, having been forced to evacuate the island, "driven out" and "destroyed."

I am arguing that the *Prophetia* offers an ambivalent image of the Britons: lost, destroyed, driven out, yet nonetheless resilient, resistant, enduring. The commentator shows an ambivalent fascination with powerful images of British restoration; yet he also works to circumscribe their symbolic power. The commentary tells a complicated history that links a (desirable) British resistance with a (deplorable) British tyranny. In the end, of course, Cadwall and the Britons are undone. The commentary makes clear that this undoing stems neither from the ferociousness of the enemy Saxons nor from the treachery of powerful sovereigns, but from the communitarian frailties of the Britons themselves. In this account, intra-British rivalries open the door to Britain's ultimate undoing. Such stories are common in national histories, texts that frequently recount how foreign invaders gain successful entry into a house divided against itself. In a prophetic text dating from a period of fractiousness like that of the Wars of the Roses, such a tale could provide a rationale for disciplining recalcitrant aristocrats.[12]

In emphasizing the barrenness of the Britons as community, yet also emphasizing the power of British resistance to Saxon invasion, the commentator negotiates the politically provocative implication that the Welsh Britons might have a future claim on British group identity. Unhooked from links with Welsh political claims on a future identity and rule, British resilience and endurance through loss can be activated for different set of sovereign fantasies. This negotiation demands that the Welsh figure as both Britain's native and Britain's past people be already imbricated in loss; as the vestige of a native history, the Britons can offer the promise of a direct insular lineage, but not a future of (Welsh) recovery. It is important for this commentator, in other words, that the power of British resilience remain tied to the loss of the British community's future. And this returns us to the commentator's anti-Welsh politics to which I alluded earlier.

In later portions of the text, the commentator explicitly denounces the possible implication that the resistant Britons in the Welsh mountains have any future claim to a centralized English throne. This claim, known as the "Breton Hope," was a repetitive motif in Welsh vaticination. The commentator of the *Prophetia Merlini* omits the "Breton Hope" prophecy in his borrowings from Geoffrey's *Historia*. Instead he recounts how the Saxon King Egbert "deposed the brasen image" of Cadwall that the Britons hoped would "chace away the Saxons." And in the commentary to prophecy eleven, a "voice from hevyn" tells Cadwall's successor, Cadwalader, the "last king of Bretons" that "it is not the will of god that brentons [sic] regne no lenger ne nevir recouer the lond til the tyme the reliques of thi body and of other seyntes be found and brought from Rome unto bretayn" (73).[13] The commentary for prophecy eleven links the future of Welsh sovereignty with the pieties of pilgrimage, and not the politics of home rule. British restoration occurs not through magical sovereign resurrections or movements fueled by political ardor, but through the return of religious relics from the Holy See.

There is additional evidence as to the text's orthodox politics. On the basis of details of the text's penultimate prophecy (no. 37), editor Eckhardt surmises that the commentator may have "wished to avoid any association [with] the house of Percy . . . reputed to be seeking the throne" (Introduction, 28–29). The Percies, of course, were infamously allied with Glyn Dŵr and Mortimer (and against Henry Bolingbroke) in stories of the Tripartite Convention; the Tripartite Treaty—purporting to divide the kingdom among Percy, Mortimer, and Glyn Dŵr—was historically (if spuriously) linked to the prophecies of Merlin.[14]

In his depiction of the Britons as both surviving insular subjects and historically conquered objects, the commentator of this *Prophetia Merlini*, tries to circumvent rebellious uses of the prophecies of British return. The Britons continually reemerge as a presence on the island, in the farthest reaches of Wales. Despite devastating and repeated losses, the remnant Britons remain together in the heart of the realm. Unlike many vanquished native peoples, they are assigned a stable and local identity, not a diasporic, peripatetic one spreading to the ends of the earth. Separated from the center of power, they are nonetheless deeply interior to the realm. They constitute a continuous insular presence. The Britons lose, but are not lost. A poor and defeated Welsh remnant inhabiting the mountains and borders of the island still dwell in an insular interior (however marginalized) withstanding famine, plague, and Saxon invasion.[15]

These vanquished Britons remain tokens of a beleaguered insular past. The version of the island's early history available in the commentary to the *Prophetia Merlini* resists Welsh "oppositional" strategies at the same time that it heroizes an insular heritage that has proved resistant through loss.[16] And yet this poignant tale of poverty, hunger, and defeat is only half the story: the prophecy also crafts a sweeping genealogy; it enumerates insular rulers one after the other, attesting to how doggedly kingship over the island has survived through the consistently disastrous and fractious past. A history of the stability of sovereign power through loss to British community can console a culture anxious about the instability of its changing identity.

The symbolic riches of this Welsh survival through devastating defeat become fantasmatically useful to sovereigns and aristocrats in Britain anxious about their own futures. By the second half of the fifteenth century, images of British restoration become a strategic feature of Yorkist claims to legitimate succession.[17] In Edward IV's *Long Pedigree*, for example, succession becomes a recovery of a native identity, a return to a British sovereignty untainted by non-insular culture.[18] Manuscript Bodley 623 gives a particularly striking view of such a genealogy and the prophecies it deployed. This manuscript contains "a chronology of the world from Creation to 1464 in the form of a chart" that juxtaposes prophecies with specific interpretations of them. The "Breton Hope" is included, followed by an explanation that from Cadwalader's time, "the rule of the Britons has lapsed, but that it has now descended ead Edwardum 4 verum heredum britanie" (58); an adjacent diagram records Edward IV's link to Cadwalader in genealogical form. One portion of the manuscript depicts the details of succession from the fifth century to the fifteenth, noting a dramatic shift in insular identity during Edward IV's reign. Eckhardt describes the genealogy:

At A.D. 448 in the chronology, there appears an entry for Merlin's prophecy to Vortigern, just below the entry for the accession of Marcianus as emperor. At A.D. 530, there occurs the statement that in this year Merlin told Arthur about the Six Last Kings to come; . . . [An] angel's prophecy to Cadwalader (another version of the "Breton hope," from the end of Geoffrey's *Historia*) occurs at A.D. 680, with a reference there to its fulfillment in 1460. After 680, the column that has been labeled "Britannia" is labeled instead "Anglia," in recognition of the Germanic conquest. It continues to be labeled "Anglia" until the accession of the new "British" King Edward IV, at which point, in tacit fulfillment of the prophecy that "nomine bruti vocabitur insula" (from the *Prophetia Merlini*), the column is labeled "Britannia" once more. (58)

With Edward's succession "Britannia" reclaims the island as its home; the reign of "Anglia" explicitly gives way to the return of the "British" that Merlin had prophesied long before.[19] From the long view of history, Edward IV did not finally supply the native pedigree sufficient to render him a believable redeemer returned. The Yorkists would lose the throne in the "readeption" of the Lancastrian Henry VI. And yet in Edward's attempt to fabricate such credentials he identifies the legitimate crown with an insular British past rather than a continental Plantagenet one.

When English kings craft genealogies based upon older Welsh forms and popular Welsh political hopes, they deploy what Michael Taussig calls, with reference to a later colonialism, "the magic of mimesis." In copying those forms English sovereigns "share in or acquire the property of the represented" (46). English sovereigns and English devotees of the Merlin prophecies revel in the rich magic of a past of British return, or borrow the poignancy and energy of British loss, while continuing to gain the political and economic riches of a Welsh colony. Such uses point to the dependencies of the conquerors upon the people they rule.

The *Prophetia Merlini* imagines a heritage of British people hidden within the island's interior, and implies that changes in particular sovereign bodies do not unrecognizably, or devastatingly, change the heart of Britain. Such a "native" insular past evokes a powerful British identity. To consider further the nature of this identity, imbricated both in loss and in restoration, I turn to the most popular (and melancholy) prophecy of English sovereignty, the Middle English Prose *Brut* version of the prophecy known as the "Six Kings to Follow John."

Apocalyptic Warnings: The Six Last Kings

According to Lister M. Matheson, the Middle English Prose *Brut* chronicle was "the most popular secular work of the Middle Ages in England," the abundance of its manuscripts in Middle English "exceeded only by that of the manuscripts of the two Wycliffite translations of the Bible" (210). Until such time as a comprehensive comparative analysis of the 172 manuscripts listed in the *Manual of Writings in Middle English* is finished, Matheson's current catalogue of variants remains authoritative. He designates four basic versions, as follows: the Common Version (based on the Anglo-Norman Prose *Brut*, usually ending with the Battle of Halidon Hill in 1333, but with continuations, some of which bring the chronicle up to 1461); the Extended Version (adding details taken from the *Short English Metrical Chronicle*); the Abbreviated Version (a shortened account with elements from both the Common and Extended versions); and what he calls "Peculiar Texts and Versions" (a miscellaneous category including Latin *Bruts* translated into English, idiosyncratic reworkings of English texts, and smaller texts based on the *Brut*).[20] The first volume of Brie's

EETS edition of the *Brut* offers the Common Version, a chronicle up to 1333. The prophecy of the "Six Last Kings" occurs here, first as Merlin's prophetic utterance to King Arthur, and later in specific interpretations linked to the English kings Henry III, Edward I, and Edward II. Because of a modern unfamiliarity with this prophecy so very familiar to nearly all fifteenth-century English chronicle writers, I quote a lengthy (abridged) version from the Prose *Brut* text:

How Kynge Arthure axede of Merlyn Þe aventures of vj the lastekynges Þat weren to regne in Engeland, and how Þe lande shulde ende.
[The lamb]   "Sire," quod Merlyn, "in Þe ȝere of Incarnacioun of oure Lorde M CC xv Þere shal come a lambe oute of Wynchestre Þat shal haue a white tong and trew lippis and he shall have wryten in his hert Holynesse. This lambe shal . . . haue pees Þe most parte of his life, & he shal make one of Þe faireste places of Þe worlde Þat in his tyme shal nouȝt full ben made an ende. . . . And in Þe ende of his lif, a wolf of a straunge lande shal do him grete harme . . . And Þe lambe shal leue no while Þat he ne shal dye. His sede Þan shal bene in strange lande, and Þe lande shal bene wiþout gouernoure a litill tyme.
[The dragon]   And after him shal come a dragoun mellede wiþ mercy and ek wodenesse, Þat shal haue a berde as a good, Þat shal ȝeve in Engeland shadewe, and shal kepe the lande from colde and hete . . . He shal vnbrace iii habitacions, and he shal oppen his mouþ toward Walys. . . . This dragoun shal bene holden in his tyme Þe best body of al Þe worlde; & he shal dye besides Þe Marche of a straunge lande; and Þe lande shalle duelle faderlesse wiþouten a gode gouernoure; and me shal wepe for his deþ; wherefore, 'allas' shal bene Þe commune songe of faderles folc, Þat shal ouerleuen in his lande destroiede.
[The goat]   And after Þis dragone shal come a gote . . . Þat shal haue hornes & berde of siluer; and þere shal come out of his nosbrelles a drop Þat shal bitoken hunger & sorw, & grete deþ of Þe peple; and miche of his lande . . . shal be wastede. . . In Þat same tyme shal dye, for sorwe and care, a peple of his lande, so Þat many shal bene oppon him Þe more bolder afterward. . .
[The boar]   Aftre Þis goote shal come out of Wyndsore a Boor Þat shal haue an heuede of witte, a lyons hert, a pitouse lokyng; . . . his worde shal bene gospelle; his beryng shal bene meke as a Lambe. In Þe ferste ȝere of his regne he shal haue grete payne to iustifien ham Þat bene vntrew; and in his tyme shal his lande bene multipliede wiþ Aliens. . . . And he shal whet his teiþ vppon be ȝates of Parys, and vppon iiii landes. Spayne shal tremble for drede of him; Gascoyne shal swete; in Fraunce he shal put his wynge; his grete taile shal reste in Engeland softely; Almayne shal quake for drede of him . . .
[The second lamb]²¹   After Þis Boor shal come a lambe, Þat shal haue feete of leede, an heuede of bras, an hert of a loppe, and a swynnes skyn and herde; and in his tyme his land shal bene in pees. . . . Þis lambe shal lesein his tyme a grete parte of his lande Þrouz an hidouse wold; but he shal recouer it, an ȝif an Lordeship to an Egle of his landes . . .

[The mole]   After Þis lambe shal come a Moldewerpe acursede of Godes mouÞ, a
caitif, a cowarde as an here. he shal haue an elderliche skyn as a goot; and vengeance
shal fall vppon him for synne. . . . Than shal arisen a dragoun in Þe North, . . .
and shal meve werre aȝeyens Þe forsaide Moldewerpe . . . Þis dragoun shal gadre
aȝeyne into his company a wolf Þat shal come oute of the West, Þat shal bygynne
aȝeynes Þe Moldewerp in his side;
Þan shal come a lyon oute of Irlande, Þat shal fal in company wiÞ ham; and Þan
shal tremble Þe lande Þat Þan shal bene callede Engeland, as an aspe lef . . . and
after he shal leue in sorw al his lif-tyme; and in his tyme Þe hote babes shullen
bicome colde; and after Þat shal Þe Moldewerp dye aventurly and sodenly—allas,
Þe sorwe!—for . . . his seede shal bicome pure faderles in straunge lande for euermore, and Þan shal the lande bene departede in iii parties, Þat is to seyn to the
Wolf, to Þe dragoune, and to Þe lioun; and so shal it bene for euermore. And
Þan Þis lande bene callede 'Þe lande of conquest,' & so shal Þe riȝt heires of
Engeland ende."

The prophecy catalogues England's fall from glorious sovereign wholeness: beginning with a utopian scene of rule (indebted to images of the
Lamb and New Jerusalem from the book of Revelation) the text devolves
to a recurring vision of a desolate, fatherless folk. Occasional moments
of peace always give way to misery, England overflowing with loss; held
by strangers; overrun with "Aliens"; shaking like an aspen leaf; under
shadow; turned cold; a land of hunger and sorrow; a wasted land; the
land of conquest. Animal-kings allegorize English monarchs of the Plantagenet dynasty of the thirteenth and fourteenth centuries, beginning with
Henry III. Amid his narration of the events of Henry III's reign, some
hundred pages after Merlin's audience before Arthur, the *Brut* author
(following the Anglo-Norman text) identifies Henry as the lamb of Winchester, Edward I as the dragon, and Edward II as the goat. None of
the continuations of the chronicle included in Brie's text (taking us from
1333 variously into the fifteenth century) continue the prophecies through
to their end. By logical extension, however, the remaining three animal-
kings, the boar, the second lamb, and the mole must follow as Edward III,
Richard II, and Henry IV as the last of England's kings.

Any chronicler or member of his audience in the years beyond the
death of Henry IV knew, of course, that Henry was not the final monarch.
Like many unfulfilled prophecies, this one should have lost its power once
the events it foretold failed to transpire. And thus Henry V's succession
should perhaps have put an end to the "Prophecy of the Six Last Kings";
this may explain why the interpretations of the last three prophecies are
omitted from the *Brut* continuations. Yet the prophecies of "the end of

this land" did not, in fact, die out even after events had proven England's survival.

Scholars analyzing the use and purpose of the "Prophecy of the Last Six Kings" have focused attention on the historical story of the "Tripartite Convention," or the "Tripartite Indenture" an account of which is found in a chronicle of the reigns of Richard II and Henry IV.[22] The Tripartite Convention was, as mentioned earlier, the name given to the possible alliance between Percy, Mortimer, and Glyn Dŵr against Henry Bolingbroke. This story (most famously told in Shakespeare's 1 *Henry IV*) purports that this rebel alliance was inspired by the "skimble-skamble stuff" of prophecy. Scholars had long assumed an historical link between the "Prophecy of the Six Kings" and the prophecy putatively used by the Glyn Dŵr faction; those links, however, have been compellingly called into question. In a subtle analysis of the manuscript and textual history of "Prophecy of the Six Kings," T. M. Smallwood argues that, in its Middle English version, the text was not used for the propagandistic purposes so many scholars have assumed. Smallwood compelling argues, in fact, that unlike their Anglo-Norman sources the Middle English versions of the "Six Last Kings" display a particularly striking lack of propagandistic interpolations.[23] She questions whether the history of the "Tripartite Convention" is itself authentic, remarking that it might be "no more than a fantasy, . . . suggested by the 'Prophecy of the Six Kings' itself" (592).[24]

Smallwood argues that Welsh vaticination (which she calls the "common currency" of medieval Welsh politics) not this Middle English prophecy supplied Glyn Dŵr's prophetic material. Even as she points to the dubious nature of the "Tripartite Convention," Smallwood documents the longstanding power of Welsh vaticination for imagining an alternative to English insular sovereignty. "Propagandistic and hortatory use of prophecy had been a feature of native Welsh culture for many centuries before Glendower's time. . . . It is to this enduring Welsh tradition of political prophecy that we should [look] for an understanding of an outburst of propagandistic prophecy, evidently hostile to the English crown, in the "rebel" areas of Wales early in Henry IV's reign" (592). Given these traditions, what are we to make of the inclusion of a prophecy recounting the end of England's sovereignty in the most popular English history of the fifteenth century? The fact that Caxton and other scribes and printers did not remove the prophecy as archaic, flawed, or out dated might suggest that prophecies of loss to English sovereignty, quite apart from particular propagandistic uses of them, had captivated cultural imagination in fifteenth-century Britain. How are we to understand an English fascination with a genealogy of losses, a train of sovereign fathers leaving their land behind?

The prophecy envisions catastrophic community, the death of "the people" and the loss of the sovereign as father. At the death of the rule of the Dragon we read: "And þe lande shalle duelle faderlesse wiþouten a gode gouernoure; And me shal wepe for his deþ; wherefore, 'allas' shal bene Þe commune songe of faderles folc, þat shal ouerleuen in his lande destroiede" (73). In the reign of the Goat, "þere shal come out of his nosbrelles a drop þat shal bitoken hunger & sorw, & great deþ of þe peple" (73). With the reign of the Mole, "þan shal tremble þe lande þat þan shal bene callede Engeland, as an aspe lef" (75). And at the death of the Mole, "sodenly – allas, þe sorwe! – for . . . his seede shal bicome pure faderles in straunge lande for euermore . . . . And þan þis lande bene callede 'þe lande of conquest,' & so shal þe riȝt heires of Engeland ende" (76).

In the previous section of this chapter, I argued that the commentator of the *Prophetia Merlini* linked loss with *British* community so as to negotiate the provocative implication that the Welsh, formerly the Britons (the past tense is crucial), had any right to a future of insular sovereignty. In the "Prophecy of the Six Kings," loss resides in England; "England" becomes "the land of conquest." These words offer a trace history of English Conquest, as both a colonial legacy suffered and a conquest forged. From one view, "þe lande of conquest" claims that England, shaking like an aspen leaf, is itself a conquered land, thus alluding to a history of Norman invasion. But England is also "þe lande of conquest" in another sense, since English boundaries (although differently at different historical moments) have been forged through the sword.

Positioned in a double, middle space, both conquered and conqueror, England's sovereignty is fixed in the most mournful trajectory possible. As if in response to this history, the "Prophecy of the Six Kings" mourns the loss of a common sovereign English father as unpreventable, in need of the mournful cries of its folk community. England's six last kings cannot provide the enduring power and symbolic protection that the Briton's King Cadwall, even in death, offered to his people. Both conqueror and conquered, English sovereign death offers no fantasy of security. Yet consolations still follow English loss, returning in other formulations. The train of lost sovereigns offers hope for recovery, not through sovereign resurrections, but through the newly communitarian work of a mourning people. A unified song of mourning can compensate for sovereign imbecilities. Sovereign loss is thus transformed through a singular cultural production, a common song of longing created in response to this loss. Unlike the representation of the Britons in the *Prophetia Merlini* (who have powerfully resistant sovereigns, but are a painfully barren community), this account of sovereign endings promises that the end of a community of English sovereigns nonetheless forges a bond among a field of folk. The song of an English "folk" community rises amid the ashes of sovereign loss.

This image of newly common folk survival forged through loss would be powerfully resonant during times of English sovereign troubles. By the late fifteenth century, England's loss of French holdings will urge a domestically circumscribed and insular "native" identity; yet by that time any notion of an historic, insular, surviving Britain will have already been troubled by Glyn Dŵr's rebellious use of Welsh prophecy. Thus late medieval English relations vis-à-vis the "Britons" involve the most delicate and poignant kind of fantasy, one that joins the preciousness of "British" insular survival (and thus a history of Welsh resistance to Anglo-Saxon and to Norman colonialism) with a denigration of British resistance to a later English rule. "British" identity conjoins Welsh survival with Welsh loss, so as to separate the power of images of Welsh survival from the dangers of Welsh rebellion. Triumphant and angry predictions of Welsh revenge, predictions in Welsh vaticinative poetry that detail specific "oppositional" hopes for sovereign rule turn, in Middle English prophetic texts, into a melancholy apocalypticism.

Precisely because such efforts deploy prophecy for a productive English future, it is important to remember that, particularly during the early part of the century, some had more cause to mourn than others: the Welsh would remain under suspicion of sedition, their dealings with the English rigorously constrained. Legal discourse and statutes from the post-Glyn Dŵr years describe the Welsh as a perfidious people like "the wild Irish, our enemies." The infamous penal statutes of the early fifteenth century circumscribed the powers and activities of Welshmen as Welshmen. According to those laws no Welshman could buy land in England or in the "Englishries" within Wales; no Welshman, or Englishman married to a Welsh woman, could hold office in Wales; no Welshman could carry arms on the highway, or in any market or town; no Welshman could hold a castle or fortress, neither could men of mixed race; no Welshmen could bring legal suit against, or be used as a witness to secure the conviction of, an Englishman. R. R. Davies describes this body of legislation as both "more comprehensive by far than any other issued hitherto" and "more specifically racist in character" (*Conquest*, 458). While intermarriage between Welsh and English had long been a corollary of English and Anglo-Norman rule, in the wake of the Glyn Dŵr rebellion such intercultural practices became illegal.[25] This legislation was a distinct shift from earlier policies which had depended upon English and French-speaking Welshmen and Anglo-Welsh Lords for the governance of the area of the March.

The prophecies of England's "Six Last Kings" emerge in conversation between Merlin the prophet and the British King Arthur. Arthur, linked both to sovereign power and to apocalyptic fantasies of sovereign decline, encodes late medieval fantasies of desolation and recovery. The multicultural history of Arthur's legends—particularly the French, Welsh, Scots, and English pasts to which it alludes—provides a horizon against which an ancient and enduring British landscape can be imagined. Late medieval contestations over Arthur's sovereign heritage nonetheless make Arthur's Kingship (and the prophecies spoken during it) crucial to a large, and culturally diverse, audience. Prophetic prose and poetry point with clarity to the tragedies and losses of that tradition.

Communitarian Futures

The preceding discussion suggests that prophetic fascination with kings (living and dead) can, perhaps paradoxically, impel the imagination of a future people joined together. In these fifteenth-century prophetic texts, fissures in sovereign genealogies, breaks and fractures to stable kingship produce fantasies of communitarian futures: the Britons from the *Prophetia Merlini* hold London against Saxon invasion thanks to the power of Cadwall's dead body; in the "Prophecy of the Six Last Kings" the loss of English sovereign stability inspires a popular common song. These texts point to the links between monarchical (dynastic) genealogies and the "horizontal" bonds among a populace. On one hand, such images might be read to corroborate the generally accepted notion (thanks to Benedict Anderson's *Imagined Communities*) that horizontal bonds among peoples evolve only after belief in monarchical stability recedes. I am arguing, however, that Anderson's implicitly evolutionary model cannot account in a satisfying way for the dialectical movement between fantasies of monarchical loss and the image of a communitarian future produced as the work of mourning. It is crucial to remember, moreover, that these futuristic imaginings of identity occur in the context of intense contestations over the meaning of the nation that is to be. And so I turn to consider the difference such a history of difference makes for understanding fantasies of a once and future identity.

In *Imagined Communities*, Anderson argues that shifting notions of community, governmental organization, and history coalesced with the rise of capitalism and developments in vernacular printing to produce the spread of national forms.[26] Anderson argues that consciousness of dynastic monarchical formulations and typological notions of history must pass away before a sense of the nation as imagined community develops. Yet the evolutionary (even teleological) model of history that impels this account means that the losses crucial to Anderson's study figure simply as sensibilities passing away before the inexorable march of time. The mournful prophecies described in this chapter encode (and at times demand) the repetitious sufferings of particular cultures, particular bodies in the wake of conquest and war. Through their interest in lost sovereignty and in temporal repetitions these prophetic texts show that dynastic consciousness and typological notions of history encode the future nation as a work requiring mourning. By emphasizing mourning here, I do not mean a vague nostalgia for a lost golden age. These narratives are much too poignant, too deeply sad, to support such a conclusion. I mean instead that these narratives insinuate that the consolidation of a united insular future produces communitarian bonds precisely by producing, and using, experiences of loss. Widespread experiences of loss unleash, in this case, substantial energies that can be captured for unification.

These prophetic texts also display (as early as Geoffrey of Monmouth) the relevance of the imagination of a community of sovereigns (a monarchical "imagined community" across time) to the imaginings of territorial spaces. In both this and the previous chapter, I have endeavored to suggest that the imagination of a community of sovereigns across time enables a subsequent imagination of a community across the space of a realm. I am, therefore, arguing for a dialectical, rather than sequential or teleological, relationship between typological histories, dynastic monarchical polities (the site of vehement and repeated contestations precisely over questions of legitimate rule at various times throughout the Middle Ages), and horizontally "imagined communities" of national identity.[27] This is not to say, of course, that fifteenth-century (or earlier) communitarian arrangements are identical to later sets of affairs. It is to say, however, that imaginings of identity exist through contested oppositional debates about centralization before such differences are subsumed (or disavowed) in explicitly centralized narrations of a nation disseminated to a widespread reading public.

While aware of the strengths of Anderson's analysis, Sara Suleri similarly criticizes the evolutionary chronology of colony and nation he deploys for its implicit condescension toward colonized groups. She argues that such models "merely replicate in inverse order an enduring imperial stereotype, which suggests that empire confers the rationality of nationhood on its prerational subjects" (*Rhetoric*, 8–9). Emphasizing instead the "intimacy of the colonial setting," Suleri argues that national imaginings occur through "the dynamic of imperial intimacy," where "an idea of nation that belongs neither to the colonizer nor to the colonized" is produced (9). In Suleri's formulation the imagined nation constitutes its own kind of otherness; it is an "alterity to which both subjugating and subjugated cultures must in coordination defer" (9). In contrast to Anderson's linear model, Suleri's formulation of intercultural dynamism can accommodate a nexus of passionate, oppositional contests over the definition of the culture that a national future might encode.

The relation between imagination, contestation, and England's future legible in the prophetic texts examined in this chapter remind us, moreover, that for imagining a nation the future is crucial. And in a century marked by worries of inheritance and disputes over sovereignty, fantasies of England's future would be of special concern. Texts of prophecy, simultaneously gesturing toward past, present, and future, deploy what R. W. Southern called a "the chief inspiration of all historical thinking" (160).[28] The double structure of memory and futurism in prophetic texts and sovereign genealogies makes identity available for the present and future by speaking its "truth" in the past. It thus marks what I will call a "cultural anamnesis," a psychic and communitarian moment of remembrance powerful enough to affect a still uncertain future.[29]

This role of futuristic ambiguity for cultural identity offers, *contra* Anderson, a conflictual, and non-teleological, history of national imaginings. It also provides an example of what Gilles Deleuze and Felix Guattari call a "reverse causality," a set of relations "which are without finality but testify nonetheless to an action of the future on the present" (*A Thousand Plateaus*, 431). Prophecy's role in late medieval history makes explicit how a futuristic vision of the recovery of a fully united British island can effect insular politics well before such an identity is recognizable in explicit hegemonic narrations of the nation. That is, the prophetic image of a Britain "united from sea to sea" can impel activities both in anticipation of, and in defense against, a united English hegemony coming into being. The possibility of an insular English future wholeness—English control over the entire Welsh principality, for example—helped inspire Glyn Dŵr's revolt as an attempt to ward off such a future. In Henry Tudor's triumph, insular union between England and Wales becomes anticipated as a threshold crossed, a prophecy apparently fulfilled by the succession of a Welsh man to the English throne.[30] When Deleuze and Guattari remind us that, "to ward off is also to anticipate," they encourage us to see in striking relief how the activities of Owain Glyn Dŵr and those of Henry Tudor might be more intimately connected than has traditionally been acknowledged. Proclaimed the Royal Prince of Wales by his followers in September 1400, Glyn Dŵr claimed to be the *Mab Darogan* (Son of Prophecy) returning to rescue the Welsh in their darkest hour; in August 1485, Henry Tudor likewise was acclaimed the *Mab Darogan*, appropriating the national banner of the Welsh dragon on his way to claim an English throne.

Antagonistic traditions of the use and interpretation of prophecy thus display one of the paradoxes of late medieval historiography: while sovereigns required the symbolic flexibility offered by prophecy to sponsor imaginary ties to a continuous community of British sovereigns (and thereby to legitimate their kin-based claims to the throne), this same flexibility was useful to rebel leaders and to the enemies of the powerful. Prophetic symbolism was actively deployed in the service of conflicting political agendas. Managing the "truth" of such politically charged claims would become increasingly important to sovereign succession and to the status quo. The *Prophetia Merlini*'s attempt to craft a union across time thus also registers its attempt to declare historical verisimilitude, "a desire to demonstrate that about other matters also 'Merlin said soth'" (Eckhardt 42).[31]

Considered as a kind of late medieval historiography, moreover, prophecy can prompt a reconsideration of the uses of typological repetition.[32] Traditional accounts of medieval historiography (accounts to which Anderson is indebted) emphasize the medieval historian's tendency to prize the confluences and repetitions of history rather than its disjunctions and differences. This has prompted the view, advanced most famously but by no means exclusively by Peter Burke, that the medieval sense of history was less sophisticated than the "renaissance sense of the past."[33] While scholars no longer accept Burke's assertion, assumptions about the radical differences between medieval histories and those of the early modern period persist (as Janet Coleman has recently shown) in scholarship as well as in university curricula.[34] Nonetheless, as Coleman points out, histories in various periods rely upon notions of similarity as well as difference. In a recent consideration of the contemporary privileging of "difference and its relation to a demand for 'heteronormativity,'" Louise Fradenburg argues that this "alteritism [of the present to the past, of the 'modern' or 'early modern' periods to a pre-modern medieval one] functions within current historicist practice precisely to stabilize the identity of 'the modern'" ("Pleasures," 378).[35] This is, moreover, exactly the status of the "medieval" in Anderson's work. It functions to stabilize the identity of "nation" and "modern" as mutually defined and defining.

Stabilizing that identity literally means jettisoning the oppositions that also produced it. At a time when innovations in historiographic practice (the vernacular chronicle) and textual production (the printing press) dramatically increase popular access to stories of Arthur, questions of interpretive accuracy will also increase dramatically. This may explain what Eckhardt describes as a "demystification" of Merlin's prophetic ambiguity by fifteenth-century chroniclers and the commentators. The Middle English commentary on the *Prophetia Merlini* claims an orthodox version of the magician's words. It turns symbolic ambiguity into a singular historical "regime of truth." That text, unlike Monmouth's *Historia*, redirects the ambiguities of prophecy into a monotonous and hackneyed version of a genealogy of kingship. The historical truth it registers is entirely sympathetic to England's continued attempts to consolidate a colonizing hold over the variety of its regions. In the midst of a growing audience of readers, the indeterminacy of prophetic ambiguity and futuristic visioning proved increasingly dangerous.[36] Attempts to demystify Merlin's voice, to explain carefully and unequivocally the precise meaning of every prophecy, hope to ensure no one could misunderstand the proper historiographic truth they tell. They try to ensure that no one like Collingbourne could use prophetic cryptographs to insult a monarch, or that no one like Glyn Dŵr could ever again employ prophecies of a "Breton Hope" to gather an army in insurrection against an English king.

"Let us sit upon the ground," intones Shakespeare's Richard II, "and tell sad stories of the death of kings" (3.2.155–56). Shakespeare's words prompt Lee Patterson to remark that "the relationship between monarchy and tragedy is reciprocal" (*Negotiating*, 229). The train of England's "Six Last Kings" and the encrypted image of Cadwall's dead body encased in brass point to the tragedies of kingship; but these narratives hint as well at the victories and privileges that accrue to a tragic male sovereignty. More precisely, they suggest how deeply some sovereign victories—triumphant fantasies of survival beyond death—are linked to a sovereign's time to die. Images of sovereign death and endurance testify to a cultural endurance valuable because it was against all odds.

Late Middle English Arthurian romance gives those losses a full and, I will argue an even more poignant, narrative emplottment. I will read romances of Arthur for the kinds of privileges and pleasures imagined through the tragic tales of one legendary king. I suggest we consider more fully the poignant uses of a tragic insular kingship for a fantasy of insular contestation that will often preserve English rule, but can still, from time to time, offer substantial power to critique it. If a tragic king Arthur inspires our compassionate pity, the readings of Arthurian romance in the next two sections will remain mindful of the bodies and pleasures sacrificed to his service.

PART II

Romancing the Throne

CHAPTER THREE

Disavowing Romance

Colonial Loss and Stories of the Past

I N the "Proem" to his 1482 edition of Ralph Higden's *Polychronicon*, a history of Britain, William Caxton praises history's inclusiveness, its powerful witness of "triumphal victories of all manner [of] people":

Historye is a perpetuel conservatryce of thoose thynges that have be doone before this presente tyme and also a cotydyan wytness of bienfayttes, of male faytes, grete actes, and tryumphal vyctoryes of all maner peple. And also yf the terryble feyned fables of poetes have moche styred and moeved men to pyte and conservynge of justyce, how moche more is to be supposed that historye, assertryce of veryte and as moder of all philosophye is moevynge our maners to vertue.

Caxton defines history as the conservation of a past into perpetuity, and as a daily witness capable of "moving our manners to virtue." The distinction he makes between history and poetry is one of degree rather than kind, emphasizing certain attributes that history proper shares with imaginative fables. As Paul Strohm and others have shown, history's claim to truth during the late Middle Ages was affectively combined with the poetic. History is, in these accounts, an intense and intensely honest kind of poetry, a genre whose affective power serves, rather than compromises, its claims to the truth.

Caxton's words suggest that even by the fifteenth century, a period identified with shifts in medieval historiography and the increasing importance of vernacular chronicle, history and fable remained close familiars. In place of what will later become a categorical opposition, Caxton raises the issue of proportion. He names poetic fable not to discount it, but to borrow motivational power from it. Both Charles Kingsford and Antonia Gransden remind us that literate audiences desired vernacular (and "nationalistic") stories about the past, tastes which could be satisfied equally by romance and chronicle.[1] While it may be no coincidence that Caxton stakes history's reputation on its intimacy with poetic fables, his emphasis upon history's claim to truth suggests that the terms of this intimacy were increasingly complicated for history writers, or at least their editors, perhaps because of the enormous popularity of fables.

Caxton's confidence that history always yokes affect to truth seems striking, especially in light of the more anxious moments in the history of British historiography. Castigations of the imaginative excess of Geoffrey of Monmouth remain repetitive and persistent.[2] The Tudor historians will later insist upon history's solid identification with truth, and romance's identification with fantasy. Yet history's link to truth telling is not the only contrast embedded in Caxton's remarks. He lists the specific attributes of history emphasizing comprehensiveness through the opposition of good to evil (cotydyan wytness of bienfayttes, of male faytes). History offers daily witness to both good and bad, and the oppositional character of this inclusion implies that history leaves nothing out. Yet the next item renders Caxton's list a good deal less exhaustive: he modulates from the rhetorical comprehensiveness of "good deeds and bad deeds," to a repetitive and singular focus on the great and victorious ("great acts and triumphant victories"). Repetitious elaboration replaces categorical exhaustiveness; contrasting breadth gives way to comparative detail. Caxton, to put it bluntly, does not preserve his parallelism. The misstep seems striking given the rhetorical direction of the passage. His omission of categories here implied (petty, shameful acts, and devastating losses) is even more notable, written at a period known for its "savage battles, ruthless executions, and shameless treasons" (Watts, 110).[3] Caxton's definition of history is thus haunted by the repression of treason and devastating loss. History's link to glorious victory, in other words, is here enacted through a repression of the kinds of stories "triumphant" nations require and hope to produce: histories of the devastating losses visited upon the vanquished. Caxton implies (perhaps unconsciously) that history is, par excellence, the genre of the winners. Those winners claim the power not only of affect but of truth.

If Caxton's view of history suggests a determinedly (even overdeterminedly) triumphalism, the Middle English genre of Arthurian romance poignantly narrates those categories here disavowed: shame, treason, and irrecuperable loss. Unlike their earlier continental or Celtic counterparts, late Middle English romances of Arthur obsessively repeat the tragedy of Arthur's death and fellowship. This repetitious delectation of the tragic end of an illustrious insular king constitutes a historiographic counterpoint to accounts of Britain's triumphant greatness. It offers, I will argue, a means to read the materiality of loss as a heritage of the past. What are we to make of this insular romance sub-genre's obsession with tragic loss? What can these poetic British histories tell us about the preservation of loss within traditions of the past?

To answer these questions I turn to a slightly earlier time, and to the Alliterative romance of Arthur most closely identified with the chronicle tradition and with tragedy, the *Morte Arthure*. I first analyze the poem's often cited gesture to Arthurian "chronicle" and "romance" traditions so as to consider how the expansive power of Arthur's story helps constitute it as communitarian fantasy. Next, I read the interrelation between imperial ambition and intimate loss in the representation of Arthur's rule over insular Britain and continental Europe. Following a critical trajectory first established by Lee Patterson, I will read this poem as a meditation on the meaning of history, that is, a historiography. I will also disagree with Patterson's implication that, as tragedy, the Alliterative *Morte Arthure* gestures only fatalistically to the impossibility of historical progress, suggesting instead the important anti-triumphal politics of the poem. The *Morte* poignantly attends to innocent suffering, even as it troublingly suggests that some innocents are more deeply mourned, and worthier of rescue, than others. Borrowing Sara Suleri's notion of romance as a colonial genre, I will argue that this text encodes the "unending longing and loss" of late medieval colonial encounters. Disavowing the loss and longing of romance from history proper enables narratives of glorious and triumphant survival to stand as the truth of history.

"Romance/Chronicle" and the Alliterative *Morte Arthure*

The Alliterative *Morte Arthure* survives in a single copy in Lincoln Cathedral MS 91 (the Thornton Manuscript). The poem, usually identified with the Arthurian "chronicle" tradition, tells the story of Arthur's impressive exploits abroad as the downfall of insular Britain. Arthur is here the monumental, indeed imperial, ruler of Britain and Europe. The poem opens upon the king's New Year's feast at court in Carlisle. The festivities are interrupted by the arrival of emissaries sent by the Emperor Lucius from Rome who demands Arthur pay him tribute. The feasting continues (with the Roman visitors welcomed as Arthur's guests), while the king holds council with his closest allies and chief knights. Arthur's advisors, pledging their loyalty and military support for the King, recom-

mend not tribute, but war. As the king prepares to leave for battle on
the continent, he appoints, despite his wife Gaynor's (Guinevere's) special pleading, Mordred as England's viceroy and her protector. Arthur's
military successes against the Giant at Mount St. Michael and later against
Lucius's advancing army are rendered in substantial and palpably realistic
detail. Success against Lucius does not satisfy the king who, following a
rout of Lucius's army in France, continues his conquering drive toward
Rome itself. Arthur ceases finally at the Pope's request, after securing the
promise that he will be crowned Emperor in Rome. Military triumph
on the continent, however, quickly transmutes into civil war at home:
after a fateful dream prophesying his downfall, word reaches Arthur that
Mordred has opportunistically usurped the throne, and taken Gaynor as
wife. Arthur gathers his remaining troops and hurries back to defend his
insular title. The ensuing battles on both sea and land devastate both forces
and usher in the tragic deaths of Arthur's beloved Gawain, the treasonous
Mordred, and the king himself. The dying Arthur orders that his body be
taken to Glastonbury for burial, and bequeaths his throne to Constantine.
The main episodes of the poem are inspired by Geoffrey of Monmouth's
Historia (in part through their rendering in Laʒamon's *Brut*), but the Alliterative poet draws upon a rich variety of medieval texts and traditions. The
poem will later serve as a source for Malory's "Tale of King Arthur and the
Emperor Lucius."

Arthur's demise in the Alliterative *Morte Arthure* results from a
complex dynamic of international and domestic affairs registered in the
sovereign's own territorial ambitions. This version of Arthur's death foregrounds the geopolitics of his downfall as (in part) a result of his expansive
militarism: the king's obsession with militarism abroad sets the stage for
Mordred's treasonous advances at home. The other standard version of
Arthur's death, usually termed the "romance" tradition (read in the Stanzaic *Morte Arthur*, examined in Chapter 5), emphasizes Arthurian tragedy
as a largely domestic affair, the result of the sovereign's ineffectual management of his closest familiars. While the distinction between Arthurian
"chronicle" and "romance" traditions can be useful, we should be cautious
of reading these differences as generic oppositions. The Alliterative poet
does not, in fact, seem to do so.

At a crucial turning point in the narrative (one frequently noted by
critics), the poet construes Arthur's legacies with a doubled reference to
both traditions. Following Arthur's conquest of Rome, and just before he
hears news of the rebellious Mordred, Arthur has a prophetic dream, his

second in the poem. Arthur sees himself positioned on Fortune's Wheel, one among the group of kings known as the Nine Worthies; as Fortune's Wheel turns, the king witnesses his fall from glory to desolation. The dream episode evokes issues important to the larger poem: Arthur's tragic fate follows that suffered by other monumental sovereigns (the great Alexander, for example); the poem at least implicitly (and perhaps, as some have argued, explicitly) questions Arthur's culpability in this fate. The immediate context raises not Arthur's guilt, but his expansive textual appeal. Interpreting his sovereign's dream, Arthur's philosopher reminds us that Arthurian tales have been a durable vehicle for "romance" and "chronicle":

This sall in romance be redde   with ryall knyghttes,
Rekkenede and renownde   with ryotous kynges,
And demyd on Domesdaye   for dedis of armes
For Þe doughtyeste Þat euer   was duelland in erthe—
So many clerkis and kynges   sall karpe of ȝoure dedis
And kepe ȝoure conquestez   in cronycle for euer! [ll. 3440–45][4]

[This [story] shall be read in romance with royal knights/ Reckoned and renown with warlike kings/ and deemed on Doomsday for deeds of arms/ As the boldest that ever dwelt on earth/ Thus (So) many clerks and kings shall tell of your deeds and keep your conquests in chronicle forever!]

Critics have persisted in reading the terms "romance" and "chronicle" as implicitly opposed here; yet the poet's words offer little evidence of that opposition. As in Caxton's account of history's link to poetic emotion, the Alliterative poet imagines the chronicle-romance relation as one of shared interests. He foregrounds the textual similarities between the genres rather than their differences. The doubled reference seems a determined one, moreover, especially since the dream episode borrows from a variety of different kinds of texts. According to editor Mary Hamel, Arthur's dream of Fortune's Wheel constitutes one of the most highly crafted literary episodes in a highly crafted poem.[5] The poet condenses reference to chronicle and romance, alongside motifs from philosophy, dream vision, and moral tract. Although himself a widely read and learned writer deeply engaged with various kinds of sources, the poet explicitly emphasizes Arthur's expansive textual legacies in these two terms.

The distinctions between "chronicle" and "romance" legible here are quite subtle.[6] Romance, mentioned first, takes a narrative and logical priority; however, the description implies a dialectical, rather than strictly oppositional, relation between the two kinds of texts. Romances spread Arthur's renown, extending his popularity through stories of his "deeds of arms"; chronicle "keeps" those deeds forever. The poet implicitly identifies romance with medieval scenes of reading, suggesting the power of the story to captivate and fascinate a readership. Chronicle accounts, on the other hand, link with official acts of writing, with the preservation of such captivating stories in the "official" statements of clerks and kings.

When the poet recasts his diverse sources into the double terms of "chronicle" and "romance," he points to the power of Arthur's image to instruct and edify through both "official" and "popular" texts. The poem offers a concise image of how, in Arthur, the popular appeal of unofficial texts circulates even within legitimated "official" stories. Romance offers, as in Caxton's prologue to the *Polychronicon*, an important source for a common tradition. Even more, the relation of romance to chronicle described here can be read to suggest that romance precedes (indeed causes) chronicle: if one reads the "so" of line 3444 as a causative connector (thus) rather than an intensifier (so many), then the passage suggests that the popularity of romance impels the work of the chroniclers. Reading one popular story helps produce another official text. This account of a productive (and dialectical) relation between romance and chronicle resonates with the reception history of Geoffrey of Monmouth's *Historia*, and with the Merlin Prophecies examined in Chapters 1 and 2. To be sure, this process reverberates with worries by some that popular fables might masquerade as official truth. Yet popularity is, we should recall, utterly useful to the powerful who benefit from popular belief in officially sanctioned fables.

We find again, as we did with Monmouth's *Historia*, Arthur's link to a narrative tradition situated within the official-popular nexus that, according to Lauren Berlant, has the power to structure national fantasies. When the Alliterative poet emphasizes the twofold character of Arthurian textual traditions, he suggests the important inclusivity of such conjoined textual modes. The inclusivity, breadth, and textual largesse of the Arthurian tradition remain in the narrative foreground. The poet gestures to the cumulative cultural effect of the Arthurian tradition, a tradition that is at once repetitive and recursive, yet also variable and diverse.[7]

Of course, as the controversies and ambiguities of Geoffrey of Monmouth's text (according to Julia Crick, a text reviving in popularity in England during the late fourteenth and fifteenth centuries) suggest, rela-

tions between official and popular accounts of the past were as frequently
contentious as they were cooperative. When the poet foregrounds the con-
gruence of concerns among various kinds of Arthurian texts rather than
the formal distinctions between them, he gestures to a history of textual
competition. There is evidence to support such a reading elsewhere in the
Middle English corpus. Cultural competitions between official and popular texts, and their relation to truth claims, are crucial to the plot of the
Stanzaic *Morte Arthur*. So while I will address this text in Chapter 5, I
wish to pause here to note the Stanzaic poet's specific concern with the
power, and the occasional falsity, of official versions of the truth.

Truth claims converge on romance poetry throughout the Stanzaic,
but especially in the episode of the poisoned apple. When a Scottish visitor
to Arthur's court dies from eating a poisoned apple innocently handed to
him by Arthur's queen, the official story at court proclaims Guinevere's
guilt. From the start, however, the poet has made clear Guinevere's innocence (of this crime at least); as readers of the romance we know both that
the poisoned apple was the result of a nefarious scheme of an unnamed
"squyer in the court," and that the squire's intended victim was not the
Scottish visitor, but Gawain. At the burial of the accidentally poisoned
Scotsman, however, Guinevere's guilt becomes official "truth": a "crafty
clerke" inscribes the queen's apparent guilt "with lettres droughe" into the
stone of the dead man's tomb. On the strength of those letters the innocent
queen is officially rendered guilty. The Scotsman's brother can seek redress
from Arthur and very nearly succeeds in obtaining the queen's death as
punishment for a murder in which she had no part.

The Stanzaic poet, a writer who takes pains to insist upon the
importance–and the veracity–of his version of events repetitively insisting
that his story is "no fabul," contrasts the official and false declaration of
Guinevere's guilt in poisoning the Scottish knight with the "true" story
of Guinevere's innocence offered by the text of the romance itself. The
readers of that romance are shown that an "official" version of events, even
one written in stone and on a dead knight's tomb, offers neither the most
satisfying, nor the most accurate, account. Thus the Stanzaic poet depicts
a conscious competition between the truth claims of official texts and the
truth claims of romance. His poem implicitly argues that romance, because
of its ability to deal with the complicated subtleties and machinations of
court politics, can offer an apparently more satisfying and, indeed, accurate
account of Guinevere's real guilt before the Arthurian court.

Considered as a set of interpretive competitions, the differences among these texts suggest another way to think about the flexibility and diversity of Arthurian traditions. What does this flexibility, this capacity to cross the apparent competitions between "romance" and "chronicle," and between "popular" and "official" cultures, suggest about notions of British community or of a British past? If Arthurian romance is large enough, ambitious enough, for diverse appropriations made by diverse audiences, how might we reconsider its encyclopedic character?[8] Why would narratives of the tragic end of a legendary British king resonate powerfully with such a wide audience? Competitions between popular and official texts raise questions of interpretive legitimacy and accuracy. Indeed the Stanzaic and Alliterative versions of Arthur's death offer two very different accounts not only of the proximate causes of Arthur's downfall, but the details of Arthur's, and especially Guinevere's, guilt or innocence.

Questions of loss and punishment, of guilt and innocence are, of course, fundamentally questions of interpretation, and they were obviously no less controversial in the late Middle Ages than they are today. These issues are important to the Alliterative poet. Critics have long debated whether this poem is critical of Arthur, with some construing the poem as an implicitly pacifist text. While I would read the poet's passion for the details of war as more a glorification than a critique of battle, I agree that there are momentary critiques of kingship. I am more interested in the line of interpretation first established by Lee Patterson's reading of this poem as a prolonged meditation on the inescapable repetitions of history. The poem depicts Arthur as a great man trapped by forces even he cannot control: indeed, the tragedy of this romance obtains as much because of Arthur's greatness as because of his fate.

To return to the text of Arthur's fateful dream, the Alliterative poet mentions romance and chronicle not long after an important reference to Arthur's wartime actions. That is, just forty lines before Arthur's philosopher emphasizes the ethical problems of warrior kingship: "Thow has schedde myche blode, and schalkes distroyede, / Sakeles, in cirquytrie, in sere kynges landis [You have shed much blood, and destroyed men/ guiltless, in arrogance, in various king's lands] (ll. 3398–99). This is a textual moment often cited by those reading the poem as a pacifist critique of war. There is here, of course, an accusation of the arrogance of sovereignty, a sin to which Arthur falls victim. Yet the poet raises guilt only in terms of its opposite, emphasizing not Arthur's guilt, but the guiltlessness of Arthur's victims. If the poet wishes to critique the king's personal wrongdoing, why foreground guiltlessness, even that of Arthur's victims?

When the poet raises the question of guilt not in terms of Arthur's actions but of the tragedy of guiltless victimization, he points to a problem more deeply troubling even than arrogant kingship: the historical trauma of innocent suffering. At poignant issue here is the wholesale slaughter of the innocent in "sere kings lands." To be sure, Arthur shares culpability for this, but this seems a limitation, a tragic failing, of a nonetheless very great king. There is less a sustained critique of one sovereign's guilt than a tragic delectation of the human fragility even of this greatest sovereign. Arthur, for all his magnificence, cannot save the guiltless; even he is complicit in the slaughter of the innocent. The poet does not offer more detailed critiques of Arthur's limitation; perhaps that is because he cannot respond to innocent suffering with ethical aphorisms about sovereign excess.[9]

Patterson reads the poem's concern with these kinds of questions as fundamentally historiographic: "the poem insists that what must be raised to significance is not a schematic outline of events, but the historical world in all its random particularity" (*Negotiating*, 213).[10] Reading this as a historiography – "the meaning of history per se" – Patterson sees here, "a vision of history that undermines the very possibility of history":

> The poem sees the past as harboring a legitimizing authority of such value that it must be retained even if it costs the present its own historical identity. Arthur must be another [Emperor like] Alexander even if it means that his career will enact the same curve of aspiration and disappointment. Not that this risk is lightly undertaken. The fear of recursion haunts the poem, and if it sees the past as uniquely valuable it ascribes to the present a desire for ascendancy, an ardor for selection and control that would grant to the past only so much survival as the present would wish. (222)

History narrates the past as fated, as that which cannot be avoided, a historiography encoded in eternally turning Fortune's Wheel. Yet this admittedly pessimistic view of historic repetition only, as Patterson puts it, "undermines the very possibility of history" if by history we mean a progressive, evolutionary, model of time in which survival signals progress (living beyond trauma) and never repetition (the residue of a trauma encrypted).[11] Yet repetition need not be read only for its dismal view of the impossibility of progress; repetition is also, as theorists of traumatic memory have reminded us, a memorialization of victimization. This, I would suggest, is part of the recursiveness of Arthurian tragedy. The repetitive desire for stories of tragic kingship gestures toward the dismal fact that some histories are stories of repeated constraint, repetitive failures. The image of a tragic history that eludes our desires for escape, moreover, reminds us that suffering and victimization are meted out inequitably: trauma is too often repetitively visited upon certain bodies and certain peoples. Moreover, the slaughter of the innocent in many lands is, not infrequently, the very part of history that the progressivist national rhetorics seek to disavow.

Progressivist historical chronologies have been the subject of recent critiques by scholars such as Sara Suleri, K. Anthony Appiah, and Anne McClintock. They identify the historiographies of progress developed in the nineteenth and twentieth centuries with the production of Western thought in the context of empire. In the rest of this chapter, I will argue that the *Morte Arthure*'s representation of an imperial Arthur alongside the poet's unwillingness to allow historic trauma to be surmounted encodes traumatic memories of conquest. I will read this romance for its attention to traumatic longing and loss, cultural failures and catastrophic endings. This poignant view of the past gestures to a history of trauma beyond consolation. Such texts do the work of mourning: resisting the ideologies embedded in certain kinds of historical explanation, these texts remind us that explanations are frequently complicit in the cultural demand that victimized subjects accept, and hence submit to, their losses as somehow "necessary." [12] In the final section of this chapter, I will also suggest that although the poignancy of this poem resists progressivist demands for a triumphal history, the poem nonetheless encodes an ideological program for appropriate and inappropriate mourning. This ideology has everything to do with gender, with the poem's representation of knightly masculinity and female pathos.

We must note, however, that in its tragic and traumatic pessimism, the Alliterative poet's view of history diverges from Caxton's. History as traumatic memory cannot so easily, as Caxton will later put, "move our manners to virtue." The tragic, traumatic losses from the past are, in fact, precisely the aspects of history that Caxton's prologue to the *Polychronicon* disavows. Arthurian romance, on the other hand, encodes the past as mournful, distressing, and inconsolable. The Alliterative poet remains less confidant than Caxton does that past woes might be recuperated for the common weal. Yet when the poet embeds his attention to Arthur's textual power within the highly crafted literary episode of Arthur's dream, he nonetheless suggests that dreams of sovereign demise might still be culturally useful.

Lost Empires

Given these remarks, it is unsurprising that the *Morte Arthure* is described as both a magnificent and a profoundly tragic text.[13] From the poem's opening, moreover, trauma and loss link to colonial legacies and desires, comparing Arthur's power to the ancient claims of Rome. By the end of the text's first hundred lines Arthur and his court must respond to a powerful challenge from that Empire. Lucius insists that Arthur is his subject; Arthur contests Rome's view, arguing his own claims to imperial sovereignty. Arthur wryly dismisses Lucius's demands, claiming himself Lucius's overlord. This argument alludes to the tradition known as the *translatio imperii*, the history (also at times contested) of the westward transfer of Rome's imperial power so as to recover an empire of "universal" territory and scope.[14]

The poem's opening catalogue of Arthur's geographic possessions suggests that Arthur commands a power on the order of Rome; yet even at this early stage the image of a lost empire shadows Arthur's international rule. When the ambassadors from Rome disrupt Arthur's feasting, they speak of Lucius by his imperial title "Lucius Iberius" in an anxious command designed to gain the tribute Lucius lacks. Arthur rebuffs the command and, unruffled, offers the ambassadors a seat at his feast. The scene thus foregrounds the fragility of Roman claims, at least in Arthur's Britain. Lucius's challenge, of course, contests Arthur's preeminence as supreme ruler even there. The possibility of losses to insular Britain, and the problem of sovereign insecurity of the kind that worries Lucius, are thus present from the poem's beginning. Moreover, despite the expansive praise of Arthur's power, there are hints of the troubling prehistory to Arthurian rule, a prehistory linked to Arthur's (famously ambiguous) paternity. Arthur has "covered the crown of that kith riche, / of all that Vter in erthe aughte in his tym" (ll. 28–29). Arthur's need to "recover" his father's crown gestures to the well-known troubles of Uther's rule as well as to contestations over Arthur's inheritance following Uther's death. When the poet hints at these problems even as he catalogues Arthur's massive powers and territories, he links colonializing annexation with a troubled genealogy of British fragmentation and loss.

As with many texts of the Middle English Arthurian tradition, we are flung here immediately into a scene of loss. For while the *translatio imperii* tradition offers a rationale for legitimating claims to universal and united territorial possession, the confrontation between Lucius and Arthur at the text's opening points not to a secure imperial title, but to an empire in pieces. Although his loyalties certainly lie with Arthur, the Alliterative poet does not offer specific evidence for the superiority of either sovereign's claim to be overlord of the other; we see instead a contested empire, and an imperial unity already gone. Imperial wholeness will, in the end, elude both kings; by the time Arthur gains the crown of Rome, insular Britain will be in open rebellion. The security of Empire has already unraveled; imperial unity is already gone.

Arthur of course stands against Roman imperial sovereignty; his war with Lucius is an explicit attempt to reverse his ancestors' earlier submission to Rome. Yet his efforts will have traumatic consequences for the island kingdom. Britain's insular stability will be compromised by Arthur's ambitions for sovereignty over all of Europe, a fact that some have read as crucial to the poem's critique of warmongering. Geoffrey of Monmouth, we recall, offered the past image of a united *tota insula*, a lost insular wholeness available for future recovery. I will read the Alliterative poet to suggest instead that some fantasies of wholeness–here of an international, putatively "universal," European empire–endanger another kind of unity, that of Arthur's insular home. Arthur's claims to Roman rule, his fantasy of the recovery of a "universal" European empire, will put the sovereign integrity of a "native" British island at risk. Lucius's demands, and Arthur's successful refusal of them, are thus important to this text's representation of Arthur as an imperial sovereign. Yet they also provide a means to measure loss against loss. The poem will recommend a shrinking of monumental, European, and "international," sovereign ambition into the circumscribed space of an insular realm. The borders delimiting Arthurian geography constrict. The international, imperial scope of triumph thus contains its own tragic limits. Arthurian sovereignty lost on the continent can nonetheless deploy loss so as to calibrate desire for imperial sovereignty in an "insular" home.

The poem constructs its condensation of sovereignty spatially and geographically, both as a result of its larger narrative structure, and in its descriptions of Arthur's realm. The earliest catalogue of the lands of Arthur's rule (see lines 30–47), overwhelming in its detail, renders Arthur a grand international emperor. Beginning with Arthur's holdings in the far north of Britain (Orkney and the "outer isles"), the list moves southward to the continent, "with special reference to the English territorial gains in the war [with France]" (Hamel 254). The poet turns, however, to greater geographic (and insular) specificity in his very next lines:

Then rystede that ryall
Suggeourns Þat seson
In Bretayne Þe braddere
Sythyn wente into Wales
Sweys in to Swaldye
For to hunt at Þe hartes
In Glamorgan with glee,
And thare a citee he sette
That Caerlyon was callid . . . (ll. 53–61a)

and helde Þe Rounde Tabyll,
to solace him seluen
as hym beste lykes;
with his wyes all,
with his snell houndes
in thas hye laundes,
thare gladchipe was euere.
be assentte of his lordys

[Then that royal rested and held the Round Table/sojourns that season to pleasure himself/ in Britain the broad as he likes best;/ then went into Wales with all his people/ goes into South Wales with his quick hounds/ for to hunt at the hart in those high lands./ In Glamorgan for amusement where joy was ever./ And there a city he established with the assent of his lords/ that was called Caerlion.]

A broad list of European holdings mutates into the particular specificity of "Bretagne Þe braddere," Britain the broad. The description retracts geographically from a catalogue of continental locales to a snapshot of insular ones; the text effectually drops the reader in the spot where the catalogue has begun, moving backwards into the details of insular holdings: to Wales, then smaller yet, South Wales, to Glamorgan, and finally, to the particular city of Caerlion. The earlier expansive list organizes the names of Arthur's territories in ways that suit the alliterative line. Here the poetry guides the reader along a journey back, with each line more particular and local than the one before.

This insular return, moreover, exudes pleasures. Britain is the "broad" place Arthur loves best, where he takes his "solace," a word with rich medieval associations in the aesthetic delights of literary romance. This fond description emphasizes the expansive breadth of Britain, a place of sport and amusement; it is, moreover, an explicitly Welsh landscape radiating joy and gladness, the home to an extraordinarily just and peaceful rule. We glimpse the glad fellowship of the Round Table, and a city built through the communitarian assent of lords and king. If the previous list of Arthur's holdings is designed to impress us with his sovereign reach, this snapshot of a city in Wales offers a romantic view of the local pleasures of royal (male) fellowship. These are the pleasures of a utopian community absorbed with vitality and pleasure. And this is the fantasy some still seek in images of a healing Arthurian space, hungry for the recuperation promised by (and commodified in) vacation tours of "Arthur's Britain" today.

The *Morte Arthure* offers a poetic account of Arthurian trauma and loss that nonetheless, at moments like this one, foregrounds the pleasures of Arthur's Britain in Wales. The power of this insular space becomes increasingly important and deserving of rescue as the poem progresses although most of the text's action will take place overseas. Furthermore, the constriction from the expanses of European places back to the insular space of "Bretagne Þe braddere" parallels the larger structure of Arthur's military campaign and the narrative that recounts it. Arthur's eventual return home, after he has conquered imperial rule itself, will tragically produce not communitarian wholeness and healing, but desolation, death, and loss. The tragedy of Arthur's loss is imagined most poignantly when the insular unity he once forged, with all its utopian pleasures, devolves into ruin.

Arthur's power as conqueror of all Europe, thus, serves as the measure of his sovereign greatness; Arthur's communitarian pleasures in Britain serve as the measure of his sovereign loss. Rebecca Beal has suggested that this poem borrows the power of Rome through such comparisons and contrasts: "When Arthur decides to march on Rome, the poem constructs him as the representative of a civilization fully equal to the one he opposes" (40).[15] According to Beal the construction of Arthur's "civilizing" mission is accomplished in part through the grisly comparison with that figure designed to represent utter barbarism: the giant of Mount St. Michael who eats the flesh of children. The excessive force of this contrast, at the beginning of Arthur's journey to vanquish Lucius, renders Arthur's civilization well above "not just the rudeness of the giant, but the glory that was Rome" (Beal 41). Yet once Arthur's glory is established as comparable to the Roman imperial model, the poem turns immediately to the heart of its tragedy: the loss of Arthur's insular community and Arthur's insular rule. Arthur's final defeat, moreover, returns us to images of the excesses of conquest, and thus, as Beal argues, resonates with the episode of the giant who consumes children. When, in the final episodes of the poem, Arthur orders that Mordred's children be slain, as Beal writes, "the difference becomes blurred between the king and the giant whom Arthur himself condemned 'Because that Þow killide has Þise cresmede childyre' [Because you have murdered these christened children]" (41). The paradox of sovereign violence erupts through such morbid repetitions, as the putatively civilizing force of conquest ushers in a recurrence of innocent slaughter.

In a recent provocatively ambitious reading of the episode of the cannibalistic Giant of Mount St. Michael rendered in Geoffrey of Monmouth's *Historia*, Geraldine Heng reads this lurid romance episode as encoding a traumatic memory of cannibalism reported, or alluded to, in various accounts of the First Crusade. Identifying this textual matrix with the "genesis of Arthurian Romance," Heng reads romance as "effect[ing] specific forms of cultural rescue" (99), encoding a history of Europe's guilty and traumatic relations, specifically with the East: "Romance represents a medium that is neither wholly fantastical nor wholly historical, but in which history and fantasy collide, the one vanishing into the other, almost without trace, at the location where the advantage of both can be most easily mined. For romance does not repress or evade the historical—as has sometimes been claimed—but surfaces the historical which it transforms and safely memorializes in an advantageous form, as fantasy" (126). Heng's formulation of the collision between history and romance, her reading of how history "vanishes" into fantasy, brilliantly foreground the poignant ways that fantasy can safely memorialize atrocities. Her work thus offers one way to understand the complicated relations between fantasy and history, romance and cultural politics. And Heng may well be right that stories of the "shock of communal trauma" of cannibalism in the Levant during the First Crusade return, transformed and "safely memorialized," in romance fantasies of cannibalistic giants overcome by imperial power. She, thus, contributes to scholarly efforts to understand how and why colonial histories are so deeply interested in the figure of the cannibal.

I would not disagree with Heng's suggestion that fantasy can sometimes serve racist and utterly oppressive ends, but I am unconvinced that such a view of fantasy accounts for the "genesis" of Arthurian romance, or satisfyingly summarizes the relations of romance to history. My study suggests that alongside its ability to coordinate a "cultural rescue" deployed sometimes in the service of deeply conservative—Eurocentric and heterosexist—ideologies, Arthurian romance also encodes subversive possibilities and potentialities, utopian visions that gesture to another site of colonization, this time from Europe's western fringe. I wish to account for the ways in which Arthurian fantasy offers utopian rescue and hope for the beleaguered and the conquered. For if history, at times, "vanishes" into fantasy, it also borrows the imaginative expansiveness of fantasy to tell a coherent story. I am suggesting we might consider fantasy not only for its well-documented abilities to surface racist and oppressive exoticisms, but for the power that its fascination with difference offers in the utopian hope of imagining the world differently. The complicated relations between history and fantasy, moreover, tendentiously position fantasy as the other to imperial "regimes of truth" precisely because of that utopian power. This is why the history-making fantasies of a dominant culture often "vanish" into narratives of history proper, while the fantasies of minority, or non-dominant, groups simply vanish altogether; they are willingly lost as "unreal," or to recall William of Malmesbury's words, as "the ravings" of a perverse people. In the context of cultural contestations over truth and fable, contestations that persist in the ways English fantasmatic uses of Arthur still count as history more frequently than do the uses of Welsh or Scots ethnic minorities, Arthurian utopianism was powerful enough to be culturally dangerous. From the view of this long-lived historic contestation over Arthur, moreover, William of Newburgh's "sententious rebutt[al of Geoffrey of Monmouth's] sensational fictions" claimed that certain ways of imagining the world were illegitimate. This was not at all, as Heng terms it, "an absurd spectacle" even if it was, as Heng also suggests, "futile and impossible" (126).

Heng's analysis does, however, implicitly raise for my study the problem of how various medieval scenes of conquest coalesce. I have been arguing that the Alliterative *Morte Arthure* provides one view of those collocations. It reminds us to examine the links between the invisibility of Europe's "internal primitives," the linguistic minorities encoded yet also lost through the logic of the notion of "Europe," and Christendom's colonizing project against "pagans" and "infidels" in the East. We may be tempted here to judge loss against loss, conquered against victimized, forgetting that experiences of disruption and conquest are incommensurable. But such a procedure would merely duplicate the "divide and conquer" tactic of imperial rule. Indeed, the imperialist politics of the Alliterative *Morte* argue that we make exactly those imperialist divisions, offering a double view of Empire so as to suggest that some losses are of less consequence than others. Rather than duplicate that argument, however, I wish to examine what it means that this text alludes both to an Eastern Empire and a Western one. How do the losses embedded in this poem contribute to the process by which, as Felicity Riddy puts it, "Arthur shifted from being one of the conquered to being one of the conquerors" ("Contextualizing," 57)?

Having gained imperial stature through both his victory over the Giant of Mount St. Michael and his conquest of Lucius's forces, Arthur imports even the excesses of imperial sovereignty back to Britain. Traumatic events occurring first on the continent now return as insular devastation. And the defender of the innocent has now become their victimizer. Beal reads the "lesson" of the poem in implicitly imperialist terms: "even the ideal king who bears the weight of civilization pays dearly for his power. It is not only the *Aeneid* which suggests that civilization must be paid for in blood: in the Alliterative *Morte Arthure* those who represent civilization pay as dearly as civilization's antagonists do to ensure the continuity of a culture" (41). Beal's remarks return us to the tragic trajectory of the poem, and to the hopeless historiography Patterson describes. Her gesture to the *Aeneid* is not coincidental; it reminds us that a historiography of Roman imperialism, and the legacies of Roman rule and Roman literary tradition, haunt Middle English accounts of a British past. These texts are quite literally the traumatic ancestors of Geoffrey of Monmouth's *Historia*. The legacies of imperial Rome erupt in this poem as another kind of traumatic return, finally and most devastatingly, destroying the happiness of Britain the broad.

Yet the trauma of innocent suffering evoked by this poem also reminds us of the unjust and horrific methods used to ensure cultural continuity. In a structure that links international success with insular demise, the poem implicitly argues that excessive desires for "universal" empires can destroy a utopian, explicitly insular, realm. The most horrific victimizations, or so the Alliterative poet implicitly tries to convince us, occur not in Europe but on insular British soil. The poem may well critique Arthur's arrogant ambitions but it does so not on behalf of all the innocent who suffer, but only those British innocents deemed worthy of rescue. When, in the poem's final moments, Arthur demands the slaughter of Mordred's innocent children the text reminds us again of the sovereign's complicity with such suffering.

Despite his interest in innocent suffering, even this poet does not poignantly linger over the murder of Mordred's babies. The insular rebels are made to resemble Lucius's forces, implying that civil war in Britain is a tragic return of a history that has already transpired elsewhere. Yet as much as the resemblance between Lucius's army and Mordred's establishes the recurrence of history as tragic, such historic similarity and repetition is quickly recast through phobic representations of Mordred's allies as "saracens" and "pagans." The poem struggles to discriminate between the innocents (like Mordred's babies) who can be easily sacrificed and those whose passing registers as a catastrophic kind of loss. This discrimination is accomplished in part through the poet's description of mourning.

Some innocent victims in this poem are more deeply mourned than are others. The most extensive consideration of the death of an innocent occurs at what some have called the most tragic moment of the poem: the death of Gawain. At the grisly scene of Gawain's death, Arthur, his beard covered with blood from kissing his dead kinsman, laments Gawain's "sakles" [guiltless] passing. In a speech reminiscent of the philosopher's earlier lament for innocent suffering, Arthur mourns Gawain's bloody mutilation and, within the space of seven lines, declares Gawain's guiltlessness twice:

"For blode" said the bolde kynge   "blynn sall I neuer,
Or my brayne to-briste   or my breste oÞer!
Was neuer sorowe so softe   that sanke to my herte;
Itt es full sibb to my selfe,   my sorowe es the more—
Was neuer so sorowfull a syghte   seyn with myn eyghen!
He is sakles, supprysede   for syn of myn one."
Down knelis Þe kynge   and kryes full lowde,
With carefull contenaunce   he karpes thes wordes:
"O rightwis riche Gode,   this rewthe thow beholde,
Þis ryall rede blode   ryn appon erthe!
It ware worthy to be schrede   and schrynede in golde,
For it es sakles of syn,   sa helpe me oure Lorde!"
                                  (ll. 3981–92)

["For blood," said the bold king, "cease will I never,/ Before my brain bursts in two or my breast either;/ Was never sorrow so soft that sank into my heart./He is full kin to myself, my sorrow is even more—/ was never so sorrowful a sight seen with my eyes!/He is guiltless, surprised because of my own sin."/ Down kneels the King and cries full loudly,/ with sorrowful countenance he utters these words:/ "O righteous rich God, this sorrow thou beholds/ This royal red blood runs upon the earth!/ It were worthy to be recovered and enshrined in gold, / For it is guiltless of sin, so help me our Lord!"]

Arthur's first words respond to his companions who demand that he mediate a grief they call womanly ["to wepe als a woman it is no witt holden"

(l. 3978)], a grief which has, in a particularly grisly image, moved the king to slather his beard with Gawain's blood. Arthur's language returns again and again to images of blood, his own and Gawain's; he evokes the traumatic fragmentation of the body wounded in battle, registering death as gruesome, bodily, bloody mutilation. But, as Arthur's speech also implies, part of the tragedy of Gawain's loss involves his kin relation to his king: "For blode," declares Arthur, "blynn sall I neuer." The Middle English term "blod" refers both to bodily fluid and to noble lineage. Repetitively focusing on blood, first his own and then Gawain's, Arthur words link bloody death with royal lineage as family inheritance. In his grief over this most intimate familial loss, so excessive because his ties with Gawain are so close, Arthur imagines his own sovereign's body in fragments, his brain and body "tobrest." In mourning Gawain's innocent death, Arthur fantasizes the atomization of his sovereign body. He thus anticipates not only his own bodily mutilation and demise, literally his bloodletting, but also the loss of his royal genealogy, the end of a British blood line.

Gawain's guiltlessness, emphasized here, links his death with the tragedy of traumatic repetition foretold by Arthur's philosopher. Yet here the tragedy of innocence has distinctly aristocratic, indeed royal, valences. Gawain's guiltlessness alludes again to Arthur's traumatic sovereignty. Yet this scene also signals a larger set of cultural contestations (and competitions) over the meaning of Arthur's image as a sign of sovereignty. The king suggestively imagines his own body in fragments, blood spilt, brains and breasts bursting open. Images of bodily fragmentation, according to Jacques Lacan, occur to structures of identity at times of psychic disruption; they signal the "aggressive disintegration" of the sense of identity ("The Mirror Stage," 4). Elsewhere Lacan describes what he calls "imagos of the fragmented body," in other words, "images of castration, mutilation, dismemberment dislocation, evisceration, devouring, bursting open of the body" as a means to refigure "aggressive intentions" ("Aggressivity in Psychoanalysis," 11). Through these imagos the subject copes with the fundamentally alienating processes of identification, particularly in the demand that identity be imagined as a singular, and unified, icon of wholeness, a fiction of subjectivity that disavows aggressive drives and impulses. Imagos of the body in fragments, thus, engage the disciplinary demands of identification. They allude to the aggressive resistances, and to the contestatory pain, of the subject's tortured desire for, yet alienation from, its belief in itself as whole and unified.[16]

Arthur is not, however, just any subject. His royal status, and the emphasis at this textual moment upon the loss of royal blood, suggests a specifically sovereign fantasy of identity at issue. And thus I wish to extend Lacan's account of the subject per se to consider how Arthur's body in fragments engages with the sovereign *as* subject, and the sovereign as *subjected* to the aggressive impulses of his subjects. (This is, to be sure, one way to read Arthur's failure vis-à-vis Mordred.) As I will make clearer in a moment, Arthur's iconic image, here in fragments, can be read to allude to disputes and aggressive contestations over the interpretive uses of Arthur that I have addressed in the previous two chapters. They point to competing "identities" of Arthur and to the various sovereign fantasies that circulate around him.

Before explaining more precisely how these structures of identification may be at work in Arthur's fantasy of his own body in fragments, two important textual moments also pertain to Lacan's formulation, and it is to these images that I now wish to turn. In the council scene that follows Lucius's challenge, Arthur's vassals repeatedly vow their allegiance to Arthur on the "holy Vernacle," or the cloth of Veronica. According to an eighth century legend, much venerated in the fourteenth and fifteenth centuries, Veronica used a cloth to wipe the face of Jesus on his way to crucifixion; to repay her kindness, Jesus left the imprint of his face on her cloth.[17] The cloth of Veronica was a relic reputedly lodged in Rome and, hence, a medieval symbol of pilgrimage to Rome. The literal appropriateness of the symbol for Arthur's war with Lucius seems obvious, since in vowing loyalty to him, Arthur's forces declare a kind of pilgrimage to Rome.[18]

Some medieval traditions of the "holy vernacle" resonate with Lacan's notion of the "imago," from the Mirror Stage, especially since the "holy vernacle" was imagined to carry the fidelity of a perfect image of Jesus, a perfect display of faithful identification, an iconic reflection. Gerald of Wales, perhaps to contrast with what he saw as (other) spurious relics of the crucifixion, glossed the name of "Veronica" to mean "vera-icon" or true image.[19] In medieval terms, then, when the various sovereigns pledge their loyalty to Arthur on the "holy vernacle," an image of perfect fidelity and true resemblance, they promise perfect fidelity to Arthur's rule. They identify themselves as mirror images, true icons of Arthurian sovereignty. When leader after leader vows on the "holy vernacle" they implicitly position themselves as united, not through their loyalty to one another, but through their absolute fidelity to, and identification with, Arthur.

We might, however, read this iconic image of an international force united in loyalty to Arthur through a vow on the "true icon," as embedding an anxiety not only about Arthurian unity, but also about the problem of Arthurian "truth." Indeed, there is more than a little irony in depicting such a united force in agreement over Arthur and his image at a time when questions about Arthur's image, who owns it and who can legitimately use it, are hotly contested. There is evidence, moreover, that such contestations are important to the Alliterative poet as well, particularly in his use of certain sources. Before returning to the image of Arthur's body in bloody fragments, I turn to the second pertinent icon of Arthurian sovereignty in the poem, the heraldic image traditionally associated with Arthur as Pendragon, the figure of the golden dragon.

According to Geoffrey of Monmouth, the golden dragon was Arthur's standard. On the basis of that identification a series of English kings, notably (and for this poet most recently) Edward III, marched and fought under the Pendragon banner. Yet, despite this tradition, the Alliterative poet follows the lead of another of his sources, *The Siege of Jerusalem*, and shifts the dragon banner from Arthur's heraldry to that of the Roman Emperor Lucius. In this he departs from his chronicle sources. Suggesting a dating of the poem about 1400, editor Hamel explains the shift in the following way:

> There would have been no particular reason for rejecting his chronicle sources in favor of *Siege* during the reign of Edward III or for some time thereafter, but there may well have been compelling reasons for doing so around the year 1401. Edward III, that very "Arthurian" military leader, was the last English king (before the Tudors) known to have taken a dragon-banner into battle, at Crecy in 1346; thereafter the emblem fell into disuse until Henry VII revived it. In the interim, perhaps inspired by Geoffrey's account of Arthur the Briton, Owen Glendower adopted both dragon-ensign and dragon helm among his emblems; . . . If the [poet] were completing his poem during this period, he might well have felt a double warrant for the change: not only did *Siege* tell him matter of factly that "a grete dragoun of golde" was the Roman emperor's sign, but an open rebel to English royal power had adopted the golden dragon for his own. Indications are that this change came late in the process of composition . . . It creates a certain ambiguity about the significance of the dragon in the poem as a whole, ambiguity that further revision might have clarified. (53–54)

The shift in the image of the dragon—from Arthurian standard to Roman imperial one—hints at the early fifteenth-century cultural contestations embedded in Arthur's tradition. There was, as we have seen, a long-standing Welsh textual tradition that, alongside Geoffrey of Monmouth, inspired Glyn Dŵr's use of the Pendragon standard, a fact which indicates that, between Edward III and Henry Tudor, the Pendragon standard did not, "go into disuse," as Hamel claims, but was actively used by those contesting, rather than proclaiming, Plantagenet rule.[20] With these contestations in mind, we are now ready to return to the moment of Gawain's death and the question of Arthur's sovereign identity, a sovereign body in fragments.

Arthur's fragmented body fantasmatically encodes disputes over Arthur's "true" identity, and the identity of Britain's legitimate kingship. The image of a bloody Arthur split in two alludes to blood spilt in contest over the image of Arthur, and to anxieties about a united Arthurian tradition. We might recall, at this point, that the turn of the fifteenth century was a time when English fortunes in the war with France were on the wane, and when fears of French invasion were increasing. Both Welsh soldiers and Scots patriots (to whom Arthur's image was also important) fought against the English and alongside the French in that war. The *Morte Arthure* alludes to these shifts and to the cultural disputes they signify. But I am also suggesting that the Alliterative poet's interest in Arthur's continental success against "saracens" and "pagans" and the loss of Arthur's insular brotherhood in a tragic war against a similar insular force encodes anxieties about the future of England's sovereignty vis-à-vis insular ethnic difference. On the one hand, the poet turns to events on the continent as a preamble to a story of insular loss and fragmentation. This implicitly argues that continental excesses open the door to insular decay, a structure that obscures the fact that insular aggressions might develop from the problems and pleasures of insular relations themselves. Yet linking insular decay with continental war, while offering as many have suggested a critique of war overseas, also shows us how stories of international brotherhoods converge upon intimate contestations and the socio-political fragmentations they signify. I do not mean to suggest that international brotherhoods are not crucial here—the example of a French-Scots-Welsh alliance of fighting forces obviously suggests otherwise. But in the context of a complicated triangulation of English, Welsh, and Continental relations, European international affiliations and insular British ones might be, not opposed to one another, but intimately related.

Critics have called the moment of Gawain's death the climax of the Alliterative *Morte Arthure*. And many have noted that the poet's use of expansive and grisly detail in this scene surpasses the description of the death of Arthur. In emphasizing the tragedy of Gawain's death through images of Gawain's spilt blood and Arthur's fragmented body, the text, I would argue, memorializes the loss of a certain kind of Arthurian identity and identification. This moment casts Arthurian loss as a loss of family, native, and insular heritage, the tragedy of an insular ruler with poignant ties to native kin. Moreover Gawain, close kin of Arthur, is linked only one hundred lines before he dies to the Welsh site earlier identified with utopian insular rule, "Glamorgan and Wales" [Glamour, of Glayslonde, ll. 3862]. Glamorgan, here tied explicitly to Gawain's overlordship, appeared earlier as the site of Arthur's pleasurable communitarian court, Caerlion. Gawain's larger cultural identification with Welsh Arthurian traditions—and, in this poem, Gawain's explicit links to utopian Welsh locales—identify his loss with the loss of Arthur as legendary ruler from the "West Isles." In light of this poet's identification of the dragon banner with Lucius, the mournful moment of Gawain's death resonates with the loss of Arthur as Pendragon, a loss linked to Welsh fantasies of sovereign return that, by the early fifteenth century, will inspire separatist Welsh rebellion against the English crown. Gawain's death encodes the loss of the utopic insular spaces and intimate kinship demarcated by Britain's broad isle. In other words, the Alliterative *Morte Arthure* mourns, through Gawain, the loss of an implicitly Welsh Arthur.

While the poet moves Arthur to the continent to show him both Rome's heir and the Golden Dragon's rival, thereby implicitly renouncing Arthur's Welsh connection, perhaps because that connection has also been bound up with an important fantasy of a united, healed and whole British *totius insulae*, the loss of this Welsh Arthur must nonetheless be mourned. The Alliterative *Morte Arthure* mourns Arthur's tragic defeat as most crucially the loss of an insular community composed of loyal fellows and native kin. As William Matthews has remarked about the moment of Gawain's death, "[Arthur's grief and] contrition are not for his pride of conquest nor for the carnage it had wrought abroad . . . but rather for the loss of his own men" (382). Such a measure of loss against loss, of course, hints at a xenophobic ethos of the kind that will mark later, particularly fascistic, nationalisms. Insularity, as here, can verge on provincial loves and hatreds, read in the phobic descriptions of Mordred's allies, the "Saracens" and "pagans" who resemble Lucius's united continental forces. The poem offers here another moment to view the collocation of the insular and the international, of colonial aggression against the East and desire for British insular space. Categories of foreignness converge on categories of unbelief.[21]

The issue of Gawain's guiltlessness, and the sacredness of his guiltless blood (blood that, like the "precious" blood of the Christ, deserves preservation in a golden reliquary) contrasts, of course, with the guilt of Arthur's other kinsman. Mordred's actions, along with the composition of his fighting forces, offer a means to discriminate between Arthur's guiltless kin and his guilty ones. The insular family dynamics continue since Mordred, a figure also identified with the "West Isles" and "Celtic" spaces of Cornwall, Ireland, and Wales, is in the chronicles Gawain's brother or half-brother. It is Mordred, of course, who kills Gawain, in an image of the tragic insular violence of brother against brother. It is important to recall here, particularly at this moment, how tightly the circle of adversaries has constricted. In a poem that begins with foreign senators and two international fighting forces locked in combat overseas, we find ourselves at last within a deeply intimate royal circle, within intimately related familial antagonists. We are back within the once utopian realm of insular Britain with fighting spaces that are narrow, tightly circumscribed, compressed.

Mordred's guilt, moreover, is born of intimacies, if treasonous ones. While Mordred's closeness to Arthur is not figured in this poem through the excessive closeness of incest (Mordred is Arthur's nephew and not his incestuous son here), Mordred's guilt converges nonetheless on adulterous sexuality, particularly on his excessive closeness, not to Arthur, but to Arthur's wife, Gaynor. Those moves make it clear that insofar as this text imagines an historic legacy of identity out of the insular fragmentation of Arthurian Britain, that imagined community offers little hope for Gaynor's happiness.

Loss, Gender, and Colonial Romance

In a formulation that seems uncannily pertinent to the preceding discussion of the Alliterative *Morte Arthure*, theorists of postcoloniality argue that "nation" and "empire" are mutually defined and defining. As Gauri Viswanathan has put it, postcolonial critics search for ways to insert "imperial" into "national" without "reducing the two terms to a single category." They seek to "challenge the assumption that what makes an imperial culture possible is a fully formed national culture shaped by internal social developments" (190). The Alliterative *Morte Arthure* shows the collocation of the insular with the international European scene. In this poem the European fantasy of a "universal" empire on the scale of ancient Rome helps construct an imperial rule to be imported back to an insular realm.

Imperial power is, however, only imported back as a shattering set of losses. The affective tensions of those losses remain important to the poem's denouement. They also return us to the poem's fatalistic historiography, to the trauma of victimization, and to the sufferings of the innocent. This kind of romance historiography, as Sara Suleri notes, provides a particularly resonate site to display the tragedy of the colonial setting. Suleri argues that colonial romance "decode[s] the colonized territory through the conventions of romance, reorganizing the materiality of colonialism into a narrative of perpetual longing and perpetual loss" (*Rhetoric*, 10).

The *Morte Arthure* is just such a colonial romance. In place of material contestations over claims about Arthur's sovereign power, we find a melancholic tale of the loss of Arthur's greatness. In place of specific details of how the Welsh Britons lost rule over themselves, if not the island, we find a tale of the tragic theft of Arthur's coronation sword. In place of the story of how the Plantagenet dynasty lost territory in France we find the account of Arthur's death upon his insular return. In place of an account of how increasingly harsh English laws repudiate Welsh language, law, and custom, we hear the fated, inexorable passing of Gawain, and of the king whose communitarian court was held in Glamorgan. The loss of this Arthur points to, yet also avoids, a specific history of material losses. Through its narrative of tragic loss, the *Morte Arthure* calibrates desire for a glorious British king and for the united insular realm he was believed to have ruled.

The Alliterative poet copes with such losses in part through his historiographic concern over the suffering of the innocent. The trauma of those tragic repetitions, moreover, is encoded in the registers of gender and sexuality. The scene of Gawain's death places Arthur's mournful rites within the context of the sex/gender system. It suggests that the tragedy of Arthur's kingship is most satisfyingly evoked in gendered and sexualized terms. In fact Arthur's display over Gawain's dead body is profoundly homoerotic:

Than gliftis Þe gud kynge   and glopyns in herte,
Gronys full grisely   with gretande teris;
Knelis down to þe cors   and kaught it in armes,
Kastys vpe his vmbrere   and kyssis hym sone;
Lokes one his eye-liddis   Þat lowkkide ware faire,
His lippes like to þe lede   and his lire falowede.

*   *   *   *   *   *   *   *   *   *   *   *   *

Than swetes the swete kynge
Swafres vp swiftely,
Till his burliche berde
Alls he had bestes birtenede
Ne had sir Ewayne comen
His bolde herte had brousten
"Blyne" sais thies bolde men,
Þis es botles bale,
It es no wirchipe, iwysse,
To wepe als a woman
Be knyghtly of countenaunce,
And leue siche clamoure,

and in swoun fallis,
and swetely hym kysses
was blody berown,
and broghte owt of life.
and othire grete lordys,
for bale at Þat stownde.
"thow blodies Þi selfen!
for bettir bees it neuer.
to wryng thyn hondes;
it es no witt holden.
als a kyng scholde,
for Cristes lufe of heuen!"

(ll. 3949–54; 3969–80)

[Then the good King groaned gruesomely and wept great tears/Bent kneeling to the body embraced it/Cast up his visor quickly kissed Gawain/ Looked at his eyelids now cast shut/ His lips like lead and his complexion pallid;/ Then the sweet king sweated and sank in a faint/ But staggered up suddenly and solemnly kissed Gawain/ Till the blood bespattered his stately beard/ As if he had been battering beasts to death./ Had not Sir Ewain and other great lords come up,/ His brave heart would have burst then in bitter woe/ "Stop," these stern men said, "You are bloodying your-self!/Your cause of grief is cureless and cannot be remedied./You reap no respect when you wring your hands/To weep like a woman is not judged wise./ Be knightly in demeanor, as a monarch should,/and leave (aside) such clamour, for the love of Christ of heaven."]

Although scenes of brotherly affection between knights are common in the pages of Arthurian romance, Arthur's is a striking display. Scholars of medieval sexualities have taught us, of course, that chivalric culture can accommodate a wider range of knightly masculinities than modern readers might expect. As E. Jane Burns puts it, courtly "masculinity and femininity are not impermeable or mutually exclusive categories" (127). She suggests, moreover, that "even within the heteronormative model of Arthurian romance, which tries relentlessly to construct men as knights and women as ladies, we find ample evidence that gender might be better understood as 'queer' in Eve Sedgwick's definition of the term," although "sexuality's component elements remain more open for men than for women in the Arthurian world" (127).[22]

If the *Morte Arthure* allows Arthur a flexible, homoerotic masculinity, it also notes a transgressive aspect to Arthur's display. This is evident, in particular, with reference to Arthur's mourning, at the moment when Arthur's companions castigate his "womanly" excess: "To wepe als a woman," they entreat their king, "it is no witt holden" (l. 3978). Even if the companions are unsettled by Arthur's affectionate kisses and bloody embrace, their words turn to gender as a critique, not of Arthur's love for Gawain, but of the means he uses to mourn him. The onlookers attempt to discipline their king through a gendered matrix of mourning. Women weep excessively, while kings bear their grief with "knightly" demeanor. "Be knyghtly of countenaunce," the companions insist, "als a kyng scholde" (l. 3979). This ideology of gender and mourning recurs elsewhere in chivalric texts, as for example, in the modest mourning of Theseus over the hapless tragedies of Chaucer's *Knight's Tale*.[23] Sobered by his companion's response, Arthur rises from Gawain's lifeless body to display his manliness as king, fighting again, reminding us of the links between sovereignty and virility, so as to recover his usurped and "unclede" (l. 4196) sword, Clarent. It is important to note that Arthur's mournful display is imagistic and rich; his display as sovereign mourner is deeply satisfying both to Arthur himself, and to the poet who describes this moment. And if the king's companions remind him that his masculine duties require that he leave aside this weeping, those knights also console their king. Arthur's all male fellowship, moreover, suggests he redirect his grief toward the satisfying violence of the battlefield, and in righteous indignation at his usurper. He can transform the victimization of Gawain, and the apparent passivity of his mournful weeping, into the activity of war. Violence against one kinsman can apparently compensate for the loss of another.

Such are, I would argue, the gendered consolations of Arthur's tragedy. And we must note that while the few women represented in the Alliterative *Morte Arthure* are also linked with scenes of loss and desolation, they are allowed neither the satisfying aggression nor the righteous violence available to the king. Much earlier the Giant of Mount St. Michael has killed a beautiful duchess who, along with the old widow who mourns her, had no power to help herself. Traumatically victimized herself, the widow who meets Arthur can only imagine a repetitive future of victimization. "Carefull careman," she says to Arthur at his arrival, "thow carpez to lowde! May ȝone warlawe wyt, he worows vs all" [Unfortunate man, you speak too loudly. / Yon savage creature may know, he will kill us all] (ll. 957–58). Unable to envision any hope for rescue, much less self-defense, the widow warns Arthur against even the slightest self-assertion: a raised voice. She insists that he will lose any battle he attempts; and she cynically assumes that Arthur, like knights generally, is motivated primarily by a self-interested desire to increase his reputation. The widow's hopelessness as she mourns her beloved duchess, so starkly different from Arthur's mourning of his beloved Gawain, reminds us that some kinds of traumatic victimization, some kinds of innocent suffering, do not allow a belief in the possibility of rescue, let alone hope for recovery.[24] The widow offers a poignant image of a traumatic victimization that forecloses the very possibility of escape, or of resistance.

Gaynor's position throughout this poem is likewise linked to loss, and unlike the tragic romanticism of Arthur's lament over Gawain, she too is offered little hope for consolation. Early in this text, and at the news of Arthur's departure, the queen displays, through tears and lamentation, both her loyalty to Arthur and her anxiety about her future. "All my lykynge of lyfe," she says, "owte of land wendez, /And I in langour am lefte, leue ȝe, for euere. /Why ne myghte I, dere lufe, dye in ȝour armes, / Are I þis destanye of dule sulde drye by myne one?" (ll. 695–704) ["All my pleasure in life goes out of this land/ And I am left in misery, without you forever. / Why might I not, dear love, die in your arms/ before this destiny of dole I should suffer on my own?"] Gaynor's mournful devotion to Arthur, her prophetic fear about their future, does not convince her king. Despite her entreaties, Arthur abandons her to Mordred; she can only, and pathetically, beg her king not to leave her "in misery" suffering alone "this destiny of dole." Like the old widow, Gaynor is rendered both amazingly prescient and helpless to effect the fate of sovereignty. She registers for us the lamentable future absence of Arthur, predicting uncannily a tragic insular future and her own frightful destiny. Scholarly tradition has been less interested in Gaynor's mourning than in her apparent guilt as Mordred's co-conspirator. Yet because of this moment, this poem opens the possibility that Gaynor may be falsely accused. For if Arthur seems to settle on Gaynor's guilt when he asserts that only she could have given Mordred access to his wardrobe and hence to his coronation sword, the poem nonetheless, in its final moments, hints that there might be more to the story. At his death Arthur suggests that Gaynor may, herself, be an innocent victim and he wishes her well. At such a moment the poem alludes, if in only the most tenuous way, to a competing version of Arthur's fall, one that might find room to consider Gaynor herself an innocent sufferer left unprotected and unable to help herself.

Arthur's largesse in this final moment, thus, obliquely reminds us yet again of the tragedy of innocent suffering. Arthur's triumphant valor, briefly glimpsed in the wake of Gawain's death, soon disappears. This time it is Arthur who is imagined widow-like; comparing himself to that doleful state, the once great king gives a moving account of the end of his legacy:

"I may helples one hethe	house be myn one,
Alls a wafull wedowe	Þat wanttes hir beryn;
I may werye and wepe	and wrynge myn handys,
For my wytt and my wirchipe	awaye es for euer!" (ll. 4284–87)

[I am helpless upon the heath, lodged by myself,/ As a woeful widow that longs for her children; I may curse and weep and wring my hands/ For my wisdom and my worship is gone forever.]

Arthur, a mournful mother rather than a tragic father, wrings his hands for the loss of his children. The once powerful Arthur, alone on his heath, startlingly seems more akin to the biblical Rachel than he does to the raging Lear. The image of the widow is important here: it links Arthur to the earlier widow at Mount St. Michael (this poet alone makes that grieving older women of the tradition a widow); and it recalls the poet's emphasis, at line 3154 and following, on the weeping of widows who, in the wake of Arthur's wartime conquests, wring their hands in pain. Widows were, of course, a group explicitly protected under Arthurian chivalry. Here widows signify, however, not the promise of rescue, but the trauma of repetitive victimization, the innocent suffering sponsored by, and also encoded in, Arthurian sovereignty itself.

Instead of providing widows refuge, the image of Arthur as the widow Rachel who weeps for her children recuperates the promise of justice offered by the Arthurian chivalric code for its sponsoring sovereign. The image rescues Arthur from the earlier implications that he was solely and personally responsible for innocent slaughter. This moving moment, along with Arthur's equally moving display at Gawain's death, argues that Arthur is both victim and victimizer. And so we return finally to the question of traumatic repetition, and the problems of a history that cannot imagine future progress.

Insofar as we can, because of that traumatic repetition, attend to the very things that Caxton's view of history seems anxious to occlude (the problem of innocent suffering, of the petty, shameful deeds of apparently great men, of the losses and failures of the past) the Alliterative *Morte Arthure* offers a means to critique history's narrative triumphalism. In its reminder that even the most glorious of sovereigns, those acclaimed forever in chronicle and romance, produce, indeed depend upon, innocent victims whom they might (or might not) decide to rescue, this poem offers moving testimony to the victims of chivalric culture. It is testimony that we cannot, given the poem's poignancy, refuse to hear.

Yet we must also attend to the fact that innocent victimization was not meted out equally. For while Arthur felt, at the end of his life, like a mournful widow weeping for her children, he was not one in fact. He was not, after all, imprisoned and helpless, repetitively victimized so that he had no hope of any future recovery. Arthur's traumatic end is the culmination of an exciting, and vigorous, life; it is not, as in the case of Gaynor, the female victims of the Giant of Mount St. Michael, or Mordred's babies the final indignity in an endless history of longing, loss, and despair.

Thus if romance, as the genre deeply attuned to longing and to loss, reminds us of all the incivilities and cruelties that history proper longs to forget and struggles to disavow, it nonetheless designates its own victims. Examined as a colonial genre, Arthurian romance can help us to consider the politics of tragedy and loss, and help us to recall that some peoples and some bodies have suffered loss more tragically (and more frequently) than have others. In the next two chapters I analyze those losses more specifically, examining the longings of the Arthurian love plots both for the alternative possibilities and pleasures they create, and for the structures through which they assign guilt and blame.

CHAPTER FOUR

"In Contrayez Straunge"

*Sovereign Rivals, Fantasies of Gender, and
Sir Gawain and the Green Knight*

IN the previous chapter I argued that the Alliterative *Morte Arthure* registers the longings and losses of a colonial romance, displaying the value of insular British community precisely through a tale of its loss. The Alliterative *Morte*, moreover, imagines insular difference as both intimate and lethal: Mordred, Arthur's trusted nephew, uses his intimate connections to the royal circle to take advantage of the king's absence with devastating consequences for an entire kingdom. *Sir Gawain and the Green Knight*, another alliterative poem, one written around the same time, construes insular intimacies in less catastrophic, if no less complicated, terms. This time a loyal Arthurian intimate (Gawain) successfully negotiates a complicated position within a fractured regnal community.

The previous chapters emphasized the contestations over Arthur's meaning in broad cultural terms, terms that I have been linking to antagonisms over an insular heritage and, hence, to an imagined sovereign community. This chapter examines the ways that Arthurian romance encodes these contestations subjectively, that is, through a story of a particular subject negotiating the poignant complications of belonging. There is already a scholarly tradition linking *Sir Gawain and the Green Knight* with "community, virtue, and individual identity," to borrow the words of David Aers. Yet if *Gawain* tells a story about what it means for a knight to belong to Arthur's fellowship, the poem also fascinates its readers with exotic others from mysterious places that turn out in the end to be not very far from Camelot at all.

Sir Gawain and the Green Knight only became a standard of the Middle English literary canon in the nineteenth century, yet readers ever since have delighted in the formal elegance of its plot. The story opens on Arthur's spectacular New Year's feast, the young king's demand for entertainment, and a marvel appropriate for the occasion. He will not be disappointed in the amazing Green Knight who arrives, sumptuously dressed in gold and green, challenging Arthur to a beheading match. Gawain takes the floor on his sovereign's behalf, swiftly beheading the marvelous green man who amazingly retrieves his severed head and demands a rematch, one year hence at the Green Knight's Green Chapel. In due time Gawain journeys as his sovereign's representative to the mysterious vicinity of the Chapel, only to find instead the more humble castle of Bertilak de Hautdesert. Waiting here for the appointed time of his rematch, Gawain enjoys a series of intimate encounters with Bertilak's Lady, encounters structured through an "exchange of winnings" game Gawain plays with his host. On the third and final morning of Gawain's encounters with Bertilak's lady, she offers him a girdle endowed with the magical power to protect a knight's life. Although Gawain has pledged to relinquish everything he receives from Bertilak's Lady (in exchange for Bertilak's winnings in the hunt), Gawain is silent on the matter of the girdle. When Arthur's knight presents himself at the Green Chapel the next day ready to receive his blows from the Green Knight, he wears the protective girdle. The girdle becomes, instead, the sign of Gawain's dishonor when Gawain's marvelous challenger reveals that he is, in fact, Bertilak. The events at Hautdesert have constituted the real test of Arthurian chivalry and honor. The Green Knight's awesome display at Camelot the year before is now revealed to have been devised by Hautdesert's true power, Morgan le Fey, who is also Arthur's sister (and thus Gawain's aunt) and whose jealousy toward Queen Guinevere has inspired the elaborate trick. Gawain resists Bertilak's laughing invitation to join the fellowship at Hautdesert and, after unleashing his fury at Morgan in particular and women in general, returns to Camelot chastened by his adventure.

Gawain thus gives us a view of the magic by which the stranger becomes the familiar, the exotic "other" revealed to be as close as kin. This is a time when the exotic body of a Green Man converts into commoner form, and the wild geographies of "contrayez straunge" modulate into the apparently more "civilized" space of region. In the following chapter I will suggest that such transformations allude to the problems and pleasures of an intimate frontier, a borderland between linked, yet also distinct, insular cultures. Contextualizing *Gawain* and the region of its provenance as border spaces, I will argue that the poem offers traces of both the exoticism and resistance that structure an insular intercultural setting. Negotiating those regional and ethnic differences, *Gawain* ultimately imagines the stable identity of a past British community by shifting emphasis from exotic ethnic otherness to what the text would have us see as the more crucial difference of gender. An otherness of female to male, the gendered otherness of Morgan le Fey and her rule to King Arthur and his court, helps Gawain cope with differences temporarily marked as exotic. This disappearance of one kind of otherness in the appearance of another, moreover, occurs through tests of Gawain's honor and loyalty. My reading will thus suggest that relations of cultural heterogeneity that have often been forgotten in readings of this Middle English text, are in fact embedded in it. *Gawain* itself seems invested in producing such forgetfulness. And this may explain why scholars have not yet linked the poem's interest in what I will argue is a colonial exoticism to its well-documented concern with Gawain's ethical position as "honorman."

Before proceeding to those details, I wish first to situate them with regard to the ethnographic discourse about the Welsh in circulation by the time the *Gawain*-poet wrote, through a brief analysis of Gerald of Wales' *Description of Wales*. While certain kinds of medieval ethnic difference may have been imagined (as Robert Bartlett argues) in the "malleable" terms of language, law, and custom, Gerald's text at times demonstrates that discourses of law and custom can nonetheless anxiously guard nearly absolute boundaries between peoples. Turning next to the Middle English poem, I address the cultural complications of the borderland between England and Wales, the hyper-militarized region of Lancashire and Cheshire, the area of *Gawain*'s provenance. I will ground my reading of the poem's strategies of disappearing difference in the region's role as a militarized frontier society, and an ethnically heterogeneous locale.

Ethnic Virtue, Ethnic Vice: The Case of Gerald of Wales

In his groundbreaking analysis of the colonial legacies and multicultural relations at the heart of the medieval "making of Europe," Robert Bartlett argues that medieval categories of ethnicity were largely conceived in cultural, rather than biological, terms. He writes, "while the language of race—gens, natio, blood, stock, etc.—is biological, its medieval reality was almost entirely cultural" (197).[1] There is a good deal of evidence—much of which Bartlett himself supplies—to support such a claim; medieval accounts of ethnic difference repeatedly emphasize the cultural practices of language, law, and custom, rather than the physiological terms found in the nineteenth century. And cultural attributes, as Bartlett reminds us, are subject to change: "Customs, language and law share a common characteristic: all three are malleable" (197).

We must be careful, however, not to exaggerate what such a distinction, and the malleability it implies, must have meant during the Middle Ages. Evidence culled from medieval descriptions of "others" does not necessarily suggest that the malleability of language, law, and custom provided for greater ease or tolerance about boundaries between peoples; indeed, the possibility that one could change one's language, laws, and customs could, and frequently did, become a demand dominant cultures placed upon ethnically marked groups. Moreover, the contrast Bartlett makes between biology and culture deserves further attention. Biology offered a powerful vocabulary for supporting racism during the nineteenth century precisely because science was an influential cultural discourse at the time. While discourses of biology and science were neither as influential nor as well developed by the late Middle Ages as they were in later centuries, this does not preclude the existence of other powerful vocabularies to support and justify ethnic and cultural chauvinisms. As Bartlett's important history of medieval ethnicities shows us, biological essentialism is only one way of conceiving of the differences between people. We still need to ask what powerful medieval cultural discourses circulated around the categories of race. Were there discourses that played the role science played in the nineteenth century?

Gerald of Wales's *Description of Wales* suggests that an answer might lie with religious discourses of virtue and vice.[2] Written in the twelfth century, this text might qualify as the earliest example of British ethnography. Divided into two contrasting parts, Gerald's text describes Welsh characteristics through a doubled rhetoric of virtue and vice. The text's first section recounts "all the good points which redound to [Welsh] credit and glory" (255), describing Welsh "boldness, agility and courage," "natural acumen and shrewdness"; here we read of Welsh love of music and song, their poetic and literary talents, their respect for their most ancient "British" heritage. Part II deplores the Welsh as "sunk in a deep abyss of every vice" exemplified by a list of evils including "perjury, theft, robbery, rapine, murder, fratricide, adultery, incest, homosexuality" (265). ["Qualiter enim poenitentiam nedum peregisse dicentur, quos tot peccatis vitiorumque voragini datos, perjuriis puta, furtis, latrociniis, rapinis, homicidiis et fratricidiis, adulteriis et incestibus, obstinata de die in diem amplius malitia implicitos videmus et irretitos"] (228).[3]

The list of Welsh virtues points to a series of apparently "natural" talents as well as to cultural customs and values. The catalogue of "sins" that follows ascribes the degradation and poverty of the Welsh people to a long-standing moral disorder rather than to their long-standing relation with an English (or Anglo-Saxon or Norman) monarchy. Gerald identifies Welsh abjection, moreover, with one apparent sin in particular: "It was because of their sins, and more particularly the wicked and detestable vice of sodomy that the Welsh were punished by God and so lost first Troy and then Britain" (264). ["Praeterea, peccatis urgentibus, et praecipue detestabili illo et nefando Sodomitico, divina ultione tam olim Trojam quam postea Britanniam amiserunt"] (227). Despite the determined confidence of his pronouncement, despite the righteousness of the scriptural exegesis surrounding the accusation, Gerald immediately equivocates, remarking that "for a long time now this vice has ceased among the Welsh and hardly anyone can remember it" (264–65) ["veruntamen multo jam tempore adeo a Britonibus enormitas illa prorsus evanuit, ut ejus etiam memoria jam apud eos vix habeatur"] (228). The fantasmatic "sin," quickly there and gone, disappeared so long ago that memories have ceased to record it. Gerald's charge is troubled at the very moment of its utterance. Yet for all this ambiguity, and for all the anxiety this equivocation might suggest about Gerald's own position as "native informant," he still manages to deploy both the "sin" and Welsh repentance of it to challenge Welsh hopes for a triumphant return to the throne of Britain:

[The Welsh] boast, and most confidently predict, that they will soon reoccupy the whole island of Britain. It is remarkable how everyone in Wales entertains this illusion. According to the prophecies of Merlin, . . . [t]he Welsh will then be called Britons once more and they will enjoy their ancient privileges.
In my own opinion this is completely wrong. . . . The fact that the Welsh have now given up homosexuality, which they were unable to resist in their more prosperous days, must be attributed, not to any improvement in their morals, but to their indigence now that they are exiled and expelled from the kingdom of Britain. (265)[4]

On one hand, Gerald depicts a changeable people. The Welsh have "given up" the sin that apparently led to their conquest. Yet change has its limits. Welsh morals have not improved despite evidence to the contrary. Pointing to changes in habit, Gerald still insists that the Welsh remain intransigent.

Pious appearances can hide recalcitrant hearts. Cultural habits, for all their malleability, hide a moral turpitude that here seems immutable. Both malleable and obdurate the Welsh nonetheless remain other to Britain. In fact, Gerald implies that the Welsh will *only* change their ways so long as they remain other to Britain. The possibility of Welsh transformations does not here undermine ethnic otherness; indeed ethnic separation, "expulsion" and "exile," are requisite to change. Intrinsic ethnic differences remain.

In this account, conquest chastens behavior while leaving hearts unmoved. The usefulness of poverty and degradation—exile and expulsion—for weaning the Welsh away from their apparently wilder ways offers a colonial cautionary tale. Welsh "crime" resulted in monumental losses, losses that have made it impossible for the Welsh to continue living in error. While this indigence may not produce moral rectitude, it apparently prohibits a continuation of the vices to which a prosperous Welsh fell victim.[5] By implication, acts that produce indigence (acts like conquest) become refigured as ways of chastening an inherent ethnic immorality. Welsh indigence is, thus, a morally superior state to Welsh prosperity; and the rehabilitation gained is not credited to Welsh virtue. Only loss at the hands of the apparently righteous English can save these wild Britons from themselves. Conquest is refigured as salvation.

In his analysis of what he terms Britain's "internal colonialism," Michael Hechter argues that England's efforts to subdue the regions of a "Celtic Fringe" "involve[d] dominations by a 'racially' and culturally different foreign group, imposed in the name of a dogmatically asserted racial, ethnic, or cultural superiority, on a materially inferior indigenous people . . . [where] a complex of racial or cultural stereotypes [serve] to legitimate cultural superordination" (30). Throughout Gerald's text, stereotypical designations of Welsh vice are linked to critiques of law and custom. Indeed, many of the "sins" with which the Welsh are charged have their roots in differences between Welsh and English law. For example, Gerald accuses the Welsh of "the crime of incest" in that "they have no hesitation or shame in marrying women related to them in the fourth or fifth degree and sometimes even third cousins" (263). Yet this practice, as James Dimock points out, while deviating from the requirements set out by canon law before 1215 remains true of many legal systems today (xlvii). Gerald's critiques imply at times England's moral superiority over their Welsh subjects; they thus pave the way for Welsh malleability before the importation of English law and custom. The fact remains, however, that while Gerald classifies Welsh ethnicity in terms of cultural laws, habits, and practices, rather than in the biological terms which will fuel later discourses of race, stereotypes of a vice-ridden Welsh still function as, in the terms of Henry Louis Gates, "a trope of ultimate, irreducible difference between cultures, linguistic groups, or adherents of specific belief systems" (5).[6]

The complications—even contradictions—implicit in Gerald's representation of Welsh ethnicity point to the fantasmatic character of categories of ethnic difference. These discourses encode social ideologies in complicated ways; they cannot be thought to offer us direct access to an unmediated "medieval reality" of ethnicity. It is precisely because of such complications that we might usefully consider theories of colonial difference, as well as the work of medievalists on such topics. Theorists of postcoloniality remind us, for example, that "tropes of indissoluble difference" work to manage an otherness between peoples that is neither indissoluble nor absolute. Anxieties about difference attend upon what Suleri has termed "the intimacy of the colonial setting" and recur in images Bhabha describes as "ambivalent." Such representations offer, Bhabha argues, an " 'otherness' which is at once an object of desire and derision, an articulation of difference within the fantasy of origin and identity" ("Other Question" 19). To be sure, intimacies between Welsh and English have a much longer history than do the intimacies that Suleri and Bhabha describe. In geographic terms, moreover, Welsh and English are near neighbors, their spatial intimacies more immediate (if not more intense) than those that would obtain for an overseas empire. We noted in Chapter 1, with regard to Geoffrey of Monmouth's *Historia*, the historically significant complex of shared fantasies and political contestations across the spaces and identities designated by "Welsh" and "English." Despite, if not because of, such a combination of shared dreams and political contests, the castigation of an immoral Welsh derisively claims cultural difference from their potential conquerors as intrinsic and nearly essential. In so doing the Welsh are tendentiously located "outside" the very Britain they are actively engaged in contesting.

The ambivalence of Gerald of Wales's descriptions of virtue and vice simultaneously justifies Welsh malleability before English law and custom while, paradoxically, insisting upon Welsh difference.[7] In the Middle English poem written nearly two centuries later, *Sir Gawain and the Green Knight*, ambivalent representations of ethnic difference like these recur, if with a good deal of subtlety, and to happier effect. I move now to a consideration of the colonial complications registered not only within the poem, but in the history of the region from which it came.

Territorial Spacing

Sir Gawain and the Green Knight can help us examine, as Michel Foucault puts it, how "space is fundamental in any exercise of power" (144). Like many Middle English Arthurian tales (and unlike their French counterparts), *Gawain* specifies its relation to a particular region in some detail. Hautdesert rises on a landscape far from Camelot; the Green Chapel casts a different shadow than either the stately elegance of Camelot or the intimate delights of Bertilak's hall. Despite this, no one has yet considered the relation of the text's interest in regions—exterior as well as interior; wild as well as domesticated—to its other often scrutinized obsessions, namely the honor and identity of Gawain as Arthur's knight and (in more recent accounts) the gender and sexual politics of an honor system which registers identity as always formed in relation to a community and its surroundings.[8]

The poem negotiates heterogeneous territories and the social, political, personal, and economic interests they produce, within a subtle set of cultural affiliations. Critics have long argued over the poem's complicated combination of Welsh and French borrowings.[9] The opening of *Gawain* links geography to conquest by gesturing to an empire of *longue durée*. Brutus's conquest of Britain parallels the establishment of Rome; and the move westward from Troy, described with startling quickness, lists classical colonies: Troy, Rome, Tuscany, Lombardy, and Britain. Yet we hear Arthur's name in its Welsh form, despite Latinized (Arthurus) or French (Artu) alternatives that were available and, according to editors Tolkein and Gordon, more popularly in vogue at the time:[10]

> Siþen þe sege and þe assaut watz sesed at Troye,
>   Þe borȝ brittened and brent to brondez and askez
>
> . . . .
>
> Hit watz Ennias þe athel, and his highe kynde,
>   Þat siþen depreced prouinces and patrounes bicome
> Welneȝe of al þe wele in þe west iles.
> Fro riche Romulus to Rome ricchis hym swyþe,
>   With gret bobbaunce þat burȝe he biges vpon fyrst,

And neuenes hit his aune nome, as hit now hat;
    Tirius to Tuskan and teldes bigynnes,
Langaberde in Lumbardie lyftes vp homes,
    And fer ouer þe French flod Felix Brutus
On many bonkkes ful brode Bretayn he settez with wynne,

. . . .

Bot of alle Þat here bult, of Bretaygne kynges,
Ay watz Arthur Þe hendest. (ll. 1–2; 5–15; 25–26)[11]

[After the siege and the assault ceased at Troy/ the city destroyed and burnt to wood and ashes/ . . . It was noble Aeneas and his high kindred/ that afterward subjugated realms and became lords/ of almost all the wealth in the West Isles. / When noble Romulus made his way quickly to Rome/ with great pride that city he built upon first / And named it (with) his own name, as it has now;/ Tirius (went) to Tuscany and dwellings (he) founds/ Langaberde builds up homes in Lombardy,/ And far over the French sea Felix Brutus on many wide shore established Britain with joy./ . . . But of all of Britain's kings that ruled here,/ in all ways was Arthur the most noble.]

Such an opening is striking even if critics have long tried to familiarize it for us, explaining it as a predictable moment of medieval classicism.[12] This account tells us little about France, Britain's most recent colonizer and a culture with Arthurian traditions important to the *Gawain*-poet. With the briefest of allusions ("Þe French flod") the poet figures France as an adjectival marker for a distance crossed, not itself a crucial player in British history; it sits one step removed from a genealogy of Arthur "Þe hendest."

The *Gawain*-poet thus lays claim to one version of British history, specifically combining the Welsh with the Classical, while nearly eliding the French. He makes his audience view Arthur's famous court within the horizon of a Roman Empire that literally passes over Gaul. A Welsh "Arthur" sits at the heart of Trojan inheritance; the identity and origin that so preoccupies a court poet like Geoffrey Chaucer in this case includes a sovereign with Welsh credentials. This link is legible in Geoffrey of Monmouth, but as the opening scene to an Arthurian adventure tale it is not as entirely predictable as literary history would have it. Chaucer's *Wife of Bath's Tale* imagines Arthur's time as long since past, but invokes the land of Faerie rather than a tragedy from classical antiquity. The Stanzaic *Morte Arthur* begins with loss, but one that belongs wholly to Camelot's recent history of grail quest. The Alliterative *Morte Arthure*, equally imperial in the tenor of its commencement evokes conquest not as a heritage of Trojan losses, but as part of Arthur's war with the Emperor Lucius. Emphasis here upon Arthur's insular locale crafts a commonalty between centralized classical concerns and provincial Welsh ones, between a Trojan inheritance and a British *totam insulam*. For all this poem's well-documented indebtedness to a panoply of French and Anglo-Norman texts, Arthur's relation to France, here both implied and repressed, is not one of easy identification. (Such ambiguity is unsurprising given the poem's context, written during the Hundred Years War in a region filled with soldiers.) The repressed French will return in this text, of course; but when the poet hedges his French connections he suggests that France may not be the only, or even the primary, cultural affiliation he desires his readers to see.

"British" cultural collocations remain heterogeneous. It is well accepted by now that the poem also inherits, however incompletely, a number of motifs from Welsh tradition.[13] Moreover, and crucial to colonial considerations, *Gawain* is peppered with historically specific English names for Welsh places, most notably in the description of Gawain's journey in Fitt II. Arthur's knight rides "Þurȝ Þe ryalme of Logres . . . ful neghe into Þe NorÞe Walez," passing by "alle Þe iles of Anglesay . . . ouer at Þe Holy Hede . . . in Þe wyldrenesse of Wyrale" (ll. 691; 697; 698; 700) [through the realm of Logres . . . approaching into North Wales . . . [by] all the isles of Anglesay . . . over at Holy Head . . . into the wilderness of Wirral]. Logres, according to editors Tolkien and Gordon, derives from the Welsh (Lloegyr) for England; the geographic references situate Gawain, an emissary from a court in England, in transit through North Wales. His route shares a good deal with Gerald of Wales's description of the usual itinerary through Wales, and with accounts of Henry II's 1135 invasion.[14]

Moments like these point to the poet's specific interest in Wales and a history of conquest. But why does a king with a Welsh name sit on a throne in Logres—England? We still need to understand the role Arthur's Welshness plays vis-à-vis Gawain's journey into the "contrayez straunge" of North Wales (l. 713). Arthur's court in Logres has all the trappings of centralized power; that apparent contradiction here again blends Welsh difference with historic British identity. The figure of a Welsh Arthur as heir to a British throne in England simultaneously invokes Welsh sovereignty and English centrality.[15] This combination can only allude to England's desires for—its conquest and incorporation of—Welsh culture and language. Gawain's journey westward develops those allusions. In the wild Wirral,

> wonde Þer bot lyte
> Þat auÞer God oÞer gome wyth goud hert louied
>
> . . . .
>
> Mony klyf [Gawain] ouerclambe in contrayez straunge,
> Fer floten fro his frendez fremedly he rydez.
>
> . . . .
>
> So mony meruayl bi mount Þer Þe mon fyndez,
> Hit were to tore for to telle of Þe tenÞe dole.
> Sumwhyle wyth wormez he werrez, and with wolues als,
> Sumwhyle wyth wodwos, Þat woned in Þe knarrez
> BoÞe wyth bullez and berez, and borez oÞerquyle,
> And etaynez, Þat hym anelede of Þe heȝe felle.
> (ll. 701b-2; 713–14; 718–23)

[few lived there/ that either God or the man with a good heart loved./ . . . Gawain overcame many cliffs in strange regions/ Far removed from his friends, as an alien he rides./ . . . So many marvels by the hills there the man encounters/ it would be too tedious to tell even a tenth of it./ Sometimes with dragons he wars, and also with wolves,/Sometimes with trolls that dwelt amid rocks/ Both with bulls and bears, and boars other times,/ And giants that pursued him from the high fells.]

Dragons, trolls, and giants walk these woods. Representations of wild territories like this one are common in ethnographic discourse, in Gerald of Wales and in the travelogues of Mandeville. Significantly, despite brief mention of Gawain as "alien" ("fremedly he rydez"), the scene foregrounds not Gawain's strangeness, but the otherness of Wales to Arthur's knight. Gawain represents his king in a wild place. His journey's length makes clear that the dangers of foreign strangeness lie far from the heart of Camelot. And the poet's extensive description indicates that the distance placed between Arthur and Welsh wildness is valuable to him.[16]

Sarah Stanbury has noticed the exoticism of this description, and the narrative shifts that she recognizes are entirely pertinent to colonial concerns: "In the first part of the scene (ll. 715–23) Gawain is a traveler in exotic lands, 'contrayez straunge' where space is undifferentiated and unmarked by known boundaries. In the second part (726–32), however, space closes narrowly in on him. The effect of this shift is to mark experience as contingent on space and vice-versa; the narrative effects a modal translation in which meaning is inscribed chiefly through the senses of sight, touch, and hearing" (106). An exotic and undifferentiated countryside narrows on a bounded and known territory.[17] As Gawain travels between those spaces—indeed, the beauty of the description of his harrowing journey suggests something of its value to the poet—we are led from wilderness and into region, as territory civilized and ruled. Such a movement parallels annexation, where a putatively unmanaged and unnamed territory is mapped and an accounted region "civilized." This description deploys what Jacques Le Goff once called "the great contrast" of the Middle Ages, namely, the contrast "between nature and culture, expressed in terms of the opposition between what was built, cultivated, and inhabited (city, castle, village) and what was essentially 'wild'" (58). Wild geographies imply an absence of culture within them, seeming almost to invite the conqueror's apparently civilizing impulse.[18]

For all the strange ferocity of this wild Welsh landscape, the Green Knight's menace is nowhere seen or heard:

> And ay he frayned, as he ferde, at frekez Þat he met
> If Þay hade herde any karp of a knyȝt grene,
> In any grounde Þeraboute, of Þe grene chapel;
> And al nykked hym wyth nay, Þat neuer in her lyue
> Þay seȝe neuer no segge Þat watz of suche hwez of grene. (ll. 703–7).

[And ever he inquired, as he went, of the men that he met/ If they had heard any talk of a green knight/ on any place thereabout, of a green chapel;/ And all said no to him, that never in their lives did they see a knight that was of that hue.]

The Green Knight's obscurity in the very place that Gawain has been sent to look for him may well foreshadow the fact that we (with Gawain) will later discover him to be none other than an ordinary regional lord.[19] But it also hints at what I am arguing is one of the central issues this poem takes on. That is, exoticism, otherness, ethnic difference is fantasmatic; it appears and disappears. Yet within the context of this ferocious landscape Gawain's inability to find his Man of Green seems more dangerous than comforting. A hidden adversary in "contrayez straunge" offers risks beyond the ken of even this most confident knight. Moreover, even territorial wildness suddenly vanishes when Gawain, still trembling at his wild surroundings, magically sees the vision of Hautdesert: "Nade he sayned hymself, segge, bot Þrye, / Er he watz war in Þe wod of a won in a mote, /

Abof a launde, on a lawe, loken vnder boȝez/ . . . a castel þe comlokest Þat
euer knyȝt aȝte" (ll. 763–65; 767) [The man had not but signed himself
(with the sign of the cross) three times/ before he was aware in the wood of
a dwelling with a moat/ above a glade on a hill, shut behind branches/ . . .
the most beautiful castle that ever a knight owned]. Within the brief space
of four lines craggy snarls of mossy hawthorn transmute into a handsome
castle on a hill. The rapidity of this transformation is both exciting and
discomforting. It suggests how quickly places of wildness can give way to
civilized institutions. Yet, as the poem will eventually make clear, Gawain
is neither surer nor safer in the comparatively familiar location of these
courtly surroundings than he was in the strange and wild countryside.

According to Michael Bennett, journeys such as Gawain's were not
uncommon in the region and at the time the *Gawain*-poet wrote. By the
last quarter of the fourteenth century, territorial exploitation of Wales was
becoming increasingly crucial to the strategies of the English crown. When
Richard II's rule came under siege, he turned to his patrimonial lands in
Wales—lands outside the purview of Parliament—as his primary financial
resource, establishing himself in exile in Cheshire. In the process parts
of Northeastern Wales "were joined to the county palatine of Cheshire"
as a new "principality," with confiscated Welsh lands given as rewards to
Richard's loyal supporters (Thomson 162–63). In 1385 at least four Welsh
castles had Cheshire men installed as their constables; in the same year
many more men from the region took part in Richard II's expedition to
Scotland (Bennett, 167). Bennett describes the "careerism" of Cheshire and
Lancashire men who hoped to, and often did, gain prestige and prosperity
thanks to the military opportunities available to them. Soldiering became
an "agent of social mobility" during the time, a "part-time occupation
and supplementary source of income for able-bodied men from all social
classes" (162–63). Bennett identifies the *Gawain*-poet with Richard II's
provincial court and the border region between England and Wales—a
region he describes as sharing "a long and confused history of coloni-
sation, conquest and cultural assimilation" (10). Cheshire and Lancashire
men became the military arm of English rule in the area of Wales most
intimately associated with Owain Glyn Dŵr's rebellion. And against the
threats of a rising Welsh separatism, those colonial emissaries could parlay
their middling position between an English crown and a Welsh populace
into economic and political privileges. Bennett describes "a whole series
of soldiers from the northwest" who served as sheriffs of Welsh counties
"acquir[ing] lands and lordships in border areas" (179, 180). R. R. Davies

notes an intensification of intercultural exchanges between "Welsheries" and "Englishries" during the time, describing familial alliances between the Palatine states and communities of the Welsh March.[20] Cheshire and Lancashire were thus a frontier country where diverse "cultures and people met, confronted, and adjusted to each other; . . . (yet) where the distinction between native and settler . . . still remained basic in governance" (Davies, "Fragmented Societies," 89). The migration and settlement of Cheshire and Lancashire men into Wales, moreover, prompted Anglo-Welsh marital engagements as well as military ones.

We tend to think of regions of intercultural interaction as places marked by strident oppositions: conquered vs. conqueror, ethnically marked culture vs. dominant one, "Celt" vs. English. Scholars of medieval frontier societies suggest the complications to this view. Yet the history of the region of the Welsh march points to yet another complication that troubles the apparently easy split between "English" and "Welsh." The uses a centralized crown made of this Northwest region and its soldiers shows us how and why regional warriors not themselves entirely identified with central power might decide to risk their lives to further the crown's interests. In the process it suggests that colonial intimacies can involve heterogeneous, and not just dual, loyalties. That is, we should not necessarily assume an easy cultural identity between a London-based court (even one in exile) and northwest regional soldiers fighting on its behalf. Regional customs, dialects, and loyalties can make powerful claims on categories of identity.

Despite their unique geopolitical position, late medieval Cheshire and Lancashire are not usually considered sites of ethnic diversity. Yet the social and political complications outlined above suggest that this region offers a particularly striking view of relations between medieval cultures; it can thus make legible the dynamism of regional difference. Indeed, it may well be one of the legacies of colonial rule that medieval regional geographies, even in borderlands, are not usually considered places of difference.[21] Such an assumption implies we can distinguish absolute boundaries between the Welsh and the English. Yet by the fourteenth and fifteenth centuries English-Welsh intimacies on those frontiers were troubling the categorical differences between these peoples. As I will shortly demonstrate, *Sir Gawain and the Green Knight* examines the ways ethnic otherness can appear and disappear. The *Gawain*-poet depicts the exotic "other" as part fantasy, a figure who can sometimes seem to be a marvelous Green Man, sometimes an ordinary regional lord.

Cultural heterogeneities—like those in this text and its context—pose troubles to identity. Issues of identity have been important to *Gawain* scholarship. David Aers links space with identity when he reads Camelot and Hautdesert as "the split between domains and spaces [that] has generated a split in forms of consciousness, a split in obligations and . . . divisions in the knight's identity" (165); he helpfully considers the poem an account of "community, virtue and individual identity" (153). I would argue that the poem inflects those nouns with a regional accent. The problems of Gawain's virtue and his individual or group identities take place in an area culturally in-between wild Wales and the court; but the subsequent obligations Gawain must juggle, for most of the poem, remain threefold.[22]

Like a number of readings of the poem, Aers' account foregrounds the narrative's structural doubleness; Camelot and Hautdesert are signs of Gawain's doubled identities, public and private. Yet spatially the text itself is even more complicated. This narrative only comes upon doubleness as a final resolution to the problems that it raises to Gawain's honor, agency, and identity.[23] During most of the romance the reader, like Gawain, is aware of not two, but at least three sets of players and places: Camelot, the Green Chapel, and Hautdesert; Arthur, the Green Knight, and Bertilak; Guinevere, Morgan le Fey, and Bertilak's Lady. The *Gawain*-poet locates the poem's central action, moreover, explicitly on the border in between Arthur's locus and the Green Knight's; Hautdesert, the place of Gawain's testing, is the border between Camelot and Wirral. As the romance progresses these heterogeneities are domesticated into the doublenesses so many critics describe, so that by the end of the romance we find out that Bertilak *is* the Green Knight, and that Morgan's powerful aggressions are directed against Arthur and Guinevere's court. This crucial structural move—from heterogeneity to doubleness—moves the poem's readers from the multiplicity of region and ethnicity to the doubleness of gender. This, I argue, becomes the means whereby the *Gawain*-poet juggles the complications of identities and agency on a colonial frontier.

Sovereign Contests

A series of important territorial concerns thus coalesce in *Gawain*: a Welsh-named Arthur stands for "British Sovereignty" over the whole island; the regions of North Wales figure as places of vanishing wildness. Exoticism occurs, at some points in the poem, as a geographic quality;

yet upon the Green Knight's arrival at Camelot, geography links with ethnicity. The foreignness of the marvelous man's home converges on questions of his kin: "To quat kyth he becom knwe non þere/ Neuer more þen þay wyste from queþen he watz wonnen" (ll. 460–61). [To what family he belonged they knew not/ no more than they knew from where he had come]. And as much as the Green Knight's extravagance delights Arthur's court, it also challenges the king's agency. The visuals of sartorial splendor offer evidence of the knight's powerful parity with, even superiority over, the sovereign he challenges. We are persuaded of the knight's majesty by a description imposing in physical detail alone:

> Ande al grayþed in grene þis gome and his wedes:
>   A strayte cote full streȝt, þat stek on his sides,
> A meré mantile abof, mensked withinne
>   With pelure pured apert, þe pane ful clene
> With blyþe blaunner ful bryȝt, and his hod boþe,
>   þat watz laȝt fro his lokkez and layde on his schulderes;
> Heme wel-haled hose of þat same,
>   þat spenet on his sparylr, and clene spures vnder
> Of bryȝt golde, vpon silk bordes barred ful ryche,
>   And scholes vnder schankes þere þe schalk rides;
> And alle his vesture uerayly watz clene verdure,
>
> .   .   .   .
>
> Aboutte hymslef and his sadel, vpon silk werkez
>   þat were to tor for to telle of tryfles þe halue
> þay were enbrauded abof, wyth bryddes and flyȝes,
>   With gay gudi of grene, þe gold ay inmyddes.
>
> .   .   .   .
>
> Wel gay watz þis gome gered in grene,
>   And þe here of his hed of his hors swete.
> Fayre fannand fax vmbefoldes his schulderes;
>   A much berd as a busk ouer his brest henges,
> þat wyth his hiȝlich here þat of his hed reches
>   Watz euesed al vmbetorne abof his elbowes,
> þat half his armes þer-vnder were halched in þe wyse
>   Of a kyngez capados þat closes his swyre.
> (ll. 151–61; 179–86)

[And all arrayed in green this man and his costume:/ a straight tunic, very narrow, that clung to his body/ a fair mantle over it, lined on the inside/

with plain fur evident, all of one color/ with bright ermine, pure white, and (on) his hood also/ that was thrown from his head and laid on his shoulders; . . . /And all his clothing indeed was pure green,/ Both the stripes on his belt and other bright stones that were richly set in his fair garments/ About himself and his saddle, embroidery upon silk./ It would be too tedious to tell half of the trifles/ that were embroidered on it, with birds and insects/ With gay ornamentation in green with gold always mingled./ . . . A great beard as a bush over his breast hung/ that along with his splendid hair that extended from his head/ was trimmed al about, above his elbows/ (so) that half his arms underneath were covered in the way of a King's cape, that closes at the neck.]

In a description resonant with earlier images of wild geographic space, the Green Knight's magnificent body carries signs of the natural world. We also see vestiges of courtly dress, the sartorial accoutrements of knighthood. Ermine-trimmed cape and hood, gold spurs, bands of silk, an impressive mane of hair and beard together convince us of the Green Knight's majesty. While the knight is nowhere called a king, he dresses like one with a "king's cape" fastened at his neck. We get no comparable description of Arthur though he is sovereign of the occasion; indeed the poet foregrounds the visitor's majesty in ways which, as some readers have suggested, critique Arthur's sovereignty as ineffectual, even childish. In contrast to the prodigious majesty of the exotic Green Man, Arthur and his fellows seem, as the Knight himself taunts, "bot berdlez chylder" (l. 280) [but beardless children].

This implicit critique of Arthur's sovereignty suggests that the poem is not simply a royalist exercise. Yet neither does the poem invest in any simple opposition between the knight's spectacular performance and Arthur's royal essence. If the Green Knight's challenge casts the visual majesty of knight in competition with the dynastic majesty of king, the sumptuous splendor of Arthur's table dislodges any simple opposition between lineage and virtue. Arthur and the Green Knight both enact what Georges Bataille calls "expenditure", a "sumptuary process of social classification" (119); both use the New Year's festival as an opportunity to display power ostentatiously, showing themselves to be rivals in rank and standing. The knight's bodily expenditure, viewed in the astonishing titillation of his decapitation and survival, squanders "as much energy as possible . . . to produce a feeling of stupefaction" in the company (Bataille, 119); the court sits stone-still (l. 432), speechless (l. 244), astonished (l. 301), even

Arthur full of wonder (l. 467). Moreover, the Green Knight's beheading and survival means that he can magically vanquish death even while
displaying it; such a combination performs the doubleness of the king's
(two) bodies. He lives despite mortal blows to his crowned head. When
he performs the doubled role required of the sovereign, the Green Knight
matches Arthur's power with his own, challenging Arthur's sovereignty
with his own sovereign pretensions.

Difference merges with similarity. The stranger is, after all, a Green
Knight familiar with the demands of courtesy, honor, and the practices
of chivalry. He is, nevertheless, a *Green* Knight, decked in gold and ermine and frighteningly huge. Both like them and different from them,
the stranger delights as much as he dismays. This ambivalent image of
the challenger—both menacing and marvelous—resonates with Homi
Bhabha's description of mimicry, wherein an ethnic or racially different
figure, becomes "a subject of a difference that is almost the same, but not
quite." "Mimicry," Bhabha writes, "is at once resemblance and menace"
("Mimicry," 127). The Green Knight brings both resemblance and menace
to Arthur's court. In him we see the exotic other from the Western reaches
of the isle whose rule and power rival Arthur's; we also see an image of
chivalric aping, a display of sovereign trappings almost right but not quite.

There are important differences between the fabulous exoticism of
this moment in medieval romance and the "post-Enlightenment" discourse
that Bhabha reads. For one, Bhabha's mimicry surfaces what he elsewhere
calls "sly civility," an ambivalent response to a historically specific English
colonial acculturation. The Green Knight's *in*civility (readers usually call
him discourteous) is, famously, not so very sly. His bold insults will later
be replaced by Bertilak's good-humored politeness. Yet one could argue
that Bertilak (and Morgan's) trickery in displaying the (illusory) extravagance of the Green Knight's challenge might be itself a kind of slyness:
a performance designed to register a threat even to a self-obsessed court
like Camelot. Ultimately, moreover, the plot's resolution will mean that
Gawain, an emissary who has moved between "home" and "away," returns
home to face the prodigious imbecilities of Arthur and his community. The
Gawain-poet, in other words, incorporates elements of the Green Knight's
insolence in Gawain's ironic and sad view of the court upon his return. In
so doing the poem comes close to enacting its own "sly civility."

There are, in addition, important formal differences between medieval
romance and the texts that Bhabha reads. Romance encodes the fantastic and magical, although as Fredric Jameson, Peter Haidu, and a host of
others argue, this makes it no less historical or material in its concerns.[24]

Bhabha reads texts infused with realism, and his notion of colonial mimicry explicitly points to the fantasmatic slippages in the putatively rational, indeed bureaucratic, dictums of empire. He suggests how fantasmatic effects criss-cross even the soberest governmental discourse. The moments of discourteous mimicry in this medieval romance suggest a view from the other side: that is, that serious, imperial aggressions and (as I will make clearer in a moment) equally serious colonial resistances might criss-cross in the fantastic visions of romance. Thus, if Bhabha's work offers a view of how the colonial historical archive is filled with fantasy, a medieval consideration of colonial mimicry can offer a view of how romance fantasies might encode a kind of colonial historical archive.

In the case of *Sir Gawain and the Green Knight*, moreover, this scene of discourtesy is also a scene of contestation. Both exotic marvel and challenger of Arthur's sovereignty, the Green Knight offers a particularly concise symbolization of those intimate (yet also ambitious) contestations within an English-Welsh Arthurian scene. The Green Knight's challenge to Arthur mounts a condensation of two medieval discourses—where an exoticist discourse of monstrosity and the counter-hegemonic discourse of Welsh traditions converge in concise and startling ways. Traces of hegemonic exoticism and traces of an oppositional sovereignty intersect, not only in the delights and slippages in the figure of an exotic Green Man, but in the ways that this image alludes to the historical agency of Welsh claims to "British" sovereign figures and forms. The condensation can thus offer an emergent scene of, to quote Benita Parry, "the native as historical subject and agent of an oppositional discourse" ("Problems," 44). My reading of this provocative scene from *Gawain* rethinks the Green Knight's challenge as an exotic colonial image that nonetheless "challenges, subverts, and undermines the ruling ideologies . . . [a] speech and stance [that] refuses a position of subjugation" ("Nativism," 176). *Gawain*, thus, offers a dialogic space rich in centralized ideology and oppositional discourse. It thus suggests that a postcolonial approach to medieval romance might amplify textual condensations, making visible traces of medieval "counter-hegemonic" moves.

Although the previous remarks follow some of Benita Parry's critiques of Bhabha's work, Bhabha's notion of mimicry nonetheless remains important to my analysis. There are two reasons for this. Unlike other ways of signifying multiple identities (as Gloria Anzaldua's "mestiza," recently recommended by Jeffrey Cohen as preferable to Bhabha's terms), "mimicry" connotes a resistant edge that remains, pace Parry, useful for a consideration of oppositional agency. The Lacanian psychoanalytic valences of "mimicry," moreover, figure identity formation through a complex structure of identification and aggressivity, a combination of special importance for the intimate scene of English-Welsh relations. But there is another implication of Bhabha's "mimicry" that also particularly suits my analysis. While "mimicry" suggests a way of construing resistant agency within the colonial setting, it also encodes (often without noting the effects) a gendered exclusivity. Diana Fuss and Anne McClintock have each pointed out that Bhabha's "mimicry" seems exclusively male, as suggested by the title of the essay, "Of Mimicry and Man." As an implicitly male term, Bhabha's "mimicry" thus registers a masculine oppositional civility. As the next sections of this chapter will eventually make clear, I am arguing that the *Gawain*-poet is interested in exactly this kind of masculinist oppositional agency; Gawain's (and Arthur's) masculinity will be important compensatory features of Gawain's willing return to Camelot.

Masculine opposition ultimately becomes a means to register male autonomous agency. Such moves also help explain the poem's concern with the problems of Arthur's youth, and I turn briefly to this question. The opening scenes at Camelot confront a young, self-indulgent king with the prodigious size and grandeur of a bold challenger.[25] A number of readings of Arthur's youth and the New Year's setting emphasize the optimism of both; yet when they do, they ignore a host of medieval discussions of sovereignty in which youth figures as a troubling quality for a king.[26] The implications of Arthur's youth resonate, for example, with concerns surrounding Richard II's minority, himself a sovereign by age ten. Chroniclers of the period devote considerable attention to the question of the realm's stability, as when Adam of Usk links the instability of Richard's reign to the king's tender age:

During this King Richard's reign great things were looked for. But he being of tender years, others, who had the care of him and his kingdom, did not cease to inflict on the land acts of wantonness, extortions, and unbearable wrongs. . . . According to the saying of Solomon: "Woe to thee, O land, when thy king is a child," in the time of the youth of the same Richard many misfortunes, both caused thereby and happening therefrom, ceased not to harass the kingdom of England, as has been before said and as will hereinafter more fully appear, even to the great disorder of the state and to the last undoing of king Richard himself and of those who too fondly clung to him. (7; 10)[27]

The devastation of Richard's rule—and the unhappiness it brings to both the sovereign and his familiars—began with those "who had the care of him." Their intimacies with the boy-king meant that "acts of wantonness, extortions and unbearable wrongs" were able to "harass the kingdom of England" unto its "great disorder" and Richard's "last undoing." The trouble of a child-king is figured here as a trouble with relationship. His inability to stand autonomously without the entanglements of those who "too fondly cling to him," destroys his sovereign power and England's great order. Richard's problem—the problem of sovereign minority generally—is an excess of relationship. He is overly dependent, overly vulnerable, overly implicated in the apparent wanton affections of others. His boyishness means that he cannot stand on his own; a manly king would be, by implication, one who can dispatch royal authority without bothering to consider the interests or opinions of his familiars. The authoritative adult king is the entirely autonomous one.

Visions of entirely autonomous and independent kings are, of course, fantasies of sovereignty. Rulers, whether king or queen, adult or child, are positioned amid a nexus of relations of both kin and courtesy. The history of gender and power told about medieval rule frequently ascribes autonomy and independence (and the strength of the royal will) to strong and virile male rulers. Good rulers are imagined as the best of men: mature, decisive, autonomous, independent, reasoned, and adequately passionate about their women and their wars. Bad rulers are, by contrast, boys, women, and feeble old men. Dependence figures as the opposite of virtuous rule; it is consigned to (male) youth and dotage, and to women. Usk links the "wanton" caretakers of Richard's youth with the king's later lack of independence, implying that Richard's love for his intimates marks a refusal, in short, to be a man. Richard's kingly manhood is deficient for the same reasons that those of a mama's boy would be: he will not put behind him the entangling affections of childhood.

Such a story told, in this case well after Richard's deposition, exile, and death, was in the air in the last decades of the fourteenth-century. The "Merciless" Parliament of 1388 executed eight of the King's "favorites," including Sir Simon Burley, Richard's tutor from boyhood. More than forty of Richard's advisors and familiars were banished on account of the king's excessive dependence upon them.[28] Within such a context, the *Gawain*-poet's emphasis upon Arthur's boyishness can be read to register an alarm for, and certainly alertness to, sovereign ineptitude and court instability.[29]

Arthur's court, nonetheless, has the power to bestow sumptuous feasts; yet Camelot's need for a "marvel" as a catalyst to Arthur's dining pleasure—and Arthur's inability to provide one himself—suggest that cen-

tralized courts like Camelot require exotic intruders to grant them access
to their pleasures. R. R. Davies has pointed to the role similar delectable
feasts played in England's colonization of Ireland, where the opulence of
an imperial court (specifically Henry II's Christmas feast held in a festival pavilion outside Dublin) was aggressively offered in gift to the native,
and soon to be subjugated, people.[30] Arthur's banquet shows as well that
sovereigns require delighted audiences before whom they can spend their
fortunes as one means of making their power palpably real.[31] In the scene
of Camelot's New Year's feast, moreover, Arthur's dependence upon the
importation of foreign goods and services is sustained in the poetic description of the imported canopy Guinevere sits arrayed beneath, made:
"Of tryed tolouse, of tars tapites innoghe/ Þat were enbrawded and beten
wyth Þe best gemmes" (ll. 77–78). That beautiful accouterment is brought
from markets overseas, the cloth from Toulouse, and the silk from Tharsia,
a region, according to Norman Davis, identified in *The Travels of Sir John
Mandeville* as adjacent to Turkistan in the Levant (75, n. 77). The opulence
of Arthur's court links explicitly to the colonizing impulse of European
desires for exotic riches from other lands.

   The competition between Arthur and the Green Knight thus figures a
competition about power as masculine agency. In his challenge to Round
Table fellowship, the Green Knight matches his virile physicality against
Arthur's courtly power, a power based upon wealth and reputation rather
than achievement. In the process we are momentarily presented with two
kinds of male agency: the Green Knight's, autonomous and virile, and
Arthur's, frivolous and ineffective. But why is this impressive Green Man
finally shown to be commanded by a jealous female? What are the ramifications of the link between Green Knight's awesome display and the
desire of Morgan le Fey? To answer these questions we need to examine
the intimacies of Gawain's fortune as Arthur's heroic representative in that
middle place between Camelot and the Green Chapel. I turn now to what
comprises the bulk of the romance itself, the events and conversations at
Hautdesert, and Gawain's relation with Bertilak and his Lady.

Entangling Alliances

   Gawain encounters Bertilak's hospitality in regions and bedchambers
far from home. In the text's middle section, the heterogeneities of Gawain's
obligations to Arthur, Bertilak, Bertilak's Lady, and the Green Knight con-

verge in tests of his identity and agency. The three-fold scenes of Gawain's exchange of winnings with Bertilak show two kinds of male power: the virile ferocity of Bertilak's hunts alternate with the more delicate intricacies of Gawain's mornings with Bertilak's Lady. Those domesticated scenes are as gripping in their knotty complications as the hunt scenes are for their riotous freedoms. While the effect of the textual juxtaposition of forest and chamber is, as many have noted, to establish a relationship between the two scenes, the juxtaposition of tracking and trysting also renders intimate complications of men with women as the far more threatening of the two.

At Hautdesert, Gawain's relation not to Bertilak but to Bertilak's wife constrains his agency. On the second day of the games, the troubles come together with particular force.

> "Sir, ʒif ʒe be Wawen, wonder me Þynkkez,
> Wyʒe Þat is so wel wrast alway to god,
> And connez not of compaynye Þe costez vndertake,
>
> . . . .
>
> "What is Þat?" quoÞ Þe wyghe, "I wysse I wot neuer;
> If hit be sothe Þat ʒe breue, Þe blame is myn awen."
> "ʒet I kende yow of kyssyng," quoÞ Þe clere Þenne,
> "Quere-so countenaunce is couÞe quikly to clayme;
> Þat bicumes vche a knyʒt Þat courtaysy vses."
> "Do way," quoÞ Þat derf mon, "my dere, Þat speche,
> For Þat durst I not do, lest I deuayed were;
> If I were werned, I were wrang, iwysse, ʒif I profered."
> "Ma fay," quoÞ Þe meré wyf, "ʒe may not be werned,
> ʒe ar stif innoghe to constrayne with strenkÞe, ʒif yow lykez."
> (ll. 1481–83; 1487–96)

["Sir, if you are Gawain, it seems to me a wonder/ A man so well disposed always to goodness/ does not know how to perceive the demands of society"./ . . . "What is that?" said the knight, "I do not understand./ If it is true what you say, the blame is my own."/ "Yet I instruct you in kissing," said the beautiful lady, "Wheresoever he finds favor is proper to claim (it) quickly/: this is fitting for every knight who practices courtesy."/ "Cease," said the doughty man "my dear, from that speech,/ For that dare I not do, lest I were denied;/ If I were refused, I would be wrong, indeed, if I made the request." "Indeed," said the beautiful woman, "you may not be refused./ You are strong enough to constrain with force, if you wish."]

Their conversation pertains to desire and choice, to the limitations imposed upon Gawain's honorable actions. Gawain's refusal to ask the Lady
for a kiss suggests to her that he is a fraud. Gawain parries her challenge
with a courteous assessment of the dilemma of his agency: in making advances, he might be refused; and any refusal could show him to be in the
wrong, proving, in fact, that he has not mastered the particulars of poli-
tesse. "If I were werned," he argues, "I were wrang, iwysse, ȝif I profered."
The double use of the conditional ("if I were werned; . . . ȝif I profered")
emphasizes the limitations of Gawain's autonomous activity. As a stranger
and a representative of Arthur, Gawain juggles a complicated nexus of relations; he cannot predict with any surety the responses his behavior might
evoke. The Lady responds to Gawain's worries by reasserting his agency in
superlatively masculine terms: he is, she asserts, strong and "stif" enough
to constrain her with virile strength. Physical strength and masculine stiff-
ness become the means of asserting knightly agency. Yet in the process
Bertilak's lady makes it impossible for Gawain to continue his refusals
and claim an unfettered masculine agency. Her testimony to his manliness results in nothing less than Gawain's submission to her wishes. Her
reassurances prompt Gawain's capitulation to her desires. When the Lady
links masculinity with agency so as to make Gawain submit, she shows us
that images of masculine strength nonetheless encourage the pliability that
sovereignty power demands.

Histories of colonial conquest narrate the agency of imperial militarism in just such terms: virile imperial power overcomes a feminized native
resistance, a power frequently (and unfortunately) figured in metaphors of
sexual conquest and rape. These metaphors of rape, Sara Suleri argues, obscure the significance and the intricacies of homosocial relations between
the colonizer and the colonized.[32] This insight could cause a reexamination
of the fantasmatic charge of homosexuality in Gerald of Wales's ethnography. While I do not wish to conflate what Suleri means by homosociality
with Gerald's description of what he would have us see as Welsh depravity,
both works suggest the pertinence of categories of same-sex relations to
analyses of ethnic difference. Studies of ethnicities need to consider the
intercultural complications between men as readily as they examine the
intercultural complications between men and women. Categories like mis-
cegenation, for example, tend to assume that race-mixing is only fraught
in its heterosexual form, and thus imply that heterosexual relations across
ethnicities are more complicated, and more anxious, than are intercultural
relations between men or between women. This implication, as I will make

clear, is exactly the resolution *Sir Gawain and the Green Knight* seeks; it bifurcates heterosexual relations from intercultural ones so as to suggest that the former are more complicated, and more dangerous, than are the latter. While relations across regional and ethnic difference occur here between men, these intimacies, as we shall see, seem less troubling than are their erotic heterosexual counterparts. In view of Caroline Dinshaw's recent reading of the homosocial palpitations of the kissing game between Bertilak and Gawain, I would argue that what she describes as "the romance's particular investment in [heterosexuality]" focuses our attention on heterosexual complications so as to divert attention away from the complications to agency posed by relations between men.[33]

The scenes between Gawain and Bertilak's Lady display, as Geraldine Heng has argued so compellingly, that the power and agency of women in *Gawain* constitute much more than a poetic "subtext." Impressively challenging the priority given to the manifest masculine competition, Heng reads "the sedimentations of female desire" situated "in the repeating moments where masculine command slips and misses" ("Feminine Knots," 501). Yet in her understandable emphasis upon recovering the power of the "feminine" text, Heng does not investigate the misogynist consequences of locating "feminine" power as the corollary to masculine failure. For it is crucial in this text that Gawain is *not* constrained by his submission to Arthur, Bertilak, or the Green Knight, but by his submission to Bertilak's Lady. The "feminine text" that Heng identifies, and the powerful woman who commands it, tricks Gawain into submission with the illusory image of a masculine power which (apparently) cannot be refused. A female's desire delimits male agency, displacing the anxieties of masculine control prompted by submission per se onto the demands of powerful women. Along the way the text splits complications away from the intricacies of relations among men. This text would have us see that male agency is compromised across the difference of gender and not the differences of region or ethnicity. Such an image of male agency forestalls anxieties about the constraints of agency amid the complications of the borderland.

Bertilak's lady's desire and the desires of Morgan le Fey are at the heart of this text's solution to the problems that ethnic and regional difference poses to masculine command per se and to the complications colonial relations between men pose to masculine agency. The gender strategies are compensatory. Gender takes center stage so that the complicated ethnic and regional differences of the poem's earlier moments—between a centralized sovereign (Arthur), a colonial emissary (Gawain), and a sometime "exotic" other (Bertilak-the Green Knight)—can disappear in favor of an easy split between "masculine" agency and "feminine" aggression. And this is why Gawain directs his infamous anti-feminist diatribe against not the entanglements of men with men, but the entanglements of men with women. Bertilak's revelation that he is the Green Knight and that his court is ruled by Morgan le Fey rescues Arthur's sovereign power from the Green Knight's earlier challenge—by marking Arthur's rule as unequivocally male. If the Green Knight's challenge has raised questions about Arthur's power, Bertilak's obedience to Morgan, a dangerous and aggressive female commander, reveals that the knight's exotic masculinity is illusion. The text would have us see the Green Knight's virility as a show that hides female command.

Heng reads Bertilak's "astonishing excursus" into the details of Morgan's power as a "celebratory testament" to her as "the goddess" ("Knots," 508). Yet in nearly the same breath Bertilak reminds Gawain that Morgan is his aunt: "ArÞurez half-suster,/ Þe duches doʒter of Tyntagelle, Þat dere Vter after hade ArÞur vpon" (ll. 2464b-66a). Morgan is celebrated as goddess briefly and only once; the text specifies in some detail Morgan's precise kin relation as Gawain's aunt. Hautdesert and Camelot are thus revealed as literally kin to one another. The Green Knight's exotic strangeness proved to be fantasmatic; ethnic heterogeneities finally modulate into nothing more than the differences of an extended family. Thus, and somewhat ironically, by the end of the poem, the Green Chapel and Camelot are not only split, but also joined as cognate kin. Gawain's choice is now between devoted submission to his mother's sister, and a return, wiser and older, to the court of his mother's brother. Poised between uncle and aunt, between regional court commanded by a woman and centralized court ruled by a man, Gawain's choice of loyalties is made to seem remarkably easy. In the midst of Gawain's final encounter with the Green Knight, this revelation resolves the problems and challenges that the exotic stranger once posed to Arthur's court. The Green Knight, whose ties to family and land were earlier scrutinized and questioned, is ruled by Gawain's own female kith and kin. Morgan le Fey's ultimate responsibility for all these events sponsors Gawain's ability to repudiate Hautdesert (and its pleasures) as the realm of the ("evil") female.

By the time the conjoined figure of Bertilak-the Green Knight finally invites Gawain to stay with him at Hautdesert—raising the question of Gawain's loyalty and duty to Arthur—the choice facing Gawain is marked with the difference of male to female. Gawain can choose again the king he has been representing all along, reassured by the difference that gender makes that his choice encodes male power. Bertilak offers a more emasculated alternative, remaining enthusiastically enamored of Morgan's power. The Green Knight submits and, apparently, loves doing so.[34]

While Morgan's power produces Bertilak's enthusiastic submission, Arthur's sovereignty can accommodate both Gawain's loyalty and his wry disdain. Yet for all the complications of the position of knights on a border between, the text finally renders masculine agency as a solitary matter. In terms of his relations at court, Gawain is left with a private sense of the irony of his position. Gawain's solitary image riding home at the end of the poem thus points to how well this male aristocratic subject survived the vicissitudes of community across region; he has now gained autonomy and integrity despite the instability, immaturity, even the naiveté of the sovereign he is charged with representing. When Gawain finally does return home, blushing with shame at the girdle, the symbol of his failures abroad, the courtly company misreads both him and it. Naively Arthur and "alle Þe court als/ Laȝen loude Þerat, and luflyly acorden/ Þat lordes and ladis Þat longed to þe Table,/ Vche burne of Þe broberhede, a bauderyk schulde haue" (ll. 2513b-16). The distance between the court's response and Gawain's indicates both the limitations to Arthur's view and Gawain's independence from their opinions. Managing nonetheless to belong he remains aloof from their enthusiasms.

Yet if Arthur's court, by the end of the text, emerges as naive, Morgan's haunting image at Hautdesert serves to undermine any earlier indication that Arthur's kingship, when compared to the Green Knight's virility, is effeminate. Round Table knights may foolishly decide to don a green garter as a sign of their union, but they are not managed, as Bertilak apparently is, by a jealous female pulling strings from behind the scenes. Arthur's sovereign agency is not compromised by the intimacies of his affection, for this text offers us no view whatsoever of Guinevere's perfidy or Lancelot's seductions. And if the text at moments calls into question—and thus resists—the power of a centralized court, it finally recapitulates Arthurian sovereignty as the only reasonable alternative because it is rightfully male.[35]

The poem's resolution implicitly, if also ambivalently, favors Arthur's sovereign powers. *Sir Gawain and the Green Knight*, thus, offers a view of how medieval fantasies of ethnicity and gender can produce submissions to an English sovereign centrality. And if it has been difficult to see the colonial elements here, this is because the poem's narrative strategies deploy a misogynist gender hierarchy to help us forget moments of exotic difference. Recent readings of the poem have suggested the ways this poem might be critical of the royal culture it describes; I am suggesting that insofar as this poem makes it utterly easy to forget differences of region or ethnicity, or ultimately construes Arthur's court in homogeneous terms, those critiques entwine with colonial consolidations. But this does not mean, of course, that we must follow the poem's resolution, believing that the Green Knight's or Morgan's challenge to Arthur's hegemony is merely illusion. If Gawain's final return to Camelot reasserts his (ambivalent) loyalty to the conservative and authoritative politics of a centralized monarchy,[36] we are also left with Morgan's power intact and with the echo of Bertilak's laugh.

Bertilak's Laugh

The poem's last look at Bertilak-the Green Knight discloses that, whatever has happened to the Green Knight's exoticism, the kindnesses and pleasures at Hautdesert do not fade away. Gawain blushes with shame before Bertilak because he accepted the Lady's girdle as a safeguard for his survival before the formidable opponent he was to meet the next day. Bertilak does not, however, chastise Gawain's apparent weakness; his answer reverberates with a compassionate understanding of a knight's desire to survive. ("Bot for ȝe lufed your lyf; Þe lasse I yow blame," "But that you loved your life; I blame you the less [for that].") A subject from the central court, Gawain persists in reading his own desire to survive as shameful; evidently the shame of accommodation is particularly fraught for this emissary from a centralizing power.

In long debating Gawain's "sin" or "dishonor" in accepting the Lady's girdle, critics have been deeply unsympathetic to a knight's desire to survive. In this they have colluded with Camelot's demand that knights display the purest loyalty and virtue. Bertilak's sympathy for Gawain, his laughing invitation that Gawain stay at Hautdesert, and "make merry" with those who love him there, on the other hand, resists Camelot's demands for unswerving and pure loyalty. Part of the challenge Hautdesert can still raise to Camelot can thus be read, even at the poem's end, in Bertilak's compassion and kindness, in his apparent unconcern with either Gawain's pure virtue or his pure loyalties.

Such a reading suggests that if the textual strategies of *Sir Gawain and the Green Knight* establish male autonomy through its misogynist opposition to female relation, the subtle accomplishments of the *Gawain*-poet offer plenty of power to critique the demands of the state. This ambivalent, complicated view of sovereignty does not serve a clearly royalist agenda. It mounts instead an ambivalent recuperation of bold challenge for a subtle, interior (if also exclusively male) form of resistance. This poem displays the poignant problematics of survival in borderlands. Gawain's fears for his survival mark the structure of his desire as pertinent to intercultural encounters. In the complicated intimacies of the borderlands survival demands the accommodations to intimate relations, the kind of flexibility Gawain displayed, what R. R. Davies calls "coexistence and change." Yet within such a context, strategies of accommodation and survival can nonetheless open a space for resistance. For Gawain's accommodating acceptance of the green girdle also hints at his resistances to both Bertilak's command that he disclose everything, and to Arthur's demands that his heart, like his identity, remain courageously pure. We might, thus, view Gawain's "failure" with more sympathy than he does himself, and remain attentive to the poignant resistances within it.

Sara Suleri argues that intimacies across difference are constitutive for imagining a nation. In the intimate locale of the frontier, colonized and colonizer live side by side; those familiarities, moreover, construct and confer identity. She asks, "is nation in itself the alterity to which both subjugating and subjugated cultures must in coordination defer?" (*Rhetoric*, 9). With Suleri's figuration in mind, Welsh and English interaction in march towns, at regional marketplaces, on the battlefield, or in the narrative tropes of a Middle English poem become the multiple places where unity is forged from ethnic heterogeneities. Colonial union becomes an act of cultural synchronicity, a coordination of capitulation. The particularities of the late medieval scene examined here might make us wonder whether the idea of a "British" insular wholeness was an "otherness" to which cultures in England, Wales, Cheshire, and Lancashire in the late Middle Ages deferred. During the period leading to Glyn Dŵr, a category like "Britain" may have been as vexed a one for various English peoples as it was for the Welsh since it required a coordination of (at least) two different identities into a new third term. Such coordination, to be sure, would be founded in part on attempts to differentiate the "wild" Welsh from the "civilized" English so as to insure that an English identity remained intact, apparently unaffected by its intimate relations with, and its desire for, those others.[37] Rhetorics of distance and differentiation—the desire to separate "Welsheries" from "Englishries" in late medieval histories, or in the case before us to determine once and for all which parts of *Gawain* are Welsh or English—efface the familiarities, shared dreamings, common spaces of household and story. They efface as well the dialogue of imperial demand and colonial resistance.

Gawain also shows us, furthermore, that as an imagined community the Arthurian chivalric brotherhood genders relationship, opposing it to autonomy. It links the former with heterosexual women and the latter with heterosexual men. This splitting purchases an autonomous male power by marking women as more deeply linked to the problems and passions of relational attachments. Such a gendered and heterosexual imagined community disavows the relational complications within which all subjects find themselves. It tendentiously implies that brotherhoods, unlike heterosexual unions, can accommodate movement across difference of region or ethnicity. The special complications of relationship and women have been read in colonial histories that emphasize the problems of cultural mixing in heterosexual terms; they likewise appear in psychoanalytic formulations of what Deleuze and Guattari call "the dogma of Oedipal theory"; they are legible in literary histories of the romance genre that continue to associate tales of love, especially by the late Middle Ages, with the desires and powers of women. With this reading of *Gawain* in mind, we might wonder how deeply this version of literary history is indebted to a colonial inheritance; we might wonder to what extent histories of female desire for the late Middle English romance sediments subsequent "failures of masculine command" that attend upon intimacies across differences other than gender. In the next chapter I will suggest the tragic consequences of such structures in times of war. The Stanzaic *Morte Arthur* offers poignant evidence that the tragedy of Arthurian romance depends upon its gendered politics.[38]

CHAPTER FIVE

Dangerous Liaisons

Disloyalty, Adultery, and the Tragedy of Romance

Passion means suffering, something undergone, the mastery of fate over a free and responsible person. . . . Passionate love, the longing for what sears us and annihilates us in its triumph—there is a secret which Europe has never allowed to be given away; a secret it has always repressed—and preserved! Hardly anything could be more tragic; and the way passion has persisted through the centuries should cause us to look to the future with deep despondency.

—Denis de Rougemont, *Love in the Western World*

Now thou leviste for hyr sake
alle thy dede of armys bold.
I may wofully wepe and wake
In clay tylle I be clongyn cold.

—Guinevere to Lancelot, Stanzaic *Morte Arthur* (ll. 748–51)

D ENIS de Rougemont characterizes the Arthurian adultery story, specifically as told through the tale of Tristan and Iseult, as the ultimate marriage of passion and pain, and as mythic testimony to the West's powerful tendency to understand desire as bound to loss and lack—in short, to death. His work suggests that, as genres, tragedy and romance might not, as in the literary history of the epic, oppose one another; he points to romance as intensely tragic, and to a tragedy resonant with romantic overtones.[1] When de Rougemont links passionate suffering and ecstatic triumph, fervently affirming that "hardly anything could be more tragic," he reminds us that representations of tragic passion give us pleasure. De Rougemont powerfully insists that western culture desires this conjunction, even delights in it. In his thinking, moreover, these desires are "profoundly connected with our liking for war" (55). Such a suggestion, made as it was during World War II, calls for a profound rethinking of war not as fate, but as an exercise of Western culture's deepest desires.

But the rhetoric of de Rougemont's lamentation over the union of love with war and death, despite its purported desire to reveal as horrible the secret of a "passion sprung from our dark nature" (22), frequently verges on the rhapsodic and reinscribes the conjunction of love and death as productive for heroism. With images of light and heat de Rougemont invests passionate suffering with nobility, marking as "triumph" that which "sears" and "annihilates." And if he is able to see how Western subjects desire a union of love with death and desire war, he is not concerned with how this desire might itself be produced by Western culture for those subjects. Indeed his reflections never engage questions of who might gain—or lose—from the production of such desires. The chilling imagery of Guinevere's moan to Lancelot with which this chapter also begins, on the other hand, figures death not as an heroic obstacle intensifying love's passion, but as the consequence of years of melancholic desolation, the ultimate embodiment of ceaseless woe. As she puts it, "I may wofully wepe and wake/ In clay tylle I be clongen cold." Guinevere's speech implies that the tragic pleasures of heroism are produced at a devastating cost. Her words suggest that when it produces the desire for love and death within its heroic subjects, Western culture might be demanding the deaths of other, non-heroic, bodies. For bodies like Guinevere's the fact of death does not occasion the bright triumph of desire: these bodies suffer ignobly and their deaths register, not as bright productions of heat and light, but as the very substantiation of cold, moist decay.

Guinevere's figuration of her own disconsolate end within the Stanzaic *Morte Arthur* intimates that de Rougemont's model of passionate heroism might be a particularly gendered one. The Stanzaic narrates the famous story of the devastating consequences of Guinevere's love affair with Lancelot; yet it also poignantly depicts the ease with which Arthur's knights willingly rest all their communitarian troubles as Guinevere's feet. The tradition of the Arthurian adultery plot, the famous story of the destruction of Arthur's utopian brotherhood on account of the illicit loves of his wife, offers the ultimate version of romance tragedy. Destructive female desire proves to be one of the most common motifs of Arthurian romance. The tradition persistently narrates the ignoble suffering and frequently the guilt of its female characters. Guinevere, Morgan le Fey, and others emerge in the critical tradition, and frequently by the end of the romances themselves, as deadened and deadly; their deadliness, moreover, endangers relations among their heroic sovereigns, fathers, and lovers.

A brief review of the story told in the Stanzaic *Morte Arthur* will be helpful here. When Arthur decides to increase his fame by holding a tournament, Lancelot eventually attends, but only in disguise. Winning the tournament, Lancelot is wounded and subsequently takes refuge with the Earl of Ascolot, whose daughter Elaine falls in love with him. Out of compassion for Elaine's unrequited love, Lancelot leaves his armor with her, armor that Gawain (who later comes to search for the missing Lancelot) recognizes as that of the tournament champion. Elaine tells Gawain that Lancelot has been her paramour, misinformation that Gawain reports back to Guinevere who, upon Lancelot's return, jealously rebukes and banishes him. The romance then turns to the episode of the poisoned apple, and begins to focus insistently upon the question of Guinevere's guilt. Guinevere inadvertently gives a poisoned apple intended for Gawain to a visiting Scottish knight who dies as a result. The dead knight's brother demands redress and Guinevere is very nearly burned at the stake for a murder she did not commit. Guinevere is eventually cleared of the death of the Scottish knight, rescued by Lancelot's return to Camelot and his victorious trial by battle against the dead knight's brother. The remainder of the romance details what the poem sees as Guinevere's actual guilt before Arthur's court, as Arthur's knights, led by Agravain (Gawain's brother), conspire to prove her perfidy to Arthur by catching her in an amorous liaison with Lancelot. Once Arthur is presented with incontrovertible evidence of their adultery, Arthur's brotherhood splits in pieces. In the midst of Arthur's war with Lancelot, a tentative peace is nearly reached until Gawain intervenes to convince the king that his feud with Lancelot must continue. Arthur follows Lancelot to battle with him in France, and in Arthur's absence Mordred usurps the kingdom. The final battle (now between the forces of Arthur and the forces of Mordred) ushers in the death of Arthur and the dissolution of Camelot.

The famous Arthurian adultery triangle links the dissolution of brotherhood to heterosexual love, and thus to women. It might be said to constitute the shadow of what Eve Sedgwick identifies as the nexus of homosocial desire. It is by now a critical commonplace to remark that intimacies and desires between heterosexual men require the protective mediation of the female. Sedgwick calls this the structure of "homosocial desire" and her term has become a common way of marking a relation between masculinity and femininity. The dependence of male community upon "the traffic in women" has been long noted by cultural theorists, and is itself the subject of some of the most important recent feminist and queer revisionary thinking.[2] Sedgwick helps us see, to borrow an Arthurian example, that Arthur and Lancelot navigate their homosocial desires through their mutual loves for Guinevere. However, such an emphasis also overlooks the power of Guinevere's words in the Stanzaic, as well as the intense passions of Arthurian women throughout the tradition. Women desire in these texts. Their hearts quicken with longing for their paramours. Crucial figures in the Arthurian corpus, women constitute much more than a kind of switching station in an electrical current of male-to-male attractions. Lancelot's heroism is produced in part by Guinevere's admiration for him; he becomes engaging to us because he is desired by, as well as tortured by his desire for, his sovereign's consort. Arthurian knightly virtue needs the admiration of a female audience, and this, as we shall see, provides us with a way of rethinking the identification of women with romance as a genre.

The version of literary history that links the romance to women readers and patrons implies that female subjects, when given access to means of production, desire to produce and consume narrations not just of love, but of a love that proves graphically deadly for women.[3] In the Stanzaic *Morte*, Guinevere's words imply the terrifying and gendered consequences of construing lethal destruction in terms of intimate relations. With de Rougemont's work and Guinevere's words in mind, this version of literary history situates female desire in a suicidal impulse: women apparently desire a genre that allows them little hope for survival and no hope at all for triumph; women apparently delight in narratives that figure their deaths in graphically ignoble terms. Yet the conjunction of death with love, while often associated most specifically with (masochistic) women, I will argue in this chapter, might better be understood as a desire produced by and productive for a military culture.

Lancelot's love for Guinevere as portrayed in the Stanzaic *Morte Arthur* offers exactly the kind that of tragic passion de Rougemont links to "our liking for war." For de Rougemont the tragedy of such passion involves its overwhelming power; passion manifests "the master of fate over a free and responsible person." His formulation, not entirely dissimilar from medieval theological accounts of how the soul stands slave to its cupidities, situates passionate love as the opposite of a (nearly absolute) autonomous agency. De Rougemont glories in the romance of such a passionate (male) heroism; yet he also helps us remember that these particular, intimate drives and desires monumentally effect the world. Stories of Arthur's tragic end likewise bring psychic structures to bear upon history, the personal into relation with the political, and through the adultery plot render devastating cultural dissolution and royal disaster as a function of intimate passions. Arthur's inability to hold his community together is all the more poignant when disastrous mutiny comes from the intimacies of his affections. As much as love is fraught with obstacles here, love becomes itself an obstacle to a community's productive agency, even survival.

I begin with de Rougemont because his comments hint at both the psychic and the cultural power of the tragedy of Arthurian adultery. In the following chapter, I wish similarly to account for the complex attractions of the Arthurian adultery plot in psychic and cultural terms pertinent to the late fourteenth century. I also wish to suggest that there is a gendered structure of blame and victimization embedded in the longstanding identification of women with the messy (and destructive) complications of love. I will show that this structure of victimization (emerging in accounts like these as a trouble with women) is produced by and productive for chivalric military culture. In Chapter 4, I argued that such traditions emerge in *Sir Gawain and the Green Knight* so as to disavow the complications of intimacies among men. In that poem, Gawain's sense of his own psychic autonomy from Arthurian command is purchased by imagining heterosexual relations, unlike homosocial ones, as more profoundly constraining, intimate attachments more deeply unfree.

Psychoanalytic conceptualizations of individuation, which have likewise sought to explain the complications of a subject's agency in relation, account in part for the persistent identification of women with relationship rather than autonomy. And so I turn first to these theories. Following that analysis, I read the Stanzaic *Morte Arthur* for its desolate view of love in the time of war. In the third and final section of this chapter, I suggest the ways in which these issues might help us understand the tragedy of Arthurian romance as a particularly gendered one.

Loving Subjects

The most famous (or perhaps infamous) version of the constraints imposed by love available in psychoanalytic theory is, of course, the Oedipal drama, the primary structure within which the subject is understood as negotiating both freedom and attachment. According to this version of early love, the child desires the mother, wishing to supplant the rival parent's claims to her; the child must, however, according to the structure of the family romance, renounce such desires, submitting instead to the disciplining structures of the paternal relation. Psychic health and maturity (according to this trajectory) require a renunciation of libidinal desire for the mother; such renunciation is understood to be necessary for productive (adult, autonomous) survival.

Strict use of what Gilles Deleuze and Felix Guattari call the "dogma of the oedipal theory" thus opposes relational dependencies (particularly those of childhood and those linked with the mother) to the greater autonomy of the individuated (and by default male) adult. In critiquing this strand of Freudian psychoanalysis in their *Anti-Oedipus*, Deleuze and Guattari argue that the Oedipal narrative constricts the subject's desire for the entirety of the world into a narrow (overdetermined) desire for the mother. Deleuze and Guattari thus show the narrowing of the subject's desire onto the mother as a psychic-social production, one demanded by the capitalist organization of the family as romance. The Oedipal drama is, for Deleuze and Guattari, what desire looks like under the particular conditions of capitalist economic and social structuring. Klaus Theweleit pushes the pertinence of Deleuze and Guattari's analysis of desire by reading the *Male Fantasies* of proto-Nazi, military men of pre-Hitlerian Germany, a group known as the Freikorps. Following upon Deleuze and Guattari, Theweleit argues that when autonomous (male) subjectivity is opposed to maternal relation, relationships with women are experienced by men as suffocatingly dangerous, in other words, as lethal. Such psychic structures turn "desiring-production" (Deleuze and Guattari's term for desire's link, not to lack, but to the production of the world) into what Theweleit calls "murderous-production."

Feminist revisions of this trajectory on relationship and autonomy are likewise pertinent here. In *Black Sun: Melancholia and Depression*, Julia Kristeva implicitly links literary images of "death-bearing women" with the literary productivity of male authorship. Kristeva also, however, links women with the apparent dangers of too much relation, arguing that the gender similarity between mother and girl-child makes the female subject's separation from the mother a more arduous psychic task than it is for the male. From Kristeva's Lacanian perspective, moreover, separation from the mother is the prerequisite for the subject's entrance into language and culture. For the male subject, the demand to repudiate maternal relation produces, according to Kristeva, recurring fictional and artistic images of the "death-bearing woman" as "sublimatory solutions" and "lucid counter-depressants" (25). For the female subject, however, the construction of the mother as death-bearing involves a simultaneous construction of the self as death-bearing, a process which marks female desire as imbricated in "a hatred locked up within" the female which "kills . . . slowly" (29). Yet Kristeva's theorizations of motherhood, as Louise Fradenburg argues, amount to "a narrative imperative for the feminine subject . . .[that foregrounds] the uncertainty of her participation in culture" ("Our owen wo to drynke," 92)—an imperative that, again as Fradenburg demonstrates, inscribes loss, mourning, and gender identity in the service of masculinist privilege.[4]

If psychoanalytic formulations have tended to oppose relationship to autonomous subjectivity, they can also (as Deleuze and Guattari's work points out) give testimony to the multiplicity of desire and the workings of agency amid a nexus of drives and forces. Kristeva's story of repudiation and individuation constitutes only one version of what Teresa de Lauretis calls the "incessant material negotiations" going on in the seam between the ego and the world; it is a version, nonetheless, based upon a normative male, heterosexual desire. In a deft rereading of what she calls Freud's "passionate fictions," Teresa de Lauretis has read Freud's second typography of the psyche (the ego, id, and super-ego), as the site of the production of normative behavior—the site of the infamous "normal sexuality" Freud is said either to promote or merely describe—in relation to which other desires and behaviors are marked as "perverse." Examining the uses of a metaphor of particular resonance to our immediate concerns with cultural and social relations, de Lauretis explores the ramifications of Freud's description of the ego as "a frontier-creature, . . . try[ing] to mediate between the world and the id, to make the id pliable to the world and, by means of its muscular activity, to make the world fall in with the wishes of the id" (*Ego*, 55).[5] In attending to the dynamic seams between interior and exterior, de Lauretis (unlike de Rougemont) offers access into the complications of agency as always in relation to society and culture. Thus unlike Theweleit—who seems to evaporate the military context of his Freikorpsmen when he moves into the psychoanalytic register—de Lauretis's reading of Freud's ego frontier keeps desire and culture in dynamic interaction. These terms seem particularly apt for understanding Gawain's agency that, as I argued in the previous chapter, produces its apparently autonomous and heterosexual masculinity in the midst of its submission to a centralized authority.

Such a positioning also reminds us that Gawain's complicated agency in *Gawain* engages its audience for a host of reasons, not the least of which would be the psychic and cultural complications of agency per se, as well as the particular complexities of the agency of an honorman on a frontier.

Kristeva's work implies that before a male heterosexual audience images of "death-bearing women" might excite a greater sense of masculine agency. Yet if this is true, the traditional association made between the romance and women's desire needs to be rethought.[6] The image of women as death-bearing, I will argue, promotes a particular version of female subjectivity and female agency which, because of its use of loss and sorrow, serves a heterosexual and masculinist military culture working to consolidate its power in a time of war. The association of women readers with desires for the misogyny of romance is in danger of simply duplicating this version of female subjectivity.

The Stanzaic *Morte Arthur* offers the sovereign image of the death-bearing woman embodied in Arthur's queen. The relation of Guinevere's desire to the adultery plot, within which her desire is voiced, suggests both the complications of such an image of female desire and the material stakes involved in promoting it. As we will see, this version of subjectivity and relationship copes with the complications of a developing English nation through its designation of female desire and female victimization.

Love in the Time of War: Female Desire in the Stanzaic *Morte Arthur*

The Stanzaic *Morte Arthur* is a text centrally concerned with issues of loss and war and, in contrast to the twelfth-century French text credited as its source (*Mort Artu*), this late Middle English poem figures female desire for virile knightly violence as productive for military relations among knights. For the most part, however, critics have limited their attention to analyses of the text's role as source for Malory's "Book of Sir Lancelot and Queen Guinevere"; the extent to which the stanzaic poet modified his source material has not yet been adequately addressed, despite the sense in the work of scholars as diverse as J. D. Bruce, writing in 1928, and P. F. Hissiger, writing fifty years later, that *Le Morte* deserves such attention.[7] Revisionary trends in Arthurian studies, moreover, have resulted in increasing efforts to situate this work within the social or political cultural context prevalent at the time of its recension.[8] Yet the concern this text, an English adaptation of a French original, evidences for the constellation of desire, death, and war, inscribed, as it was, in the midst of a prolonged war between England and France, seems to call for an analysis of the complexities of its narrative aims and their cultural function. What might be at stake in the translation of a French prose account of the death of a mythic British sovereign and the dissolution of his famous court during the century of the Hundred Years War? Further, given our concern with gender, how might Kristeva's analysis be complicated by locating the production of representations of death-bearing women within a horizon of seemingly ceaseless war? What might the image of a woman as a melancholy victim who can never kill gain for a culture engaged in battle? What might be involved, finally, in attempts to displace and remake this kind of desire as a desire produced by women and for women?

Female desire and its apparent collusion in the production of war preoccupy the poet of *Le Morte Arthur*, and this text depicts a culture dependent upon battle—both the war games of tournament and the apparently more serious diversions of foreign war—for its sense of honor, and even identity. Rival knights matching strength on some field of combat seems to be imagined as a cultural necessity early on in this text; it is a necessity voiced by the text's central female character, and potentially most important victim, Guinevere. In the first scene of the poem, Guinevere, apparently fearful for the court's loss of prestige now that the Grail has been achieved, suggests that Arthur stage a tournament so as to prevent the Round Table knights from possible obscurity. Addressing her husband in the quintessentially intimate locale of their bed, she conceives of tournament as both a remedy for current ills and a nostalgic recovery of the court's past:

> The kinge in bed lay by the quene.
> Off aunturs they byganne to telle,
> Many that in þat land had bene . . .
> "Sir, your honour bygynnys to falle
> That wount was wide in world to sprede,
> Off Launcelott and of other all
> That evyr so doughty were in deed."
> "Dame, thereto thy counsell I calle,
> What were best for such a nede?"
> "Yiff ye your honoure hold shalle,
> a turnement were best to bede." (ll. 18–20; 25–32)

The poet inaugurates his text with an assertion of Arthur's waning honor, the loss of what "wount was wide in world to sprede." Guinevere's rhetoric of fame lately spreading, now falling implies a width and breadth to Arthur's influence, suggesting the once considerable scope of his sovereign sway. In their spatial orientation, the poet's verbs (falling, spreading) give a geographic cast to sovereignty, intimating that Arthur's powers demand territorial acquisition, or at least geopolitical influence peddling. This geographic emphasis is, of course, somewhat standard in the Middle English tradition. This rhetoric of Arthur's narrowing fortunes mirrors the location of this conversation within Arthur's private chamber. When he locates the conversation between king and queen in bed, the poet constructs fame both as an intimate concern of sovereignty and as a sign of sovereign power functioning in a domestic scene. A loss of fame causes domestic concern; such loss is best remedied by domestic activity. The problem of a sovereign's falling fame in the world "out there," is a problem the culture can try to address through the production "in here" of the spectacle of domestic war games. Conceived within a king's personal domestic scene, the tournament identifies Arthur's realm as interior space, a military community bounded by precise borders of space and time.

This construction brings the wide world into a circumscribed domestic scene; its spatial rhetoric, moreover, brings the space of domestic desire into relation with the space of military spectacle, addressing the anxiety of a culture (like England in the late fourteenth century) facing the fragility of its domestic borders. In the transition from foreign grail exploits to domestic tournament the poet brings foreign war into relation with domestic spectacle, suggesting that sovereigns like Arthur who lead a community of warriors, must manage a complicated series of allegiances both at home and abroad. We see here, then, a collocation of international and domestic concerns not unlike the relationship drawn in the Alliterative *Morte Arthure*. Again Arthur's fellowship is endangered in the aftermath of his successes. Yet whereas the Alliterative *Morte* worried over Arthur's excessive aggressivity, here the sovereign's lack of aggressive display, and the concomitant neglect of his admirers overseas, poses problems. The poem thus offers a view of the troubles not of too much military activity, but of too little.

Significantly the poet locates this recommendation for the recovery of Arthurian fame in Guinevere's mouth, thereby characterizing tournament as a response to a *woman's* assessment of the danger of loss and *her* hope for a restoration of male and "national" honor. Such a location links tournaments, and by extension wars, to Guinevere's ambitions; here, female desire for male honor and the spectacle of male combat motivates and supplies the creative germ for Arthur's activation of knightly aggression. Guinevere's reference to Lancelot—the knight who, as a variety of critics have pointed out, any fourteenth-century audience would identify as her lover—combined with the poet's setting of this discussion in the marriage bed eroticizes tournament for a female spectator. It also points to the problems of Arthurian domesticity: Arthurian domestic relations, a late medieval audience would recognize, are significantly less stable than they might at first appear. The triangulation of Guinevere, Arthur, and Lancelot—already implied in Guinevere's opening words—evokes the problem of multiple loves and reckons female desire as multiple. From the poem's very beginning multiplicities of desire haunt the conjugal unity of king and queen; and given a medieval political theory that figures the relation of king to subject with tropes of marriage, fissures in the union of this sovereign with his most beloved subject insinuate that Arthur's union with his knights is likewise compromised by competing loyalties and multiple desires.

This representation of female erotic desire for tournament is absent from the French source. That text begins with a fuller narration of the Grail and identifies tournament with Arthur's desire that his knights not lose the military vitality gained during their years of quest.[9] In his revisions the Middle English poet remakes a male sovereign's desire for male prowess into a female sovereign's erotic desire for the display of knightly power. The translation works to occlude the extent to which Arthur desires violent spectacle. This displacement of male erotic desire onto the female (a conflation of the audience required by the tournament with author requiring it) is, moreover, reinscribed within the critical tradition. Lee C. Ramsey asserts, despite a lack a textual evidence to support his claim, that Guinevere's request for the tournament is based on the fact that, "in actuality, she wants to get [Arthur] out of the castle so that she can have a meeting with Lancelot" (128). In fact, the text makes no such suggestion and while Ramsey's reasoning is plausible, he ignores the fact that the text explicitly identifies the desire for such a secret meeting as Lancelot's. When the tournament takes place, it is Lancelot who dissembles, feigning illness and staying away from the tournament, so as to arrange a secret rendezvous with the queen. Ramsey's reading, thus, reduplicates and extends the displacement of male erotic desire onto female desire, a move upon which, I am arguing, the Middle English poet founds his text.

The Middle English poet translates male desire for tournament into female desire. Such a translation proves, moreover, especially provocative in the historical context of the Hundred Years War. During periods of extended war, sovereigns would find it useful to project their desires for violence onto a populace, thereby deflecting critiques of their violence and war.[10] This mystification of sovereign desire, as we will see shortly, has particular uses for a culture fantasizing its identity as a domestic "British" community, an assemblage of insular cultures conceived against a "foreign" continental adversary. I turn now to the particular context of violence in the fourteenth century, the Hundred Years War.

Chronicles from the period of the Hundred Years War likewise display female desire as enabling for male aggressivity. In narrating the military fortunes of Sir Eustace D'Aubrecicourt, for example, Froissart links Eustace's valor in war to the love of one Isabel de Juliers,[11] displaying how powers of affection activate a military virility:

This Sir Eustace performed many fine feats of arms and no one could stand up to him, for he was young and deeply in love and full of enterprise. He won great wealth for himself through ransoms, through the sale of towns and castles, and also through the redemption of estates and houses and the safe-conducts he provided. No one was able to travel, either merchants or others, or venture out from the cities and towns without his authority. He had a thousand soldiers in his pay and held ten or twelve fortresses.

Sir Eustace at that time was very sincerely in love with a young lady of high breeding, and she with him . . . This lady was still young and she had fallen in love with Sir Eustace for his great exploits as a knight, of which accounts were brought to her every day. While he was in Champagne, she sent him several hackneys and chargers with love letters and other tokens of affection, by which the knight was inspired to still greater feats of bravery and accomplished such deeds that everyone talked of him." (161–62)

Froissart places Eustace's success in violent encounter not in the litany of material acts Eustace performs (demanding ransom, restricting trade, commandeering property), not in the thousand male bodies that comprise Eustace's "forces," but instead in the force and potency of his youthful ardor. Isabel's military aid rests in the inspiration provided by her love letters as much as in the materiality of the horses and goods she sends him. But this depiction of female love as enabling for the war effort stands in tension with Froissart's account of the sack of Limoges (1370), where it is not female desire, but scores of dead female bodies—alongside those of children, and men "who were too unimportant" to have deserved such vengeance—that invests war with its potency and vigor (178). These bodies serve as the matter upon which an English "righteousness" gets quite literally made real.[12] Such an account reminds us that while female desire for male militarism may contribute to a sense of male potency, in a war culture, it is dead bodies, whether female or male, that war requires and produces. The relation between love and death in Froissart's account implies that the benefits for, and the necessity of, such a conjunction lie within a military culture. In that case de Rougemont may have it a bit backwards: it is not our innate "dark passions" that produce "our liking for war"; the union of love with death is a conjunction that, at least in part, is produced *by* a war culture, as much as it is productive *for* such a culture.

In the *Morte Arthur* the representation of feminized and multiple erotic desire implies that gendering desire during times of war can serve particularly nationalistic ends. Questions of insular community and cultural allegiance emerge explicitly in the text of the Stanzaic *Morte Arthur* with the appearance of an unnamed Scottish knight who, while sharing the intimacies of Guinevere's table, dies from eating a poisoned apple which the queen has accidentally given him. As I have already noted in my discussion of this moment in Chapter 3, the poet makes Guinevere's innocence clear, along with the fact that the poisoned fruit was intended for another, apparently more local, victim: "a squyer in the courte hath thought . . ./with a poyson þat he hath wrought/To slae Gawayne yif that he mighte" (ll. 840; 842–43). The text enacts a double set of substitutions: the "Scottisshe knyght" stands in for Gawain, displacing the murder and victimization of a member of the court onto the murder of a Celtic visitor; second, the Queen stands in for the unnamed squire, substituting her innocence for his guilt. This second substitution again displaces male aggressive desire (of the squire toward Gawain) as female desire, and here the poet makes the politics of that substitution entirely explicit. The explicit displacement witnesses Guinevere's innocence of this particular crime; yet the text will trade the surety of her innocence in this case for an opportunity to develop the sense of her greater sin against Arthur and his community.

The question of the queen's guilt becomes the dominant focus of the next few sections of the narrative and the poet repeatedly reminds his audience that, at the burial of the Scotsman, a "crafty clerke" inscribes the queen's apparent guilt "with lettres droughe" (l. 877) into the stone of the dead man's tomb. Those letters mark the Queen as guilty; they enable the Scotsman's brother to seek redress from Arthur and very nearly succeed in obtaining the queen's death as punishment for murder. As the narrative progresses the court moves further and further away from any sense that Guinevere might be unjustly accused, believing increasingly in the materiality of the Scotsman's tomb and the persuasive letters of the clerk. This injustice heightens the textual drama as Lancelot rides in, at the last minute, to rescue Guinevere from public execution; her innocence functions here, in part, to focus our attention on the power of Lancelot's heroism and the pathetic inadequacy of Arthur's perceptions, indeed, of his justice. But in making explicit the clerk's role in establishing Guinevere's guilt, the text stresses the importance and the near incontestability of written words about the dead, whereby fictions are made into historical fact. The poet implies that the keeping of records—an activity useful to "national" governments—can, in fact, make fiction into history, rendering innocence as guilt. Yet the poet's assertion of Guinevere's innocence at the death of the Scottish knight also works to compel our belief in her other guilt later on. That second accusation brought against her must be true, and the text displays with horrifying clarity an investment in the assumption that even those unjustly accused are likely guilty of some other crime and, thus, probably deserve whatever punishment they are judged worthy to receive.

Guinevere responds to the accusation of murder (and to the eagerness with which the court accepts her guilt) with tears of desolation, entreating Arthur's knights to take up her cause against the Scotsman's brother. Guinevere's position, surrounded by a court willing to believe whatever it likes, thus shares certain correspondences with Gawain's position at the end of *Gawain*. Yet where Gawain's distance from his comrades' opinions in *Gawain* founds his self-conscious male autonomy, Guinevere's distance from the views of her community here marks her only as the court's pathetic victim. When Arthur's knights refuse to help her they make explicit what they see, and what the text would have us see, as Guinevere's real guilt at Arthur's court: she has, out of jealousy over what she believes to have been Lancelot's amorous attentions toward the Maid of Ascolat, banished the greatest of knights from round table fellowship. The poet's representations of Guinevere's desperate pleas to Bors, Lionel, Gawain, and Ector, alongside the fury of their refusals, suggest—by virtue of both the severity of her sufferings and the repetitive assertion of her guilt—that he delights in Guinevere's abasement and sympathizes with the fury of Sir Bors' words: "'Madame,'" he sayde, "'by crosse on rode, /Thou are wele worthy to be brente'" (ll. 1348–49). Such vengeful obduracy implies that if Arthur's court culture, and perhaps chivalric culture in general, bases its claims of righteous justice upon its purported commitment to rescue the innocent, that commitment rests upon the culture's ability to decide who it will designate as guilty, and thereby deservedly lost, and whom it will name innocent and deserving of rescue.[13] These are exactly the kinds of decisions soldiers make in wartime when they decide, as the Prince of Wales did during the sack of Limoges, that civilian populations are guilty of treason and, thus, "deserve" to be slaughtered.[14]

But while the court's assumption of the queen's guilt emerges as a central problem for this text, the exchange of the Scottish knight's death for Gawain's drops almost immediately from mention. This substitution, on its face, implies the displacement of local rivalries onto foreign visitors, but such a reading ignores Gawain's Welsh or Scottish connections and the possibility that, given the larger Arthurian tradition, a fourteenth-century audience might view Gawain and his brothers themselves as not entirely English.[15] If so, the substitution of the Scottish Knight for Gawain might have to do with identifying "Celtic" others, whether Welsh or Scots, as interchangeable. Such a substitution identifies Gawain with a knight "of an unkouth stede" (l. 851), foregrounding Gawain's relation to unfamiliarity and foreign strangeness.

Indeed the poet's substitution of one "Celtic" knight for the other suggests an intensity of identification between the two on rhetorical as well as narrative grounds. In describing why the murderous squire sets the apple near Queen Guinevere, the poet writes, "For he thoughte the lady bright/wold the beste to Gawayne bede/But she it yaff to the Scottisshe knight/For he was of an unkouth stede" (ll. 848–51). Here "Gawayne" and "the Scottisshe knight" perform the same linguistic function, indirect objects of Guinevere's gift. I would suggest that in part this poem works to demonstrate that Scottish "foreigners" and Welsh "intimates" aren't so very different from each other after all—the poet's immediate omission of this substitution from the later story certainly renders such substitutions narratively inconsequential. The fact that both Gawain and the Scottish knight become associated with murderous intrigue implies that the presence of either brings lethal dangers to knightly solidarity. The ramifications of this association will produce Arthur's death and the dissolution of the Round Table in the face of a complicated series of kin and court allegiances, which Gawain fails to negotiate well.

The extent to which Gawain, as a result of his reactions to these various obligations, emerges as the villain of this text, as he does in the readings of nearly all the critics, may reflect the poet's wish to discredit him, and, by extension, his Welsh background. If Gawain is the villain this seems to be because he embodies an overly rigid loyalty to Arthur, and to the loyalties required of cognate kin: Gawain refuses to allow Lancelot to be restored to the Round Table because he is determined to avenge his brothers' deaths and his uncle's honor. Gawain's "inflexibility" and "rigid personal idealism," in the words of Brian Stone, "take Arthur away from his seat of power and open the way for Mordred's treason" such that Gawain "reaches beyond the grave in loyalty to his king" (179). Stone literally figures Gawain's loyalty as lethal, and while the text displays some sympathy for Gawain's position, it simultaneously suggests that in his apparently overzealous attentions to kinship obligations, Gawain unleashes deadly forces both toward himself and his king.

But what might be at stake in the poet's desire to discredit a Welshman as inflexibly loyal to his mythic sovereign during a period of England's war with France? Such a suggestion seems particularly ironic in time of war, when cultures usually delight in the kind of intense and unflagging loyalty Gawain embodies. A centralized English authority finds itself fearing violent aggression on multiple fronts: the Scots are waging border wars against English attempts at territorial expansion northwards; Owain Glyn Dŵr is gaining momentum for his nearly successful attempt to dislodge aspects of English hegemony in the north of Wales. By the late fourteenth century, English efforts in the Hundred Years War are increasingly unsuccessful and England fears invasions from the continent. In the midst of these complexities a culture would be interested in producing in its male subjects, particularly its nominally Welsh ones, an absolute personal loyalty to a centralized sovereign, and a willingness to change loyalties in order to assure the survival of the state. Arthur's knight must be willing to switch his affections from kinship to kingship; he must display a willingness to forgo kin bonds, and obey the symbolic order of the state; he must be willing to sacrifice even his personal integrity if such a sacrifice serves his sovereign's pleasure.

This representation, occurring at the time when Glyn Dŵr is employing the figure of Arthur as a representative of former Welsh glory, and in the service, not of an insular "British" identity, but of a provincial Welsh separatism, argues against any project, like Glyn Dŵr's or like that of the Scottish barons, dependent upon an overly rigid loyalty to a "Celtic" kin identity.[16] This may be why, in this version of the death of Arthur, there is no promise of salvific sovereign return. As a king identified with a Welsh or Scots past, Arthur's fellowship must pass away. This *Morte*, from beginning to end, constructs Arthur as a sovereign whose glory is fading, whose judgments are flawed, whose knights prove treasonous even at the very moment of their sovereign's death. This Arthur's court, moreover, is fatally wounded from within; such a construction of internal siege mirrors the problems of a British "nation" trying to define itself within certain borders, fearful that those boundaries might themselves prove lethal.

Internal morbidity, we recall here, is crucial to the episode of the Scottish Knight where death comes from a deadly and invisible poison ingested within his body, attacking silently and invisibly. The knight receives this poison, moreover, from the hands of an intimate and a woman; it is Guinevere who passes on the poisoned fruit, however unknowingly. We return, then, to this text's concern with female desire and its connection to lethal aggression. From the outset of the tale Guinevere's position, as we have seen, has been complicated by a multiplicity of desire, a diffusion of interests in a number of directions at once. Unlike Gawain, Guinevere refuses to choose between competing claims upon her affections, and here questions of loyalty and desire work to elaborate further the absolute personal loyalty required of Gawain as knight.

While the text worries about Guinevere's multiple affections, the problems she raises to knightly community can be resolved by the text's tragic romanticism. The multiplicity of Guinevere's affections proves useful in mediating the military relations between men; Guinevere's passion, her desire (with all its various objects) emerges as necessary to a heterosexual war culture. Her attentions to the Scottish Knight and the dilemma of her imminent execution activate the glory and heroism of Lancelot, her apparent rescuer. And as Brian Stone points out her "attachment to her royal spouse [despite her love for Lancelot] is one of exemplary loyalty on every public occasion" (180). Finally the multiplicities of Guinevere's affections work to enliven both sides of the battle between Arthur and Lancelot. Lancelot and Arthur fight over her, even if both are destined to lose her. This double empowerment Guinevere offers to both sides of the battle explains, in part, the function of the adultery plot within the Arthurian tradition: as a moral exemplum, the adulterous triangle between Arthur, Guinevere, and Lancelot stresses the dangers of females with multiple loves, suggesting by implication that proper affections are single-hearted and that appropriate desire is focused on a solitary libidinal object. Yet the sexual politics of Guinevere's multiple loves, the identification of multiple affections with a changeable female, also ensures that the trouble of multiplicity can be remedied by the loss of a woman; it is Guinevere who will be repudiated and lost. If Arthur and Lancelot both end the tale as tragic (yet noble) heroes, their nobility is linked to the loss of Guinevere. And this, I would argue, works as a convenient way of warning against the dangers of multiple affections while marking an efficient economy of the tragic: here, the loss of one woman is productive of two tragic heroes, which helps explain what appears to be the deadlock between Arthur and Lancelot until Mordred's treachery intervenes to direct Arthur's attention homeward. Indeed, when Mordred attempts to usurp his uncle's throne, he too tries to enliven his military might with Guinevere's love, attempting to coerce her into becoming his bride. That he fails to overpower Arthur, in this version of the story, may be related to Guinevere's refusal to submit to him; the poet associates her stratagems for avoiding Mordred's demands with the beginnings of his defeat.

Thus despite her absence from any of these battles, the text of *Le Morte Arthur* wants us to see Guinevere's affections, unlike Gawain's, as enabling for military potency. In such a system women must remain loyal not to any sense of their own desire, but to a quickening of male aggressivity; they must impassion the war machine by passionately loving their soldiers. But representations of a multiply desiring female also implicitly argue that females need to be managed and controlled. At the end of this tale, we are left with the image of Guinevere eternally lost in sad, disconsolate weeping: "Therein she lyved an holy lyffe/in prayers for to wepe and wake/nevyr after she cowde be blythe" (ll. 3570–72).

This text, I argue, pits desire for Arthurian community (and a fantasy of British sovereignty) against the multiple (and polymorphous) affections of women. It suggests, along the way, that the erotic desire that activates militarism will be, by definition, heterosexual. This constellation of love with war asks women to perform, on behalf of "unified identities," an eroticization of heroic violence so as to legitimate militarism in the service of "our women and children." Such a structure remakes the frequent victims of war into its authors, displacing an eroticization of military violence for male warriors onto the very bodies of those frequently subject to its fury. In the process lethal war is remade as salvific; slaughter becomes designated as rescue. The violence of this kind of community—its link of love with death—requires that females take on the work of mourning, envisioning a female subject "abandoned within herself and [one who] can never kill outside herself" (Kristeva, *Black Sun*, 30). Love in time of war marks women as inherently unable to defend themselves or return violence for violence, maintaining military culture as a bastion of male (hetero-sexual) virility, and inscribing in women the putative necessity, even the unavoidability, of their victimization.[17]

The Tragedy of Romance: Gender, Genre, and Agency

If, as de Rougemont implies, Arthurian romance gives us a satisfy-ing narrative of our powerlessness over our own passionate attachments, that powerlessness has remained invested in images of women as either dangerous or deadened. And while the story de Rougemont tells about passion and culture gives us a glimpse of the strictures that interior drives and desires demand of us, he fails, as we have seen, to view those desires in relation to the cultural and social horizon that helps to produce them. For if agency is always in relation, the relations within which it operates frequently deploy desire to promote the privilege of those whose bodies are thought to matter.

In Part II we have seen how a male heterosexual subjectivity pur-chases the fantasy of its autonomous agency through a gendered splitting. Male heroism, invested in loss, gains a rough and ready agency, a tarnished heroism by displaying its separation from women. In *Sir Gawain and the Green Knight*, Gawain's disillusioned autonomy gains its claim to agency by distancing itself from the complications of relationship and by deni-grating power in relationship as a problem with females. That version of male heroic agency helps to manage the dependencies that a government like Richard II's will have upon its Palatine states by showing a centralized knight like Gawain to be a bastion of self-conscious agency despite the flaws and weaknesses of the centralized court from whence he takes direc-tion. *Gawain* deploys female desire so as to display the complications of a male frontier agency while splitting it from the apparent dangers of rela-tionship and accommodation. It depicts the fantasy of a borderland subject during a period of increasingly intense intimacy between aristocrats from a central court and those from the provinces. It shows the anxieties that intercultural union and desire pose to autonomous agency at a time when English subjects are engaged in monitoring and governing the outlying regions.

While *Gawain* takes on the troubles of the subject as a figure in-between various communities, the Stanzaic *Morte Arthur* imagines rela-tional troubles within a community as a single domestic fellowship. Along

the way this text displays how the foreign exploits of war gain a coherent, if also fragile, sense of union in masculine and military terms. And in
the midst of a war with France and increasing acts of colonial resistance,
the Stanzaic *Morte Arthur* genders agency and desire in a culture at war:
women's desire for knightly valor and strength is seen to propel masculine
virility, and knights are protected from realizing the extent to which their
bodies do not matter to the sovereign powers who are willing always to
risk losing them in battle.

These uses of gender remind us of the fantasmatic character of tales
of dangerous Arthurian liaisons. Arthurian romance offers a late medieval
audience of men and women imaginative access to the affections and disaffections of community; it provides a place to explore the delights and
horrors of group identity, of uniting and dividing, of the violence and pleasure of incorporation and accommodation. And when those violences and
pleasures put at risk the fantasy of a purely autonomous sovereign British
power, these texts offer a view of the vicissitudes of personal affections as
complications wrought by women. This story tries to gain political and
military agency by casting complicated intimacies as a story of love, and
not a story of war and conquest. This story of a political male agency
opposed to a relational female passivity has long been told. It recurs in the
history of epic and romance, where the former displays the potency of male
militarism, while the latter gives a view of the intimate complications—
and ultimately the dangers—of females and their loves.

Yet, as this chapter demonstrates, the splitting of private affections
from public deeds is finally undone in the story of Arthur. The genre's
complicated multiplicity and its repetitious adultery plot displays the relation of the heart to the world, of affect to nation. It displays, too, how
representations of male military power or of heroic masculinity depend
upon representations of female desire as disordered and destructive. We
have seen, to put this in psychoanalytic terms, how male subjectivity uses
a final female victim as a way of distancing itself from the complications of
the frontier position of its own ego. And in a militarized culture, like that
of late medieval England, representations of relationship as dangerous to
autonomous agency can impel aggressive activity both on the battlefield
and in the pages of its texts. In the next section we view the ways Arthurian
romance can help a military subject cope with the intimacies in which he
is enmeshed and compensate for the submissions, the necessary losses, he
must endure.

The extent to which this structure constitutes Arthurian romance as a genre marks the extent to which that genre proves tragic, especially for women. And if the romance has been traditionally associated with women as producers and consumers of culture, in its tragic moments it renders the female subject entirely unheroic in her suffering. In her case "tragic silence" may not be, in the words of Walter Benjamin, "a storehouse of an experience of the sublimity of linguistic expression" (109), but a hopeless surrender before the massive fact that no one cares to listen. Her words, in contrast to this silence, might carry a subversive potential, at least insofar as they remind us, as Guinevere's words did at the start of this chapter, that cultures produce certain kinds of literary, or political, projects on the bodies of dead women.[18] And if, like de Rougemont with whose words this chapter also began, we feel a "deep despondency" as we look toward the future, perhaps this is because those same cultures produce in us the inability to imagine more compassionate alternatives. We might instead endeavor to reclaim love in the time of war for a politics based, not on the tragedy of fate, but on the creation of possibility.

PART III

Insular Losses

CHAPTER SIX

Military Intimacies

The Pleasures and Pains of Conquest

I N Part I of this study, "The Matter of Britain," I argued that the imagination of Arthurian sovereignty over the whole island of Britain conveyed, as early as Geoffrey of Monmouth, contestations over the meaning and ownership of (past and future) insular rule. This differential history, moreover, narrativized in late Middle English traditions of Merlin's prophecies deployed tropes indebted to Welsh vaticination and a past Welsh resistance to loss. Imagining a future community became the work of mourning, "the common song of fatherless folk."

In Part II, "Romancing the Throne," the poignant story of Arthur's death in civil war (from the Alliterative *Morte Arthure*) encrypts such mourning for a traumatic historiography that can contest the narrative triumphalism of later English histories, precisely because it reverberates with the longing and loss of colonial romance. Yet through the death of the "innocent" Gawain, the Alliterative *Morte* mourns the loss of the Arthur of Welsh tradition and, consequently, of the explicitly oppositional uses of Arthur's images. The alliterative poem *Sir Gawain and the Green Knight* takes up the problem of Welsh opposition from a different angle, negotiating the intimacy of Welsh and English in borderland spaces. Arthurian community emerges in this text as an affinity between men pliable enough to withstand travel between "home" and "away." The Stanzaic *Morte Arthur*, also concerned with homosocial community, nonetheless offers sustained attention to Guinevere's suffering, thus suggesting that the romance adultery plot is produced by and productive for chivalric community. The first two parts of this book, moreover, read the imagined community of Britain through the triangulations of England, Wales, and France.

Part III, "Insular Losses," moves to the mid-fifteenth century, to England's insular regions, and to military relations during the "Wars of the Roses." In the current Chapter 6, I examine militarism in four texts—two based in London, two from the north—written during a period denigrated in traditional histories for regional violence, disunity, and aggression. I first analyze the tensions between violence and pleasure in the London-based texts *Knyghthode and Bataile* and the Love-Day pageant of 1458. These texts figure union in the intimacies produced by violence, a construction that serves regional and hierarchical privilege.

This material serves as a backdrop for my consideration of two Arthurian tales written in the North during approximately the same period, *The Avowing of King Arthur* and *Awntyrs off Arthure at the Terne Wathelyn*. Because of their northern provenance, these romances usefully complicate what would otherwise be an exclusively southern—and metropolitan—view of militarism. Elaborating the relations between individual warriors and centralized sovereigns, the romances allow a detailed reading of the gender implications of knightly fellowship, linking insular militarism with both regional privilege and the annexation of land. They explore how intimate relations among knights, kings, and ladies can serve the powerful pleasures of the sovereign. Arthur's role as a centralized military sovereign around whom knights desire to—and are required to—unify suggests the stakes in crafting national union through military activity, and from a series of neighboring regions.

In the present chapter I examine the nexus of militarism and land, intimacy and aggression, and pleasure and violence to complicate traditional understandings of the geography of insular union. Male rivalry and violence emerge as productive for community. Yet this model of community nonetheless depends upon female bodies to mark the limits of its violence. Female rivalry and violence is coded as nonproductive; female victimization disavows the fact that military communities often also demand the victimization of men. I turn first to the union of intimate accord and aggressive threat marked by the Love-Day pageant of 1458.

Intimate Aggressions

Mankyndys lyfe is mylitatioun,
And she, thi wife, is named Militaunce.
  —*Knyghthode and Bataile*, ll. 96–97

The representation of violence is inseparable from the notion of gender.
  —Teresa de Lauretis, "The Violence of Rhetoric," 240

In March 1458 on the feast of the Annunciation, warring Yorkists and Lancastrians celebrated a temporary reconciliation and truce, or
"Love-Day." During this pageant, argues R. Dyboski, the Middle English
verse adaptation *Knyghthode and Bataile*—a reworking of Flavius Vegetius
Renatus's fourth-century treatise *De re Militari*—was initially inscribed,
perhaps presented to the Lancastrian monarch Henry VI.[1] A handbook
of military strategy set in verses of heroic meter, *Knyghthode and Bataile*
instructs military leaders in the training and deployment of knights while
apparently working to inspire its audience with the grandeur and justice
of Henry VI's sovereignty. In the assessment of Dyboski, editor of the
text, it serves as a useful source for details about late medieval military
organization.

About its status as poetry, however, Dyboski appears less sure. Even
as he recommends the text for its romantic descriptions of battle, he critiques the poet's "crude" Latinate language. The text's accurate depictions
of medieval tournament and chivalric knighthood serve, thus, as "touches
of refreshingly romantic colouring, . . . oases in vast stretches of sheer
Latinity" (xxx). The unpleasant crudity of the language of Latin antiquity
(and military technique), in contrast to the more pleasurable delicacies of
a chivalry identified as English, delimits this text's aesthetic power. Dyboski's reading of *Knyghthode and Bataile* thus opposes the pleasure of
chivalric spectacle to the pains of military strategy.

The disjunction between spectacle and strategy—and pleasure and
pain—likewise haunts accounts of the Love-Day pageant. Historians interpret the pageant's display of peaceful spectacle and military strategy to
signal its failure as politics. These accounts describe it as a failed spectacle
of peace, producing an intensification, and not an enervation, of military
activity in and around London. When Henry VI called for the reconciliation, promising to convene a council at Westminster, he had just recently
raised the troop of royal archers in London to some 13,000 strong.[2] During
the months preceding the reconciliation, large numbers of Lancastrian and

Yorkist magnates along with their men gathered in and around the city. Ralph Griffiths describes the difficulties this posed to the Lord Mayor and Sheriffs who strove to ensure that war did not erupt, despite the intimate proximity of enemy factions to one another (*Henry VI*, 805–8). It was, according to chroniclers of the time, only with the greatest difficulty that the closely quartered rival troops were prevailed upon to postpone their aggressions until the king's council could meet.[3] The spectacle celebrating the rivals' reconciliation displayed friendly intimacies between the, now putatively former, enemies. The pageant's procession to St. Paul's Cathedral displayed rival factions arm-in-arm: Lord Somerset walked with his enemy Salisbury; Exeter processed with Warwick; Henry's Queen Margaret of Anjou followed behind her consort hand-in-hand with the Duke of York.[4] This figuration of enemies purported to replace the aggressions of rivalry with closeness born of trust and friendship. But in the context of the militarized zone of London such spectacle appears, at least to historians like A. J. Pollard, "an empty charade" (23).

Pollard decries the Love-Day as "charade" because of his sense that the rivals remained deeply invested in militarism, despite their reconciling rhetoric. Yet certainly a concern with military strategy is no surprise given the political insecurity of this fifteenth-century Lancastrian monarchy. Pollard's characterization of the truce as an inauthentic performance, moreover, invests in an absolute difference between the intimacies of friendship and the violence of battle. He assumes that aggression and factionalism have no place in the friendly space of reconciliation; harboring aggressive desires at such a time constitutes the falseness of charade. The intimacies of authentic friendship must, in this view, banish aggression to produce vicinity, proximity, and unity.

Pollard's designation holds, however, only if we assume that unity always signals affection. The Love-Day suggests instead a dynamic interplay between intimacy and aggression, proximity and distance. That the physical nearness of armed enemies proved potentially dangerous to the London citizenry reminds us that war requires a physical intimacy between enemies. The display of friendly intimacies in the midst of an armed encampment may be read as a strategic combination of militarism and peace, one designed to preserve London as utterly unlike the field of battle. Historical testimonies from the London chroniclers emphasize the excessive number of soldiers housed in the city for the event. In the context of hoards of soldiers swarming in and around the city, a procession of peaceful intimacy offers a model for a soldier's demure urban behavior.

Following the important battle at St. Albans—an engagement occurring no more than a day's journey north—and as a spectacle suited for a London audience, the Love-Day might help regionalize violence, banishing its dangers from London, relegating it to the apparently less valuable— and less "civil"—regions further north. A procession of enemies arm-in-arm through the London streets demonstrates that these rivals can display civility and manners in the proper places; and they can take the scrappiness of their fighting "outside" to the apparently wilder peripheries. It declares a peaceful ruling class's possession of London as their territory, a space appropriated for their uses. By identifying the London streets as a place where rivals move as friends, the spectacle marks London itself as a space of peace and order where the bodies of the bitterest rivals remain peaceable and orderly, no matter how well armed they might be.[5]

Such considerations can help explain the preoccupation with numerical specificity in chronicle descriptions of the time. The concern with quantitative evaluation in both the Love-Day accounts and in recent histories of the period suggests that the quantifiability of damage may have been a problem during the period itself.[6] Appraisals of how much damage a war causes can be, of course, matters of opinion. A Londoner, for example, might find damage to the city of London a disaster worthier of note than any damage, however extensive, to the town of Hexham in Northumbria.[7] As Anthony Goodman points out, very little attention has been paid to the "regional consequences of rebellion" since most histories of the Wars of the Roses depend almost entirely upon evidence from London chronicles. For Goodman, "[London Chroniclers'] general lack of a sense of civic and personal involvement [in the Wars of the Roses] is a valuable indication of wealthy Londoners' experience of the wars [as inconsequential], but cannot be taken as a pattern of Englishmen's experience generally" (197).[8] When one considers the location of most of the war's grisly battles, northern and western "peripheral" counties fared considerably less well than did economic and cultural centers like London. London's relative stability during the period would have depended, in fact, upon the existence of other sites for battle.

Pollard's description of the Love Day "charade" hopes to banish uncontrollable aggression from the reunion of rivals, suggesting that knightly intimacies follow stately configurations. Such disciplinary structures preserved London as an especially valuable space. In marking intimacies among knights as demure, safe, and orderly, moreover, the Love-Day pageant also hints at the sexual politics of war. The gendering of peace read in the spectacle, for one thing, displays affection in heterosexual terms: it was, after all, Margaret of Anjou, and not Henry VI, who walked arm-in-arm with their archrival, Richard of York. Margaret's role in the pageant employs heterosexual coupling as a metaphor for peaceful unity. This coupling can be read to imply that warriors who join together in friendship nonetheless retain their masculine potency. Heterosexual union becomes, in *Knyghthode and Bataile*, a figure for war, and marital unity becomes a trope for military relations: "Mankyndys lyfe is mylitatioun, / And she, thi wife, is named Militaunce" (ll. 96–97).

Margaret's role in the pageant displays this collocation of wifely militancy as well. Joined with Henry's rival, the Duke of York, Margaret stood in for Lancastrian factionalism. This allowed Henry, as crowned Sovereign, to remain above the mutabilities of all such apparently "narrow" concerns. Margaret's value as a place holder for Henry's involvement in factional politics continues to be written in histories about this period, histories that frequently contrast the "vindictive savagery" of the queen's ambitions with the peaceability, even holiness, of her enfeebled spouse (Haswell, 15). It may thus be no coincidence that a union performed by a queen called the "she-wolf of Anjou" by some of her contemporaries might be so easily denigrated as "barren" (Ramsey, 209).[9]

Traditional accounts of chivalric culture tend to reproduce, rather than analyze, the sexual politics of these relations. In his *Memorials of the Most Noble Order of the Garter*, for example, G. F. Beltz delights in knights swearing a common brotherhood, marking their intimacies with rituals like those associated with marriage:

[Knights] having each caused a vein to be opened, mingled their blood in token of indissoluble friendship. Others obtested the purity of their reciprocal obligation by the most sacred religious acts. As if members of one family, they wore similar apparel and armour, desirous that, in the heat of battle, the enemy might mistake one for the other, and that each might thus participate [in] the dangers by which the other was menaced. By brotherhoods of this character, the sovereigns, under whose banners they enlisted, were enabled to achieve the most daring warlike operations. (xxviii)

Descriptions of martial loyalty resonate with the language of marital relations, and the signs of intense identification among knights—an exchange of bodily fluids, religious ritual, appropriate dress—correspond with the signs of wedding contract, a union also creating "members of one family," through "sacred religious acts." Knightly intimacies are "pure" in their "reciprocal obligations"; "indissoluble friendship" marks knighthood as both permanent and productive. But the structure of this relationship, while conceived as generative and immutable, rests on the principal of mutability, the possibility of sacrificial death: knighthood here manages a mutual participation in one another's lives through participation in the possibility of death, that is, through the apparently noble act of renouncing one's life for the life of a brother knight.[10]

For Beltz the substitution of knight for knight proves desirable precisely because it produces a sovereign's "most daring warlike operation," displaying a ruler's military potency and virility.[11] Such images are implicitly indebted to texts like *Knyghthode and Bataile*, where militarism figures as the close consort of mankind, claiming holy unity, just as the church under the light of Jesus:

> Sumtyme it was the gise among the wise
> > To rede and write goode and myghti thingis,
> And have therof the dede in exercise;
> > Pleasaunce heryn hadde Emperour and Kingis.
> O Jesse flour, whos swete odour our Kinge is,
> > Do me to write of knyghthode and bataile
> > To thin honour and Chivalers tavaile.
>
> Mankyndys lyfe is mylitatioun,
> > And she, thi wife, is named Militaunce,
> Ecclesia; Jhesu, Saluatioun,
> > My poore witte in thi richesse avaunce,
> Cast out therof the cloude of ignoraunce,
> > Sette up theryn thi self, the verrey light,
> > Thereby to se thi Militaunce aright (ll. 89–102).

The union of man with militancy figures under the Christian God's protection; the poet of such a union seeks divine inspiration and guidance for his task. The awkward, even ungrammatical, insertion of the word "Ecclesia" in stanza two—an emendation present only in this adaptation— emphasizes militarism as a corporate and communal bond, and echoes, as the editor notes, "the old watchword, *Ecclesia Militans*," the Church Militant (112). This military community, like the marital bond, is a divinely sanctioned union of soldiers.

In the next stanzas of Part I, the band of loyal knights figures as a host of archangels loyal and obedient to the divine. As these descriptions merge so too, the poet proclaims, earthly knights loyal and united as one band join with God's archangelic forces, undoing the loss Paradise sustained "by Lucyfer falling" (l. 163). The poet devotes thirty-five lines to this exaltation of unity and loyalty as angelic, and to the demonization of its opposite: disloyalty and disunity among earthly knights refigure Satan's battle.

Yet the text also registers anxiety about the very unity it embraces, turning next to circumscribe its limits. Within the space of five lines a glorified "ooste of hem for [Goddes] perfection" divides along regional lines. Northerners, with "more blood and lesse wit," evidence "hardinesse" "to fight & blede," while Southerners, with "more wit . . . & lesse blood" are "reserve[d] to labour & to lore" (ll. 173–79). While loyal unity supplies militarism's holiness and potency, military regulations intervene to insure that these holy unities not extend to actual scenes of battle. This army—not incidentally based on a Roman imperial model—finds a unity of soldiers from different regions useful so as to save southern soldiers from the injuring and bleeding that war requires. Military rescue of southern warrior bodies requires that their northern counterparts not be saved. Northern bodies, with their apparently greater store of blood and hardiness, can afford the violence of battle that southern bodies cannot. Unity thus ideologically channels regional privilege. Regional privilege is naturalized as divinely ordained. This kind of ordering makes regional actors into intimate companions for the purpose of preventing certain bodies and certain regions from sustaining pain and loss.[12]

Marital relations become a useful metaphor for martial ones in the text of our fifteenth-century poet/translator, usefulness that may have to do with the fact that "marriage" offers a way of imagining union that can nonetheless protect certain kinds of privileges. As sociological analyses of domestic violence have demonstrated, the intimate closeness of marital alliance provides no guarantee whatsoever that the sacrifices their relations exact will be mutual ones.[13] It is, thus, no coincidence that *Knyghthode and Bataile* is as quick to imagine the tactical limits to union as it is to imagine the benefits union can perform. But this points to a crucial paradox within the category of union itself: while union's utopian power rests on a powerful image of commonality, mutuality, and equality, its economic and social structuring orders relationships by caste and place, emphasizing the differences and not the similarities among its members.[14] When a text like *Knyghthode and Bataile* produces a picture of unity ordered as regional privilege, it simultaneously suggests that unity needs a specific geographic elaboration to be useful to centralized power. The poet suggests, in other words, that the kind of sacrificial intimacy that Beltz celebrates can sometimes prove horrific, that is, if a southern body is mistaken for a northern one.

Yet if *Knyghthode and Bataile* claims unity through a delicate negotiation of privilege, Part III of the poem repudiates disunity as utterly disastrous. The twenty-ninth stanza links disunity with regional longing: "Sumtyme amonge an ooste ariseth roore. / Of berth, of age, of contre, of corage/ Dyvers thei are, and hoom thei longe sore" (ll. 1174–76). As much as *Knyghthode and Bataile* extols soldierly affections, it simultaneously characterizes love, and love for "home" in particular, as dangerous to military power, implying a regionalism to homesickness, and suggesting—despite a tradition linking warrior mettle with love of homeland—that military loyalty requires that particular homes and loves be renounced. The army responds to the dangers of homesickness with nothing other than the exacerbation of militarism: "Wherof ariseth it? of ydilnesse. What may aswage it best? Good bisinesse" (ll. 1179–80). The unification of military forces thus becomes the goal of military activity in a circular structure that suggests why armies might be so adept at finding enemies.

Militarism thus safeguards a sovereign against the dangers of regional ties. Some twenty-five stanzas catalogue military work as "remedie" for "when thei are asonder" (l. 1188). Military leaders "commende, and exercise, and holde hem inne"; "with discipline of armys [they] holde hem undir." The text is quite specific in its recommendations: train "of dart, baliste, and bowe and cast of stoon"; as fearless knights, who "course a myghti hors with spere and shelde"; make them "to falle a grove or wode, and make a gate/ . . . and make a dike, and hewe a doun/ a cragge . . ./or dowbil efte the dike abowte a toun;/ To bere stoon, a boolewerk forto make/ Other sum other gret werk undirtake;" teach them to battle at the trumpet's sound "toward batail blewe up 'Go to, go to!'/ The clariouns techeth the knyghtys do" (ll. 1193; 1200; 1202–4; 1206–8; 1282–83). The work of war disciplines an army to work as one "hole multitude" (l. 1237). War's "[g]ood bisinesse" banishes remembrances of past homes and peacetime loyalties, ensuring that soldiers sacrifice themselves for the fiction of union and for the hierarchical and regional privilege that union signals.

With this in mind we can see that the sacrifices of military union are neither as mutual nor as easily achieved as Beltz's idealized portrait of the Order of the Garter suggests. In detailing union as a delicately managed set of relations, *Knyghthode and Bataile* shows union to be both perilous and precious. Yet because of its ability to redirect a soldier's loyalty, military activity emerges as useful for a culture trying to modulate regional identities into centralized ones. But a knight's flexible affections require careful managing. If we can change our loyalties from home to crown, we can likewise change them from one crown to another, or from one military general to the next. Our loves must only be as flexible as the sovereign desires them to be. The dangers and the benefits of a warrior's flexible loves mean that military union is constantly in need of forming and re-forming; it is a relationship fond of reinvention and constantly in need of staging and display. Unity is not, even—perhaps especially—in the name of "nation," or "homeland," a *fait accompli* so much as it is a performance that must be repeated both in space and in time, by a horizontal field and a genealogical lineage of particular bodies.

This may help explain why the Love-Day of 1458 displayed such repetitive obsession with the geography of English insular union. In addition to pageant and poem, a ballad commemorated the event, too, emphasizing a peaceful consolidation of insular regions, this time requiring the exile of felonious disunity to France:

> In Yorke, In Somersett, as y undyrstonde,
> In Warwikke also ys love and charite,
> In Salisbury eke, and yn Northumberlond,
> That every man may reioyce the concord and unite.
> Now ys sorw with shame fled yn to Fraunce,
> As a felon that hath forsworne thys long;
> Love hat put owte malicius governaunce,
> In every place both fee and bonde.[15]

The apparently shameful pleasures of violence are associated with France, England's historic enemy. The ballad imagines a loving English insular fellowship, emphasizing a peaceful union among specific English localities: in York, in Somerset, in Warwick, from Salisbury to Northumberland. Such specificities reflect the identities of the key players in the Love-Day accord; but they also corroborate a concern with union across English insular space, from its northern regions (York) to its southern ones (Somerset), and back again (Salisbury to Northumberland). Like the unified army depicted in *Knyghthode*, the ballad represents union in explicitly northern/southern terms.

But the ballad also suggests that peaceful unity between north and south depends upon France. This seems an especially notable detail given contemporary evidence of xenophobic diatribes against Henry's French queen, Margaret of Anjou. Despite the symbolism of Henry's marriage and his coronation in Paris as a bolster to his claim of sovereignty over areas in France—realms his father and grandfather claimed to have won in the final decades of the Hundred Years War—England's continental claims are weakening. Banishing violence onto French shores, the ballad encodes a longing for the putatively unified (and thus peaceful) space of insular rule. The ballad thus repeats, if in a slightly different way, the geopolitical activity of the Love-Day pageant. There is, of course, an ideological tension between such desires for insular peace and the militarism of *Knyghthode and Bataile*. If, as the preceding discussion makes clear, military activity was crucial to a hierarchical union of north with south, the utopian insular union imagined in the ballad disavows regional privilege by suggesting that "malicious governance" has been put out "of every (English) place," residing instead in France.

In the earlier chapters of this study, I have contextualized Arthurian stories in the efforts of the English crown to elaborate its power over its "internal colonies," specifically Wales. The regionalism just discussed suggests that joining northern with southern regions proved an equal challenge for British sovereignty during the period.[16] If this is so then analyses of mid fifteenth century British militarism must usefully engage northern texts as well as southern ones. In fact northern romances of Arthurian relations amplify the specific troubles of union during the period; they also explicitly link the troubles of union to English borderlands. *The Avowing of King Arthur* imagines union in an aggressive, yet affectionate chivalric brotherhood under the sway of a centralized king. *Awntyrs off Arthure at the Terne Wathelyn* connects those intimate aggressions with the materiality of region and land, and with sovereign policies of annexation. Both of these texts demonstrate a view of union structured through relations of gender.

Masculinist Military Interiors

On the basis of its language as well as provenance *The Avowing of King Arthur* raises the issues of literary regionalism. Editors identify the language as northern original, situating the text in one of the four "northernmost counties, the northernmost tip of Lancashire, [or] the northern two-thirds of Yorkshire"; the manuscript has also been given a Lancashire provenance, dating most likely from the third quarter of the fifteenth century (Dahood 28–29).[17] The poem dramatizes Arthurian unity through a story about boundaries and loyalties—the "insides" and "outsides" of Arthur's fellowship. A new knight joins Arthur's brotherhood, while the loyalty of earlier members must be tested.

The narrative is organized around a story of the loyal vows famous Arthurian knights (Gawain, Kay, and Baldwin) pledge to their king. These vows ostensibly celebrate the geographic integrity of Arthur's realm and the virtuous integrity of his inner circle. Arthur begins with a vow of his own: he will serve his subjects by destroying a ferocious boar ravaging the borders of Inglewood Forest. The King immediately demands that his best knights do likewise: Arthur's close familiars must design their own vows, mirroring their sovereign's commitment to the strength of the realm. Gawain and Kay make the first reply:

> Gladdely grawuntutte Þay.
> Þen vnsquarut Gauan,
> And sayd godely agayn,
> "I avowe to Tarne Wathelan,
> To wake hit all nyȝte."
> "And I avow," sayd Kaye,
> To ride Þis forest or daye;
> Quoso wernes me Þe waye,
> Hym to dethe diȝte!" (ll. 129–36)

The text at first appears to suggest an untroubled homosocial unity among these brothers-in-arms. Arthur's request is granted "gladdeley," and Kay and Gawain's vows to protect the land of Arthur's realm, Terne Wathelan and Inglewood Forest—two spaces of the northwestern border regions— cohere with Arthur's vow to kill Inglewood's boar. The scene seems to foreground an untroubled loyalty among Arthurian warriors. Until, that is, Baldwin takes his turn:

> Quod Baudewyn, "To stynte owre strife,
> I avow, bi my life,
> Neuyr to be ielus of my wife
> Ne of no birde bryȝte;
> Ne werne no mon my mete,
> Quen I gode may gete;
> Ne drede my dethe for no threte,
> Nauthir of king ner knyȝte." (ll. 137–44)

Baldwin's speech suggests that the reason for all this vowing may not be the celebration of an already peaceful union so much as the remedy of a troubled one. Baldwin's aim ("[t]o stynt owre strife") explicitly raises the problem of disunity, although exactly how and why strife arises, or how his vow might work to end it, is left unclear. When the poem raises the issue of distrust among knights at this early moment of their vowing, it suggests Arthur's court is troubled in its interior, and not just from forces outside it like wild boars or, later in the romance, trespassing recreant knights. The subject of rivalry between the knights, moreover, drives the entire narrative, furnishing the text's most exciting and entertaining scenes. While disunity suggests a threat to Arthur's band, this rivalry is also valuable, producing the most exciting narrative elements. Rivalry between warriors fascinates for its violent pleasures and for the narrative opportunities its complications provide.

Baldwin's vow, unlike Kay's, Gawain's, or Arthur's, does not pertain to the geographic integrity of Arthur's realm, however. Instead Baldwin promises to perfect his own interior and, in so doing, to help create a harmonious brotherhood. The Arthurian territory to which Baldwin pledges himself is the territory of a particular chivalric heart. The vowing plot thus suggests that a knight's interior spaces are just as important as are the geographic spaces that the knight patrols. To be sure, Baldwin's attention to interiors is hardly unique within chivalric discourse. The relation of a knight's interior (his honor, his virtue) to his exterior (his body in spectacle, his appearance and prowess on display) runs throughout late medieval discourse on chivalry, underwriting both its violence and its sexual politics. Yet in positioning Baldwin's vow as a challenge to his fellows and his King, *The Avowing of Arthur*, implies that certain loyal interiors compete, rather than collaborate, with a sovereign's desire for territorial control. Later in the story, this competition will move Kay, Gawain, and Arthur duplicitously to test Baldwin's virtue. The *Avowing*, predictably, will eventually show that well-ordered exterior spaces (sovereign territories) depend upon well-ordered interior ones (knightly hearts). And yet I want to examine why this is a story of splits between insides and outsides. Why does Baldwin's vow seem at first to challenge Arthur's virtue? And how might a romance describing a split, at least initially, between a militarized exterior space and a military man's interior virtue function for a culture interested in militarism's ability to unite men across regions?

We turn, then, to a scene central to the poem and not untypical in the pages of romance, where a bumbling Sir Kay, fulfilling his vow to Arthur, attempts to rescue a weeping woman from the hands of a recreant knight, Sir Menealfe, who threatens to rape her. As we might expect, given Kay's legacy as Arthur's most frequently denigrated representative, Kay fails, managing to become, like the weeping woman, one of Menealfe's prisoners (ll. 279–336). As a result Kay himself requires rescue. Enter Gawain who fights and defeats Menealfe, on behalf of both a victimized Kay and the victimized maiden. With Gawain's triumph, Menealfe and the maiden both become members of Arthur's court. The poem repetitiously asserts the importance of the nameless woman, mentioning six times that all of these battles were fought "be chesun of this birde briȝte" ["for the sake of this beautiful woman"] (ll. 295, 318, 323, 362, 502, and 544). Yet the ensuing interactions have little to do with her, and it remains unclear how she benefits, if she does at all, from the encounters. Indeed, Kay quite literally stands in her place; he becomes the object of Gawain's rescue, while she drops almost entirely from mention. The relationships developed throughout the text are, moreover, almost exclusively homosocial: Kay and Menealfe; later, and quite a bit more happily, Menealfe and Gawain; and finally, Menealfe and Arthur. Despite the text's apparent confidence in the happier fate of the nameless maiden at Arthur's court than at Menealfe's hands, moreover, the court welcomes the knight who just a few stanzas earlier threatened to rape his prisoner, an act explicitly forbidden by Arthurian chivalry.

Menealfe's membership in Arthur's troop enlarges the Round Table, extending the exterior size of the fellowship. Yet, given Menealfe's treatment of the woman, his addition to Arthur's band also troubles the integrity and virtue of the group. These developments suggest that the earlier split between Baldwin's devotion to interior virtue and Arthur's attention to exterior space represents not an opposition between two aspects of rule so much as a problem at the very heart of a growing fellowship. This text's concern with the geography of Arthurian spaces—and with conflicts in the border regions of Inglewood Forest—gestures to the problem of maintaining integrity despite the intrusion of strange creatures (boars, unknown knights, foreigners) into its spaces. For while Arthur's fellowship will grow through the incorporation of Menealfe, the community thus produced will be in crisis. To what extent will the addition of this recreant knight change the nature of Arthurian chivalry?

In fact one could read Menealfe's transformation from recreant to brother to mean that Menealfe's threat has been transferred from the

woman he led as captive to Arthur and Arthur's court, just as Kay's champ-
pioning of the "birde briȝt" transferred Menealfe's threat from the woman
to Kay. The text displays the logic of this substitution when Gawain arrives
explicitly determined to rescue not the woman but Kay. Danger transfers
from the body of the woman to the body of the knight, and in rescuing
Kay, Gawain rescues Arthurian knighthood. Thus it is no surprise that
finally, despite the text's repetitive insistence that this battle performs its
violence "for the sake of the woman," knightly concern for her proves so
thin that it vanishes in favor of warrior solidarity. This solidarity incorporates the former enemy into the fellowship by making the woman whose
interests this rivalry apparently served vanish altogether. Such a narrative
suggests yet another way in which military intimacies function across the
boundaries military culture works to sustain: soldiers, even those who
fight against each other, frequently have a good deal more in common
with one another than they do with the civilian populations they purport
to protect.

The incorporation of a former rival into Arthur's fellowship thus necessarily produces anxieties about a split between outsides and insides, a
split this text treats through the difference between Arthur, Gawain, and
Kay's vows and Baldwin's. The instability of categories like "recreant" in
these relations—read in Menealfe's relatively easy transformation from foe
to friend—fall out in opposite ways. If former enemies can easily become
friends, then former friends can likewise, and just as easily, become enemies. In the context of such fluidity—and in the midst of relations where
designations of "friend" or "foe" depend on the pleasures of the sovereign
overseeing them—warriors will likely remain cautious of trusting their
brothers, any one of whom might come to displease their king. And these
knights will be wary of displeasing their monarch lest they become designated "recreant" and banished from fellowship. The structure of these
knightly relations is, therefore, disciplinary: rivalry between knights—
what amounts to a "split" within the brotherhood—destabilizes knightly
bonds, ultimately accomplishing a "union" of knights only through their
loyalty to the pleasures of their sovereign, and their obedience to their sovereign's will. Union in this case first splits so as to perform a particular kind
of joining with the sovereign at the center. In *The Avowing of King Arthur*,
the split between Menealfe, Gawain, and Kay proves useful to Arthur; it
ensures that these three knights will unite in their oath of loyalty to their
sovereign and not to each other.

The disappearance of the weeping maiden from the text does not, however, imply her triviality with respect to the cultural work it describes. When *The Avowing* displays the maiden's disappearance as a function of knightly fellowship, it simultaneously suggests the necessity of her presence. Indeed, the paradox of Menealfe's incorporation figures clearly as paradox only when we read from the maiden's perspective, only when we consider Menealfe as a continued threat for her safety. Her interests and perspective must be banished if Menealfe's prowess is to be available to King Arthur. When her interests vanish from textual mention, the narrative implies that Menealfe's danger to Arthur's court has likewise vanished. As the figure whose body carries the threat of violence, the weeping woman must be made present in order that she disappear. The occasion of her disappearance signals the very instrumentality of the cultural work she performs.

Nonetheless, Menealfe's incorporation into the fellowship continues to require the feminine mediation: Arthur's queen mediates his oath of fealty to Arthur. Guinevere commands the moment when "Þay fochet furth a boke/all Þayre laes for to loke" (ll. 565–66), finally transforming recreant knight into legal comrade. This transformation of foe to friend suggests that Arthurian brotherhood has the power to reproduce itself— to add to its numbers through knightly conquest—although it also requires women to serve as mediators of that reproduction. And this helps to explain the importance of the law book here.[18]

When the romance *The Avowing of King Arthur* connects the reproduction of knightly fellowship to a sovereign act mediated by the law, it likewise suggests the crucial power of law to make and legalize relations of reproduction. Representing the law's power to transform recreance into fellowship is one way of representing its power to transform the illegitimate into the legitimate, the bastard into the rightful heir.[19] If Menealfe's transformation seems altogether too easy—his shift from Gawain's hostage to Arthur's knight takes less than six lines—this moment serves to suggest that women's role in reproduction is mediated by law, a law which may produce the very illegitimacy this text gives it the power to transform.[20] But we still need to explain more precisely why women become the mediatrixes of this transformation. How do the gender complications relate to the split between Baldwin and his fellows?

The relation of gender to the thrill and troubles of violence thus far have been read through the functioning of women's disappearance within the romance. In the test Arthur and his knights eventually pose to Baldwin women are no less crucial, coming now to figure as the sign of excessive

rivalry and aggression which must be disavowed. Baldwin's climactic testing, and the story he tells following it, figure rivalry through the pleasures
of female beauty. His story suggests that an overzealous attention to exteriors is far less dangerous for knights than it can be for beautiful women.
Arthur, Kay, and Gawain test Baldwin's honor by planting a fellow knight
in bed with Baldwin's wife; Baldwin passes Arthur's test by not growing
angry over such circumstantial evidence. Pressed to explain his amazing
patience, Baldwin relates a tale of lethal, female jealousies.

Baldwin's tale within the tale recounts the deaths of two beautiful
ladies at the murderous hands of a third. The solitary surviving beauty
gains the undivided attention of five hundred knights because she murders her two (apparently more beautiful) companions and competitors.
At the beginning of his story Baldwin makes clear that the women are
at court to serve the knights; he implies, too, that such service relates to
their beauty. His brief (and vaguely eroticized) account of the first murder
depicts rivalry and jealousy as erotic and lethal, pleasurable and dangerous.
In his description of the second murder, the deadliness of female rivalry,
while troubling for the knights who watch provides even more explicitly
erotic delights:

> And for Þo werkes were we wo,
> Gart threte Þo othir for to slo.
> Þenne sayd Þe tone of Þo,
> "Lette us have our life,
> And we schall atte ȝour bidding be
> As mycull as we all thre;
> Is none of ȝaw in preuete
> Schall haue wontying of wyfe."
> Þay held us wele Þat Þay heȝte
> And diȝte us on Þe dayliyte
> And Þayre body vche nyȝte,
> Withoutun any stryue.
> Þe tone was more lovely
> Þat Þe toÞer hade envy.
> Hur throte in sundur prevely,
> Ho cutte hitte wyth a knyfe. (ll. 940–55)

The representation of the death scene immediately following the women's
vow to submit "Þayre body uch nyȝte," makes explicit the sexualization

of their servitude. Moreover the image of women killing one another for the apparent privilege of singular access to the beds of some five hundred soldiers seems at once both an amazing (masculinist) fantasy, and an interesting reversal of what might be described as the traditional, if traditionally male, story of the romance. There a protagonist distinguishes his heroism by performing his superiority through a spectacle of violence; such display, moreover, gains for him the admiration and devotion of a hoard of female spectators.[21]

The story of the deadly beauties apparently functions for Baldwin as a cautionary tale; Baldwin's reading of the tale suggests the similarities between rivalries among women and rivalries among knights: "Forthi ielius schall I never be," Baldwin declares, "For no siȝte þat I see,/Ne no buirdes briȝte of ble;/Ich ertheli thinke hase ende" (ll. 985–88). The wording seems striking in the context of the story Baldwin has just told. In Baldwin's tale death comes from treachery and violence; Baldwin's aphorism ("Ich ertheli thinke has ende") implies instead a more inevitable view of mortality. The deaths represented in his tale, however, suggest something altogether different from a fated, irresistible demise. They suggest that envy and jealousy over exteriors can prove deadly for rivals. But they simultaneously suggest that such rivalry serves (quite literally in this case) the erotic needs of a band of knights. The problem here is that as much as rivalry usefully invigorates military relations—that is, it is one of the main ways knights reproduce themselves, add to their numbers in just the way Menealfe joined Arthur's troop—it can also destroy knightly bodies. In terms of the tale within the tale, this is another way of saying that as much as the knights at the court in Baldwin's story are horrified by the actions of the lone surviving murderous woman, they also desire her in their midst.

The structure of gender within the story Baldwin tells links the dangers of violent aggression with the pleasures and passions of beauty, translating "anxiety into desire" (Bronfen, 62). If rivalry between knights risks lethal dangers, figuring that rivalry and danger as somehow linked to beauty can rework knightly anxiety and fear about death into desire, however ambivalent, for death as sublime beauty. A soldier's anxiety that he will not be able to resist death transmutes into an image of death as, simply, irresistible. But the story of dead beauties also works to mediate the very possibility of knightly demise: while both the knights and the women use aggressive intimacies against their rivals, it is only the women who die. Figures of dead beauties ward off the lethal possibilities for soldiers, imagining such dangers visited instead upon nonknightly, nonheroic bodies.[22] Such gender splitting enables Baldwin, Arthur, and his knights to attend to the fascinations and pleasures of rivalry while fantasizing their own safe protection from the death those rivalries might bring. It may be no coincidence that the occasion of the telling of this tale figures the final solidarity among Arthur and the gang, including the newly initiated Menealfe. The juxtaposition of the murdering women with the final fellowship of "kinge and his kny3tis all" (l. 1133) marks knightly aggression as life-giving by suggesting that it is the structure, and pleasures, of feminine rivalries that produce death.

If *The Avowing of King Arthur* has earlier suggested that Arthur's band might be split, the poem ends by suggesting that untroubled Arthurian unity is a masculine accomplishment. Community emerges as a brotherhood that can accommodate a certain amount of male difference. This romance celebrates the pleasures of knightly aggression by banishing the possibility of any ultimate division onto beautiful women. It suggests, moreover, that violent rivalries invigorate masculine militarism, and that imaginative tales told among knights produce the intimacy of knightly togetherness by recounting violent death as something they witness, rather than experience. Displaying the function of the tale that Baldwin tells, the poem constructs an important cultural function for itself; it grants to fantasy and imagination, and to the structure of the romance, the important task of imagining ways around paradox and contradiction.

The usefulness of violence, and stories about it, for creating hierarchical relationships of union recalls issues raised by *Knyghthode and Bataile*. There, the loyalty of warriors to their leader is linked with the disciplining "good bisinesse" of war. With *The Avowing* in mind, telling the tales of romance seems a part of war's work of unifying troops: such texts can train knightly loves and loyalties, and protect knights from their anxieties about the violent dangers of war. The intimacy read between masculine militarism and the beautiful female victim also recalls the metaphor of marriage from *Knyghthode*. In this romance, joining foes as friends depends upon splits between knightly rivals as well as upon their reconciliation. Relations of union, marital and martial, cleave in both senses of the term: some relations will split and separate, so that other relations can adhere.

Splitting and joining will be particularly difficult for those, like the authors and scribes of this text, inhabiting borderlands where complications of loyalty and identity compound. When *The Avowing* links the testing of loyalties with the protection of a border space like Inglewood Forest, it links military brotherhoods to the materiality of region and land. These regional relations emerge even more explicitly in another romance from the North inscribed in manuscript during approximately the same period, *The Awntyrs off Arthure at the Terne Wathelyn*. This romance links marriage to militarism and to policies of annexation; it depicts the pleasures of a centralized sovereign who rests his practices of land distribution and regional control on the violence of knightly rivalry.

The Body of the Knight and the Pleasures of the King

Two distinct romance episodes structure the plot of *Awntyrs off Arthure*. In the first section an eerie, blackened ghost of Guinevere's mother visits Guinevere and Gawain during a howling storm. She has come back from the grave to warn them of the wages of sin. The second episode recounts the conflict between Sir Galleroun of Galloway and Gawain over the rightful ownership and occupation of land that Galleroun inherited from his father, land that Arthur has nonetheless given to Gawain.[23] While the romance has been read as two discontinuous episodes, various commentators have suggested structural similarities between these two sections.[24] I will argue that both shorter tales share a thematic concern with land; both episodes explore the significance of land to sovereignty, and examine the pleasures and pains of the sovereign's territorial ambitions.

In its opening adventure this text explicitly pairs representations of land with remorseful female lust and with losses to sovereign power. When Guinevere's mother returns from the grave to warn her daughter and Gawain of the consequences of lustful appetites, she uses the story of her fate as an exemplum for them, characterizing her former glory, and thus the bitterness of her losses, in geographic terms:

> Quene was I somewile, brighter of broes
>
> . . . .
> Of al gamene or gle Þat one grounde growes
> Wele gretere than Gaynor of garsomes and golde
> of pales, of powndis, of parkes, and of plewes
> Of townes, of towris, of tresoures untolde,
> Of countres, of castells, of cragges, of cleves.
> Now am I cauyte oute of kiÞe to cares so colde;
> Into care am I caughte and cachede in clay (ll. 143; 145–51).

This catalogue of things Guinevere's mother held as queen foregrounds the spaces of her sovereignty. This queen's wealth and power stretch from the aristocratic sites of the palace to the peasant's field; they bound the narrow circumferences of tower prisons and the broad mercantile space of towns; they span "civilized" fortifications and the "wildness" of craggy cliffs and gorges. The poem does not figure Guinevere's mother's lost glory through images of an opulent court; nor does it list the jewels, silks, or satins often associated with regal women. Land signifies both the glorious wealth of aristocratic privilege and the unbelievable breadth of a realm. And the loss of these glories links the apparently sinful and disfigured female body with sovereign loss.

This constellation of categories resembles the figuration of power, land, and the hag in "The Tale of Florent" from John Gower's *Confessio Amantis*, a resemblance that reminds us of the connections between Guinevere's mother's ghost and the tradition of the loathly lady. As it will be helpful to examine the loathly lady motif in some detail, I turn now to a brief discussion of Gower's "Tale of Florent," an important contemporary analogue to Chaucer's *Wife of Bath's Tale*. Florent, a knight and cousin to an emperor journeys through the Welsh border marches and engages in combat with Branchus, a young marcher lord. When Branchus dies in their battle, his angry family in retribution for the death of their son force Florent on a quest, offering to grant him his life if he can determine what it is that women most desire. After a series of adventures Florent comes upon the loathly lady, a horrendous, disfigured, and ancient woman who promises the answer to Florent's quest so long as he agrees to marry her. Gower's description emphasizes, even delights in, the monstrous decay of the hag's hideous body, detailing its ugliness inch by disgusting inch.[25] He does not, however, represent her as a helpless or poverty-stricken wretch. On the contrary her physical appearance contrasts with the rich control she keeps "of land, of rent, of parke, or plough." Gower's rhetoric stakes the lady's ugliness against her landed wealth, contrasting her sexual undesirability with her economic power and prestige. When it does so, Gower's tale links libidinal pleasures to economic gain. This text argues, moreover, that a warrior can seek material wealth as compensation for a loss of sexual pleasure. Such a structure marks marriage as the site for the exercise of propertied possession and not love, thereby connecting territorial power with marital alliance.

Annexation of territory serves as a link between the marital and the martial here. The "Tale of Florent" imagines a certain kind of marriage as a surrogate for war. A union between the bodies of warrior and hag remedies the conflict between an emperor's kin and an enemy in the borderlands. Florent's willingness to marry the hag appeases the family of his enemy, and stands in for a battle between his family and theirs. Moreover, Florent's ambivalence about the marriage registers in violent fantasies: he imagines his bride's death, conjecturing that, if only he could be rid of her, he could gain her land; he imagines the hag as his prisoner, banishing her to an island far from help or rescue. This substitution of marriage for war marks the female body as particularly liable for violence; the pleasures of such violence can be read in Gower's apparent delight in displaying the horrific wretchedness of the hag's decaying femininity.

The context of war, moreover, links the hag's horrible body, as Florent's adversary, with the wounded body of the enemy. This suggests that while stories of the loathly lady explicitly trade on images borrowed from the tradition of courtly love, they also seem edged in militarism. Like the courtly love tradition, the "Tale of Florent" depicts a male body suffering the denial of its libidinal desires. Unlike most of the courtly love tradition, however, the tale of the loathly lady conceives the suffering and pain of the male lover in the coercion of his desire, and not the lack, or obduracy, of a beloved. If only, the tale implies, the knightly lover could lack such a horrible lover. If only such a brave and youthful (male) body could remain aloof before such hideous, aging (female) decay.

The repudiation of physical decay constitutes the structure of the loathly lady motif; in most versions of the tale, including Gower's, the knight's dilemma is solved once the hag's horrible form magically modulates into a stunningly beautiful bride. And of course such a transformation occurs only once the knight has first explicitly repudiated his desire for a beautiful body. This repudiation implies that the loyal warrior will be willing to submit his body to the physically hideous. When the dutiful knight finally gains everything—he gains the lady's land through his conquest of her; he gains her as beautiful by conquering his desire for beauty—we are shown the rewards of his willingness to forego his own desire for beauty and pleasure.

The knight conquers of the lady (and her land) by managing his own desire. He conquers her by conquering his aversion to her. Florent, thus, also stands as the well-ruled subject, a man willing to submit his desires and have them remade for the sake of conquest, and in order to gain land, power, and prestige. In Gower's version, moreover, Florent is nephew to the emperor, a fact that inhibits Branchus' family from exacting vengeance on him. Florent's successful conquest of land converges on his successful conquest of himself. The promise of the lady's transformation consoles the knight willing to remake his desires in the hope that his single-minded loyalty to the emperor will be rewarded.

In her discussion of the loathly lady in the Thornton manuscript romances, an analysis which includes *Awntyrs off Arthure*, Fradenburg links the transformation marked on the body of the loathly lady with sovereignty itself. She argues that the loathly lady's transformation depicts the utopian transformations promised by right rule. The loathly lady figures "a way of imagining a conflict whose outcome is nonetheless predetermined" (253). "The aging, loathly woman," Fradenburg continues, "who desires sovereignty over her husband in 'The Wife of Bath's Tale'; the unstable Venus of the Judgement of Paris, whose gift might not be a true gift; the blackened purgatorial ghost of *The Awntyrs off Arthure*, once beautiful but terribly transformed through sexual corruption and infidelity; and indeed, the wanton bride Israel might all be 'in the end beautiful' when fidelity to the right man, a willingness to be ruled by him, are revealed" (253–54). Willingness to be ruled rightly promises, through the loathly lady motif, massive transformative powers. The transformation of the wild and horrible "lady of the land" through right rule alludes to the transformative power—although not from all perspectives "beautiful"—of sovereign territorial annexation. Like the apparently wild "lady of the land," the space of wilderness can be similarly transformed into a well-ruled sovereign realm. Insofar as the knight witnesses this transformation, he stands as sovereign for—and in some versions becomes sovereign of—the body of the lady. By ruling his newly beloved, he rules the realm in small.

But the knight, as we have just noted, has also had to remake his desires to produce those transformations. He, too, has had to submit. In so doing he is reminded that the power he wields over the lady is not held merely at his pleasure. When Florent joins with the body of a hag in a legally sanctioned marriage, he demonstrates his willingness to exchange marital vows for the sake of the emperor. The tradition of the loathly lady moves us thus to recognize the heterosexist demands of such images of sovereign control: control of the land and control of the realm can be shown when warrior bodies submit to the state's need for heterosexual kinship. In a formulation that resonates with Klaus Theweleit's explication of the "male fantasies" of militarism, soldiers console themselves for their submission to the state by controlling the bodies of their women in its reproductive service.[26]

Such observations may help to explain the complications of plot we
see in *Awntyrs off Arthure*, and it is to this romance that we now return. The poet's description of the awful body of the ghost of Guinevere's
mother—a body that seems, in the vividness of its description, considerably more substantial a horror than its status as ghost would suggest—
imagines the woman as deadened and deadly. Guinevere's mother stands as
the sign of a horrific, and isolated, future born from sin. The feminization
of the sinful splits the cloying dampness of fleshy putrefaction from the
virtuous masculinity of warrior heroism. The warrior, whether Gawain or
Florent, displays life in terms of a virile male potency; his liveliness, moreover, emerges as utterly different from the death in war that he confronts
and transcends. In this ideological contradiction, the warrior's work is the
opposite of war. His touch can transform shriveled hags into revitalized
beauties.

Fradenburg argues that the transformation of the loathly lady usually
offers the promise of rule as redemptive; yet *Awntyrs off Arthure* makes
no such promise. There is no final marriage here, no female body turned
fantastically from aged hag to stunning beauty. If this is so, then it seems
fair to read this northern borderland text as pessimistic about the possibilities for a well-ruled sovereignty in the Arthurian borders, and it is
here that this text complicates the picture of masculine militarism we have
been examining. Despite its gesture to a tradition of utopian sovereign
transformations, this text foregrounds the failure of Arthur's realm. But
unlike the tradition that figures Arthur's failure as a matter of intimate
intrigues and forbidden sexual pleasures, this romance displays royal failure as a consequence of Arthur's territorial policies. Arthur's failure is an
eventuality produced by his excessive appetite for annexation, and because
the intimacies of his realm require such acquisitions.

Guinevere's mother links ambitions for land to sovereign failure when
she prophesies a dark future for Arthur's fortunes, cautioning Gawain
against a single-minded submission to the demands of militarism.[27] In a
set of lines reminiscent of Arthur's prophetic dream from the Alliterative
Morte Arthure, the ghost's prophesy critiques Arthur's property rights,
listing the "fele kinges londes" where Arthur's army has violently "de-
foulene Þe folke," claiming "riches over reymes withoutene eny righte" (ll.
261–62). Guinevere's mother warns that Arthur's covetousness will result
in treason and envy visited upon the breadth of Arthurian localities: on
Carlisle (l. 289), on Dorsetshire (l. 295), and on Cornwall (l. 301). Her
final prediction figures danger and treason literally growing up at Arthur's

court: "In riche Arthures halle/The barne playes at Þe balle/Þat outray shalle you alle,/ Derfely Þat day" (ll. 309–12).

The ghost's prophecy of a treacherous child at court implies that Arthur's court schools its own disaster, a disaster linked to play, to childish pleasures. We recall too that in most versions of the story the child of Arthur who brings about his downfall is his bastard son. And, after all, Arthur's own patrimony can be read as legally suspect: in some versions he is called a bastard son as well. The implications of intimate treachery and its relation to conquest of land drive the narrative of *Awntyrs off Arthure* and here, I would suggest, we might usefully consider the second episode as a gloss upon the first.

In the romance's second episode a Scottish knight, Sir Galleroun of Galloway, challenges Gawain to mortal combat in hopes of winning back his family's property. Gawain has taken possession of Galleroun's patrimony, land that was given to Gawain by King Arthur in payment for Gawain's valorous service to the realm. When Galleroun and Gawain prove equally matched in the violent combat that is to decide their fortunes, and when both appear equally wounded, Guinevere, at the request of Galleroun's distraught lady, intercedes with her consort pleading that he end the joust and reward both champions. Arthur's response displays how deeply his sovereignty is structured around policies of land grants and through tournaments like this one. He grants another set of lands to Gawain so that Gawain, mirroring the gracious sovereignty of his liege, can return his Scottish rival's patrimony.

In both moves the text ironically figures Arthur's kingship as generous. For Galleroun, Arthur's "gift" of land through Gawain suggests Arthur's ambition to mediate the familial relations of Scottish inheritance. In other words, the tournament shows an exchange of land as a means to display Arthur's power: Galleroun's possession of Galloway becomes something which serves the king's pleasure; Galleroun's inheritance— something which Arthur had nothing whatsoever to do with—becomes ironically refigured as Arthur's gift. Arthur's generosity to Gawain suggests the problems of land distribution by sovereign whim:

"Now here I gife the," quod the king,
"Gauan tresoure and golde
Glamorgans landis, with grevis so grene;
The wirchipe of Wales, to welde and to wolde
With Gryffones castell, kirnelde so clene;

And the Husters Haulle, to hafe and to holde
Wayford and Waterforde i Wales, I wene
Twa baronnes in Bretayne with burgesse full bold." (ll. 663–69)

Arthur appears to have a solution to the problem of two worthy knights competing for the same land; it is a solution based upon the further annexation and conquest of more land. Arthur's sovereign arrogance extends so widely that he simply grants another region to Gawain by royal writ. This apparent solution displays the problems of annexation and promises the recurrences of battle. Of course, those who hold the title to these lands in Wales will likely travel, as Galleroun has done, to reclaim their lands from Gawain's possession—thereby suggesting that Arthur's court will witness this same tournament battle over and over again. Yet this may not, at least in the short run, constitute much of a problem for Arthur the King.

While the romance implicitly critiques the ideology of Arthur's land policies, the text is not particularly critical of militarism per se. The tournament battle between Gawain and Galleroun offers a beautiful scene of violent display. The text delights in both the excitement and horror of the bloody fray:

Hardely Þene Þes haÞeleseone helmes Þey hewe;
Þei betene downe beriles and bourdures bright.
Shildes one shildres Þat shene were to shewe,
Fretted were in fyne golde Þei failene in fighte.
Stones of iral Þey strenkel and strewe;
StiÞe stapeles of stele Þey strike doun st[r]iyte.
Burnes bannene be tyme Þe bargane was brewe,
The dougheti withe dyntes so delfully were dight. (ll. 586–93)

Armor glitters; shields glisten with golden filigree; the violence of warriors literally showers the field with precious stones. Such a description foregrounds the pleasures of watching. Moreover, it suggests that warrior bodies explode in the heat of contest to produce showers of gold and gems, not bloody heaps of flesh. And if the wounds Gawain and Galleroun suffer are grievous and grisly, the splendor of this spectacle seems, in the context of this kind of poetic description, judged worth the price. This is the kind of military picture in which chivalric romance glories.

Yet while the poet of *Awntyrs off Arthure* may delight in these putative glories, the poem is finally critical that they are used exclusively for

Arthur's territorial pleasures. When the narrative connects this tournament to the annexation of land—a practice which it has already decried as "riches wonnen withouten eny right" thanks to Arthur's greedy appetites—it foregrounds the injustice of a sovereignty that trades upon such pleasures. Galleroun's battle with Gawain suggests a problem at the heart of Arthurian structures of knightly reward. It is, however, a problem that doesn't seem to bother Arthur so long as he has knights like Gawain willing to risk deadly and painful wounds to display the integrity, and the wealth, of Arthur's rule. Arthur depends upon his knights' willingness to display their bodies in violent spectacles of military might.

With this in mind, one must remember Guinevere's mother's prophecy of Arthur's disastrous fall. Despite the ghost's mention of the treachery of Mordred, Arthur emerges not as the tragic sovereign from the Stanzaic *Morte Arthur* or from Malory, whose fatal flaw lies in the naive trust he places in his intimates. Arthur is instead, as in the Alliterative *Morte Arthure*, a conqueror whose policy of annexation, land "wonnen . . . in war with wrong wile" (l. 421), produces disaster. Even more, this text shows us that annexation encodes the pleasure of a sovereign who uses military men for his personal entertainment if also to protect the integrity of his realm. Arthur, finally, seems unconcerned about the particular bodies and particular losses sacrificed to his pleasure.

Such a picture of the injustices of imperial sovereignty seems altogether appropriate to the Northwest provenance of the romance. Geographic references to borderlands pepper this text, references which, when they can be identified, seem to involve the regions surrounding Cumberland and the southwest corner of Scotland. Rosalind Field suggests that Galleroun "shows the reluctance of an independent lord to be assimilated into the scheme of centralized royal power" (66); Helen Phillips, following Field's lead, remarks that "it is tempting to see in the Galleroun episode a fictional reflection of English imperialist expansion" (9). In the end, however, Phillips dismisses the pertinence of this connection on the basis of manuscript dating and a lack of linguistic evidence. "There seems nothing that points to Scottish rather than English authorship," Phillips writes, "[and t]he poem's language appears to have been northern Middle English, with no features that can with certainty be said to have been exclusively Scottish at the period, and the Scottish places mentioned are large and well-known" (10).[28] And yet the lack of a definitive Scottish identification need not preclude a concern with the landed policies of centralized monarchies. A Middle English poet, especially one working in the northern border counties, might be just as concerned as would be a Scots poet with the uses centralized royalty makes of its outlying regions. Such a poet might find the memory of a century-old series of battles between the English and the Scots a useful metaphor for its struggles with a London-based aristocracy deploying regional alliances and identities ("Yorkists" and "Lancastrians") in its battles over centralized power.[29] Scotland's function as metaphor enables a northern literary culture producing the tale to contest a centralized image of sovereign power, represented in this text by an Arthur greedy for land. As metaphor for regional concerns, Scotland offers a means at once to resist English moves toward centralization and at the same time to deny that English centralization complicates northern loyalties at all.

While I read this romance's concern with regional localities and landed disputes as pertinent for the period of the mid-fifteenth-century—a time when regionally inflected disputes erupted into "open rebellions" against the king and "private wars" between local magnates were on the increase—it is significant that the structure of the narrative mediates evidence for this connection in favor of its attention to first Scottish and then Welsh concerns.[30] This mediation does not imply the irrelevance of regional concerns to the narrative, however. Insofar as reference to losses in Scotland and, once Galleroun has defended his patrimony, the prediction of losses in Wales displaces northern anxieties of English centralization, they can suggest that a policy of "internal colonialism" has consequences for intra-English relations as well as for Anglo-Scots, or English-Welsh, ones. That is to say, an English crown's attempts to consolidate power over a region like Wales affect relations among other regions throughout the island as well. It provides an image of unity to which all those on the island of Britain must submit. When the English crown attempts its unification with Wales, it implicitly performs a joining on behalf of a variety of English regions, northern as well as southern. Thus, England's conquest of Welsh regions can provide, among other things, an opportunity for the unification of Lancaster with Somerset, York with Warwick and Salisbury. Northern regional concerns during such a time thus emerge as both linked to, yet distinct from, Celtic regionalism. And this is one way to read the regionalism of *Awntyrs off Arthure*.

In its beautiful display of tournament rivalry, and Arthur's pleasure in watching, *Awntyrs off Arthure at the Terne Wathelyn* illustrates the relation of annexation and unification to sovereign pleasures in the practice of violence. This romance demonstrates, moreover and finally, how the integrity of a loyal knight's body might come to represent the integrity of the body of the realm.[31] When Gawain agrees to fight Galleroun he stakes his title to the lands in question on his body's ability—and willingness—to withstand the violence and prowess of his Scottish rival. His wounded body testifies to his belief in Arthur's sovereignty and in the practices by which such sovereignty is constituted. But the relation of this romance's second episode to its first—the relation, in other words, of Gawain's encounter with Galleroun to his encounter with Guinevere's mother's ghost—suggests that the Gawain who rides valiantly against his Scottish rival has already remade his desire to serve Arthur's demands. Gawain displays his loyalty to Arthur by using his body against Galleroun. And thus he is easily moved, at Arthur's pleasure and by Arthur's writ, to turn over land he's just been given in exchange for the promise of new lands. The fact that Gawain may be forced to fight over and over again for the land Arthur promises implies that he is fighting not for his own desires or his own land, but to serve the king's scopophilic pleasures and system of political reward.

It is not surprising, given the likelihood of such repetitions, that the violence depicted here demands that wounds be quickly healed. It is significant that both Gawain and Galleroun regain the wholeness of their bodies by the end of this romance; their dreadful wounds are quickly healed: "þe wees that werene wounded so woþely, I wene/ Surgenes sone saned, soþely to say" (ll. 692–93). Gawain and Galleroun come away from the grisly battle remarkably whole, their bodies intact and their relationship repaired. And Galleroun, like Menealfe from *The Avowing of Arthur*, becomes rather easily incorporated into the Arthurian fellowship. Gawain's and Galleroun's bodily wholeness becomes, by the end of the romance, a useful synecdoche for the unity and integrity of their community.

In this romance, as in the one examined previously, military might becomes the means for joining foes, creating wholeness, communion, and relationship. Chivalric culture deeply prized bodily perfection in its soldiers, an image of wholeness, once again, depending upon gendered relations.[32] *The Book of the Ordre of Chyualry* (translated and printed by William Caxton) will describe these relations thus:

A man lame or ouer grete or ouer fatte or that hath ony other euyl dissposycion in his body For whiche he may not vse thoffyce of chyualrye is not suffysaunt to be a knygt. For hit shold not be honest to thordre of chyualrye yf she recyued a man for to bere armes whiche were entatched corrupt & not myghty. For so much noble & hyghe is Chyvalry in hyr honour that a squyer lame of ony membre how wel that he be noble and ryche & borne of noble lygnage is not dygne ne worthy to be receiued in to thorder of chyvalrye. (63–65)

Chivalry, gendered feminine, desires an ideal male form, banishing the wounded and the infirm from her company. Their exile makes it possible to forget that chivalry will produce, in fact must produce, lameness and bodily "corruption" if it is to be successful in its battles. Yet when chivalry is gendered female, the ideal knight's relation to militarism becomes, through "her," explicitly heterosexual. This is, of course, the formulation of *Knyghthode and Bataile*: "Mankyndys lyfe is mylitatioun,/ And she, thi wife, is named Militaunce" (ll. 96–97). These texts deploy militarism as a means of uniting difference, yet also as a gendered and sexualized venture. And if the first conjures the dangers of a knight's wounding only to banish them, the second raises marital intimacies as if to declare that martial pleasure must be only heterosexual.

These metaphors make clear links between a knight's masculinity and his heterosexuality; they cast knights as masculine by imagining the institutions they embrace (chivalry, war) in feminine terms. War, personified as a female spouse, stands between the violence of military men; violent pleasures occur when soldiers unite with "war" as event, not through the intimate physicality of brothers-in-arms. Militarism is thus claimed for a heterosexual potency; military power becomes male heterosexual virility. War is thus thought to bond males together safely, uniting male bodies in exciting configurations, while simultaneously reasserting its commitment to female objects of desire. "Deviant" pleasures thus haunt the homosocial relations of such a culture. Yet masculine power, as both these texts also make clear, remains also haunted by the possibility of a warrior's death, wounding, or humiliation.

During the fifteenth century violence and battle come to be viewed as a means of joining regions into a single realm, and whole bodies of knights who once were rivals come to signify the singularity and wholeness of the united aristocratic fellowship, the idealized body of the realm. This structure imagines violence as creative for community. Dependent upon traditional heterosexual structures of relationship, these images also gesture to other kinds of pleasures. Arthurian romances, when read in the context of other texts from the same period, however, suggest cultural tensions and ambiguities, even anxieties, about the militaristic unity violence provides. Yet they also show that the communities created by centralized sovereigns demand absolute personal knightly loyalty. During times of insular instability, sovereigns long for a knight like Gawain, as he is depicted in these romances, a knight always willing to subsume his pleasures in violence on behalf and for the sake of his lord.

Finally, the fact that these texts of Arthurian romance make legible the relation of militarism to categories of the ruler's pleasure serves to remind us that those training warriors in the intimate pleasure of "appropriate" violence frequently remain distanced from violent encounter themselves. The judgment that some violence is "appropriate" often depends upon the protection such judgments afford the bodies of a privileged few. When Arthur the King watches the splendor of the tournament from the safety and luxury of his space in the pavilion, his vantage provides access to the power and energy of battle while protecting his body from its dangers. And just as these romances display Arthur's preservation from the dangers of violent encounter, so did the Love-Day pageant work to preserve London as a space of special economic and cultural value, protected from the harm of regional faction. Destruction during such spectacles of violence are not, thus, indiscriminate; commanders-in-chief work hard to distinguish the regions and bodies that deserve preservation and rescue from those that can willingly be sacrificed. The shame of this kind of violence may not lie in the fact of its pleasure, but in the relationships of apparent "unity" and "peace" that purchase the bodily pleasures of kings by sacrificing the bodies of their subjects.

CHAPTER SEVEN

"Necessary" Losses

Royal Death and English Remembrance

And whan they were at the watersyde, evyn fast by the banke houed a lytyl barge wyth many fayr ladyes in hit, and emonge hem al was a quene. And al they had blacke hoodes, and al they wepte and shryked whan they sawe Kyng Arthur. Now put me into the barge, sayd the kyng. And so he dyd softelye, and there receyued hym thre quenes wyth grete mourning.

—Caxton's Malory, "The Death of Arthur," 591

THIS tableau ends William Caxton's 1485 edition of Thomas Malory's tale of Arthur. The queens in Arthur's cortege promise healing for his wounded body; weeping and shrieking they deliver him beyond the treachery of civil war to Avalon. Malory's scene of feminine melancholy, penned in the 1460s, poignantly grieves for Arthur. The weeping women extravagantly mourn the dismal scene, standing in for all who love this sovereign. The grandeur of their grieving preserves the trauma of Arthur's end. Unlike the king who goes perhaps too gently, the sorrowful sisters register Arthur's loss as inconsolable. Malory emphasizes the poignancy of Arthur's death and not a hopeful Arthurian afterlife. Arthur's sad sisters nonetheless mediate the sovereign's crossing from Camelot to Avalon, from Civil War to other possibilities, offering a technology of change poised for the future.

The 1485 edition of Malory's Arthurian compendium grants Malory's text, *Le Morte Darthur*, its own material afterlife through the mediation of William Caxton's press. Caxton's publication of Malory's *Morte* coincides with the close of a crucially changeable period for insular English society. Within the space of forty years, the crown passes six times from sovereign to successor. During the same period the commons rise in insurrection, rioting in London both before and after Jack Cade's rebellion

(1450). The later fifteenth century is noted for its cultural innovations, if also for its changeabilities: Caxton's press, new technologies of court and monarchy, the development of vernacular prose, of "national" histories, and the emergence in London of an increasingly diverse population of foreign merchant immigrants.[1] Change, innovation, and instability worry the author of *The Libel of English Policy* who, a few decades earlier, had fretted over England's weakness: "[W]ee be frayle as glasse," that poet lamented "and also bretylle, not tough, never abiding" (182).[2]

The *Libel*-poet fears England's fragility, the mutability of its fortunes. Malory, as if in response, offers the mournful story of insular mutability, of an archaic sovereignty passing softly away. Arthur's passing—its "necessary" losses, its apparent consolations—mark the subject of this chapter. I will read Malory's interest in death and passing as evocative of British territorial losses, both insular and continental, which ground a unified, insular future. Arguing that William Caxton's 1485 edition solidifies Arthurian sovereignty as English, I begin with an analysis of the tendentious Englishness of Caxton's Prologue. In Caxton's edition, a legendary sovereign biography consolidates centralized English and London-based power, preserving Arthur as the sovereign who sits at Winchester. Turning next to Malory's book I (titled in Caxton's edition "The Birth of King Arthur"), I suggest why it is Merlin's prophetic futurism (and not, as we might expect, Arthur's bonds of kin) that convinces recalcitrant nobles to unite under Arthur's legitimate rule. In the chapter's second section I read the uncanny doublenesses in the "Tale of Balin" to signify the problems that such unifications raise for unruly subjects, in a tale that portrays centralized loyalty to a single leader as both deadly and desirable.

In the third section, I read Malory's story of the Sangreall as a means of displaying the loyal submission explored in "Balin" as an attribute of virtuous hearts, moving unity inside particular bodies, a distinctly male interiority able to survive civil war and sovereign loss. Arthur becomes, in the process, encrypted in English male interiors. The necessary losses and consolations of Arthur's passing suggest a particular English identity as a question of hearts willing to suffer devastating losses. For Malory's account narrates a profoundly sad tale. In its mournful delectation of Arthur's loss, Malory's *Morte Darthur* allows us, like Arthur's sad sisters, to remember the alternative traditions lost, inconsolably, in the wake of unification and centralization.

Arthur's English Encryptment

The fifteenth-century English crown suffered, as we have noted, enormous "problems of continuity." As is well known, the legal response to those problems emerged in a discourse of the King's Two Bodies, by which the crown came to refer legally to "the sovereignty of the whole collective body of the realm" (Kantorowicz 273, 384). Sovereignty became a community endeavor, an office of corporate kingship explicitly claimed to be continuous. In response to a particular history of disunity and factionalism, continuity and wholeness were conjured in a fiction of time: sempiternal kingship claimed consistent rule by conceiving a temporal union of sovereigns, an imagined community of sovereigns through time. This historic royal procession offered "the plurality necessary to make up a corporation . . . a plurality . . . which did not expand within a given Space, but was determined exclusively by Time" (387).

Emphasizing sovereign community through time, the theory of the King's Two Bodies seems to render space inconsequential. Yet sempiternal rule begs questions of geography even as it tries to obfuscate such claims. In fact, geographic claims motivate its early modern uses: sempiternity was first articulated to establish Elizabeth I's legal right as sovereign to a particular space in the realm, the Duchy of Lancashire.[3] In ideological terms the theory of the King's Two Bodies uses the fiction of a sovereign community across time to solidify rule over regional insular space. Time and space converge in this legal consolidation of centralized control.

These same issues, I have been arguing throughout this study, converge in the variety of Middle English Arthurian romance. Yet through a differential attention to both time and space, the romance tradition, unlike the theory of the King's Two Bodies, registers an oppositional sovereign history. The prophetic futurism and geographic specificity of Middle English Arthurian romance can be read to critique (implicitly or explicitly) the territorial claims of the sovereigns who purport to follow Arthur.[4] Alternative traditions of Welsh vaticination and the "Breton Hope" (examined in Chapters 1 and 2) register resistance to English versions of insular kingship by invoking a different future. Alternative claims to insular territory are legible in the geographic mutations of *Sir Gawain and the Green Knight*, or in the critiques of Arthur's land policies from *Awntyrs off Arthure at the Terne Wathelyn* (examined in Chapters 4 and 6 respectively). As I will make clear shortly, Malory's *Morte Darthur* occasionally alludes to such alternatives.

Yet despite those allusions, Caxton's Malory claims a single defini-
tively English Arthurian space and time. In his preface to the *Morte*,
Caxton markets not only Malory's story and the press producing it, but
Arthur, now solidified as a centralized English sovereign. This is the "nobel
and ioyous hystorye of the grete conquerour and excellent kyng, Kyng
Arthur, sometyme kyng of thys noble royalme, thenne callcd Brytaygne"
(3), "whyche outght moost to be remembered emonge vs Englysshemen
tofore al other Crysten kynges" (1).[5] This history, Caxton argues, belongs
to the men and women of England, who deserve to hear it in their own
"maternal tongue" (3).

Arthur's English identity, in Caxton's formulation, compels the publication of Malory's account. Yet Arthur's Englishness stands here upon a
British geography marked as already long past, the difference of Britain
to England constructed as a matter of time. England, "thys noble royalme
thenne called Brytaygne" (3), claims geographic integrity as a ruled space,
a realm, that crosses temporal difference. England and Britain, present
and past, share not only space but also rule, implying continuity (and not
contestation) between past and present geography in the fact of sovereign sway. This is, as was just seen, exactly the ideological move made by
the theory of sovereign sempiternity, where temporal continuity similarly
stakes territorial claims. Furthermore, Caxton's emphasis upon language
(that this realm was once *called* Britain) renders difference through historic
philological variation. As a result, linguistic change signifies not a polyglot
(or multicultural) contested insular past, but an archaic name passing away
before its more modern variant. The name of "Britain" is the linguistic
trace of an enduring identity currently called English. Caxton's language
moves Arthur's Englishness into the place of his (archaic) Britishness. In
a standard colonizing move, Caxton pushes Arthur's alternative insular
identities into a language lost before the march of time.

Yet differences regarding Arthur resurface as Caxton next recapitulates the problem of Arthur's historicity, pointing to the longstanding
controversies over Arthur's identity. Some scholars have read Caxton's demure as insincere, an opportunistic rhetorical move designed to advertise
the importance of the book he publishes. To be sure, Caxton's business
sense, increasingly noted in scholarly accounts of his press, may well have
provoked his interest in Arthur precisely since controversy offers substantial power for a growing book trade.[6] Yet Caxton also identifies Arthur
with a particular interpretation of Arthur's rule. Hedging his bets against
the Arthurian traditions that might have caused problems for his London

consumers, Caxton tendentiously catalogues Arthur's existence as particularly pertinent to southern England. Banishing doubts about Arthur's reality, Caxton offers evidence of Arthur's body embedded in England's geography and history:

Fyrst ye may see his sepulture in the monasterye of Glastyngburye. And also in the Polychronycon, in the v book the syxte chappytre, and in the seuenth book the XXIII chappytre, where his body was buryed and after founden and translated into the sayd monasterye. Ye shal se also in th'ystory of Bochas, in his book De Casu Principum, parte of his noble actes and also of his falle; also Galfrydus in his Brutysshe book recounteth his lyf. And in dyuers places of Englond many remembraunces ben yet of hym and shall remayne perpetuelly, and also of his knyghtes. Fyrst in the Abbey of Westmestre at Saynt Edwardes Shryne remayneth the prynte of his seal in reed waxe closed in beryll, in which is wryton PATRICIUS ARTHURUS BRITANNIE GALLIE GERMANIE DACIE IMPERATOR. Item in the Castel of Douer ye may see Gauwayns skulle and Cradoks mantel; at Wyncester, the Round Table; in other places Launcelottes swerde, and many other thynges. (2)

In Caxton's formulation, Arthur's body crosses land and text. Arthur's English burial testifies in space (his sepulchre at Glastonbury) and time (in an amazingly specific citation to his resting-place in Higden's *Polychronicon*). Arthur's native identity continues to be materialized in an obsessively English land; it is thus produced here as materially English, and as historically material because of its relation to English soil. Caxton specifically mentions traditions from the south: Glastonbury, Winchester, and Dover. He remains silent as to other "diverse places of England" the other perpetual "remembrances of him." Vestiges of Arthur's community—of the body of his fellowship—give perpetual remembrance throughout a specifically southern England; alongside the histories mentioned, such specificities commemorate a British past disappeared into an English present.[7]

This territorial and historical encryptment resignifies Arthur's contested identity for an English southern centrality. In identifying Arthur's British past as coterminous with a specifically southern English present, Caxton links central England's claims to various insular spaces with its possession of British history. In these remarks, like the legal theorists crafting the theory of the King's Two Bodies, he deploys a temporal continuity of sovereigns to serve a determinedly centralized geography. Again, the imagined historical coherence of Britain to England serves to banish geographic and cultural difference. Space and time collide in an insular English identity accommodating change while nonetheless enduring coherently beyond it. This England owns Britain by owning Arthur's past.

Caxton's representation of Arthur's encryptment thus resonates beyond dynastic issues to a larger set of cultural concerns. Malory's text
is similarly broad in its attractions. In an impressive recent reading of
Malory's text and context, Felicity Riddy compellingly identifies *Le Morte
Darthur* as a "post-imperial, or even post-colonial, text, which speaks with
the voices of 'noble and dyvers gentylmen' of Malory's generation, for
whom the loss of the French territories in 1453 had been a personal disaster." Riddy reads in Malory's text the "death throes" of the chivalrous
class (73). This was a time "when the governing elites, no longer united
against the French and the Scots, first fell upon each other in the Wars of
the Roses and then reassembled themselves under the Tudors against their
own tenants. The great myth of the fifteenth-century is the gentility to
which these men all aspire, and *Le Morte Darthur* is the great repository
of that myth" (71–72). Emphasizing the important class dimensions to
England's loss of French territory, Riddy deploys the term "post-colonial"
with reference to the long-standing legacies of war and conquest between
England and France. I share Riddy's sense of the crucial role of England's
French losses in explaining the amazing popularity of *Le Morte Darthur*,
a text that would be repeatedly published into the Tudor years: in 1489,
1529, 1557, 1585, and 1634.[8]

Riddy's mention of the Tudors, however, implicitly raises a third
player in what I have been arguing is the triangulated cultural relationship
pertinent to Arthur's popularity among England, France, and Wales. The
contestations and shared dreamings between England and Wales suggest
another colonial scene to which we must attend. Alluding to this tradition
early in her article, Riddy (not unlike Caxton) reads Arthur's Welshness
primarily as a function of the past: "By the fifteenth century Arthur, who
had begun as a Celt, was an English king, and his life provided ways
of exploring the upper-class perceptions of Englishness which had been
sharpened by the Hundred Years War. The old story took on new meanings, as it had always done. The process by which Arthur shifted from
being one of the conquered to being one of the conquerors is part of
that shift in meaning" (57). Riddy usefully reminds us that the move from
conquered Celt to conquering English results from a shift in the meaning
of Arthur's identity. I would not entirely disagree with her formulation.
Yet the term "shift" implies (perhaps accidentally) a chronologically linear
(although not, it is important to note, necessarily progressivist) view of
Arthur's history. My study has been attempting to recast such chronologies with a wider look at the variability and heterogeneity of the period,

a persistent field of differences concerning Arthur's meaning that had not entirely disappeared. Moreover, I would qualify Riddy's implication that Arthur's meaning shifted unidirectionally from "Celt" to "English," to suggest that various Arthurs circulated complexly in various insular places (Welsh traditions were particular, as were Scots), including regional versions of Arthur's "Englishness." This variety, contested well into the fifteenth century, was an important part of Arthur's broad appeal. Caxton's Prologue, I have been arguing, tendentiously solidifies a specific brand of Arthur's Englishness, a brand that will, thanks to his press, quickly become the most popular Middle English version of the story. The quickness of Riddy's formulation, thus, overlooks the complicated processes of cultural contestation and transition, process that will be important (even crucial) into the Tudor years. To be sure, Arthur's ability to front centralized English concerns has a history predating the Tudors by some centuries. Yet I have been suggesting throughout this study that this is not the only history pertinent for a reading of Arthurian romance. Arthur's meaning was complicated, contested, and differently inflected in various texts. The colonial conquest of a Welsh Arthur for English sovereign centrality is not, even in the fifteenth century, a cultural fait accompli.

The history of Henry VII's succession suggests that colonial engagements were still part of Arthur's context at the time Caxton's Malory emerged. Throughout the fourteenth and fifteenth centuries, Welsh interest in legendary history, Welsh chronicle, and vaticinative poetry "flourished in gentry circles" (Roberts, "Writing," 207). Arthur still appears in Welsh poetic accounts of British sovereignty, poems that continue to contest the mistreatment of the Welsh by the English. Henry VII's successful deployment of the banner of Pendragon, moreover, resonated with both Welsh and English gentry, although for different reasons and with different hopes in mind. According to David Rees, Henry's popularity with the Welsh gentry who fought for him at Bosworth had much to do with Welsh hopes that they would receive "lasting political and economic advantages . . . such as the full privileges of Englishmen, which were denied them by penal legislation dating back to . . . Owain Glyn Dŵr" (5).[9] Henry VII activated Welsh national feeling by identifying himself with those hopes for a national redeemer, a *Mab Darogan* (Son of Prophecy). In England, Henry's use of Arthurian symbolism was less programmatic; before English gentry his claim to the throne had to be explicitly based, not on his Welsh patronym, but on his royal English genealogy traced through his mother, Lady Margaret Beaufort, descendant of John of Gaunt. Henry VII's succession nonetheless depended materially upon a Welsh fighting force and cultural feeling, even as the legality of his claim emphasized his rightful aristocratic pedigree. As Rees points out, Henry's Lancastrian claim, and historical accounts emphasizing it alone, obscure the political and historic importance of his Welsh popularity. Henry VII's succession was directly indebted to the troop of fighters he gathered on his 1485 march from Mill Bay in southwest Wales through the center of the Welsh principality and beyond the marches to Bosworth.[10]

King Henry VII would bolster the insecurity of his rule by courting the affections of the London establishment, moving forward on his promise to marry Elizabeth of York, Edward IV's daughter, whose genealogical claim to the throne was superior to his own.[11] And just as Henry VII, claiming Lancastrian inheritance, flies the banner of the red Welsh dragon at Westminster, Caxton's Malory brings Arthur home to London. Caxton's press makes stories of Arthur widely available for Londoners whose pleasures are crucial both to Henry VII's peaceful rule and to Caxton's financial stability. Caxton's press will establish the Middle English account of the popular Pendragon as a London sovereign. Arthur will, of course, reappear in Henry's use of spectacle and pageant, a program already well documented by Sidney Anglo.[12]

Riddy emphasizes the class implications of Arthur's popularity. And she identifies the colonial cast of England's relation to France, arguing in contrast to Walter Ullman, that we consider the similarities between "medieval" and "modern" imperial affairs. Yet Riddy's important analysis of Anglo-French affairs and class dynamics—dynamics that will also be important to my reading of Malory—leaves the colonial politics of insular British relations unexamined. Yet if Caxton's Malory offered diverse English soldiers access to aristocratic "gentility" in the late fifteenth century, such would also be the case for the similar class of men in Wales. Welsh loyalty was still very much a part of Arthur's popular appeal, and an important aspect of Arthur's identification, from time immemorial, with an insular native heritage.

Malory's Arthur resonates, as Riddy impressively argues, with such male, class identifications. Malory's text can also resonate with Caxton's emphasis upon Arthur's English identity; yet Malory does not simply celebrate Arthur as England's centralized monarch, at least not unequivocally. Nor does Malory register the absolute confidence in English endurance evinced by Caxton's prologue. Arthur's relation to geographic diversities will be important throughout Malory's text, but especially in the tale of Arthur's succession in Caxton's book I. In that story, aristocratic factionalism linked to region and geography is finally overcome through the popular support of the class of commoners. When the young Arthur claims the throne of his deceased father, Uther Pendragon, rival Kings from Wales, Scotland, and Ireland declare against him. Arthur does not surmount these rivals easily. Even after his succession, and at a celebratory feast held at Caerlion in Wales, Kings from Orkney, Scotland, Gore and Garloth (regions within the medieval kingdom of Scotland) challenge Arthur's rightful rule. Arthur triumphs when the commons "both ryche and poure" rise in united support of him. The description of the battle emphasizes Arthur's insularity, thus hinting at aristocratic factionalism as a function of insular intimacy:

And alweyes Kynge Arthur on horsback leyd on with a swerd and dyd merueillous dedes of armes. . . . Thenne Kynge Lot brake out on the bak syde, and the Kyng with the Honderd Kynghtes and Kynge Carados, and sette on Arthur fiersly behynde hym. With that Syre Arthur torned with his knyghtes and smote behynd and before, and euer Sir Arthur was in the formest prees tyl his hors was slayne vndernethe hym, and therwith Kyng Lot smote doune Kyng Arthur. With that his four knyghtes receyued hym and set hym on horsback. . . And thenne the comyns of Carlyon aroos with clubbis and stauys and slewe many knyghtes, but alle the kynges held them togyders with her knyghtes that were lefte on lyue and so fled and departed. (41)

A valiant Arthur is beset on all sides. Three enemy kings surround him striking at his body, his horse slain out from under him. The spatial orientation of the battle implies both an insularity to Arthur's position, and the dangerous treachery of back-stabbing: Lot brakes "out on the bak syde"; King Carados and the King of the Hundred Hands "sette on Arthur fiersly behynde hym." This king must watch his back; violent treachery comes here—as it does in the succession battles of the period—from peers of the realm in intimate proximity to a royal. Yet those peers retreat before an army of commoners who rise en masse with "clubbis and stauys" deploying whatever implements they have at hand to defend their sovereign. The image of a peasant force rising in defense of sovereign power seems a startling sovereign fantasy, especially ironic at the time, given that bands of commoners wielded clubs and staves in London riots early in Richard III's reign. During the Peasant's Revolt of 1381 and Jack Cade's insurrection in 1450 commoners also took up arms, but against, rather than for, representatives of sovereign governance. Yet while those events suggest the dangers popular rebellion pose to late medieval sovereignty, their memory also engages with the power of popular desire.

Here, as in debates about Arthur's historicity, the people are on Arthur's side. Arthur's popularity with the commons in both London and at Caerlion in Malory's text suggests the author's interest in power of the people for a monarchy whose legal ties to the throne are fragile or contested. The image of a popular army in Wales supporting an English Arthur against Scots resisters has consequences, moreover, for England's colonial ambitions and insular integrity. Loyal Welsh commoners rescue English sovereignty from Scottish aggression. Wales here supplies Arthur, the English king, with an army of commoners in defense of the crown.

Yet if Malory revels in the broad appeal of an English Arthur for the general class of commoners, his text also worries over the (albeit temporary) power of Arthur's challengers. Malory's story suggests the difficulties involved in consolidating aristocratic unity. Indeed, the legitimacy of Arthur's claim needs some defending throughout book I, and given the problematic nature of the evidence of Arthur's legitimacy, his skeptics could be wise not to be easily persuaded. Nor was Uther Pendragon's rule, the opening lines of the book suggest, entirely stable. While the story of Arthur's father seems at first to recollect the historic unity and wholeness to all England, a closer look reveals instead a unity just out of reach: "Hit befel in the dayes of Vther Pendragon, when he was Kynge of all Englond and so regned, that there was a myghty duke in Cornewaill that helde warre ageynst hym long tyme, and the duke was called the Duke of Tyntagil. And so by meanes Kynge Vther send for this duk, chargyng hym to brynge his wyf with hym, for she was called a fair lady and a passynge wyse, and her name was called Igrayne" (33). The text claims Uther's doubled sovereign title: he was king of all England, and he reigned as such. Such a claim recalls Yorkist indictments of King Henry VI said to rule England de facto, but not de jure; similar statements were made about Richard III, described in *The Great Chronicle of London*, as "kynge in dede but not of Right" (233).[13] Uther's doubled title insists that he is no illegitimate or titular figurehead. Uther's realm is cast as divided by the second clause of the opening sentence; the opening reference to de jure and de facto rule emerges, thus, as an anxious claim. Either the "all" of England Uther rules does not include Cornwall, or Uther remains only titular ruler there, his power compromised by the Duke's rebellion.

Uther's desire for Igraine offers a potential solution to his split kingdom, although not a particularly honorable one. Yet the text emphasizes neither this solution nor the dishonor of Uther's plan, but instead the powerful sovereign's powerlessness before love's tortures. Uther's desire, repeated twice, blends pleasure with unpleasure: "for pure angre and for grete loue of fayr Igrayne the Kyng Uther felle seke" (34); "[S]aid the Kynge, I am seke for angre and for loue of fayre Igrayne, that I may not be hool" (34). Intensely frustrated desire splits the sovereign in pieces.[14] In the context of the duke's regional rule and rebellion, Uther's crippling longing for Igraine points to (sexual) unification as an urgent, and painful, compulsion.[15]

Given the long medieval tradition of sexual coupling as a surrogate for war, Arthur's birth from Uther and Igraine's union could be expected to unite these former enemies unproblematically. Instead Arthur's parentage—who knows about it and when—becomes an acute problem for the early security of his rule. Even with a magician like Merlin at his service, Arthur's problems compound. When Merlin, knowing every detail of Uther's encounter with Igraine, attempts to testify to Arthur's legitimate patrimony, he describes the new sovereign as "Kyng Vther Pendragons sone, borne in wedlok, goten on Igrayne, the Dukes wyf of Tyntigail." Despite his assertion that Arthur was "born in wedlock," Merlin's is a particularly maladroit choice of words. Reminding the assembled that Igraine was Tintagel's wife merely reasserts the problem of Arthur's legitimacy at the very moment of its putative solution. Such testimony will certainly not reassure the assembled skeptics. At such moments Malory's text is determinedly equivocal about Arthur. Even if readers are meant to cheer Arthur's succession, anxieties of Arthur's paternity reverberate throughout book I. Given the secrecy surrounding the events of Arthur's birth and fosterage, even his mother Igraine's testimony is useless.

Significantly Merlin now responds with a prediction of a united future with England at its center: "or [Arthur] deye he shalle be long kynge of all Englond and haue vnder his obeyssaunce Walys, Yrland, and Scotland, and moo reames than I will now reherce" (40). Merlin's words remedy the problem of Arthur's heritage with the promise of a unified English hegemony. And in place of Arthur's troubled genealogy—and in response to the question of legitimacy—Merlin invokes a specific English future with supremacy over Wales, Ireland, and Scotland. Unlike vaguer references to Uther's kingdom, this is a specific, and colonizing, geography delineated through the realms of Wales, Ireland, and Scotland. Regions of the so-called "Celtic fringe" are obsessively conjured throughout this tale, their repetition an overdetermined assertion of the geographic unities the story's sovereign seeks. Wales and Cornwall, both sites of rebellious battle, are repeatedly named as explicit possessions of England's king. Sovereigns from Scotland, Wales, and Ireland repeatedly challenge Arthur's rightful rule, refusing to submit to a centralized King even after Arthur's sister marries one of them. Malory's confidence in Arthur's united rule seems, in light of such overdeterminations, anxious at best.

When Merlin uses the image of a united future to silence challenges to Arthur's sovereignty, he shows us how promises of a future hegemony can compensate for genealogical anxieties. Such prophecies place the imagination of a unified space *in* time, if in a future time. Imagining unification is thus shown to be a matter of both time and space, a future promise that can work, as Merlin fervently hopes, to banish genealogical doubts and the aggressive factionalism they produce. Yet given its context, Merlin's claim is more tentative than the formulation in Caxton's prologue; nonetheless space and time converge here as they did in Caxton's opening remarks. The spaces and times of these figurations do not oppose one another so much as weave a double helix, entwining and counterpointing. Malory's story of Arthur's succession anxiously addresses the problems of aristocratic factionalism by claiming that horizontally linked commoners willing to risk their lives to support their king can compensate for anxieties of legitimate inheritance. Malory gestures to the unifying power of a folk army, implying that a spontaneously united common army (specifically one in Wales) offers sufficient defense against rival kings from other places.

Malory thus emphasizes that horizontal bonds of a common class ground Arthur's support. Caxton's edition, adding to Malory's text a "table or rubrysshe of the contentse or chapytres" listing the most important events that follow, makes Arthur's story a usable reference text for such a common audience. Providing a twenty-eight page abstract for a volume comprising some six hundred pages, Caxton's rubric maps the stories that follow, as if to ensure that readers of the history of "this land then called Britain" not get lost among the details.[16] Structured as a royal biography beginning with Arthur's birth and ending with Arthur's death, Caxton's edition, Eugene Vinaver has famously argued, transforms Malory's compendium of romances into "a whole book." Scholars continue to debate whether Malory's text was itself moving in such a direction, yet Caxton's regularization and publication of Malory's text, rearranged as a single sovereign biography, can help us rethink "unity" as an activity promoted (if in a complicated way) by printing technology.[17]

Benedict Anderson has, famously, linked printing technologies with
the imaginary structure of national unities. He writes, "Nothing perhaps
more precipitated the search for new ways of thinking, nor made it more
fruitful, than print-capitalism, which made it possible for rapidly growing
numbers of people to think about themselves and to relate themselves to
others in profoundly new ways" (36). As I have been arguing, Caxton's
Malory promoted a certain version of Arthur's complex, contested tradition for a complex, increasingly metropolitan, national audience. Printing
technologies enabled the relatively inexpensive production (and thus wide
availability) of Caxton's Malory as the standardized edition of the history
of Arthur, an edition that would cast a long shadow for centuries to come.
However, I have also been suggesting that the version of Arthur's story
thus produced was not, as Anderson would have it, a radically "new way
of thinking." It amounted instead to a regionally interested account that
served the interests of a London elite and a "new" sovereign dynasty that
needed the affections of the commons—if the "rich" commons rather more
than the "poor" ones.

Anderson's key insight about the crucial contribution "print capitalism" makes to national imaginings is to the point. Yet because of the
complicated relation between regional particularity and Arthur's standard-
ization in Caxton's Malory, I take exception to the rhetoric of "profound"
and "radical" innovation here and elsewhere in Anderson's work. I am
suggesting that while there certainly were innovative aspects produced by
printing technologies, Anderson overstates his case and imagines innovation in nearly absolute terms. However, it is crucial to keep in mind that
the changes wrought by Caxton's Malory constituted not a profoundly
"new" way of thinking about Arthur or about community so much as it
constituted the solidification of certain particularly regional interests as a
front for a larger community claimed to be "national." As I noted in detail
in Chapter 6, unification often fronts narrow interests even while claiming ambitiously large, and communitarian, concerns. Caxton's Malory involves the ideological process of making particular regional interests seem,
through Arthur, to stand for the community of the whole realm.

Of course, the difficulty with which Malory's work hangs together
even in Caxton's edition suggests that unifying large, disparate, and contested story traditions (and the people who write and read them) is no easy
task. And yet, the very elusiveness of coherent artistic unity—the promise
of narrative coherence that seems here and there deferred or failed—can
become the means of cultivating a desire for it. Unfortunately, the disuni-

ties and inconsistencies of Caxton's Malory have not occasioned delight over the open-ended indeterminancies (at least until relatively recently), to say nothing of the contestations, of Arthurian history. In the context of this text's efforts to make a diverse story cohere in a single book, those moments tend to be viewed as evidence of the text's flaws. But that, again, is a reading experience that Caxton's Malory produces; this text works to make us want unity, but not because unity is entirely absent. We desire textual unity because this text makes it seems so near at hand; we desire it because Caxton's *Malory* has made it seem so possible.

If the 1485 edition of Caxton's *Malory* promotes Arthur, the central English sovereign as a front for the interests of a particular region and class, Malory's story nonetheless offers evidence that submission even to this beloved king is not unequivocally pleasurable. The central section of *Le Morte Darthur* narrates the fragility, and sometimes the deadliness, of union. In "The Tale of Balin," a particular knight, erstwhile challenger of Arthur, joins with his centralized sovereign only to die. Throughout the story of Balin desire for submission converges on death. Arthur will finally be rescued from the intimation that his united rule is death dealing. By the end of "Balin," we hear of Arthur's sponsorship not of the lethal barrenness of the Dolorous Stroke, but of the promise of Grail satisfaction. Yet Malory's text nonetheless allows us to read the tragedies and traumas that Arthurian unity entails.

Sovereign Dopplegängers: Doubling Forces

The relation of individual knights to Arthurian community emerges strikingly in Caxton's book II, "The Tale of Balin." The tale begins amid civil war, and with news of a rebellion led by King Ryons of North Wales with "a grete nombre of people." Arthur responds by sponsoring a tournament in London whereupon he is visited by the first of what will become a series of ladies. This first unnamed woman, gird with a sword from which she cannot free herself, seeks Arthur's help to find "a passyng good man of his handes and of his dedes," without villainy, treachery or treason who can "drawe oute the swerd oute of this shethe" (62–63). The adventure recalls Arthur's own past success at pulling stuck swords out of difficult places, and such an eerie coincidence is not lost on our king, who immediately tries his hand at the lady's sheath. The eeriness of this moment's return to the story of Arthur's succession continues as "moost all of the barons of the Round Table that were there at that tyme" follow him, but this time in repetitious imitation of their king's lack.

Arthur's failure with this sword inverts the circumstances of his succession, a scene in which the boy's amazing power over a stuck sword determined his right to assume his father's throne. "The Tale of Balin" doubles back on that earlier scene of sovereign success; Arthur's failure retrospectively casts a shadow. The episode revises Arthur's triumph and succession as an ambivalent occasion; its ambivalence comes back as "something which was repressed which recurs" (Freud, "Uncanny," 148). Freud identifies this kind of doubled uncertainty in feelings of the "uncanny" which result from "a conflict of judgment whether things which have been 'surmounted' and are regarded as incredible are not, after all, possible" (158). Questions about Arthur's succession, questions that have apparently been "surmounted" in book I, return in the image of Arthur's failure.

The incredible possibility of another outcome to the king's succession—Arthur's failure or Arthur's treachery—now haunts the court. The "poure knyght" who will succeed where Arthur failed and will rescue the nameless maiden imprisoned by the sword is, moreover, currently Arthur's prisoner. This knight (we will discover in good time that he is the eponymous Balin) identifies himself, in contrast to the king, as "a passyng good man . . . withoute vylonye or trecherye and withoute treason." As the jailer of this virtuous knight, Arthur may not be the virtuous Christian King of his reputation.

Christian virtue seems, moreover, particularly important here, as this is the tale that will set the stage for the obsessively Christianized Grail Quest. The "poure knight," Balin "le Saueage," is a Northumbrian soldier, eventually called "The Knight with Two Swords." He will ultimately strike the "Dolorous Stroke" on King Pellam, destroying three countries and rendering the land barren with "the peple dede, slayne on euery syde . . .[while] alle that were on lyue cryed" (75). The apocalyptic scene of loss produced by the Dolorous Stroke is the inverted twin of Grail satisfaction, later glimpsed in sweet smells and dazzling satisfactions. Moreover, Balin is a twin himself, and the personal tragedy he follows through to the end of this tale is fratricide: Balin will kill his brother Balan with the sword he takes from the woman at Arthur's court.

Balin at first figures, however, as King Arthur's doppelgänger, and Balin's fortunes eerily double the King's.[18] Like Balin, Arthur is "The Knight with Two Swords," one pulled from the stone in his boyhood, another given to him by the Lady of the Lake. Balin's death is mediated by Merlin, as Arthur's birth is mediated by Merlin. Finally, Balin's body is interred on a "litle iland," his sword "put in a marbel stone [which] . . . houed alweyes aboue the water" (78); Arthur's fatally wounded body removes to the island of Avalon, his sword Excalibur thrown back into the water out of which it came. Although the existence of Balin's twin brother eventually defines twinning as an identical physical resemblance among kin, the reader's attention is repeatedly directed toward Balin's uncanny doubling of Arthur's fortunes sustained from the tale's beginning to its end.

"The Tale of Balin" is obsessed with processes of twinning and with untimely and accidental deaths. While still at Arthur's court, Balin provokes the king's anger by killing the court's second female visitor—the Lady of the Lake, Arthur's benefactress, giver of his sword Excalibur—as vengeance for her earlier murder of Balin's mother. An Irish knight, Launceor, takes up Arthur's vengeful cause against Balin. Balin and Launceor will meet in the forest and the scene of their battle produces two more deaths: the Irish Launceor's and his unnamed beautiful paramour. The scene of Launceor's lady's death displays the text's uncanny turns. She comes upon Balin just after he has slain her lover:

[Balin] loked by hym and was ware of a damoysel that cam rydynge ful fast as the hors myghte ryde on a fayr palfroy. And whan she aspyed that Launceor was slayne she made sorowe oute of mesure and sayd, O Balyn, two bodyes thou has slayne in one herte, and two hertes in one body, and two soules thow hast lost. And therwith she toke the swerd from her loue that lay ded and fylle to the ground in a swowne, and whan she aroos she made grete dole out of mesure, the whiche sorowe greued Balyn passyngly sore. And he wente vnto her for to haue taken the swerd oute of her hand, but she helde it so fast, he myghte not take it oute of her hand onles he shold haue hurte her, and sodenly she sette the pomell to the ground and rofe herself thorow the body. (67)

The Lady's moan renders herself Launceor's twin inside and out. Two bodies, they beat with a single heart; their two hearts are encased in a single body. The scene of her death, moreover, enacts its own kind of doubleness: she weeps and moans twice; swooning once, she revives herself only to fall suicidally on Launceor's sword. While the text describes the moment of her death coming on "sodenly," the extended description of her sorrowful swooning leaves us wondering why it took Balin so long to wrest the sword out of her hand.

Balin turns away from the scene of double corpses, "ashamed that so fair a damoysell had destroyed herself for the loue of his deth," and repent-

ing himself "the deth of this knyght for the loue of this damoysel" (67).
Yet Balin's glosses on the scene strangely reverse the events. His statement
of shame transposes the lady's motives: she killed herself on account of the
death of her love, not for "the loue of his deth." Balin's formulation of
repentance, likewise, inverts the character of events. While Balin describes
Launceor's death "for the loue of this damoysel," two paragraphs earlier
the text made it clear that the knight died "to reuenge the despyte [Balin]
dyd . . . to Kyng Arthur and to his courte" (66). In the scene Balin has just
witnessed, it is the lady who dies for the love of her knight, and not, as
Balin describes it, the knight for the love of his lady.

Balin's chiasmatic reversals imply that for him these two bodies, and
their actions, are interchangeable. Indeed, it implies, as do the lady's last
words, that Launceor and his paramour are the same person. This scene
of twinning shows that doubleness can, especially in a scene of death,
represent singularity. Freud, following the work of Otto Rank, describes
the "invention of doubling" as "a preservation against extinction"; he also
links it to the disciplining function of the ego-ideal (superego) and to
"all those strivings of the ego which adverse external circumstances have
crushed and all our suppressed acts of volition which nourish in us the
illusion of free will" ("Uncanny," 141–42). Homi Bhabha and Julia Kristeva
both remind us that Freud's "uncanny" resonates with the submissions
required by national communities. Dopplegängers split acts of crushing
submission from those of apparent "free will." There is thus a psychoanalytic logic to the episode before us: Launceor's death as submission to
Arthur's kingship becomes, with his beautiful suicidal double, her freely
chosen desire for him in death. In Balin's fantasy she "destroy[s] herself
for the loue of his deth." Death is loved, embraced, freely chosen by a
beautiful lady; and the knight dies, so Balin tells us, for her love and not
from submission to a conquering king.[19]

Doubling here offers psychic protection against singular submission
to Arthur, a submission even unto death, to what Herbert Marcuse calls
"compliance with the Master over death" (76). Fantasies of gender are
crucial to this psychic protection. Here they reproduce a formula familiar
from the other romances: a beautiful lady's submission to death gains for
a Knight (in this case Balin) the fantasy of a masculine free will, while
simultaneously offering desire for beauty as a substitute for the anxiety of
death. The words on Launceor's tomb later assert that he desired his death,
his epitaph testifying that he was slain "at his owne request" by the hand of
Balin (68). Gender, death, and doubling transform submission unto death

into desire itself. Thus it is no surprise that the formerly rebellious Balin will testify to his desire for Arthur's worship at the very moment that he leaves behind the doubled dead bodies: "for he is the moost worshipful knyght that regneth now on erthe, and his loue wil I gete" (67).

Significant, too, are the geographic particularities of the episode. In the midst of a war with Wales, an Irish knight displays devotion to a king at Winchester. His devotion unto death, moreover, impels a knight from Northumberland to seek communion with the King who once imprisoned him. As Balin is transformed from recalcitrant rebel to dutiful subject, this story suggests that submission to centralized sovereignty is synergistic; one submission produces another. The image of a beautiful dead woman, moreover, marks devoted submission as desirable, beautiful, and poignant; the dead woman stands as the apparently beautiful (and desirable) devotion moving inside Balin's resistant Northumbrian heart.

Submission to Arthur's kingship remains of central importance throughout the remainder of the tale. The doubling redoubles. Immediately following the scene of remorse, Balin and his twin brother Balan appear together, worrying together over "the deth of the Lady of the Lake, and how Kyng Arthur was displeasyd" (67). They determine to "preue [their] worship and prowesse" (67) upon King Ryons with whose rebellious aggressions, we may remember, the tale began. "We wil helpe eche other as bretheren ought to do," Balan opines to his brother. Yet we have already been warned that Balin will kill the brother pledged to help him. Once Balan arrives on the scene, the two figures merge in and out of one another disturbingly; indeed the multiple spellings of their names—Balan, Balen, Balin, and Balyn—make it difficult to keep track of their activities, or their words, as distinct from one another.

By the middle of "The Tale of Balin," we are anxious to have the events and characters sorted out for us; we look toward some resolution, a respite from all these confusing doubles and from the repetitive invocations of the ever-expanding "mene whyle" within which everything seems to happen. As if in response, in the scene after Balan and Balin's meeting, the narrative swerves suddenly back to Ryons, the Welsh rebel king, and to the story of the twins' victory over Arthur's greatest enemy. The battle itself takes less than two sentences. Something other than the strategies of war are at stake here. Instead of those fascinations, the moment of triumph over Ryons offers the consolation that doubles nonetheless can produce useful unities: Balan and Balin forge their union with Arthur by forcing Ryons into united fellowship with their king.

To be sure, and as we might expect, the wholeness glimpsed in the moment of Ryons's submission is fleeting. The very next episode tells of Arthur's wars this time with Ryons's brother Nero and Lot of Orkeney. Merlin now foretells that Balin will strike the Dolorous Stroke that will cause "grete dommage in [three] countrayes" (75). The text's early doubleness now verges into uncountable factioning and chaos with Merlin interjecting, now and then, moments of prophetic clarity.[20]

Unity comes and with it the tomb. At the end of the war, the families of the former enemies come together to commemorate their dead warriors:

So at the enterement cam Kynge Lots wyf, Morgause, with her foure sones, Gawayne, Agrauayne, Gaherys, and Gareth. Also ther came thyder Kyng Vryens, Syr Ewayns fader, and Morgan le Fay, his wyf, that was Kyng Arthurs syster. Alle these cam to the enterement. But of alle these XII kynges, Arthur lete make the tombe of Kynge Lot passyng rychely, and made his tombe by his owne. And thenne Arthur lete make XII ymages of laton and couper, and ouergylt hit with gold in the sygne of XII kynges, and ech on of hem helde a tapyr of wax that brent day and nyght. And Kyng Arthur was made in sygne of a fygure standynge aboue hem with a swerd drawen in his hand, and alle the XII fygures had countenaunce lyke vnto men that were ouercome.

   All this made Merlyn by his subtyl crafte, and ther he told the kyng, whan I am dede, these tapers shalle brenne no lenger, and soone after, the aduentures of the Sangrayll shalle come among yow and be encheued. Also he told Arthur how Balyn the worshipful knyght, shal gyue the dolorous stroke, wherof shalle falle grete vengeaunce. (71)

Arthur's image in tin and copper presides over twelve copper kings, fixed in iconic rule of the community which eluded him while those kings were alive. Their memento mori, twelve figures with "countenaunce lyke vnto men that were ouercome," give witness to a totality, an Arthurian completion. These rebel kings are double and mute witnesses: their dead bodies testify to Arthur's triumph. Merlin's immediate prophecy of death, the Sangreall and Dolorous Stroke, however, foregrounds the ambivalence of the moment, as does the material out of which those statues are formed. Their gold is all gilding, a beautiful overlay of baser metals. This union is all image and no substance. It is, moreover, a scene of mournful deaths. Merlin's reminder of the future Grail quest hints at an apparently more satisfying, and life giving, union still to come.

If the scene of Lot's entombment marks the ambivalence of Arthur's melancholy commemorations, Balin's earlier resemblance to Arthur provides an opportunity to repudiate the king's involvement in fratricide and civil war. Civil war will be banished by the tale's ending in Balin and Balan's final lethal encounter. When Balin accidentally kills his brother Balan, their fraternity is recognized at the moment of their double deaths in chilling figures of womb and tomb: "[T]hey made her mone eyther to other and sayd, we came both oute of one wombe, that is to say one moders bely, and so shalle we lye both in one pytte" (78). Balin and Balan's morbid reunion recapitulates their especially intense kinship bond.

Their brotherhood is dramatically intimate, its memories more intense than the usual ties of kin. Arthur, too, has unusually dramatic ties to kin. Indeed, the cause of Lot's aggression against Arthur, and thus the cause of Arthur's continuing civil war throughout "The Tale of Balin," has been that "Arthur lay by Kyng Lots wyf, the whiche was Arthurs syster, and gat on her Mordred" (70). Images of incest are also ways of registering an excessive kind of intimacy, one which, we have already heard at this point, will end in tragedy. Arthur's incestuous union with his sister produces the son who finally ruins everything. Yet by the end of Balin's tale we are positioned at the graveside, not of Arthur, but of twin Knights from Northumberland: Balan who was slain by his brother and "Balyn le Saueage, that was the Knyght with the Two Swerdes and He that Smote the Dolorous Stroke" (78).

With Balin's death the similarities between Balin and Arthur are split in two: Balin "le saueage" the wild knight, is overly aggressive and vengeful; his aggression murders brotherhood, ushering in the Dolorous Stroke. And if in its earlier doubling of Arthur and Balin, the story raises intimations of Arthur's treachery, those anxieties are temporarily banished with Balin's death. For if Arthur was treacherous and Balin righteous, as the episode of the maiden's sword implied, how could Balin produce such horrors as the Dolorous Stroke? How could a righteous and true knight be so foolish as to kill his own brother? Arthur, in contrast to a dead Balin, will sponsor the Grail quest, repaying awful destruction with regeneration, creativity, and transcendence.

"The Tale of Balin" thus provides a narrativization of union and singularity through a long and confusing deferral of those very qualities. Through its twinning and its splitting the tale considers the possibility of a king's treachery in a time of civil war, yet finally reworks anxiety about treacherous rule into confidence in a sovereign committed to holy recovery. This text thus alludes to Arthurian traditions critical of Arthur—traditions which, like Balin, hail from the north of the island—as well as to the problems that submission to a centralized authority poses to individual knights from those regions. In response to those problems, "The

Tale of Balin" displays Balin's transformation from recalcitrant North-erner to dutiful, if dead, subject. And it shows that Arthur's dopplegänger from Northumberland (the "other" Arthur read perhaps in *Sir Gawain and the Green Knight*, *Awntyrs off Arthure*) comes to serve Malory's Arthur at Winchester. "The Tale of Balin" displays narrative regularization and centralization, its losses as well as its accomplishments.

Yet the tale of Balin is a deeply mournful tale. It repetitively links regularization and centralization with death, suggesting that the sacrifices demanded by unity are profound. Balin's death can, thus, testify to the losses unity produces. It has not, however, often been read in these terms. Beverly Kennedy, for example, reads the apparent necessity of Balin's end. She writes, "Balin's heroic code of ethics and his fatalist world view must be transcended if Arthurian society is to avoid self-destruction" (9). De-scribing the categories of medieval knighthood legible in Malory, Kennedy identifies Balin (like Gawain) as the "heroic" knight, one like "Roland or Beowulf" for whom "there is nothing better than a fine weapon. Balin does not distinguish between his enemies and God's enemies" (221). An ability to blend one's perspective with God's perspective is, of course, the ideological function of Galahad's success in the Grail quest. In this read-ing, a knight like Balin deserves to be lost, unable to transform his interior in *Imitatio Christi*. The submissions gained in the name of divine imitation will become evident shortly; in Balin's case, however, his failure to remake his heart so as to repudiate vengeance (and, in Kennedy's logic, deserve sur-vival) has a great deal to do with the protections his death gains for Arthur. If Balin's death can be said to be at all necessary, Malory's text implies that its necessity serves the compensatory politics of sovereign unity.

Of course, despite Kennedy's implication that it could, Arthurian society does not avoid self-destruction either. Arthur's eventual failure means that he never does consolidate glorious unity in explicitly political terms. The inexorable drive toward Arthurian failure in Malory's text reg-isters, I would argue, less of an interest in the salvific potential of pious morality, than in the problem of loss, of endings, of hopeless impossibility. Moreover, in detailing the structure of submission as the production of such hapless, monumental losses, Malory's story also allows us, if only momentarily, to ask whether Arthur's sovereignty is worth the price it exacts.

Of course those questions may well be turned aside in Malory's move to the Grail Quest. When Caxton's Malory shifts from scenes of territo-rial fracturing to Grail ineffabilities it switches the register within which "unity" operates from an explicitly geopolitical category to a spiritually transcendent one. That metamorphosis marks unity as a kind of holy interiority, a spiritualized category encrypted in the hearts of true believers. This interiorization of desires for union, moreover, renders certain kinds of geopolitical loyalties and affiliations as usefully passing, their pleasures encrypted in the memories of their losses.[21]

The figure of Balin also, however, links loss and death with female bodies, as if to protect Arthurian culture—its identity and the history it tells—from the suffocating terrors of the grave. Julia Kristeva argues that links between the feminine and death offer "a pretext for uncanny strangeness" (*Strangers*, 185), expressed in xenophobic attitudes toward the foreigner. Uncanny strangeness, moreover, inhabits the boundaries of "the fragile . . . uncertain self"; it haunts as well the places between "imagination and reality" (*Strangers*, 188). Questions of a fragile English boundary, we noted, were a concern of the author of *The Libel of English Policy*; conflicts between imagination and reality have haunted Arthurian traditions since the days of Geoffrey of Monmouth.

In the Grail story wholeness is conjured as a transcendent, religious experience. The relation of Grail quest to Christian traditions of incarnation and resurrection implicitly argues that the death to which Balin submits is not the final word. It implies too that commemorations like the one Arthur devises for Lot's grave are flimsy, cheap duplications of the "real" thing. Freud has noted the value of religious ideals for a people, as protective compensation for the "sufferings and privations which a . . . life in common has imposed on them" (*Illusion*, 22). The Grail registers these sufferings and privations. I turn now to consider the pertinence of such religious tropes for a national fantasy, attending to the continuing elusive unity offered by the Sangreall, a unity argued to offer satisfactions beyond the most devastating loss.

Malory's Sangreall: An Imagined Community of Believers

The central books of Caxton's Malory move us from one knight's story to the next. Only at moments of explicit transition—at the beginnings and endings of the various books—are we reminded that the hero demanding our immediate attention has obligations beyond his adventuring. While the text repeatedly asserts the existence of its brotherhood, it only makes those unities palpable in the final narrative of their dissolution. As readers, we feel much like Arthur when, early in book XIII, "The Departure on the Grail Quest," he gathers his troop to bid them farewell: "Now, sayd the kyng, I am sure at this quest of the Sancgreal shall alle ye of the Table Round departe, and neuer shall I see yow ageyne hole togyders. Therfor I will see yow alle hole togyders in the medowe of Camelot to iuste and to torneye, that after your dethe men maye speke of hit, that suche good knyghtes were holy togyders such a day" (431). Arthur's formulation doubles togetherness as bodily wholeness and united community. The whole and healed bodies of Arthur's knights stand in a whole and healed fellowship. Yet the chant-like repetition of the phrase "hole togyder" intones this brotherhood as it mournfully passes. Arthur emphasizes the community's fragility; he predicts absence and loss beyond recuperation. To gain the Sangreall, Arthur's knights must lose one another; they must sacrifice particular affections for the putatively ineffable satisfactions of transcendent life.

Textually the community in Arthur's field soon gives way to unity figured through a simultaneity of Grail quests, the repetitive invocation of an unending temporal "meanwhile" during which the Grail knights search. They leave Camelot one by one, yet each seeks the same quest; each brother follows a unique series of adventures, yet all at the same time. Occasional glimpses of the Sangreall, moreover, register in satisfactions both corporate and individual, particular visions that are always part of a larger communitarian dream. Grail union thus criss-crosses a view of the particular subject with an image of transcendent community. Offering heavenly satisfactions both individually tailored and formed through collective desire, Malory's Grail quest elaborates the particularity of the subject's place in community, an imagined believing community linked to Christian theological traditions.

While Benedict Anderson precludes the pertinence of (medieval) religious collectivities like the Grail to national affections, Malory's Grail quest reverberates with the kind of time Anderson reserves for national imaginings. According to Anderson the nation requires "an idea of 'homogeneous, empty time' in which simultaneity is, as it were, transverse, cross-time, marked not [as in medieval time] by prefiguring and fulfillment, but by temporal coincidence, and measured by clock and calendar" (24). This putatively "modern" simultaneity, described as "a complex gloss upon the word 'meanwhile'" (25), results in a subject's internal awareness of the existence of a field of people linked socially and acting simultaneously despite separation. This experience of temporal coincidence and spatial dislocation, Anderson argues, becomes technologically available to citizens as readers in the eighteenth century, specifically through the novel and the newspaper.

Anderson's notion of simultaneity resonates with the repetitive "meanwhile" in which Malory's Grail quest occurs. One could object that Anderson's time of clock and calendar is not all that new in the eighteenth century, nor is it a necessarily secular mode. The medieval liturgical calendar, the monastic office, books of hours also ensured an awareness of acts "performed at the same clocked and calendrical time." Simultaneity of time across space was used in religious communities as an explicit way of creating international bonds across Europe, a fact that troubles Anderson's implication that such simultaneity is per se a national formulation. Admittedly, the awareness of simultaneity Anderson describes pertains to a reading public—his exemplum is the "typical novel plot." Readers of the novel can see that characters in the novel who don't know one another are, in fact, linked. Referring to these readers, Anderson writes, "only they, like God, watch [the characters] all at once. That all these acts are performed at the same clocked, calendrical time, but by actors who may be largely unaware of one another shows the novelty of this imagined world, conjured up by the author in his readers' minds" (26). Anderson's "new" notion of simultaneity, he would argue, complicates the simultaneity of medieval monastic communities across Europe who also use texts to imagine shared spaces of Vespers, Prime, and Compline, during Advent, Lent, or Ordinal Time.

Yet when Anderson ascribes to his readers a God-like ability to see all the events they view and link them transcendentally, he indicates links between religious notions of transcendence and national formulations. Categories of transcendental communities—and of locations "above" from which to view individuals as part of a larger, over-arching society to which they belong—have historic implications with longstanding notions of community as a spiritual union transcending the material disjunctions of space and time. In traditions of Western Europe, moreover, such formulations are deeply linked, as Kantorowicz shows, with the theology of the mystical body of Christ imagined as a community of believers. Anderson's emphasis on "firm and stable" societies which link disparate individuals, furthermore, reinscribes transcendent categories like "Christendom," or the "social" in ways that make the community's dependence upon the materiality of particular bodies disappear. His hypothetical novel plot (in which characters figured with the abstract placeholders "A," "B," "C," and

"D," engage in secret romantic liaisons) deploys abstraction in a way that obscures the physical particularity (and the physical links) between the novel's characters.[22] The awareness of similarity Anderson describes is, moreover, available to readers of Caxton's Malory, both in the Grail quest and in invocation of the time of "meanwhile" throughout the larger text. For all his interest in the importance of various "simultaneities," Anderson's account proves unable to account for the simultaneity of religious and national ties. Caxton's Malory offers precisely this convergence.

In Caxton's book XI, "The Birth of Galahad," religious and national tropes converge.[23] In the episode in King Pelles's country, Lancelot fulfills an ambiguous prophecy at which point he gains a glimpse of the Grail. Happening upon a lady imprisoned, on account of her beauty, in a cauldron of boiling water, Lancelot rescues her, whereupon he is immediately asked to rescue her country threatened by "a serpent . . . in a tombe" (400). Arriving at the tomb, Lancelot reads the following inscription written in gold: "Here shalle come a lybard of Kynges Blood and he shalle slee this serpent, and this lybard shalle engendre a lyon in this foreyn countrey, the whiche lyon shall passe alle other knyghtes." This prophecy, reminiscent of the Galfridic symbolism linked to vaticinatory typologies and political poetry examined in Chapter 2, foretells Lancelot's victory over the serpent and the birth of his son Galahad. King Pelles introduces himself to Lancelot, and Malory's intertextual allusions shift from early British symbolism to early Christian tradition:

My name is, sayd the kyng, Pelles, Kynge of the Foreyn Countrey and cosyn nyghe vnto Ioseph of Armathye. And thenne eyther of them made moche of other, and soo they wente into the castel to take theyr repaste. And anone there came in a douue at a wyndow, and in her mouth there semed a lytel censer of gold, and therwithalle there was suche a sauour as alle the spyecery of the world had ben there. And forthwithall there was vpon the table al maner of metes and drynkes that they coude thynke vpon. Soo came in a damoysel passynge fayre and younge, and she bare a vessel of gold betwixe her handes, and therto the kynge kneled deuoutely and said his prayers, and soo dyd alle that were there. O Ihesu, said Sir Launcelot, what maye this meane? Thys is, said the kynge, the rychest thyng that ony man hath lyuyng, and whanne this thynge goth aboute, the Round Table shall be broken. And wete thow wel, said the kynge, this is the Holy Sancgreal that ye haue here sene. (400–401)

Recognized as the fulfillment of Galfridic symbolism, Lancelot immediately glimpses the Grail. The Grail feast, moreover, foregrounds satisfaction through the interior spaces of castles and minds. The company contemplates the wonderful repast, and when the beautiful damsel brings forward the golden cup, they do not drink, but "kneel devoutely and [say] their prayers." The physicality of the Grail's description conceives community as individuals united in contemplation. Kneeling together, their privatized interiors join in corporate devotion. They are literally a community of believers who will long remember the vision and yearn for its sweetness.

Interiorized devotion and memory are features of late medieval mystical discourse. In medieval mysticism, visual imagery produces a sensory awareness of the divine so as to enrich the believer's union with God. According to Augustine, human beings perceive divine realities through their bodily senses, spiritual union is etched on the senses, even as sensory metaphors are described as flimsy shadows of divine ineffability. Such mystical visions were understood to have communitarian ramifications, bestowing grace not only on the seer but also on members of her religious foundation or church. Marina Warner notes that for Thomas Aquinas apparitions and visions conferred "extraordinary grace on the visionaries and through them on the members of the Church to which they belonged" (300). Visions offered, even perhaps especially during the period of Reformation, "vivid proof of God's continuing colloquium" with the believing community.[24]

Yet this religious symbolism does not, as Anderson would have it, register discontinuities to the affairs of a corporate state. For similarities between Malory's description of the Grail and late-medieval coronation ritual are equally striking. State regalia described in both the *Little Device for the Coronation of Richard III*, and the *Liber Regalis* include the Grail-like descriptions. The *Little Device* describes the "a chalis of gold, a patene of the same, a septre with the dove and a rod of gold for the Kyng, and with a septre of everye also with a dove, and an other rod of golde for the Quene" (216). The *Liber Regalis* includes a golden cup and paten, and four scepters, two with the sign of a dove atop them.[25] With the exception of the crown, chalice, paten, and scepters constituted the most important symbols of coronation (229).

Anne Sutton and P. W. Hammond point to the increasing mystification of kingship rituals during the fifteenth century. From mid-century onward, and in response to the problems of English kingship, sovereigns were likely to receive communion under both species, a privilege usually reserved entirely for priests, during the mass of coronation.[26] The grail cup has long been associated with the communion cup, and royal communicants partaking of both bread and wine surrounded by incense, satin, and gold lent credence to the view, advanced even by a sober legal theorist like John Fortescue, that following their coronations kings had grail-like powers to heal.[27] The century also saw an increased use of a specifically English holy oil for sovereign anointing (Sutton and Hammond, 9), the use of what we might call "national coronation oil." According to the standard legend, the Virgin Mary appeared to Thomas à Becket giving him oil to be used in the coronation of English kings.[28] Distinct from sacerdotal chrism used to anoint bishops and priests, a vial of coronation oil was passed down with the royal regalia, specifically reserved for English kings. The oil of Thomas à Becket, moreover, was linked to a prophecy of future English kings who would "peacefully recover certain of the old domains" (Sutton and Hammond, 8). According to Rosemary Horrox, Richard III himself was associated with a similar prophetic legend, one promising victory over Welsh and Scots, and linked to his patronage of the chapel of St. Mary's in the church of All Hallows Barking by the Tower.[29]

Developments like these prompt Sutton and Hammond to conclude that fifteenth-century England "advanced toward a theocratic theory of kingship partly due to the difficulties the English kings found themselves in once there was a disputed succession" (8).[30] The ceremonies of investiture described by Sutton and Hammond gain mystical power, moreover, through a dramatic display of secrecy and silence. At key moments—during portions of the anointing, and at communion—the sovereign was shielded behind a white silk screen. Sovereign sacramental moments figure as holy of holies, a spectacle visible only through its invisiblity as a hidden and mysterious transaction. The English crown becomes a magnum mysterium beyond even the most aristocratic gaze or touch. Yet, as Sutton and Hammond note, even the captivating spectacle of Richard III's coronation could not protect him from sovereign sacrilege: "No anointing or coronation could save Richard III's body from ignominious treatment after he lost the battle of Bosworth and allowed his 'guilt' to be 'proved' by his defeat" (11). Their statement alludes to the fact that Henry VII's victory at Bosworth would be interpreted with a different kind of royal mystification. That victory would be read as the sign of divine sanction for his kingship, a view Kantorowicz links to later articulations of royal rule by "divine right." These rituals of coronation, and the theories and legends that surround them, display national sovereign ceremonies replete with sacred figures and forms. Mysticism bolsters particular English kings against problems of communitarian instability.

These are, moreover, particularly resonate images for our consideration of Malory's Grail quest, since that story too details religious devotion
amid the instabilities of community. As Arthur's knights prepare to leave
Camelot to follow the Grail, they glimpse its mysteries once more. In
this instance, the Grail is ushered in with creaks and thunderous blasts,
accompanied by bright light and "the grace of the Holy Ghoost":

Thenne beganne euery knyghte to behold other, and eyther sawe other by theire
semynge fayrer than euer they sawe afore. Not for thenne there was no knyght
myghte speke one word a grete whyle, and soo they loked euery man on other
as they had ben dome. Thenne ther entred into the halle the Holy Graile couerd
with whyte samyte, but ther was none myghte see hit nor who bare hit. And there
was al the halle fulfylled with good odoures, and euery knyght had suche metes an
drynkes as he best loued in this world. And whan the Holy Grayle had be borne
thurgh the halle, thenne the Holy Vessel departed sodenly that they wyste not
where hit becam. (432)

Utopian brotherhood offers a uniquely individualized succor. Visual pleasures are shared brother-with-brother, while individuals savor sumptuous
delicacies entirely their own. Grail vision idealizes Arthur's knights for
one another. The sensory delights provided offer a distinctly individual,
yet also corporate satisfaction. The fellowship of the Grail promises the
satisfaction of a unity that (amazingly) also preserves particular individual
desires.

   The communitarian fellowship of Grail belief also, however, makes
the physical community vanish. In its place rises a desire within each knight
to recover the apparently perfect satisfactions they have briefly glimpsed.
Gawain takes up the charge: "We haue ben serued this daye of what metes
and drynkes we thoughte on, but one thynge begyled vs: we myght not
see the Holy Grayle, it was soo precyously couerd. Wherfor I wil make
here auowe, that tomorne withoute lenger abydyng I shall laboure in the
quest of the Sancgreal" (432). In Gawain's statement desire comes both
with the memory of a physical satisfaction given, and as a longing for
an elusive vision withheld. On the quest, individual knights display their
bravery and courage through an interiorized resolve of purity. Perceval,
Bors, and Galahad will gain ineffable signs of divine union. For them Grail
delights become, finally, the beatific vision of the face of God and a reunion of knightly brothers—Bors and Perceval, and finally Galahad—as a
communion of saints beyond earthly physicality.

   But Grail is also, and crucially, a cosmological healing for a particular

land. Logres, the Wasteland, once rendered barren by a Dolorous Stroke
is made whole:

This [grail] shyp aryued in the realme of Logrys, and that tyme was dedely werre
bytwene Kynge Labor, whiche was fader vnto the Maymed Kynge, and Kynge
Hurlame, whiche was a Sarasyn. . . . and [Kynge Hurlame] came oute and fond
Kyng Labor, the man in the world of al Crystendom in whome was thenne the
grettest feythe. And . . . Kynge Hurlame dressid this suerd and smote hym vpon
the helme soo hard that he clafe hym and his hors to the erthe . . . And hit was
in the realme of Logrys, and soo bifelle grete pestylence and grete harme to both
realmes. For sythen encrecyd neyther corne ne grasse nor wel nyghe no fruyte, ne
in the water was no fysshe, werfor men callen hit, the landes of the two marches,
the Waste Land, for that dolorous stroke. (484)

Logres's Wasteland is England's elusive shadow. The image resonates with
England's losses and haunts the fringes of England's frontiers. Just as
Arthur is the sovereign with two swords, Logres, in Malory's description,
is a country of "two realms": "the landes of the two marches." We are given
no precise indication of what geographic site is intended, despite the fact
that Malory's geographies are elsewhere quite precise. Juxtaposed against
the kind of geographic particularity one finds, for example, in Malory's
aside that Astrolat is the town "that is now in Englyssh called Gylford"
(515), Logres seems a purposely ambiguous place. Such ambiguity, a space
both everywhere and nowhere, evokes I argue a kind of national space as
related to individual believing hearts, and transcending, particular regional
geographies.

The elusive neverland of Logres uncannily doubles the geography
of Arthur's kingdom. In Geoffrey of Monmouth's *Historia*, Logres is
the name for the specific region of England. In Malory, on the other
hand, Logres emerges as the uncanny itself: literally *unheimleich*, not there,
Logres is also *heimleich*, a region Balin and Lancelot have visited before,
and a kind of home for Galahad, since Pelles, the maimed king, is his grandfather. A space of ruin poised for a cosmological healing, Logres seems
both strange and familiar. In place of geographic particularity, we are given
religious clarity: the battle in Logres is between King Labor "the man in
the world of al Crystendom in whome was thenne the grettest feythe,"
and King Hurlame, "a sarasyn." Categories of Christian holiness provide
a clear opposition between the virtuous and the villainous. Perceval's virginal sister directs Galahad to the Sword with the Strange Girdles—the
sword that will save Logres—patiently explaining the history of that holy
relic, from Adam through the biblical Kings David and Solomon. In the

midst of this tale of mystical reliquaries, armed men interrupt challenging Bors, Perceval, and Galahad as members of Arthur's court. The battle that follows testifies to Christian belief: Bors, Perceval, and Galahad are virtuous even though they slay a "grete multytude of peple" (489), who "were not crystened" (490).

The image of Christian knights "virtuously" killing the unbaptized evokes, of course, the history of Crusade. Such a picture, moreover, links Logres's healing to colonizing crusaders, who strive to inculcate belief— and gain the conversion—of the strange others who challenge them. The identification of Arthur's knights with crusading rhetoric renders the enemies of Arthur's centralized court heathen unbelievers who merit all the horrible and violent punishments aggressive Christian culture visits on apostates, heretics, pagans, and Jews.[31] Logres's healing apparently pertains to interior states of belief. With this in mind we can begin to see collocations between national identity in fifteenth-century Britain and Christian orthodoxy. Such collocations help explain why fifteenth-century Lollards were frequently charged with crimes of treason and sedition.[32] In the face of an increasingly diverse population especially in and around London, questions of belief become vibrantly evocative for an exploration of national identifications as interior states.[33]

Malory's Grail knights are, moreover, described with particular reference to interior states, and to their purity as "virgins" and "maidens." Kathleen Kelly links these repetitious formulations with descriptions in medieval gynecological tracts describing the intact membrane of the hymen in virginal girls (52–71). In those descriptions, Kelly argues, the Grail knights remain masculine figures who are loyally untouched inside, united with God and, through their shared wholeness, with one another as Arthur's best knights. Untouched knights, holy and intact, offer inviolate male interiors. Such virginal interiors can, or so the Grail story argues, heal Logres from the devastations of pestilence, war, and famine.

Through the power of such putatively pure intact belief, Logres, England's shadow, also rises from desolation. Through its destruction and healing, Logres, the Wasteland, has become both the fearful specter of England's potential barrenness and the sign of its future wholeness. The Grail quest thus implicitly argues that like Logres, England can gain generativity—the promise of a future—through an interiorized belief utterly untouched by unholy loves or impure loyalties.[34]

Significantly however Malory's text, in Caxton's edition, does not end with cosmological healing or utopian unification. It ends, instead, with

Arthur's mournful losses. What are we to make of the move to sovereign loss after the promise of the Grail? Indeed, Caxton's Malory moves all along inexorably in the direction of Arthur's death. This is, after all, the tale of *Le Morte Darthur*. Arthur's sisters, the four Queens, come together for the first time as they bear Arthur's wounded body. Morgan le Fey, the queen of North Galys, the queen of the Wasteland, and Nimue, the Lady of the Lake, carry him back to a place he has never been before. Their healing returns Arthur to an ancient heritage and family and promises a new kind of wholeness and succor in death. Arthur's transition into this different space and time, while mournful, is also belated. Remarking that Arthur has stayed too long already, one asks: "A, dere broder, why haue ye taryed so longe from me? Alas, this wound on your heed hath caught ouer moche colde" (591). These words summon the losses wrought by time passing; they summon Arthur's doleful death as a crossing into the fullness of time. Arthur's wound, perhaps a figure for the traumas and tragedies of antagonisms over Arthur's meaning, has been left untended for too long. It is time, Arthur's sad sister implies, to put the wound away.

In foregrounding the sorrow of such passings, Malory's heavy-hearted scene of Arthur's death counts loss as painful and regrettable, if also utterly unavoidable. In mourning Arthur's loss, Malory registers the traumas and tragedies of his history. At moments like these, however, Malory's text also implies (as did Caxton's Prologue) that such losses are not culturally produced, but incurred through the inexorable changes and transitions brought about by time. Yet if such a view of Arthur's loss obscures the cultural, geographic, political, linguistic contestations and antagonisms evinced throughout this study as a sign of Arthur's history, it also registers the fact that England's hopes are not glorious or progressive ones.

Malory's poignant nostalgia, as Riddy points out, registers the "death throes" of an aristocratic class, yet also, as she provocatively puts it "the larger failure of Englishness . . . the loss of empire, not just the civil war" (66). Riddy helps us see that Malory's text registers the converging loss of England's imperial holdings in France with an insular turn toward the aggressive consolidation of aristocratic holdings at home. English soldiers no longer welcome in France turned aggressively toward the regions they might dominate in England. In this context Malory's poignancy thus registers the passing of Arthur's diverse and contested regional specificity and particularity. As Arthur comes to be identified, in Caxton's Malory, with a centralized English crown, the rich variability and multiplicities of his image also pass away. Arthur's loss thus mourns the passing of cultural diversities before an increasingly national insular unity. The Arthurian adultery plot might indeed be said to register the pleasures of multiple affections, the variety of ways of "owning" Arthur and managing Arthur's love. By choosing to locate Arthur's demise with the story of Lancelot and Guinevere, Malory's text implicitly links the loss of Arthur with the time when multiplicities of affection were treasonous to a unified sovereign community.

For a fifteenth-century audience worrying about England's frailties, the weeping and shrieking queens who mediate Arthur's passing also offer images of loss that are nonetheless edged with future continuities. Female figures grant the wounded body of their brother and king access to a continuity of past with future. Klaus Theweleit argues that, like Eurydice, the woman's descent into the land of the dead can provide a male artist, like Orpheus, the promise of a continuity between past and present, a sense especially poignant during times of technological change.[35] Mourning, in Theweleit's account of what he calls "orphic literary production" thus serves to maintain a solid sense of identity even when modes of artistic production are shifting. A woman who passes over to the place of death and loss can grant to the male artist who longs for her the ability to accommodate innovative technologies while maintaining a tie with the old order that is passing away. At the time of Malory's innovative vernacular prose, and in the midst of Caxton's new printing technology, Arthur's mourning queens, along with Arthur himself, offer imaginary links able to bridge the instabilities of cultural change. When the four queens accompany this British king to a place of healing beyond all divisions they evoke the image of a whole island regained. Yet the geographic implications of Arthur's four queens suggest that the "English" continuity imagined here requires losses configured by gender and more.

To be sure the Welsh gentry who supported Henry VII's succession hoped for a kind of healing beyond the divisions of England and Wales. Yet Tudor centrality would, like national power generally, declare the joys of unification so as to serve the interests of a particular region and class. The disappointing result, from some Welsh perspectives, meant that Arthur would figure obliquely in the discourse of Welsh dissidents at least until the eighteenth century. Henry VII will, of course, name his first born son Arthur; so will Scotland's James IV at a time when that child stands directly in the line of succession.

Conclusion: The Nation and Loss

Arthur figures the sovereign as abject. In Caxton's Malory, Arthur's loss reorganizes material ruin into a story of mournful passing. Yet the losses of Arthur and the elusive wholeness his rule promises but never quite delivers become a perpetual memory that can be activated in longing for utopian community. In the story of the Grail, as we have seen, readers learn that absence can still deliver utopian pleasures, if only we remain unflagging believers. If we desire utopian healings and satisfactions, this collocation of stories suggests, we need only to believe in the passing world of Camelot and in the generativity of a whole and healed Logres.

In the context of the history of England, Wales, and France, however, a good part of the use of Arthur as a "native sovereign" lies precisely with the fact that he is gone. The narrative of Malory's *Morte Darthur*, for all its—and Caxton's—explicit rhetorical celebrations of Arthur as the greatest of British kings, joins together the most horrific aspects of a sovereign power overrun by excessive entanglements and kin-feuds. This Arthurian failure explains in part why Malory seems not much interested in Arthur's return. Arthur's traditional link with Wales, Scotland, and the north means that when he departs from Britain, the geographic specificities of this kind of rule go with him. By the time of Tudor rule various kinds of specificities—Welsh and English, Yorkist and Lancastrian—have been lost, and early modern subjects had to remake their hearts and memories for an Arthur whose court is as Winchester. The publishing history of Caxton's edition encrypts Arthur the colonizer as the one and only captivating English king.

Belief in such Englishness and in the king who represents it will, as Elaine Scarry reminds us, require the materiality of the body in pain to substantiate its imaginary fantasies. As Caxton's London readers enjoy a sad look at this King and the court he rules from Winchester, Welsh and English bodies fight and die over their belief in which man, a Yorkist or a Tudor, should sit on the throne as Arthur's heir. And if the succession of Henry VII will mean an end to the oppressive penal laws of the post–Glyn Dŵr years, the union of Wales and England apparently established by his inheritance still organizes its gains at Welsh expense. Centralized England will continue to depend upon and desire the rich resources of its regions; English aggressions against their near neighbors will continue to be written in intimate relations between a London crown and a Scottish queen, or in the history of early modern Anglo-Irish relations. In each of those contexts, Arthur's image will be raised again, deployed in popular and nationalistic ambitions—in "the matter of Scotland" and the allegorical fantasy of *The Faerie Queene*.

Yet we have seen throughout this study that while the popularity of Arthur assists both sovereigns and sovereign pretenders in their moves on the throne, the flexible uses made of prophecy and romance can also have other consequences. Caxton's edition of Malory's final Middle English account of Arthurian sovereignty, for its part, regularizes Arthur's link to an established English monarchical tradition. Caxton's Malory renders England's captivation with Arthur a matter of individualized belief and privatized devotion, a national fantasy available as an interior space in the hearts and minds of a London-based reading public.

The inconsistencies and irregularities of Caxton's Malory, of course, nonetheless remain to trouble and excite later readers. The Arthurian traditions from which Malory works, as this study has suggested, fund a rich store of variable forms reiterating what seems a single story, yet in each case with a difference. Those differences shift the meaning and emphasis of Arthur from one story to the next. Some narrative traditions critique Arthur as sovereign *inutile*; others celebrate his compassionate integrity. Middle English Arthurian legend thus oscillates between intervals of space and time commemorating a British sovereignty able to accommodate heterogeneous desires while always remaining recognizable as a singular body of tales. The combination of difference and sameness—heterogeneity and singularity—inhabits, in my reading, the uses of Arthurian romance for the production of communitarian desire. Tales of Arthur provide a national fantasy flexible enough to accommodate the variety and changeability of popular desires for "Britain" itself. Yet they also encode the losses that will, and soon, silently serve explicitly national organizations.

"Through fantasy," writes Slavoj Žižek, "we learn how to desire" (*Looking* 6). Through national fantasy we learn to desire the group pleasures of union and wholeness. To desire Arthur as King and the Round Table as cultural myth, we must also remain caught in the illusion that he fascinates because he is fascinating, and not because we have been taught to find him so. We must remain convinced that Arthur's fascination predates our eyes and hearts, that Arthur has always been there, forever poised for our gaze and ready for our desire. This durable image is also the Arthur whose vagueness slips through our fingers just as we locate him in history.

As such we are tempted to ignore the material seriousness of the tradition, even as we look to the future and to the distant past in hopes of a material recovery.

In gazing hopefully toward an Arthurian futurity, or nostalgically rehearsing an Arthurian past, Middle English tales of Arthur of Britain reverberate with longing for utopian transformations and communitarian wholeness. Yet community is also equally engaged with the disruptions, the fragmentations, the contestations and aggressions of group organizations. The disquieting slips and misses of the Middle English Arthurian tradition are equally fascinating. Those slips and misses attest to the pleasures gained by fantastic difference, by sovereign instability, by flexible disloyalty, by aggressive disunity. In as much as Arthur's story encodes a longing for the pleasures of utopian community, Arthur's tragedy in all its contradictions and missteps gestures as well to desires for other moments and other spaces. As much as these stories show us knights and ladies who long for King Arthur, they show us as well subjects who long to defy him. The fascinating magic of Morgan le Fey, the marvelous form of the Green Knight, the sturdy challenge of Galleroun of Galloway, even the poignant retreat to a magical place like Avalon, hint at desires for other places and other powers, desires that just might have utopian ambitions of their own.

Lost Books

I N *Forms of Nationhood*, Richard Helgerson links national discourse
with inclusivity. Analyzing the discursive forms that nationhood took
in Elizabethan England, he summarizes his conclusions as follows:

Those discursive forms that emphasize state over nation, power over custom and
individual conscience, are also more upper-class and male. Those that emphasize
nation over state include–and even identify with–women and commoners. . . .
Inclusion emerges as an inverse function of power. The more intensely a discursive
form concentrates on the centralized power of the state the more exclusionist it is
likely to be with regard to class and gender. And conversely, the more inclusive it
is, the greater the place it gives women and commoners, the less concerned it will
be to assert the prerogatives of monarchic rule. (297)

Helgerson's formulation, indebted to Anderson's imagined community,
sees nationhood as an inclusivist step beyond monarchical statehood and
preliminary to the development of the "nation-state." Borrowing Anderson's progressivist chronology, Helgerson thus seems to imply that the
cultural formations that followed the medieval monarchic state were more
inclusive (perhaps even more compassionate) than the organizations that
preceded them.[1]

Yet historical chronologies emphasizing the progressivist gains of
"Renaissance" histories implicitly collude with national ideologies that
render unification and centralization superior to the alternatives. And
from the vantage of this study, Helgerson's (like Anderson's) progressivist
opposition of an inclusivist discourse of "nationhood" to an "exclusivist"
discourse of monarchical statehood obscures (among other things) the extent to which nations purchase their inclusivity by demanding that some

regional or ethnic affections be lost to make way for centralization. Attention to the time before the consolidation of an "inclusive" nationhood
shows instead that the discursive inclusivity of nationhood is ideologically
suspect. When William Caxton praises King Arthur in the service of a
national future, his rhetoric of inclusion fronts particular regional or class
interests precisely through an ideological claim that they speak for the
"common" people. Similarly, when the Middle English versions of Merlin's Prophecies raise the (inclusive?) image of a common people mourning
the loss of a sovereign father, those texts translate the sovereign's loss into
unification, but this is a gain that serves not compassionate inclusivity so
much as a centralizing status quo. And when Caxton's *Malory* canonizes
a particularly centralized King Arthur for a common audience, or when
prophecies of England's Six Last Kings raise the image of a common field
of English mourners, both texts make it increasingly likely that alternative
or regionalist versions of Arthurian history will be lost, sacrificed to a regu-
larized "common" view of England's past. While discourses of nationhood
thus explicitly include and unify, it is precisely through such inclusions that
they demand the sacrifice of difference. The putatively common ground
upon which nationhood builds its rhetoric of inclusivity is first cleared by
often forgotten histories of loss and suffering.

The Middle English Arthurian tradition (even in Caxton or in the
Middle English Merlin Prophecies) offers, precisely through its delectation
of suffering and loss, a way to read both the attraction and the mournful,
material consequences of some communitarian fantasies. Such readings of
Arthurian tradition are more difficult, though certainly not impossible,
from the vantage of the early modern Arthurian epic poem, Edmund
Spenser's *Faerie Queene*. Not incidentally, this text is, as Helgerson himself notes, the primary exception to the pattern of inclusivity he observes
elsewhere. Like the texts examined in my study, Spenser's text has links to
prophecy and to a colonial setting (this time in Ireland). Yet when Spenser
deploys Arthur as England's sovereign ancestor, he is determined not to
mourn the losses produced in the wake of unification, but to show that
England's present and future claims to nationhood trace a heritage from
the most ancient British days. While Spenser eventually (as evinced by the
"Mutability Cantos" published with the 1609 edition of his poem) offers
an allegorical meditation on loss, in his use of Arthurian traditions he
elides their most deeply touching passions and attachments. In this regard
Spenser's monumental accomplishment, in all its various (and violent)
excesses, seems both more fully disciplining and disciplined than the tra-

dition from which it works. Spenser's allegory values hierarchy and order even if somewhat uncompellingly, leaving room for resistant readings.

Recently scholars have begun to debate whether Spenser's text represents a violent collusion with, or a subtle response to, England's conquest of Ireland. I would merely add that when he treats loss in the abstract allegorical figure of mutability, Spenser's text makes it difficult to see that the changes wrought by conquest are not the work of fate, justice, or time's winged chariot, but something that sovereigns and cultures work hard to produce in particular ways. From the vantage of my study, moreover, Spenser's sense of Arthur's pertinence to the work of subduing Ireland has much to do with the instrumental nature of Arthur's role in the "unification" of England with Wales. The author of *The Libel of English Policy* grants Wales a similarly central role in England's increasingly colonial future: "Be ware of Walys, Criste Jhesu mutt us kepe,/ That it make not oure childeis childe to wepe" (190). Implicit comparisons among regions of the "Celtic Fringe" structure that text, making clear the comparative stakes of conquest: "if Yreland be loste, as Christe Jhesu forbede/ Ffarewelle Wales, than Englond cometh to dredd/ For alliaunce of Scotelonde . . . and so have enmyes environ round aboute" (188). *The Libel* shows an interconnected colonial network where loss or rebellion in one region poses dangers to England's control of another.

There remain, from the long view of this history, two traumas that surface in the context of Arthurian traditions with regard to these relations. During the Tudor years, Arthur's image offered a means to manage the consent of the Welsh gentry to the official unification of England and Wales, a fact that has been read as a sign of Welsh "complicitly" with English rule. Yet such consent might instead signify not Welsh (in contrast with the Scots or Irish) weakness, but a complex set of intercultural intimacies and a long history of shared dreamings and geographic proximity along the Welsh march. This history of intercultural complexity suggests limitations to notions like "complicity," notions that implicitly privilege a purity of identity and heart.

Efforts to recover pure identities, or purer times, try to escape the work of mourning.[2] Fantasizing an intact wholeness before loss, such labor paradoxically averts our gaze from scenes of desolation, the losses wrought by conquest, centralization, and unification. Yet the Middle English Arthurian corpus treated here suffers from its own mournful history: these traditions survive to the present because they were, at a crucial moment in Tudor history, judged worthy of preservation. They were

saved from the devastating program of literary destruction promoted by
Henry VIII and identified with Tudor antiquarians John Leland and John
Bale. Traveling throughout England and Wales, Leland tragically separated
those medieval books he judged worthy of a place in England's cultural
heritage from those deemed unworthy of preservation, those that could
thus be willingly destroyed. Leland's and Bale's choices were guided by
what James Simpson thoughtfully calls the "ageist bias" (218) of Tudor
historiography. It is a scholarly project, as Simpson notes, that "at once
petrifies the past (by literally ruining it in the case of [the destruction of]
the monasteries) and provokes the desire to preserve the "monuments" of
the past" (234).

King Arthur was, of course, one of those national British monuments
deemed worthy of preservation. Arthurian poems, genealogies, and histories were on account of this judgment saved from the bonfires. We will
never know precisely what else, Arthurian or not, was lost. The surviving
Middle English corpus thus reverberates with yet another loss from which
we can never recover. David Lawton calls this "martyrdom of books" "perhaps the greatest act of cultural destruction that Britain has ever seen."
"What survived the cataclysm unleashed by Henry VIII," Lawton continues, "was a very small percentage . . . of the manuscripts there were, . . .
in an act that irredeemably divides the present from its immediate past,
today from yesterday" ("Surveying," 32). It is important that we read the
rescued romances of Arthur that do survive against this national, and
nationalizing, tragedy. Perhaps the mournful medieval tales of Arthur's
tragic sovereignty can help us to mark and to mourn the multiple destruc-
tions demanded by, yet still silently excluded from, subsequent discourses
of nation.

Notes

1. Historical and textual problems surround both "John Mandeville" (historical figure or literary fiction?) and the book of his travels, a popular text during the Middle Ages. The quote here is taken from J. O. Halliwell, ed., *The Voiage and Travaile of Sir John Maundeville, Kt. Which treateth of the Way of Hierusalem; And of Marvayles of Inde, with Other llands and Contryes*, reprinted from the edition of 1725 (London: Edward Lumley, 1839). The 1725 edition is based on the fourteenth-century MS Cotton Tit. C xvi. The statement is offered here not as an authoritative link to an authorial or historical "John Mandeville," but for its provocative collocation of imagination and subjugation. "Mandeville's" remarks cited here occur in a larger description (and as a critique of) the laws and customs of the Tartars in Cathay. It is cited in the *OED* as one of the earliest uses of the word *imagination*.

2. For an important reading of twelfth-century Arthurian historiography as "border writing" see Warren, *History on the Edge*.

3. On tragedy and Malory's *Morte Darthur*, see Larry Benson; on tragedy in the Middle English tradition generally see Patterson, *Negotiating the Past*.

4. Relations between England and France were more complicated than this formulation suggests. I will argue below that the resurgence in late medieval British Arthuriana was part of a process of distinguishing British sovereigns from their Norman ancestors and hence their French cousins. England's ongoing struggle to annex Scotland is important here. For a rich analysis of the nationalist character of medieval Scottish Arthuriana, see Goldstein.

5. On the definition of romance see W. R. J. Barron, *English Medieval Romance*, 53–56; Finlayson, "Definitions of the Middle English Romance, Parts I and II," 44–62, 168–81. Susan Crane's *Insular Romance* is pertinent here.

6. Ingledew has argued for the importance of a collocation of time and space for Geoffrey of Monmouth's *Historia*; see also Stein, "Making History."

7. For example, Knight, *Arthurian Literature and Society*; more recently, Shichtman and Carley. On Kantorowicz and the politics of kingship in Malory, see Pochoda, *Arthurian Propaganda*. Important recent accounts of particular pertinence include Riddy, "Contextualizing"; Beal, "Arthur as Bearer of Civilization"; Rosalind Field, "The Anglo-Norman Background to Alliterative Romance"; Heng, "Cannibalism"; Warren; Dean, *Arthur of England*.

8. In Geraldine Heng's recent reading of the "genesis" of Arthurian ro-

mance, fantasy figures as a means for "safely memorializing" traumatic impossibilities of crusader cannibalism. Romance, in this account, "surfaces the historical
which it transforms and safely memorializes in an advantageous form, as fantasy"
(126). See "Cannibalism," 98–174. I would not claim to offer any narrative of "genesis" or "origin, nor do I find this aspect of Heng's account convincing. I explain
these disagreements in Chapter 3.

9. Arthurian studies has also channeled antagonisms specifically across the
English Channel. During the first part of the twentieth century, Arthurian scholars
endeavored to fix Middle English narratives of Arthur as derivatives of either Celtic
or Continental originals, as a result of a larger desire to establish Arthur's "origin."
R. S. Loomis, Newstead, Jackson, Mac Cana, Gruffydd, and Gantz emphasize the
Welsh origin of many of the tales. The continental view, rendered most famously by
J. Bedier, and later by Faral and Watkin in France, and Bruce in the United States,
stresses that late Middle English versions (like the Stanzaic *Morte Arthur*, and
the Alliterative *Morte Arthure* and Malory's *Morte Darthur*) borrow heavily from
continental sources (particularly Chrétien de Troyes and the French Vulgate cycle).
The long preoccupation with isolating a Welsh or French "origin" has produced
what can only be called nationalist responses; this critical history points to some of
the limitations of accounts of generic "origin," even when figured (as in Heng's recent work) through a more flexible notion like "genesis." Ceridwen Lloyd-Morgan
suggested a number of years ago that we examine relations among traditions of
Arthurian material with greater fluidity, and volumes like *The Arthur of the Welsh*
exemplify the strength of the newer approaches. Lloyd-Morgan suggests that debates about textual transmission might tell us a good deal about relations between
Wales and France during this period. See "Continuity and Change," 397–405. The
debate over origin might also be read to surface (although differently) the Middle
English contestations examined in this book.

10. On how religious affiliations might nonetheless encode national imaginings, see Turville-Petre, *England the Nation*; for a postcolonial analysis of medieval
confidence in Christendom, see Biddick, "Technologies of the Visible"; on the
need of medieval sovereigns to manage (not just demand) the consent of the ruled,
see Fradenburg, *City, Marriage, Tournament*; for an alternative view of typology,
see Lupton, *Afterlives of the Saints*.

11. For earlier discussions of the issue see Tipton, ed., *Nationalism in the
Middle Ages*; and more recently, if briefly, Ambrisco.

12. Some thirty years ago Fredrick Barth suggested the importance of difference to imaginings of group identity. See, *Ethnic Groups*, especially 14–19; also
Warren, *History on the Edge*.

13. Emphasis upon this combination is, for instance, why Glyn Dŵr figures
so importantly here. As is well known, Glyn Dŵr's rebellion against English rule
deployed a model of the Prince borrowed from English rule, a fact that has further
complicated the already difficult question of Welsh resistance. I do not mean to
suggest that Glyn Dŵr be taken as the single, romantic token of Welsh resistance
as such. An equally important way of thinking about Welsh resistance has developed through the notion of the *gwerin*, or folk, for whom English sovereignty
remains inconsequential. Since I am examining (among other things) the shared

and contested spaces between England and Wales, I am interested in taking Glyn Dŵr's movement seriously as resistance, not "complicity." This explains as well my decision, following the lead of R. R. Davies whose work I admire, to retain the Welsh spelling of Glyn Dŵr's name. Postcolonial theories have been helpful to me because they also offer a means of analyzing the problematics of such antagonistic intimacies. For pointing out the problems with using Glyn Dŵr as a token of Welsh resistance and for a reminder of the alternatively resistant *gwerin*, I am grateful to Stephen Knight, private correspondence.

14. I argue elsewhere that such repetitions allude to traumatic histories of colonial loss, calling them "the Colonial Refrain." See my "Marking Time," especially 184–85.

15. Complicated relations among Wales, England, Scotland, Ireland, and France in the late Middle English period, moreover, display colonial relations enmeshed with national identities. National rhetorics in the late medieval period worry over categories of "union" and activities of "joining," practices also important to the love plots and knightly fellowships of Arthurian romance. Where Richard Helgerson discovers in the Elizabethan age a series of writers articulating nationhood such that "[e]very discourse of nationhood is also a discourse of self" (294), the troubles of late medieval "Britain" involve the reverse of Helgerson's formulation: the possibility that every discourse of self (Lancastrian or Yorkist or Tudor, Welsh or English or Scottish or French, Northumbrian or Kentish or Cheshire) might possibly prove to be a discourse of "nation." See *Forms of Nationhood*.

16. See for example Goldstein; Hechter, *Internal Colonialism*; Davies, *Conquest, Coexistence and Change*.

17. David Wallace has suggested that the particularities of a "New Historicist" method keep period markers firmly fixed in place, thus making it difficult to consider the history of the *longue durée*. I share Wallace's desire to revise, even abjure, period markers like "Medieval" and "Renaissance," and the connections I seek to make between Arthurian traditions and the later theory of the "King's Two Bodies" constitute an attempt to rethink notions of sovereignty across the period divide. But I am also interested in suggesting, pace Wallace, that the "European" and "international" affiliations of the late fourteenth and fifteenth centuries in Britain coalesce in interesting ways with what can be called national concerns. Rather than oppose the "national" to the "international," I seek to consider their mutual imbrication. See *Chaucerian Polity*, 4–7.

18. See her important argument for reading Malory's *Morte Darthur* as an "imperialist narrative," in "Contextualizing," especially 66–70. My project began before Riddy's article appeared, yet I remain indebted to this formulation of the problem of medieval imperialism.

19. As Leonard Thompson makes clear in *The Political Mythology of Apartheid*.

20. Robert Bartlett's influential *The Making of Europe*, for example, concludes with an emphasis upon the sharp distinctions between modern and medieval colonialisms, (an "absence of political masterminding in the colonial ventures of the middle ages" (309) that obtained in their modern counterparts, for instance) even as his larger project argues that Europe was, itself, a product of colonization. See

Bartlett, 304–14; for a critique of this trend as a reliance on Anderson, see Biddick, "ABC," 291, n.2.

21. For example, Biddick, *The Shock of Medievalism*; Davis, "National Writing in the Ninth Century"; Kruger, "The Spectral Jew"; Stein, "Making History English"; Tomasch, "Judecca, Dante's Satan, and the *Dis*-placed Jew"; Warren. See also the recent volumes *The Postcolonial Middle Ages*, ed. Jeffrey Jerome Cohen, and *Text and Territory*, ed. Sylvia Tomasch and Sealy Gilles.

22. Controversies circulate around the precise meaning of the "post-colonial," especially the extent to which, to quote Simon Gikandi, "the trope of postcoloniality sustains the delusion of historical rupture" between a time of colonial oppression and liberation. This issue pertains as well to whether and how postcolonial theories of representation, even as discourses of oppositionality, might collude with imperial epistemologies. For more on this debate see the introductions in the volume edited by Ashcroft, Griffiths, and Tiffin, *The Post-Colonial Studies Reader*, pp. 1–4; 7–11. See also Gikandi, *Maps of Englishness*, especially 14–20. I follow those who use "postcolonial" to signal an oppositional discourse. For a detailed account of this method, see Ingham, "'In Contrayez Straunge': British Identity, Colonial History, and *Sir Gawain and the Green Knight*," *New Medieval Literatures* 4 (2000), 61–93.

23. Jeffrey Jerome Cohen has argued for example that, because of its long-standing attention to the problems of progressivist views of time, contemporary medieval studies has much to offer postcolonial models of history. Cohen suggests that a model of history as "temporal interlacement," an interweaving of the differences between times with the coherences across time could "entwine disparate temporalities, supplanting the teleological chronology of more traditional history" ("Midcolonial," 5–6). Edward Said's *Orientalism* has been credited with establishing postcolonial studies as a field; on "orientalism" and medieval studies, see Ganim, "Native Studies," and Biddick, *Shock*.

24. See Bloch, Bronfen, Kristeva, *Black Sun*, and *Strangers to Ourselves*; Theweleit, *Male Fantasies, vol. I*, and "Politics of Orpheus." For the implications of these theories for a "compassionate" medieval studies, see Fradenburg, "Voice Memorial."

25. Jacques Lacan theorizes this property of fantasy and desire. On the general relation between desire and fantasy, and the necessity that fantasies appear to fascinate by virtue of their own attraction, see Žižek, *Looking Awry*, 33. British Arthurian romance thus resonates with what Lauren Berlant has elsewhere described as the structure of a national fantasy: it incorporates "overlapping but differently articulated positions" of "the official and the popular; the national and the local; . . . the collective and the individual; . . . utopia and history; memory and amnesia" (5).

Chapter 1. Arthurian Imagination and the "Makyng" of History

1. The vulgate text for Monmouth's *Historia* is taken from Acton Griscom, ed., *The Historia Regum Britanniae of Geoffrey of Monmouth* (London: Longmans,

1929). The use of this edition poses problems, of course, given the diversity of manuscript recensions; there remains no single standard edition of the *Historia*, and no scholarly consensus as to a preferred text. Precise accounts of those disagreements, diversities, and distinctions I leave to other scholars. But the question of diversity and flexibility as such will be important to the account that follows. My reading would be impossible without the monumental work at manuscript classification done by Griscom, Faral, Hammer, Dumville, Wright, and Crick. While scholars today tend to prefer Wright's edition of Bern, Bergerbibliothek MS 568, the use of the Bern (as will become clear below) raises difficulties for a study interested in the oppositional insular readings. Although mindful of its problems, I will treat Griscom's edition as an influential scholarly version of the *Historia*; yet I remain interested in the text's diverse versions. Except where noted, translations follow Lewis Thorpe, *History of the Kings of Britain*.

2. Curley suggests that the "Arthurian section of the HRB could be seen as a response to William of Malmesbury's claim about the absence of *veraces historiae* concerning Arthur," although "Geoffrey's Arthur was probably not entirely what William had in mind" (*Geoffrey of Monmouth*, 76).

3. "Hic est Artur de quo Britonum nugae hodieque delirant; dignus plane quen non fallaces somniarent fabulae, se veraces prædicarent historiae, quippe qui labantem patriam diu sustinuerit, infractasque civium mentes ad bellum acuerit" (11). Malmesbury, *Gesta regum Anglorum*, ed. Stubbs. The translation is indebted to Chambers.

4. Waswo reads the progressivist assumptions underlying the opposition of "fantasy" to "reality" in contemporary notions of "primitive" myth and "sophisticated" literature, although he emphasizes only conservative uses of fantasy, "The History that Literature Makes."

5. Allegiances to conceptions of "truth" or "fiction" fuel competing epistemologies—"objectivists" versus "constructivists," in Barbara Herrnstein Smith's formulation—that oppose textuality to materiality, placing the aesthetic delights of fiction and fancy against an intractable determinism of history. This debate addresses the material consequences of belief, evidence, and "truth," through the epistemological implications of post-structuralism. For examples that have been important to my thinking, see Herrnstein Smith, "Belief and Resistance"; Scott, "The Evidence of Experience."

6. In addition to Strohm, see Partner; Spiegel; and Goldstein.

7. Scarry argues for a more subtle relationship in which falsity and fiction constitute positions on a continuum of imagining, *The Body in Pain*.

8. For Lacan and Jameson's work, see Lacan, *Ecrits* and *Feminine Sexuality*, eds., Mitchell and Rose; Fredric Jameson, "Imaginary and Symbolic in Lacan" and *The Political Unconscious*. I am indebted to Fradenburg's formulation of the question, see especially "Wife of Bath" and "Voice Memorial."

9. See Scarry, p. 117 ff.

10. Patterson's use of the Middle English *makyng* has influenced my chapter's title. See also "Literary History"; "On the Margin"; *Negotiating the Past*.

11. In her important article, "The Wife of Bath's Passing Fancy," Fradenburg historicizes the opposition between romance fancy and realism, suggesting how

the apparently progressive move from fabulous narratives to realism as the constraint of "fancy" by truth. Fradenburg makes clear the sexual politics of a version of literary history where, as she puts it, "realism demands a kind of representational chastity" (33).

12. Patterson participates in a discourse, as he acknowledges, inspired by medieval rhetorical theory; following Ruth Morse, he links medieval historiography to theory inspired by classical rhetoric, according to which proper uses of figurative language are linked to moderation of appetites. Cicero stresses that figurative language, and hence the imagination, be modest, prudent, and reasonable; Geoffrey of Vinsauf instructs that figuration be decorous; Alberic of Monte Cassino figures improper rhetoric in terms of a badly served meal which "would disgust us, would nauseate us, would be thrown out." The rhetoric of excess employed here links overweening language to excessive appetites. Patterson's assessment of court narcissism seems to duplicate, rather than analyze, this discourse of the appetites, see *Chaucer and the Subject of History*.

13. See Žižek, especially *Sublime Object*; *Looking Awry*; "Eastern Europe's Republics of Gilead."

14. I am indebted to Deleuze and Guattari's formulation of desire as "desiring production." See *Anti-Oedipus*. It has recently come to my attention that there are similarities between this formulation and that of de Certeau.

15. Contemporary analysis of discourse about AIDS is a good example.

16. The theatricality of power has been impressively analyzed by Orgel, *The Illusion of Power*.

17. Crick's important study of the reception of the *Historia* has been crucial here, *The* Historia regum Britannie *of Geoffrey of Monmouth*. Earlier influential accounts include Griscom, and Dumville, "The Manuscripts of Geoffrey of Monmouth's *Historia Regum Britanniae*," in *Arthurian Literature*, III, IV, V. Dumville's tally of MSS has reached 211; Crick counts 215.

18. See Crick, 210–17 for an account of readership and circulation. For Geoffrey's use in later traditions see Tatlock; P. J. C. Field; Taylor; Scattergood; Keeler; Roberts; and Bromwich, et al.

19. Griscom argued pointedly against the early dismissal of the instrumentality of Welsh material, critiquing the methods, practices, and disciplinary habits circulating through the preeminence of Latinists in the field. The assumption that the language of linguistic minorities was inconsequential to medieval history writing produces a historiography—and an analysis of Monmouth's *Historia*—incapable of addressing the relation of Welsh texts to Latin ones, or, as Griscom suggests a little later, Irish and Scots texts to either. His treatment of the historiographic problem is to the point, even if the textual evidence eventually provided by later close readings of the Welsh chronicles tended to support the premature conclusions of the Latinists.

20. On the problem of imaginative extravagance, see Morse, *Truth and Convention in the Middle Ages*; Edwards, *Ratio and Invention: A Study of Medieval Lyric and Narrative*.

21. If Bede's use of Christian dating accounts for his reputation as historian,

then we need also to note that such a reputation rests upon the longstanding Christian bias, at least until recently, of Medieval Studies. In this light, the critique of Geoffrey's history seems to involve not the fact that he narrates the fantastic, so much as the nature of the fantastic tradition Geoffrey narrates. The identification of Geoffrey's work as, until recently, a "pseudo" history, seems a particularly overdetermined response to the question. See Gransden, *Historical Writing*.

22. Even favorable analyses of Monmouth imply that his text shows an embarrassing lack of restraint. In his introduction to the Welsh recension *Brut Y Brenhinedd*, Brynley Roberts writes, "[Monmouth] may have been moved by pride of race and political ideas, but his literary aim was to produce an acceptable popular book" (xxiv). Roberts's formulation implicitly opposes the popularity of Monmouth's text to its "pride of race and political ideas." I will eventually argue that these might be linked, and that producing an "acceptable popular book" constitutes important artistic agency in the face of constraint, a means of gaining authority (and influence) for a particular tradition of stories that incite cultural pride, and related political ideas.

23. Here is Griscom's vulgate: "Rogatu itaque illius ductus tam & si infra alienos ortulos. falerata verba non collegerim. agresti tamen stilo propriisque calamis contentus. codicem illum in latinum sermonem transferre curavi. Nam si ampullosis dictionibus paginam illinissem tedium legentibus ingererem dum magis in exponendis verbis quam in hystoria intelligenda ipsos commorari oportet."

24. One could, of course, read this compliment as decidedly back-handed, yet at other moments Monmouth's flattery seems sincere, if pragmatic. One dedication, for example, begins with a mention of Gildas' and Bede's "splendid treatment" (*luculento tractatu*) of historical matters. Dumville and Thorpe stress the importance of the following material included in the Bern and Harlech manuscripts of the *Historia*—manuscripts Dumville sees as more authoritative than Cambridge 1706, Griscom's choice for his edition. The inscription circumscribes the scope of Geoffrey's history with reference to other historians of the day. I quote Thorpe's translation: "The task of describing the kings [of the Welsh] I leave to my contemporary Caradoc of Llancarfan. The kings of the Saxons I leave to William of Malmesbury and Henry of Huntingdon. I recommend these last to say nothing at all about the kings of the Britons, seeing that they do not have in their possession the book in the British language which Walter, Archdeacon of Oxford, brought from Wales. It is this book which I have been at such pains to translate into Latin in this way, for it was composed with great accuracy about the doings of these princes and in their honour" (284, n. 1). For Dumville's analysis of Bern and Harlech and his quarrels with Griscom's edition, see "An Early Text of Geoffrey of Monmouth's *Historia Regum Britanniae*."

25. The question of Geoffrey's dedications is a complex one, given the diversity of manuscripts. Crick, following Hammer and Dumville, counts four manuscript traditions with various dedications. Those traditions include groups of manuscripts containing "the dedication to Robert of Gloucester, the nameless dedication, that to Robert of Gloucester and Waleran of Meulan, and finally that to King Stephen and Robert of Gloucester" (120). I will consider below the im-

plications of the multiple dedications for the flexible ambiguity of Geoffrey's text. For a recent subtle explication of these issues for Geoffrey's border writing, see Warren, *History on the Edge*, 25–59.

26. The name of this dedicatee, Alexander of Lincoln, is omitted in the "third variant," a group also known as the "pudibundus Brito," the manuscript author's term for himself. The entire Prologue to the Merlin Prophecies is, moreover, entirely lacking from thirteen manuscripts. And portions of it are lacking from four others. See Crick, 100–102.

27. On the difficulty of patronage, see Fradenburg, "The Manciple's Servant Tongue"; Shichtman and Finke, "Profiting," 1–35; also *Patronage in the Renaissance*, ed. Lyle and Orgel.

28. This discussion is indebted to Shichtman and Finke, "Profiting."

29. See Shichtman and Finke's sense of how Geoffrey's dedications play before a modern audience, 17.

30. For a full description see Jarman, "The Merlin Legend and Welsh Prophecy" in *The Arthur of the Welsh*, ed. Bromwich et al., 117–45.

31. Controversies circulate around the precise meaning of "postcolonial," especially the extent to which, to quote Simon Gikandi, "the trope of postcoloniality sustains the delusion of historical rupture" between a time of colonial oppression and liberation. This issue pertains as well to questions of oppositionality and resistance, to whether and how postcolonial theories of representation, even as "discourses of oppositionality" might collude with imperial epistemologies. For more on this see the introductions to *The Postcolonial Reader*, edited by Ashcroft, Griffiths, and Tiffin, 1–4; 7–11. See also Gikandi, *Maps of Englishness*, especially 14–20.

32. For a recent account of these complications see Roberts, "Writing in Wales," especially 183–87. The standard account of early vaticination is still Griffiths; see also Ceinwen Thomas; Glyn Roberts; Bromwich, ed., *Trioedd ynys Prydein*.

33. See for example, Otter, "Gaainable Tere," and especially, *Inventiones*. While Otter argues for the material seriousness of Monmouth's Latin fictionalizing (usefully reminding us that vernacular traditions did not hold a monopoly on imaginative expansiveness) she tends to read such fictionalizing in primarily conservative terms. Thus Geoffrey's imagination (again) comes under critique, making him "a kind of explorer or conqueror, . . . occasionally ruthless" (*Inventiones*, 81) who, as a translator of the language of the Britons, occupies a "linguistically privileged" position ("Gaainable Tere" 162–63). Her very interesting assessment of the "gaainable tere" of history does not provide a means to consider the complications of Geoffrey's border position, primarily because Otter emphasizes the different "aims" of twelfth century writing from later colonial rhetoric. Such singular attention to history as difference makes us unable to read the repetitions and recurrences of conquest at difference historical moments. It is particularly disabling for a reading of the repetitions of Arthuriana, or for a text like Geoffrey's that is, as Hanning points out, interested in "historical recurrence" (*The Vision of History in Early Britain*, 143).

34. On Geoffrey's border position, see Warren (*History on the Edge*), whose

analysis of twelfth and thirteenth-century Arthurian historiography provides the most subtle account of the complications of Geoffrey's position to date. Addressing the use and reception of Geoffrey's history among English, Welsh, and French historians of the twelfth and thirteenth centuries, Warren elegantly details the complicated borrowings and shifts, the very materiality of "border writing." Her work, a substantial advance on Otter's, shows that attention to translation and adaptation has substantial power for a "postcolonial" approach to medieval studies. Yet Warren's analysis, perhaps in part because of its understandable emphasis upon full historical accounts of Arthur, also underestimates the subversive possibilities of the Merlin prophecies. She does not address, for example, the oppositional agency of vaticination.

35. Robert of Gloucester, named in every Latin manuscript, supported the claim of his half-sister Matilda, Henry's daughter, to the throne; Count Waleran, described in a number of manuscripts as one of the "pillars" of the country, was the staunch supporter of Matilda's arch-enemy, King Stephen, nephew of Henry I and grandson of William the Conqueror. Geoffrey's political patrons, the direct descendants of the Norman conquerors, were only a generation or two away from the Battle of Hastings; and they were engaged in their own contestations over rule of the island. Those contestations recur in the manuscript variants. Most of the surviving manuscripts are dedicated only to Robert of Gloucester, Henry I's illegitimate son; yet a number survive which include the dedication to Count Waleran. One manuscript survives with a dedication to Robert and King Stephen. On the dedications see Crick, 117–20.

36. For decades scholars have tried to account for Monmouth's motives, asking why an Oxford cleric whose "racial sympathies," to use Tatlock's famous phrase, poise him between continental and insular "Britons," would produce a British *Historia* for a parvenu Anglo-Norman audience. Brynley Roberts describes Monmouth's book as an intervention into a lack of historical evidence for pre-Saxon Britain, and as a response to Anglo-Norman interest in the history of the land they recently conquered; Tatlock reads Geoffrey's history of imperialism as providing ancient "precedent for the dominions and ambitions of the Norman kings" (426); Reynolds argues that Geoffrey's text achieved its popularity because his glorification of a British past could transcend divisions between Norman and Saxon, *Kingdoms and Communities in Western Europe*; Hanning has suggested that Norman interest in a British history bespeaks a desire to compete with up-and-coming French and Anglo-Saxon traditions of "national" history writing.

37. See Ingledew, "The Book of Troy and the Genealogical Construction of History," 665–704. Ingledew also implicitly reads Geoffrey as a "colonizer"; while I would disagree, I nonetheless find Ingledew's linking of time and space a useful and important advance upon standard accounts.

38. There is a long tradition of disavowing the instrumentality of Welsh traditions to Geoffrey's text (see, for example, Tatlock, 305). The insistence that we preclude Welsh tradition from consideration tends to make the Welsh connection immaterial, inconsequential, and literally unreal. It seems to duplicate the cultural politics of William of Malmesbury's repudiation of Welsh "trifles" with which this chapter began.

39. Analyses of Geoffrey of Monmouth's use of the category of "Britain" in his *Historia* generally limit their attention to Geoffrey's racial identity in interpretations that ascribe to Monmouth what can only be described as an identity politics. Scholars conclude that Geoffrey must be of Breton stock since he apparently evidences Breton, rather than Welsh, loyalties. See Tatlock, 13–14; Roberts, Introduction to *Brut Y Brenhenidd*, xxiii. For a critique see Warren, *History on the Edge*, 25–26.

40. Regarding the conquerors' motives, for example, Geoffrey writes, "Maximianus developed an obsession with power, because of the enormous amount of gold and silver that flowed in to him daily. He prepared a fleet and conscripted every armed soldier in Britain. The kingship of Britain was not enough for him; he wanted to subjugate the Gauls, too" (139; v. 12).

41. Roberts also mentions the elimination of the Merlin prophecies from some Welsh translations, as when the author of Peniarth 44 "omits Merlin's Prophecies because they are difficult for people to believe" (113). Such incredulity could be read to suggest that the prophecies were uncompelling; it could alternately be read to signify the difficulty of the possibility of an effective resistance. See Warren for a reading of the Welsh *Brut*.

42. See Tatlock, 465; on Geoffrey's "central" position at court see 284–304. Also C. H. Haskins, 71.

43. The textual relations between Wace, Laȝamon, and Geoffrey are more complicated than this formulation suggests. For an important new reading of Laȝamon's text (from the Otho MS) see Elizabeth Bryan, *Collaborative Meaning*. On Laȝamon's association of "legitimate sovereignty with racially pure territory," see Stein, "Making History," 105–14. A more detailed consideration of Wace and Laȝamon's texts stands outside my present concern.

44. See Patterson, notes 4 and 5, p. 3.

45. See Davies, *Conquest, Coexistence and Change*. Also William Rees; Walker, *Medieval Wales*; Reynolds; and Frances Jones, *The Princes and Principalities of Wales*.

46. Hanning reads Geoffrey's work as a parody of Norman historiographic desires, (see especially 121–72). I would characterize his tone as perhaps more tongue-in-cheek.

47. Tatlock, for instance, dismisses the possibility that Geoffrey's use of the Latin *Britanniae insula* echoes the common Welsh name for the isle of Britain *ynys Prydein*, asserting that, despite Geoffrey's use of Welsh words to refer to other geographic locales, the category of "Britain" had no etymological relation to the common Welsh name for the island current at the time of Geoffrey's writing (8). I am suggesting that careful etymologies like this might encode a colonial "regime of truth."

Chapter 2. Arthurian Futurism and British Destiny

1. Robert Fayban, *The New Chronicles of England and France*, ed. H. Ellis, 672 (as cited by Scattergood, 33) includes the following account: "For his couplet deriding Richard III, Ratcliff, Catesby and Lovell, Wyllyam Collyngbourne was

put to the most cruel deth at the Tower Hylle, where for hym were made a newe payer of gallowes. Upon the whiche, after he hadde hangyd a shorte season, he was cutte down, beynge alyve, & his bowellys rypped out of his bely, and cast into the fyre there by hum, and lyved tyll the bowcher put his hande into the bulke of his body; insomuch that he sayd in the same instant, 'O Lord Ihesu, yet more trowble,' & so dyed to the great compassion of moche people." For other examples of the punishments doled out for lampooning king or court, see Scattergood, *Politics*, 21–23; 211.

2. See Scattergood, 19–21; Taylor's system of prophetic classification has become a common way to differentiate among various types of medieval prophetic literature. He distinguishes "Sibyllic Prophecies" (those using anagrams and letters to indicate the person in question) from "Galfridic" (those using animal figures for prophetic statements, as in the couplet cited here). See Taylor, 1–24. Taylor's texts of the prophecies are less trustworthy. For a critique see T. M. Smallwood, 571–92.

3. See *The Life of Edward the Second* (*Vita Edward Secundi*), N. Denholm-Young, ed. and trans. (London: Nelson, 1957), as cited and translated by Davies, *Conquest*, 436.

4. Allison Allan's work thus suggests certain complications to Lee Patterson's description of late-medieval historiography as a competition between two classically driven strains, "Thebanness" and "Boethianism." Allan points to the uses of a "native" tradition of historiography (grafted onto Trojan history) for royal pedigree in the fifteenth century. Patterson's emphasis upon Chaucer's use of Boethian and Theban material seems to ignore other traditions of history Chaucer deploys. The Wife of Bath's Tale, for example, an explicitly Arthurian text, offers an exploration of pertinent issues. See Fradenburg, "Wife of Bath's," 31–58; Allan "Yorkist Propaganda."

5. This chapter is indebted to Caroline Eckhardt's work, for available texts, for learned accounts of the relationships between later texts of Merlin Prophecies and Geoffrey of Monmouth, and for her analysis of the uses of Merlin traditions in the English vernacular chronicle. See especially, "Prophecy and Nostalgia" 109–26; "The Figure of Merlin," 21–39, and her editions of *The Prophetia Merlini of Geoffrey of Monmouth* and *Castleford's Chronicle or The Boke of Brut*. See also David Rees, Glanmor Williams. For the most part the chronicles listed here belong to a slightly earlier period than the one of my study: Robert of Gloucester's *Rhymed Chronicle*, ca. 1300; Thomas Castleford's *Chronicle*, ca. 1327; Robert Mannyng's *Rhymed Story of England*, ca. 1330. Trevisa's *Polychronicon* (in Caxton's 1482 edition) will be treated briefly in Chapter 3. Prophecies from the Middle English Prose *Brut* will be discussed later in this chapter. For dates, see Eckhardt, "The Figure of Merlin," 23–24.

6. Catalogues of medieval manuscripts attest to a significant number of similar genealogical tables yet to be carefully examined. For example Huntington Library Manuscript 264, *Genealogical Chronicle of the Kings of England*. Dating from the period of the Wars of the Roses, this chronicle "connects the history of the kings of Britain to Roman and biblical history through the Arthurian legends" (*Guide to Medieval and Renaissance Manuscripts at the Huntington Library* 228).

7. Eckhardt similarly points to the combination of "nostalgia" and "proph-

esy" in Arthurian texts produced between 1480–86, during which time Caxton's press printed two editions of the *Brut*, and, of course, Malory's *Morte Darthur*. See Eckhardt, "Prophecy and Nostalgia."

8. See Eckhardt's introduction for details of the difference between the *Prophetia Merlini* and the *Six Kings to Follow John*.

9. For a description of the manuscript, see Eckhardt's introduction, 20.

10. Some medieval traditions identified two Merlins: Merlin Ambrosius, Vortigern's prophet and Merlin Silvestris or Calidonius, linked with Scotland, who prophesied to Arthur. See Trevisa's translation of Higden's *Polychronicon*.

11. The commentary subsequently seems to confuse the names of kings Cadwallo, Cadwalader, and Cadvan from the *Historia*.

12. History emphasizing the superiority of unity over fragmentation, a story useful to national and imperial governments, returns in accounts that describe Glyn Dŵr's rebellion as part of his penchant for "making play with English faction" to the detriment of the monarchy itself. See especially Skidmore. For an analysis of how the dynamics of union, despite rhetoric to the contrary, nonetheless privilege centrality, see Chapter 6.

13. This is not, of course, a unique interpolation. It occurs both in the *Historia* and in Laȝamon's *Brut*.

14. These relations are most familiar through Shakespeare and, of course, his historical sources, Holinshed and Hall. Eckhardt notes an early basis for these associations in an earlier anonymous chronicle, *Incerti scriptoris chronicon Angliae de regnis trium regum Lancastrensium*, ed. J. A. Giles (London, 1848): 33, 39–42. See Eckhardt's introduction, 29. For the problems with this chronicle, see below, note 22.

15. There may, of course, be "oppositional" readings of this loss (as, for example, a consequence of English aggression). I am arguing, however, that this text favors English concerns.

16. On the pleasures (and utility) of loss see Bataille; on the heroization and gendering of loss (and hence its relation to male nobility) see Fradenburg, " 'Our owen wo to drynke'."

17. In her introduction to the *Prophetia*, Eckhardt suggests that the excision of the Breton Hope prophecies may have something to do with timing. Written before Edward IV's genealogies, the *Prophetia*'s author must have felt it unlikely that the Breton Hope would be fulfilled. Once Edward IV claimed the throne, and began to use fictionalized genealogies to legitimize Yorkist sovereignty, the Breton Hope became an altogether useful, if also entirely different, prophecy. The shift within a period of only a few years points exactly to the contestations I am analyzing. Nonetheless the commentary's anti-Welsh leanings suggest an ambivalence about appropriating a prophecy so deeply and recently linked to challenges to sovereign power.

18. Allan has called these texts the "Long English" and "Short English" Pedigrees. Matheson identifies six manuscripts of the "Long English Pedigree" (Bodleian Lyell 33; Bodleian e Museo 42 [aka Bodley 623]; Corpus Christi College, Cambridge 207; Yale University Library, Marston 242; College of Arms Arundel 53; and BL King's 395, containing a continuation to Henry VIII) and three manu-

scripts of the "Short English Pedigree" (Magdalene College, Cambridge, Pepys 2244; BL Add. 31950; and College of Arms Arundel, 23). See Matheson, 235.

19. Eckhardt's description of Bodley 623 is part of her contextualization of the *Prophetia*, see 56–58.

20. For recent listing of a bibliography of *Brut* manuscripts, see *The Manual of Writings in Middle English*, Vol. 8, especially pp. 2818–21. For a summary of the problems with Brie's EETS edition of the Common Version, see Matheson, "Historical Prose," 209–48. Matheson has undertaken, but not yet completed, a study of the manuscripts.

21. In many versions, the Second Lamb does not occur; the sixth king-animal is instead the Ass.

22. These chronicles can be found in British Library, MS Sloan 1776 and MS Royal 13. C.i. On the reliability of the account, Smallwood writes, "No true edition and no satisfactory account of this chronicle exists in print. It even lacks a name, being regularly lumped together with two separated chronicles for the reigns of Henry V and Henry VI, under the title *Incerti scriptoris Chronicon Angliae* . . or simply *Giles Chronicle*" (591, n.57). I have used the account in Ellis, 27–28.

23. Of the general facts of fifteenth-century production, Smallwood writes, "One cannot see any politically propagandistic motive in the multiplication of copies of the English Prose Translation [of the Prophecy of the Six Kings] in the early fifteenth-century. . . . This version, as part of the English translation of the 'longer' *Brut* chronicle, was copied extensively in the years from about 1400 onwards; but it would be fanciful to associate the popularity of the longer *Brut* with any wish to circulate the prophecy found within it, the latter forming only a very small part of the whole" (587).

24. Smallwood notes two fifteenth-century versions of the Prophecy of the Six Last Kings containing evidence of a specifically anti-Bolingbroke perspective. On the whole, however, she disentangles this particular prophecy from its association with Henry IV and the Percy, Mortimer, Glyn Dŵr rebellion. See particularly pp. 587–89.

25. On the history of Norman-Welsh interaction and inter-marriage see Bullock-Davies. For lists of the penal laws, see Davies, 457–58.

26. While Anderson is interested in noting a complex history in the development of national affections—and emphasizes repeatedly that their origins are "obscure"—he details a fairly straightforward sequence for an understanding of time that provides an answer for him. I will address the question of typology more fully in Chapter 7.

27. According to both Zumthor and Hanning, typological historiography emerges most intensely with historiographic practices of the monasteries, with the development of a secular history, often described as a twelfth-century innovation. Characterized by a use of prolepsis and typology, monastic historiography enlarged upon biblical and patristic models to include what are variously termed "national" traditions. Nearly all the analyses of Monmouth's *Historia* from which I have worked follow this line of thinking, developed in relatively recent decades. See Southern, Otter, Ingledew, Hanning.

28. Southern's analyses of historiographic mentalities of the twelfth and thir-

teenth centuries characterizes four kinds of prophecies (Biblical, Pagan, Christian, and Astrological) as linked to a medieval historical consciousness. His work usefully troubles any sense that medieval applications of prophetic texts to actual events were mere "popular mumbo jumbo," and links this to a historical thinking (beginning in the twelfth century) as the story of man's progressive development through time (a belief he claims ends during the eighteenth century). Southern displays, however, an investment in both the separation of "history" from "fiction" and in the privileging of Christian and Biblical prophecies (for their seriousness and import) over those he terms Pagan. I share neither his condescension toward "pagan" prophecies nor his confidence that historiography since the eighteenth-century has divested itself of progressivist (and rationalist) rhetorics of development.

29. I employ the term anamnesis both for its psychoanalytic and its theological connotations. In psychoanalysis, anamnesis refers to the subject's recollection of the past as a means of imagining a new kind of future. In scholastic liturgical theology, anamnesis refers to the relation between the ritual traditions of the community and the content of belief in Christ's sacrifice and death. Eucharistic transubstantiation invokes a process of anamnesis where the community, by virtue of its corporate memory, makes past crucifixion and resurrection literally present amidst believers. The links of anamnesis to Eucharistic theology resonate with links of the King's "mystical" body to the "mystical body of Christ." The King's Two Bodies is, after all, a "political theology." In both these registers "anamnesis" might be read for its relationship to the work of mourning.

30. My uses of reverse causality, limit, and threshold are indebted to Deleuze and Guattari's *A Thousand Plateaus*. Robert Young has argued for the pertinence of Deleuze and Guattari's theorizations for a "postcolonial" approach to history. See Young, especially chapter 7.

31. When the *Prophetia Merlini* uses the vague symbolism of prophecy ("and Merlin said the white dragon shall rise again"), it partakes of the chronicle form approaching "the allegory, moral or anagogical . . in order to achieve both narrativity and historicality" (White 22). Yet when the *Prophetia* offers its interpretation ("and Merlin said sooth. For the English people . . . sent into Saxony . . ."), it performs the very process of historiographic narrativization, where terse annalistic statements gain the fullness of vernacular prose historical specificity. For White's analysis of the historical form in the medieval period see *Content*, especially chapter one, "The Value of Narrativity," 1-25.

32. For Zumthor the voice of Merlin is what gained popularity for Monmouth's *Historia*. Zumthor writes, "le message sensationnel . . . la nouveauté . . . ce qui y piquait avant tout l'attention et éveillait l'intéret de l'esprit c'était les prophèties" (47).

33. Burke's claim that medieval historical writers were not critical historians (having no sense of "anachronism" for example) bolsters his claim of the origin of "modern" historical consciousness with Renaissance "humanism." For critiques of Burke see, for example, Guinée; Gransden, i, 20-1; ii, 454-55, 465; and Partner.

34. See Coleman, especially 558-99. Coleman argues that what distinguishes both renaissance and medieval notions of history from later ones is their similar em-

phasis upon historical analogue. She historicizes the emphasis upon the historical differences between periods as a function of nineteenth-century romanticism when "a sense of the lost and irrecoverable sense of the past would come to dominate the literary and historical consciousness" (593).

35. For this important and powerful argument concerning the usefulness of the doubleness of similarity and difference as a methodological requirement for a more radical historiography, see Fradenburg (with Freccero), 371–84.

36. On the possible dangers implicit in the important relation between books and authority in the rebellions of a few decades earlier, see Justice. For an important account of hermeneutics in the fifteenth century see Copeland.

Chapter 3. Disavowing Romance

1. Kingsford characterized the fifteenth century in Britain as "the threshold of a new epoch in historical literature" (7); some fifty years later Gransden would identify the emergence of the vernacular chronicle as "perhaps the most remarkable historiographical development in the fifteenth century" (ii, 220).

2. On the developing generic distinction, see Strohm, "Middle English." On scholarly responses to the generic problem of romance see Strohm, "Origin and Meaning" and Crane.

3. I borrow these terms from John Watts who offers them not for their accuracy, but for their display of longstanding views of the period. Watts notes that these terms have been replaced by a "more modern idiom" emphasizing "dynastic struggle, factional conflict, and private vendetta." The difficulties of the period of the Wars of the Roses have been, as A. J. Pollard argues, "demystified" by more careful accounts. See Pollard, 110–33.

4. The text is taken from *Morte Arthure: A Critical Edition*, ed. Mary Hamel (New York: Garland, 1984). Translations are my own, aided by Hamel's excellent glossary.

5. With that in mind it seems important to note that the poet's meta-textual reference occurs at a moment Hamel identifies as "the poet's most complex use of sources in the poem" (42). The sources and analogues to the episode of the Dream of the Nine Worthies and Fortune's Wheel span a particularly wide range of genres, well beyond the two mentioned: Laȝamon's *Brut* (chronicle) and the Vulgate *Mort Artu* (romance) are the most immediate, but also include Dante's *Inferno*, Boethius' *Consolation of Philosophy*, Jacques de Longuyon's *Voeux du Paon*, perhaps through an intermediary source, the Middle English *Parlement of the Thre Ages*. The "plurality" of this text's genre and plot include encyclopedic forms, on as grand a scale as Arthur's power. Encyclopedic sovereigns deserve encyclopedic poems.

6. Martin Ball implies the importance of this intimacy when he remarks that the poet mentions "the opposing terms of romance and chronicle in the same breath" (374). Despite Ball's interest in troubling the question of genre and the *Morte*, he seems at this moment to invest in the very opposition he wishes to trouble. In fact, Ball's own attention to what he calls the "generic conundrum" sur-

rounding the poem concludes with the caution that "univocal generic approaches to the poem lead only to hermeneutic *culs-de-sac*," suggesting that "the riddle of *Morte Arthure* is its plurality" (374).

7. Scholars tend to view medieval romance as a problematic, irregular genre, one difficult to categorize. Generic definitions are, according to some, so broad as to be useless; the etymological relation, moreover, of the modern term "romance" to the medieval "romans," (i.e., vernacular text) has led others to recommend we eschew the term entirely. These accounts emphasize the failures, limitations, omissions, or imprecisions of romance, whether in their own efforts at generic definitions, or in the texts themselves. Yet for all its generic plasticity, the romance mode also engages an almost cliched set of repetitions, what Barron calls "the same essential experiences" and "the same conventional motifs" (4). Medieval romance combines, as Susan Wittig puts it, "variability and redundance" (18). Medieval romance, in these accounts, eludes our best efforts at definition while remaining, paradoxically, an entirely predictable kind of text. This combination of "variability" and "redundance" deserves more interrogation, especially in so far as its "variability" converges on a repetitive kind of sameness. Repetition seems, in these accounts, a narrative dead-end, a failure that admirers of romance must explain away. Despite its repetition of familiar forms and figures, scholars have also positioned medieval romance at moments of crucial cultural shifts and historic innovations of tremendous consequence. See Wittig; Jameson, *Political Unconscious*. Fradenburg's reading of the Wife of Bath's Tale also positions the genre at a crucial moment of cultural transition, a result of the rise of capitalism and the creation of a certain kind of interiority.

8. Scholars of Malory have made important arguments in this regard, suggesting the usefulness and, indeed literary sophistication, of Malory's ambitious synthesizing project.

9. When, just a few lines later, the philosopher praises Arthur's textual legacies, he seems, as editor Hamel puts it, "to have been distracted from the suffering and regret of the dream-figures by the fame and glamour of the Nine Worthies" since he "manages to make Doomsday an attractive prospect" for Arthur, whom he names the boldest of them all (366). "In this context," Hamel writes, "the promise of fame in 'romance' and 'chronicle' is both ironic and illusory" (366). As Hamel implies, the philosopher's interpretation slips between castigating the excesses of sovereign conquest and praising Arthur's legacies. Yet fame is not the same as praise; nor is popularity the same as virtue.

10. Patterson, "The historiography of romance." Hamel notes, much more briefly, the historical implications of the poet's "tragic sense" (ix–x).

11. Psychological "encryptment" of a past pleasure or trauma has been theorized by Nicholas Abraham and Maria Torok, "A Poetics of Psychoanalysis," 3–17. Fiction making, they theorize, can offer a system of analogical references for the burial of a memory "of an idyll experienced with a prestigious object that for some reason has become unspeakable" (4). The unspeakable memory of an "idyllic moment" becomes "entombed in a fast and secure place," a "preservative repression . . . [set] up within the ego [as] a closed-off place, a crypt, . . . the consequence of a self-governing mechanism" (4). The subject can encase (that is, simultaneously

preserve and repress) the memory of a something that must be disavowed, all trace of it denied and disguised. The internment of this memory "without a legal burial place" (i.e., without a visible trace in the psyche of the subject) is experienced as a traumatic and double-edged loss: the loss of the idyllic moment and of any consolation its memory might bring. The loss becomes a mummified object, preserved within the subject. Its shadow "keeps on straying about the crypt endlessly until it is finally reincarnated in the very person of the subject," where it will still "remain utterly concealed" (5). For Abraham and Torok, the encryptment, no matter how concealed it remains for the subject, will haunt language and speech. In an important footnote to their essay, they point to the intergenerational—and thus, historic—effects of such encryptment. As they put it: "Should a child have parents 'with secrets,' parents whose speech is not exactly complementary to their unstated repressions, he will receive from them a gap in the unconscious, an unknown, unrecognized knowledge . . . subjected to a form of 'repression' before the fact. The buried speech of the parent becomes (a) dead (gap), without a burial place, in the child . . . . Its effect can persist through several generations and determine the fate of an entire family line" (17). That a repressed unspeakable memory can persist through several generations marks encryptment as a process of particular pertinence to the telling of a history.

12. Marcuse argues that acceptance of death encodes our "compliance with the Master over death." Submission and acceptance thus refigure our willingness to submit to and to accept the demands of the state. See, "The Ideology of Death," 64–76. Fradenburg suggests how Marcuse's insight might pertain to the larger psychoanalytic tradition, and to Medieval Studies itself. See "Voice Memorial."

13. This has been done most famously by Matthews, *The Tragedy of Arthur*.

14. On the *translatio imperii* tradition more generally, see J. H. Burns, *The Cambridge History of Medieval Political Thought*. We should note that the *translatio* tradition fueled competing fictions of Rome's legacy: rulers of both Byzantium and Western Christendom used it. For another reading of the pertinence of this tradition to the Alliterative, see Patterson, *Negotiating* especially 201 and following. The notion of imperial rule as a "universal" standard, as the reader may recall, has been used to suggest that the claims of medieval sovereigns were not colonial "in the modern sense of the term." See Ullman, "This Realm of England." Riddy suggests the limitations of this view; see "Contextualizing," 69.

15. Beal notes, albeit briefly, the ideological force of the contrast between Arthur and the giant; their battle becomes, Beal argues, "a battle between medieval versions of civilization and barbarism" (38). Especially since "where the giant literally consumes those under his rule—most notably the innocent children—Arthur wears the work of his people, products which he, like Edward III, pays well" (37). Heng, we recall, has linked the ideological force of this episode (in Geoffrey of Monmouth's version) with the encryptment of the traumatic memory of Crusader cannibalism. With Heng's work in mind, the material accoutrements of Arthur's armor remind us that another way the Crusaders "consumed" the East was through the importation of goods from overseas. Arthurian texts are filled with references to the eastern goods used to display Arthur's sovereign power.

16. Lacan writes that the "fragmented body . . . usually manifests itself in

dreams when the movement of the analysis encounters a certain level of aggressive disintegration of the individual" ("The Mirror Stage," 4). He notes, moreover, that "imagos of the fragmented body," "images of castration, mutilation, dismemberment dislocation, evisceration, devouring, bursting open of the body" represent "aggressive intentions . . . with an efficacy that might be called magical" ("Aggressivity in Psychoanalysis," 11). See "The Mirror Stage" and "Aggressivity in Psychoanalysis" from *Ecrits*.

17. Textually the vow on Veronica's cloth in the Alliterative replaces the vow found in the poet's source, the *Vows of the Heron*, where Edward III vows by Jesus' "sweet mother," the Virgin Mary.

18. This moment alludes as well to the well established links between crusade and pilgrimage, raising the question of whether the poetic force is here, as Brian Stone reads it, "ironic" (*King Arthur's Death*, 42, n.2). The legendary history of Veronica's cloth is not unlike the legendary history of the Shroud of Turin, a relic also associated with crusade, pilgrimage and the infamous history of the Knights Templar; see Malcolm Barber, *New Knighthood*. On the tradition dating back to Joseph Hammer linking the Grail Legend to the history of the Knights Templar, see Peter Partner, 156–80.

19. Giraldus Cambrensis, *Itinerarium Cambriae seu laboriosae Baldvini Cantuariensis Archiepiscopi per Walliam legationis accurata descriptio, auctore Silv. Giraldo Cambrense*, ed. David Powell (London: Bulmer, 1806). Gerald's glossing, obviously, resonates with the spiritual tradition of the *Imitatio Christi*.

20. It is interesting to note in this regard that in the midst of the scene of vowing on the "Holy Vernacle," the Welsh king vehemently repudiates another figure associated with the dragon-image, the Viscount of Rome (see lines 320–32). Such repudiation bespeaks an implicit desire to construct Welsh sovereign claims as the enemy of the dragon-bearer. Welsh claims to sovereignty over the island of Britain are, of course, implicated in Glyn Dŵr's rebellion and in his use of the dragon standard. On the earlier tradition of political adaptations of the title "King Arthur," see Patterson, *Negotiating*, 205–6. The Middle English Prose *Brut*, describes Mortimer's apparently illegitimate use of Arthurian trappings in Wales as rendering him nothing more than the "King of Folly": "ffor he was so ful of pride and of wrecchednesse, þat he helde a rounde table in Walys to alle men þat þider wolde come, and countrefetede þe maner & doyng of Kynge Arthures table; but openly he failede, ffor þe noble Knyȝt Arthure was þe moste worþi lord of renoun þat was in al þe worlde in his tyme" (262). Descriptions of Arthurian impostors cast Arthur as set-apart, unique, and utterly irreplaceable.

21. In light of Scarry's analysis of "the structure of war" (suggesting that foreignness, during times of war, constitutes a particularly intense kind of unbelief) such convergence is unsurprising (*The Body in Pain*, 128–33).

22. See E. Jane Burns, especially 125–34.

23. For a reading of mourning and masculinity see my "Homosociality and Creative Masculinity in the *Knight's Tale*," 23–35.

24. Her address emphasizes Arthur's maleness, and the unusual term careman (a word that specifically designates, as Hamel's glossary notes, a "male human being") occurs nowhere else in the poem.

Chapter 4. "In Contrayez Straunge"

1. Leaving aside for a moment the historiographic problem of what exactly we might know of the "medieval reality" of ethnicity from such discourses, I wish to acknowledge Bartlett's historical precision. With regard to such differences, however, scholars have increasingly begun to remind us of the biologically-driven medieval Christian discourse regarding Jews. Stephen Kruger writes, "that Jews are thought to be different from Christians in the very biology of their bodies suggests at least a proto-racial definition of Jewishness" (35).

2. This suggests the need for a more detailed explication of medieval conversion than can be given at the moment. See Viswanathan, *Outside the Fold*, especially pp. xi–xvii.

3. The text is taken from *Giraldo Cambrense, Cambriae Descriptio*, ed. David Powell. Translations are from Lewis Thorpe, trans., *Gerald of Wales*.

4. "Proinde quasi poenitentia jam fere peracta, et quoniam numero praeter solitum et multitudine, viribus et armis, bellorum quoque successibus et terrarum incrementis, nostris plurimum diebus adaucti sunt, gloriantur ad invicem, praedicant et confidentissime jactant, toto (quod mirum est) in hac spe populo manente, quoniam in brevi cives in insulam revertentur, et juxta Merlini sui vaticinia exterorum tam natione pereunte quam nuncupatione antiqua in insula tam nomine quam omine Britones exultabunt. Sed mihi longe aliter visum est. . . . Ut paupertati potius in hoc exilio, quo extorres fere facti sunt a regno, attribuenda sit vicii illius, quo in divitiis carere nescierant, illa carentia quam virtuti" (227–28).

5. Gerald's work also attests to the slipperiness of this structure; earlier his words have indicated that the results of poverty could, indeed, go both ways: "The natural propensities of the Welsh may well have been corrupted and changed for the worse by their long exile and their lack of prosperity. Poverty puts an end to many of our vices, but it has been known to encourage us in our wrongdoing" (255). The changes prompted by indigence offer potential dangers here. Yet if this moment points to the contradictions in Gerald's description, and ambivalences in his tone—thus offering the possibility for a more liberatory reading of Gerald's representation of Welsh ethnicity—the final moments of Gerald's *Description* makes clear the ultimate goal of his writing. His final chapters offer a manual for English conquest, recommending "How the Welsh can be Conquered," by encouraging Welsh factionalism: the Welsh "spirit of hatred and jealousy" can be of use to the would-be conqueror provided he "sow dissension in their ranks and do all he can by promises and bribes to stir them up against each other" (267).

6. Hechter's analysis of "internal colonialism" suggests that peripheral "backwardness"—and, by extension, disunity—link directly to core "progress," pointing to the limitations of the infrastructure available to peripheral regions in colonial situations. In Hechter's logic, centralization and economic monopoly serve the interests of "core" culture; thus few resources are left within the "periphery" for a simultaneous peripheral centralization and consolidation. Insofar as colonial economy and public works (roads, access to services) funnel resources into, in this case, London, little might be left to encourage or enable a Welsh populace to unify. Moreover, Hechter reminds us that colonial relations obscure

economic causal structures, with causes for peripheral "backwardness" remaining ideologically linked, not to the economic demands of the conqueror, but to cultural attributes of the conquered (33–34). Hechter thus suggests that the fundamentally opposed economic interests of England and Wales were opposed precisely because they were fundamentally linked, arguing that English annexation served a variety of English economic needs: the reclamation of arable land for cultivation, the solidification of a fighting force, the maintenance of territorial "integrity" for the sake of insular security (67–71).

7. Jeffrey Cohen has recently read Gerald's text, as his identity, through Gloria Anzaldua's notion of the "mestiza" and in distinction to Bhabha's notion of "hybridity" (an implicitly masculine figure in Bhabha's use). Arguing for the term "mestiza," like "borderland," as encoding a more flexibly multiple notion of space and identity (a place of "new and impure hybrids") Cohen resists Bhabha's "hybrid" (along with the term "frontier") as a particularly *English* literary figure. ("Hybrids," 96). I explain my engagement with Bhabha below.

8. Recent analyses of special pertinence include Aers, *Community, Gender, and Individual Identity*, 153–78; Spearing, "The Gawain-poet's Sense of an Ending," 195–215. Both Aers and Spearing challenge a tradition of christianized readings of *Gawain* that overemphasize (and even invent) the poem's religious orthodoxy. Both Aers and Spearing attend, albeit somewhat briefly, to the gendering of honor and knightly nobility in the tale. In "Feminine Knots" Heng displays "the feminine narrative folded into and between the masculine one," and argues for the power of feminine agency (500–514). Sheila Fisher argues that, despite such powers, the poem finally enacts an erasure of female power, rendering women (like the girdle) as "tokens" in the homosocial honor code. See "Taken Men and Token Women," 71–105. Dinshaw has considered the "relation of heterosexuality and homosexual relations" as part of the text's strategy of marking homosexual desires and actions as literally unintelligible. See "A Kiss Is Just a Kiss," 205–26. While Heng's, Fisher's, and Dinshaw's arguments point in crucial ways to the complications of sex and gender within the romance, none of them consider in any detail the relation of those complications region or colony. Sarah Stanbury's analyses of the "visual poetics of the Gawain-poet" attends to issues of land (particularly in her exceptionally fine reading of Gawain's famous winter journey in Fitt II) as socially constructed space. See *Seeing the Gawain-Poet*.

9. Most accounts emphasize the successful blendings of such diversities. The poem's impressive unities have attracted critical admiration for decades. See Tolkein and Gordon's critical edition of *Sir Gawain and the Green Knight*, xi–xxvii.

10. Not all readers agree with Tolkein and Gordon that this is a remarkable aspect of the poem's opening. There are a host of other examples of "Arthur" in its Welsh spelling in the late medieval period; moreover, this could as easily represent a scribal modification as a poetic choice. In the context of textual evidence of the poet's interest in Welsh territories and their relation to Arthur's court, however, the spelling takes on greater significance. Given the textual evidence I detail in the next few pages, the issue of Arthur's "Welsh" connections cannot be summarily dismissed as a mere convention. What would, after all, be the cultural meaning of such a convention?

11. Quotations are taken from *Sir Gawain and the Green Knight*, edited by J. R. R. Tolkein and E. V. Gordon, second edition, edited by Norman Davis. Translations are my own.

12. See for example, W. R. J. Barron, "Arthurian Romance," 2–23.

13. On the question of Welsh sources and analogues, see Bromwich *Trioedd*, especially 274–77, 461–63. The Welsh connection was (infamously) of interest to R. S. Loomis and Laura Hibbard Loomis, although the Loomises' work has since been discredited.

14. Bennett also suggests confluences between Gawain's journey through the Wirral and Richard II's return from Ireland in 1399 (*Cheshire and Lancashire*, 231–35). Recent datings of the poem in the 1380s, of course, make it difficult to draw direct conclusions from these similarities. I am arguing that the poem negotiates the demands of royalism, but not by enthusiastically endorsing them.

15. The question of the location of Camelot is an interesting one and, despite assertions to the contrary in the Tolkein and Gordon edition, not entirely settled. The editors write "The general direction of Gawain's itinerary is clear: since he rode into North Wales, and came 'þur3 þe ryalme of Logres,' a southern site of Camelot is to be inferred" (97, note on lines 691 ff.).

16. My interest in the ethnic implications of region is indebted to Deleuze and Guattari's "Of the Refrain" in *A Thousand Plateaus* (310–50). Their notions of "deterritorialization" and "reterritorialization" inform my reading of Gawain's journey as a kind of colonization, wherein a territory, figured as wild, is mapped, claimed, civilized. On the relation between "wildness" and medieval categories of ethnicity, see Bernheimer.

17. See Stanbury, especially 106–7. On the specifics of topographical references within the text see Ralph Elliot.

18. Ethnic discourse in Medieval Britain repeatedly figures the western reaches of Wales and the Scottish highlands, as well as parts of Cornwall as places of wildness. By the time of Glyn Dŵr, English Parliamentary debate had already taken to describing Glyn Dŵr and his supporters in terms of their wild desires and habits, imagining a Wild Celtic West peopled with "wild men." This image of a wild Welsh poised at the farthest western edge of the island shows debts to Monmouth's *Historia*. Fernandez-Armesto notes that ethnographic images of the "wild man" fueled the colonizing discourses of Crusade. He notes, moreover, the genealogy of images of Europe's imaginary "others" have their earlier doubles in texts which offer a "scrutiny of . . . Europe's internal 'primitives': . . . folk like the Basques, Welsh, Irish, Slavs, and pagan Scandinavians, whose cultures inspired mingled awe and contempt" (225).

19. For a fine analysis of the text's disorienting management of perception and consciousness (both Gawain's and the poem's readers'/hearers') see Ganim, *Style and Consciousness*, 55–78.

20. On pertinent regional and colonial politics, see Bennett; Davies, *Conquest*, and "Frontier Arrangements," 77–100; John A. F. Thomson; David Walker, "Cultural Survival," 35–50.

21. Centralized governments, and the histories written about them, tend to depict a homogeneous populace. See Davies, "Fragmented," 100.

22. See particularly Aers' compelling critique of the spiritualized readings of those he calls scholars of a "priestly caste" (153–78); also Spearing, "The Gawain-Poet's Sense of an Ending," 195–215.

23. For an analysis of the medieval debate over the honorman's lineage and virtue see James. On honor and knightly identity, see Jameson, *Political Unconscious*, 118 ff; for a psychoanalytic reading of knightly masculinity, see Fradenburg, *City, Marriage, Tournament*, 204–12.

24. Jameson, "Romance as Genre," 135–63. Haidu, 1–46, for example.

25. Stanbury argues that the Green Knight's challenge to Arthur makes the troubles of Arthur's power visible in a way it has not been before this moment: "Camelot is perhaps not as ordered, its structure not as coherently apparent as we are led to believe in the opening of the poem" (97). I am arguing that fractures in glory—in particular the relation of glory to colonial losses and gains—are legible from the outset.

26. For a summary of the critical responses to the question of Arthur's youth see Moody. On the implied critique of Arthur more generally, see Dean, especially chapter 4 "Middle English Arthurian Romances," 64–90. Nicholls defends Arthur's honor and argues that the references to Arthur's boyishness "would only have a distinctly critical connotation if used of a much older man" (116). He emphasizes instead the discourtesy of the Green Knight. The debate invests in a more distinct split between virtue and discourtesy than the text itself displays. I am arguing for a more subtle reading of the two kinds of power represented here. Other critics debate the extent to which Hautdesert can be regarded as a provincial court or as an extension of Camelot. This is, in my reading, a central question for the text (as well as its context). See Blanch and Wasserman, 176–88, for the former view, and Bergner, 401–16, for the latter.

27. *The Chronicle of Adam of Usk (A.D. 1377–1421)*, ed. and trans. Sir Edward Maunde Thompson.

28. For contemporary accounts of Richard's kingship, see Given-Wilson, ed.; for a general analysis of the problems of his kingship see his "Introduction," 1–52.

29. In an analysis that also reads the tale's pertinence to a "coming of age" masculinity, Cohen remarks, "The poem situates itself as a prequel to the Matter of Britain, set in the days before those betrayals which dismembered the court, in the days before the formation of Arthurian identity. . . . The grimly serious Green Knight [rebukes] the court['s] lightheartedness and youth" ("Decapitation," 182). Cohen's analysis of the decapitation topos points to the gendered and psychoanalytic register available within that narrative tradition, and I think his analysis can be pushed further by noting the resemblances between beheading topoi and the celtic "head of the king" motif; I would, however, trouble his implication that youth in a sovereign (as opposed to a knight) is desirable.

30. Davies discusses in particular the role Henry II's Christmas festivities held outside Dublin in the twelfth century played in gaining tribute and loyalty from local Irish rulers (unpublished manuscript, Medieval Studies colloquium, University of California, Santa Barbara, May 1992).

31. On the ways sovereign displays of fictions (masque and tournament, for

example) make its power and its pleasure "self-legitimating," see Fradenburg, *City, Marriage, Tournament*, 224–64.

32. See Suleri, *Rhetoric*, 16–17.

33. A more thorough examination of this question is limited by considerations of space. For a summary of scholarship on the medieval category of homosexuality and an argument as to its pertinence to *Gawain*, see Dinshaw, "A Kiss." She reads the "relation of heterosexuality and homosexual relations" as part of the text's strategy of marking homosexual desires and actions as unintelligible. The final paragraph of Dinshaw's article inspired my own reworking of the connection between colonial relations and homophobic anxieties.

34. Bertilak's good humor and clear delight at Morgan's command invites other readings (like Heng's) which foreground the text's fascination with women's desire and power. Delight and fascination are, of course, part of the ambivalence that I am arguing is here particularly colonial.

35. Morgan "Þe goddes," and Bertilak's Lady—whose parallel descriptions recall the hag/beauty relation of the loathly lady tradition—refigure traditions of female sovereignty from Celtic folklore, traditions that mark sovereign power as relationship itself, as a marriage between a male consort and the lady of the land. Such associations link Morgan's sovereignty to a competing tradition of rule. On the sovereign associations of Morgan le Fay, see Angela Carson; Douglas Moon; Margaret Jennings. On the similarity between the splitting of Bertilak's Lady and Morgan and the folk figure of the loathly lady, see Spearing, "Central and Displaced Sovereignty." On the uses of the loathly lady tradition in Middle English Arthurian texts, and its consequences for knighthood and conquest, see Chapter 6.

36. I agree with Aers' assessment of the "shadowy" interiority of Gawain, "bearing judgements and language that contradict" Camelot's honor code. Aers, 177.

37. Suleri's language carries vague resonances of a military register: the coordination of deference suggests a spatial mapping of synchronized troop movements. This points to a need, within analyses of colonial situations, for attention to the particularly destabilizing intimacies of military zones.

38. A slightly altered version of the material in this chapter, within a larger consideration of the uses of postcolonial methods with regard to pre-modern texts, see Ingham, " 'In Contrayez Straunge.' "

Chapter 5. Dangerous Liaisons

1. In linking passion with war, de Rougemont troubles a generic classification dating back to Aristotle, one commonly used by medieval rhetoricians like Isidore of Seville. In his *Etymologies*, Isidore places tragedy (with its epic tales of war and death) in the realm of "public acts" and the "histories of kings," while comedy (the genre of marriages and happy endings) is said to tell us the private deeds of men. Isidore writes, "Sed comici privatorum hominum praedicant acta, Tragici vero res publicas, et regum historias; item tragicorum argumenta ex rebus luctuosis sunt, comicorum ex rebus laetis" (*Etymologies*, 9).

2. Besides Sedgwick's *Between Men*, see Rubin; Irigaray; Butler; and Goldberg.

3. W. R. J. Barron, although arguing that the variety of examples of romance in England defy precise generic classifications, describes traditional histories of the romance typifying that genre as "a feminine counterpart to the personal prowess and comradeship of military heroes" (25) and "an evolutionary development in which a feminine idealism of the emotions is superimposed upon and partly displaces a male idealism of action" (27). See his *English Medieval Romance*. See also Mills et al., eds. While a variety of scholars assert that, in the words of David Burnley, "No one any longer believes in the sharp dichotomies epic and romance, heroic and courtly, which were accepted by earlier scholars" (Mills et al., eds., 175), most accounts continue to distinguish romance from epic on the basis of gender representations. While I sympathize with the desire to recover positive representations of women within the genre, these analyses remain unable to account for the complexities of production in a culture that, despite its representations of women as praise-worthy, might still be furthering a misogynist project. For an example of this kind of analysis, see Warner.

4. See Fradenburg on Kristeva's theory of motherhood and the functioning of gender in the war context of Chaucer's *Troilus and Criseyde*, " 'Our owen wo to Drynke.' "

5. De Lauretis' gloss on Freud's frontier ego can help us explain both the fascinations with relationship and the anxieties of agency already observed in *Gawain*. They will help us, shortly, reconsider the identification of women with the complications of relationship as a displacement of the complications of agency obtaining for all subjects.

6. R. Howard Bloch makes a similar observation on the suicidal nature of the identification of women with what he terms a misogynist genre, yet does not analyze it in the ways I am suggesting. See *Medieval Misogyny*, 176–77.

7. See Bruce and Hissiger's "Introduction." A few other scholars address the text, however briefly, as deserving of attention in its own right. See for example Ramsey and Stone.

8. On the whole, critical analyses of Arthurian romance that attempt comprehensive readings of those texts emphasize Arthurian stories as part of legend, analyzing them, in much the same way de Rougemont does, as expressions of a psychological, or in some cases, mytho-religious impulse within the western European psyche, an approach indebted to anthopological analysis of the early twentieth century. The most famous treatment of Arthurian traditions is Weston, *From Ritual to Romance*. Revisionary work during the past decade has emphasized political and materialist readings of particular Arthurian texts. The work of Felicity Riddy; Michelle Warren; Kathleen Kelly; Bonnie Wheeler; Jeffrey Jerome Cohen; Stephen Knight; Martin Shichtman and James Carley, is exemplary.

9. On the differences between the Middle English poem and the French prose account, see Hissiger's introduction to the Middle English critical edition, especially 9–10; for a summary of the French version, see Bruce, 369–79.

10. The *Mort Artu*'s representation of the male sovereign's desire might carry

erotic valences as well. This also implies that male prowess requires an (apparently female) audience before which it can stage the spectacle of its honor.

11. All references to Froissart are taken from the Penguin edition of his *Chronicles*, translated and edited by Geoffrey Brereton.

12. Scarry argues that violent contests provide a place—namely the body of the believer—wherein abstract cultural allegiances can be quite literally made real. See *The Body in Pain*, 60–155.

13. This text, furthermore, suggests that the practice of chivalric rescue might actually be based upon contempt for the weakness (perhaps moral as well as physical?) of the subject in need of such rescue. See Freud, "A Special Type of Object Choice Made by Men" (1910), 162–72. Also Fradenburg, "'Our owen wo to Drynke.'"

14. See Froissart, 177–78.

15. It seems safe to conclude that a late fourteenth-century audience of *Le Morte Arthur* might have viewed him in these terms, especially given the fact that *Gawain* dates from roughly the same period.

16. For a summary of the uses made by Glyn Dŵr of Arthur and the Merlin prophecies, see R. R. Davies, *Conquest*, especially pp. 447 ff.; see also Chapters 2 and 3.

17. See Fradenburg's analysis of the heroization of suffering *for* and its role in the devaluation of survival, recovery, or the suffering of those prohibited from such heroization in "'Our owen wo to drynke,'" especially 88–89.

18. I am indebted here to Bloch, "Death, Women, Power"; Marcuse, "The Ideology of Death"; Theweleit, "The Politics of Orpheus."

Chapter 6. Military Intimacies

1. Although the exact date of presentation cannot be established absolutely, Dyboski argues convincingly for a love-day presentation on the basis of a variety of textual and historical details. See his introduction to *Knyghthode and Bataile*, especially xvi–xxiv.

2. Ralph A. Griffiths, *The Reign of Henry VI*, 804–8. For contemporary accounts of London's militarization, see "Bale's Chronicle," ed. Ralph Flenley, *Six Town Chronicles of England; The Great Chronicle of London*, ed. A. H. Thomas and I. D. Thornley.

3. According to *The Great Chronicle of London*, "[T]he duke of York the Erlis of warwyk and Salysbury were sent for to london to the Counsayll, and thidir cam the forsaid duke the xxvj day of Januarii w[ith] CCCC men and was loggid at Baynardis castell. And the xvth day of bt said monyth cam therle of Salysbury with vC men and was lodgid in therber. And aftir cam the dukis of Excetir/and Somyrset with viii C men which said ii dukis lay wythowte temple barre. And therle of Northumbirland the lord Egremond and the lord Clyfford with xv C men which were loggid wythowte the towne. Wherfor the mayre with the Shyryffis Constablis and othir officers of the Cyte kepte grete wacch. In so moch that as

longe as these said lordis were at this Counsayll the mayre rode abowte the Cyte dayly and the Circuyte of Holboourn and Fletestrete accompanyed with v M men or thereabowte well and ffensibely Arayed for the warre to se that the kynges peas were kepte. And the xiii day of ffebruarii therle of warwyk cam to london from Caleys with vi C men alle apparaylid in Rede Jakettis with white Raggid stavis. And he was loggid at the Gray Freris."

4. The pageant is described in John Stowe's *Annales or A Generall Chronicle of England*, continuation by Edmund Howes (London, 1631): "For the outward publishing of this joyful agreement there was upon our Lady's day in Lent, on five and twentieth day of March a solemne procession celebrated within the Cathedral Church of Saint Paule in the City of London: at which the King was present in his habite royall with the Crowne on his head, before him went hand in hand the Duke of Somerset, and Earle of Salisbury, the Duke of Exeter and the Earle of Warwicke, and so one of the one faction and another of the other. And behinde the King the Duke of Yorke and the Queene with great familiarity to all men's fights, whatsoever was meant to the contrary which appeared afterward" (404).

5. In "Of the Refrain," Gilles Deleuze and Felix Guattari link what they call the expressive impulse to the demarcation of territory, suggesting the ways in which acts of expression (art, music, narrative, and, I would add, civic spectacle) work to circumscribe territory and declare territorial possession. As they put it: "The expressive is primary in relation to the possessive: expressive qualities, or matters of expression, are necessarily appropriative and constitute a having more profound than being. Not in the sense that these qualities belong to a subject, but in the sense that they delineate a territory that will belong to the subject that carries or produces them. These qualities are signatures, but the signature, the proper name, is not the constituted mark of a subject, but the constituting mark of a domain, an abode" (316). As an expression of peacefulness the Love-day procession claims a territory belonging to those producing the spectacle. The territorial appropriation seem all the more apt in this case, since the expressive rhythm of the spectacle involved transversing the actual territory, crossing through the streets of London to St. Paul's Cathedral. See *A Thousand Plateaus*, especially 316–20.

6. For recent revisionary histories see J. R. Lander, C. D. Ross, John Gillingham, R. L. Storey, M. H. Keen, D. M. Loades. See also the recent collection A. J. Pollard, ed., *The Wars of the Roses*, especially pp. 110–33. For attention to regionalism of violence, see Goodman, *The Wars of the Roses*; Storey, "Lincolnshire and the Wars of the Roses," 64–82.

7. Goodman notes the considerable number of battles taking place in the outlying regions of the realm: the Northumbrian campaigns of 1461–64 resulted in battles at Hedgeley and Hexham (both 1464); Townton, near York (1461); and Wakefield (1460). There were, in addition, battles at Blore Heath, near Chester (1459), and at Stoke, near Lincoln (1487). Goodman explains this lack of comment on the regionalism of London chroniclers: "The authors [of London-based chronicles] were unlikely to be concerned about the reduction of provincials to beggary" (197).

8. Griffiths corroborates Goodman's account, reading sovereign instability of the years 1456–59 as especially evident in the outlying regions of the realm but

not in London: "Bands of men roamed the country at will," Griffiths recounts, "although a few commissions were nominated to restrain and suppress them, especially in peripheral areas like the Welsh march, the far south-west, and Norfolk, the court's preoccupation with its own security limited their success in dealing with crime in the realm at large. Therein lay the real threat to the house of Lancaster, for these areas were frequently dominated by the estates and retainers of the Yorkist lords" (807).

9. While a more thorough explication of Margaret's queenship stands outside the concerns of this chapter, I would like to point to the complications of gender legible in that historiography. The relation between Margaret and Henry and the apparent gender reversals of their marriage (she, too political, too violent, too active, too strong, too much involved in the affairs of state; he, enfeebled, ill, distraught, depressed, ineffective, passive) are implicitly or explicitly critiqued in most histories about this royal couple. I am suggesting the extent to which Margaret and Henry's display of sovereign power is inextricably linked; their cultural functions are mutually implicated. Margaret's denigration in the histories thus helps produce kindlier historiographic judgments about Henry. For the dependencies of male sovereignty upon queenship, see Fradenburg, ed., *Women and Sovereignty*. For histories of Margaret of Anjou, see Haswell; Baudier; Erlanger. For Margaret's role in the Wars of the Roses, see Ross; Gillingham; Storey.

10. On the sacrificial nature of knighthood, see Fradenburg, "Sacrificial Desire in Chaucer's *Knight's Tale*," and " 'Our owen wo to drynke.' "

11. See Ingham, "Homosociality and Creative Masculinity in the *Knight's Tale*," especially pp. 24–28.

12. Goodman suggests differences between the picture of military organization offered by *Knyghthode and Bataile* and actual military tactics during the period: "It is difficult to be sure that the Vegetian advice given by the author of *Knyghthode and Bataile* about complex tactical formations and maneuvers was more than a literary fancy, as far as the Wars of the Roses were concerned. Probably masses of hastily arrayed contingents, often brought into battle within days of assembling, could only be expected to line up for a frontal assault or defense with their tradition weapons, bow and bill" (193). The gulf between idealized military organization and actual practice would, however, emphasize the value a treatise like *Knyghthode and Bataile* would have for a culture deploying militarism to unify its fighting forces. The absence of such a well-structured troop implies the important, and complicated, relationship scrappy forces might have to categories of military unity and order.

13. For a sociological analysis of domestic violence and its function as a form of familial and social control, see Maynard and Hanmer, eds.

14. On the common cultural combination of "hierarchy" with "communitas," see Victor Turner, *The Ritual Process: Structure and Anti-Structure*.

15. The Love-Day ballad is preserved in *A Chronicle of London, from 1089 to 1483, written in the fifteenth century*, edited by Nicholas and Tyrell from MSS in the British Museum.

16. Hechter's *Internal Colonialism* suggests that "The Expansion of the English State" relates to sovereign practices of English land control as early as the

annexation of the kingdom of Wessex in the nineth century. Hechter helpfully reminds us that colonial economies funnel resources into a "national" capital; he also suggests why and how cultural practices might work to obscure such economic systems (47–78). My argument in this chapter suggests links between the consolidation of England's power over Wales with a centralized (London-based) monarchy's attempt rework the vexed relations between northern regions and southern ones.

17. The text for *The Avowing of King Arthur* is taken from Roger Dahood's edition. For a summary of the northern original dialect and dating, see Dahood's introduction, 28–31.

18. Problems of legitimacy and illegitimacy emerge as a preoccupation during this time, emphasized in legal discourse from the period as well as in historical accounts of debates over succession during the period of the Wars of the Roses. John Fortescue's *De Laudibus Legum Angliae* (*Commendation of the Laws of England*), for example, deals extensively with bastardy in four chapters out of some fifty-four. See the following chapters: XXXIX: "Concerning the Legitimation of Children born before Matrimony," XL: "The Reasons why Base-born Children are not in England by the subsequent marriage legitimated," XLII: "Concerning the Rule of the Civil Law: Partus semper sequitur Ventrem," and XLIV: "Concerning the Tuition of Orphans." Fortescue, we remember, was a loyal partisan of Henry VI and was tried for treason before the court of Edward IV. For earlier reflections on law and kinship see Henry de Bracton, *De Legibus et Consuetudinibus Angliae* (Northford: Elliot's Books, 1942). Bracton's treatise, like Fortescue's, narrates precise legal requirements for ownership of land and the conditions of its transfer from husband to wife, father to sons, whether legitimate or illegitimate. Bracton delineates limitations to the conditions under which a woman can inherit, narrowing the legal requirements under which land can be transferred as gift. Issues of land ownership and transfer surfacing as legal concerns in Bracton and Fortescue seem to emerge in their imaginative form in the figure of the loathly lady; see discussion below.

19. Charges of bastardy were, of course, part of the debates over succession. Lancastrian claims to the throne were complicated, at best, as were the changing fortunes of the bar-sinister side of their family, the Beauforts (descendants of John of Gaunt and Katherine Swynford before their marriage). Although legitimized by Richard II's Act of Parliament (later confirmed by Henry IV), the Beauforts were barred from succession by Henry's letter of royal patent in 1407. It would later be decided that a letter of patent could not prevail against an Act of Parliament, in which case the Beauforts were legally able to inherit the crown.

20. On the theorization of the productivity of law, see Butler, *Gender Trouble*; and Rubin, "Traffic."

21. There is an equally interesting reversal here when one compares this scene to Yvain's sojourn at the Castle of Maidens in Chrétien de Troyes' *Yvain*.

22. I am reading this quite differently from Dahood, who explicates this moment with the following editorial note: "With her competition dead, the surviving woman has no reason to be violent and thus can become good" (117). And yet, the logic of virtue Dahood implies as self-evidently available in this text seems, at the very least, ironic. The woman's competitors are dead, in the context of the tale,

because she herself killed them. Medieval discourses of virtue, whether knightly, theological or both, invest not in the ease of unchallenged goodness, but in the value of virtue despite habit, and despite the difficulty one faces in displaying it. The "good" woman, or man, would not, then, be one who has "no reason to be violent" because the rival is dead, but one who eschews treacherous violence despite jealous rivalry, the attribute of Baldwin in the tale.

23. The view that these two episodes originally constituted separate romances has been argued most forcefully by Hanna who reads from stylistic evidence (divergent uses of iteration, stanza-linking, frequency of rhyme repetition, and of parenthetical half-lines) a distinction between *Awntyrs off Arthure*-A (ll. 1–338; 703–15) and *Awntyrs off Arthure*-B (ll. 339–702). While the thoroughness of Hanna's attention to stylistic detail makes his argument worth noting, he overemphasizes the stylistic differences between the two sections. See also Mills, "Introduction"; Hanna; for a response to Hanna, R. Allen. As to the possibility that the stylistic variation might be the work of a single poet, Hanna himself admits, "The critic must consider the poet to be either hard pressed by his chosen mode (and hence unable [in *AA*-B] to exhibit the variety of the use of the form in *AA*-A requires) or else attempting, in at least some places, a different form" (70). Disputing the particularities of Hanna's argument stands outside my concern here, yet I wish to note that his argument does conceive the possibility of poetic experimentation.

24. A. C. Spearing, for example, suggests a diptych structure, in which juxtaposition and symmetry produce unity and meaning, also pointing out that the image of Fortune's wheel is implicit in the poem's design: the opening and closing of the text are nearly identical, with a crowned Arthur dominating the poem's central stanza. For commentaries on the poem's structure and symmetry, see Benson, *Art*, 163; Spearing, *Medieval to Renaissance*, 126–30 and *"The Awntrys off Arthure"* in *Alliterative Tradition*, 183–202; Barron, *English*; and Matsuda, 48–62. For a summary of these arguments, see Phillips.

25. Gower's excessive description of the hag's hideousness is notable, too. The more familiar vehicle for the loathly lady within the Arthurian tradition is, of course, "The Wedding of Gawain and Ragnall."

26. This is not to suggest that heterosexuality and reproduction need necessarily be implicated in structures of state control. I am arguing, however, that certain ways of organizing union crucially link militarism, heterosexism, and misogyny. Kinship practice (the sovereign's dependence upon kinship structures for his legitimacy) provides a forceful constellation of these terms. Thus, historical narratives that emphasize state organization as a teleological drive "From Kinship to Kingship" obscure the dependence of later political forms on kinship structures. For a multicultural reading of the importance of kinship and the body for conservative nationalism even today, see Gutiérrez.

27. It may seem surprising that while the text makes clear that Guinevere's mother's fall came from her sexual excesses ("Þat is to luf paramour and lustes and listes:/ Þat gares me lyghte and lende loy in a lake," she says at lines 212–13), it is remarkably silent about the details. Instead of those (female) delights, this text details the links between desire in terms pertinent to sovereignty: overweening pride, desires for material pleasures, and an excessive appetite for war and conquest. This,

I would argue, demonstrates the extent to which this text is preoccupied with war and appetites for land. The poet connects sexual appetite with desire for land, yet foregrounds the latter rather more than the former.

28. See Phillips, 1–15. See also Rosalind Field, 54–69.

29. Goodman's attention to regionalism can help suggest why a literary culture in the northern border regions might find such narratives useful. If the Wars of the Roses succeeded in bringing the outlying regions into closer relationship to London, it makes sense that citizens of provincial regions would be anxious about relations between centralized monarchies and the provinces.

30. For an analysis of the kinds of violence on the rise during the period, see Keen, *English Society in the Later Middle Ages*, especially 188–98.

31. There are some useful connections to be made here with discourses of kingship from the late medieval period. Beverly Kennedy argues for the pertinence of the military category of "Knights of the King" to Arthurian tradition, stressing Malory's description of the intense identifications between knight and king. Gawain and Galleroun might justifiably be called Arthurian "Knights of the King," suggesting the intensity with which readers are meant to identify the bodies of these knights with the realm. See Kennedy, especially pp. 4–6.

32. For Caxton's text see *The Book of the Ordre of Chyualry, translated and printed by William Caxton*. Fradenburg uses Lacanian categories to analyze Gilbert de Haye's Scots translation of the same text. *City, Marriage, Tournament*, 199 ff.

Chapter 7. "Necessary" Losses

1. See Griffiths, Lander.

2. The text for *The Libel of English Policy* is found in T. Wright, ed., *Political Poems and Songs, vol. II*, Rolls Series, 14: 157–205.

3. This is according to Maitland's readings of Edmund Plowden's *Reports*, collected and written under Queen Elizabeth. See Kantorowicz, pp. 7–8. While Kantorowicz shows how the history of the concept evolved a good deal earlier, he follows Maitland's observations on this pointed articulation. Kantorowicz also notes that "Each transfer of power from Lancaster to York and back was legally interpreted as the demise of the defeated king" (13n).

4. One of the least productive debates within Arthurian studies concerns the precise location of Arthur's court. See Alcock; Ashe.

5. All quotes are taken from *Caxton's Malory: A New Edition of Sir Thomas Malory's Le Morte Darthur based on the Pierpont Morgan Copy of William Caxton's edition of 1485*, ed. James Spisak and William Matthews.

6. Matheson reads Caxton as insincere, see "King Arthur and the Medieval English Chronicles." On Caxton's marketing ability (creating demand for his editions), see Summit; Kuskin.

7. That Caxton enumerates Arthur's imperial title in European, rather than British terms, may seem at first to undercut Arthur's identification with an insular geography. Such a list, indebted to the Alliterative *Morte Arthure*, establishes

Arthur as Emperor rather than simply king. But it also elucidates Arthur's colonial aggressions as happening elsewhere, disavowing conquering relations within the island while granting Arthur the power of Emperor on the Roman model.

8. After a break of nearly two centuries, reprints begin again in 1817, and were published in 1868, 1889, 1893, 1897, 1900, 1910, 1911, and 1933. See Pochoda, *Arthurian Propaganda*, Appendix A, 141–44.

9. See David Rees; and Bennett, *Battle of Bosworth*.

10. On Henry's use of Welsh troops on his march through Wales see David Rees, especially pp. 113–26.

11. On Elizabeth of York's superior claim to the throne, see Wood, "The First Two Queen Elizabeths," 121–31.

12. See Anglo, "The British History," and *Spectacle, Pageantry and Early Tudor Policy*.

13. See Kantorowicz, 371; and *The Great Chronicle of London*, 233.

14. For an analysis see, Mary Wack, *Lovesickness in the Middle Ages*. On the gender politics of the glamour of loss for the male chivalric subject, see Fradenburg, "'Our owen wo to drynke'" and "Soft and Silken War," in *City, Marriage, Tournament*.

15. For Lacan, the recognition of a whole image in the mirror stage is always a misrecognition, a fantasmatic perception of a unity. Identity formation is a site for both aggression and affiliation. See "The Mirror Stage" and "Aggressivity in Psychoanalysis." See also my discussion of Arthur's fragmented body in Chapter 3.

16. These relations hint at the difference between Caxton's and Malory's texts, and thus allude to the famous question of whether Malory intended a "hoole book" or series of romances. In the last half of this century, Caxton's edition was supplanted in scholarly circles, thanks to Eugene Vinaver's reworking of the text of the Winchester Manuscript (published as Malory's *Works*), as a series of romances. Titles of individual tales differ in Caxton's and Vinaver's editions, as do some of the romances themselves. For a summary of the issues at stake see, Meale, "'The Hoole Book,'" 3–17. Important earlier accounts of the debate include Pochoda, *Arthurian Propaganda*, chapter I; Larry D. Benson, *Malory's Morte Darthur*; Terence McCarthy, *Reading the Morte Darthur*; and Felicity Riddy, *Sir Thomas Malory*.

17. On Caxton's editorial flaws, see "Caxton and *Le Morte Darthur*" in *Caxton's Malory*, vol. II, and pp. 601–27. For Hayden White's discussion of chronicle and history, see *The Content of the Form*.

18. Jill Mann describes parallels between "The Tale of Balin" and Arthur's "the final cataclysmic adventure" (91). Kennedy sees in those parallels the suggestion that "Balin's heroic code of ethics and his fatalist world view must be transcended if Arthurian society is to avoid self-destruction" (9). In emphasizing these similarities as doubles rather than parallels I am pointing to the ambivalence of the *Morte* itself. I am unconvinced that the text offers as neat a resolution to the problems of community, knighthood, and kingship as Kennedy suggests. See Mann, "'Taking the Adventure,'" 71–91; Kennedy, *Knighthood in the Morte Darthur*.

19. See again Bronfen. A more subversive view of the pleasures of submission have recently been retheorized by Leo Bersani, "Foucault, Freud, Fantasy and Power," 11–33.

20. On the experience of reading the *Morte* and on its use of parataxis, see Wheeler, "Romance and Parataxis and Malory," 109–32. In support of Malory's parataxis see also McCarthy; Riddy. On the limitations of parataxis, see P. J. C. Field, *Romance and Chronicle*.

21. On the process of encryptment and identity see Abraham and Torok.

22. On religious formulations of corporate identity, see Kantorowicz, especially Chapter 5, "Polity Centered Kingship: Corpus Mysticum," 193–232. On the importance of bodies and kinship to modern national imaginings of race, see Gutiérrez.

23. They converge as well in the traditions of the King's Two Bodies. As Rosemond Tuve writes, "the nature and limits of the King's sacred authority and his relation to the polity are crucial problems for fifteenth-century jurists[,] . . . anxious to determine what characterizes England as a nation and to determine what or who comprises this nation as well as to establish for posterity the means by which the nation will perpetuate itself" (340). See Tuve, *Allegorical Imagery*.

24. See Warner, *Alone of All Her Sex*.

25. These texts can be found in *The Coronation of Richard III: The Extant Documents*, ed. Anne F. Sutton and P. W. Hammond (New York: St. Martin's, 1984).

26. See Sutton and Hammond, 7, n. 28 for a mention of the debate surrounding double communion during coronation rituals.

27. See Fortescue, *Commendation on the Laws of England*; Chrimes, *English Constitutional Ideas in the Fifteenth Century*.

28. While there is some debate about the exact date when the legend of the new oil first appears, it is first used for Henry IV's coronation in 1399. On the legend itself see Sandquist; Ullman, "Thomas Becket's Miraculous Oil," 129–33. On the use of the oil in Richard III and Henry VII's coronations, see Sutton and Hammond, 7–12.

29. Horrox, 38–40.

30. For one view of Malory's particular relation to the court culture of Edward IV, see Richard Barber, 133–55. My concern with the version of Malory produced by Caxton's press precludes a more thorough attention to the specificity of Barber's analysis.

31. The relation between national identity and orthodox belief seems a particularly tendentious formulation during the time of the Lollard challenges to both religious and political authority. See Copeland's important analyses of these debates, *Rhetoric, Hermeneutics*; also Copeland, "Rhetoric and Politics of the Literal Sense," 335–57.

32. On such charges against Lollardy, see Taylor, 102.

33. On London's immigrant population, and anxieties about it, during the reign of Henry VI, see Griffiths; for similar information during periods of Yorkist rule, see Lander.

34. Shichtman similarly argues that the Grail quest is politicized, although not for the nation. He reads the semiotic politics of Malory's quest, especially in its depiction of the problems of interpretation the quest poses to Bors and Perceval. Lancelot fails because he does not interpret rightly; Gawain, finally, "exemplifies the frustration of the great majority who, although they are enthusiastic to discover meaning, find instead, ambiguity, confusion, and chaos" (177). See "Policing the Ineffable," *Culture and the King*, ed. Shichtman and Carley, eds.

35. See Theweleit, "The Politics of Orpheus."

Afterword. Lost Books

1. I am suspicious of this account of the comparative (gender) inclusivity of early modern nationhood not least because of the important and longstanding historiographic trajectory established by feminist analysis of the "medieval" and "Renaissance" divide inaugurated by Joan Kelly's incisive claim that women may not have had a "Renaissance."

2. On the desire to recover the past as a failure of mourning, see Fradenburg, "Voice Memorial," "Philology." Biddick, *Shock*.

Bibliography

Abraham, Nicholas, and Maria Torok. "A Poetics of Psychoanalysis: 'The Lost Object—Me.'" *SubStance* 43 (1984): 3–17.

Abu-Lughod, Janet. *Before European Hegemony: The World System A.D. 1250–1350.* New York: Oxford University Press, 1989.

Aers, David. *Community, Gender, and Individual Identity: English Writing, 1360–1430.* New York: Routledge, 1988.

Alcock, Leslie. *Arthur's Britain: History and Archeology A.D. 367–634.* London: Penguin, 1971.

Allan, Allison. "Yorkist Propaganda: Pedigree, Prophecy and the 'British History' in the Reign of Edward IV." *Patronage, Pedigree and Power in Later Medieval England.* Ed. Charles Ross. Totowa, N.J.: Rowman & Littlefield, 1979.

Allen, R. "Some Sceptical Observations on the Editing of *The Awntyrs off Arthure.*" *Manuscripts and Texts.* Ed. D. Pearsall. London: D. S. Brewer, 1987.

Ambrisco, Alan S. "Cannibalism and Cultural Encounters in Richard Coeur de Lion." *Journal of Medieval and Early Modern Studies* 29, no. 3 (1999): 499–528.

Anderson, Benedict. *Imagined Communities: Reflections on the Origin and Spread of Nationalism.* New York: Verso, 1983; reprint 1992.

Anglo, Sydney. "The British History in Early Tudor Propaganda," *Bulletin of the John Rylands Library* 44, no. 1 (1961): 17–48.

——. *Spectacle, Pageantry and Early Tudor Policy.* Oxford: Oxford University Press, 1969.

Ashcroft, Bill, Gareth Griffiths, and Helen Tiffin. *The Post-Colonial Studies Reader.* New York: Routledge, 1995.

Ashe, Geoffrey. *The Discovery of King Arthur.* New York: Doubleday, 1985.

Astell, Ann. "*Sir Gawain and the Green Knight*: A Study in the Rhetoric of Romance." *Journal of English and Germanic Philology* 84 (1985): 188–202.

Atiyah, Aziz. *The Crusades in the Fourteenth and Fifteenth Centuries.* Volume III of *A History of the Crusades.* Madison: University of Wisconsin Press, 1975.

Ball, Martin. "The Knots of Narrative: Space, Time, and Focalization in *Morte Arthure.*" *Exemplaria* 8, no. 2 (Fall 1996): 355–74.

Barber, Malcolm. *The New Knighthood: A History of the Order of the Temple.* Cambridge: Cambridge University Press, 1994.

Barber, Richard. "Malory's *Le Morte Darthur* and Court Culture Under Edward IV." *Arthurian Literature XII.* Ed. James Carley and Felicity Riddy. London: D. S. Brewer, 1994. 133–55.

Barron, W. R. J. *English Medieval Romance*. London: Longmans, 1987.

———. "Arthurian Romance: Traces of an English Tradition." *English Studies: A Journal of English Language and Literature* 61 (1980): 2–23.

Barth, Fredrik, ed. *Ethnic Groups and Boundaries: The Social Organization of Cultural Difference*. Boston: Little, Brown, 1969.

Bartlett, Robert. *The Making of Europe: Conquest, Colonization, and Cultural Change, 950–1350*. Princeton: Princeton University Press, 1993.

Bartlett, Robert, and Angus MacKay. ed. *Medieval Frontier Societies*. Oxford: Clarendon, 1989.

Bataille, Georges. "The Notion of Expenditure." *Visions of Excess: Selected Writings, 1927–1939*. Trans. Allan Stoekl et. al. Minneapolis: University of Minnesota Press, 1985.

Baudier, Michael. *An History of the Memorable and Extraordinary Calamities of Margaret of Anjou, Queen of England*. London: J. Bettenham, 1737.

Beal, Rebecca S. "Arthur as the Bearer of Civilization: The *Alliterative Morte Arthure*, ll. 909–19." *Arthuriana* 5, no. 4 (1995): 32–44.

Bédier, Joseph. *Les Legendes epiques: recherches sur la formation des chansons de geste*. Paris: H. Campion, 1929. 3rd edition.

Beltz, G. F. *Memorials of the Most Noble Order of the Garter*. London: W. Pickering, 1841.

Bennett, Michael J. *Community, Class and Careerism: Cheshire and Lancashire Society in the Age of* Sir Gawain and the Green Knight. Cambridge: Cambridge University Press, 1983.

———. *The Battle of Bosworth*. Gloucester: Alan Sutton, 1985.

Benson, Larry. *Art and Tradition in Sir Gawain and the Green Knight*. New Brunswick, N.J.: Rutgers University Press, 1965.

———. *Malory's Morte Darthur*. Cambridge, Mass.: Harvard University Press, 1976.

Bergner, Heinz. "Two Courts: Two Modes of Existence in *Sir Gawain and the Green Knight*." *English Studies: A Journal of English Language and Literature* 67 (1986): 401–16.

Berlant, Lauren. *Anatomy of a National Fantasy*. Chicago: University of Chicago Press, 1991.

Bernheimer, Richard. *Wild Men in the Middle Ages*. Cambridge, Mass.: Harvard University Press, 1952.

Bersani, Leo. "Foucault, Freud, Fantasy and Power." *GLQ: A Journal of Lesbian and Gay Studies*. 2, nos. 1–2 (1995): 11–33.

Beyles, Alfred, ed. *The Book of the Ordre of Chyualry, translated and printed by William Caxton*. London: EETS, 1926. Kraus Reprints, 1971.

Bhabha, Homi K. "The Other Question: The Stereotype and Colonial Discourse." *Screen* 24, no. 6 (1983): 18–36.

———. "Of Mimicry and Man: The Ambivalence of Colonial Discourse" *October* 28 (1984): 125–33.

———. "DissemiNation: Time, Narrative and the Margins of the Modern Nation." *Nation and Narration*. Ed. Homi Bhabha. London: Routledge, 1990. 291–322.

———. *The Location of Culture*. London: Routledge, 1994.

Biddick, Kathleen. *The Shock of Medievalism*. Durham: Duke University Press, 1998.

———. "The ABC of Ptolemy: Mapping the World with the Alphabet." *Text and Territory*. Ed. Sylvia Tomasch and Sealy Gilles. Philadelphia: University of Pennsylvania Press, 1998. 268–93.

Blanch, Robert L. and Julian Wasserman. "The Medieval Court and the *Gawain* Manuscript." *The Medieval Court in Europe*. Ed. Edward Haymes. Munich: Fink, 1986. 178–88.

Bloch, Maurice. "Death, Women, Power." *Death and the Regeneration of Life*. Ed. Maurice Bloch and Jonathan Parry. Cambridge: Cambridge University Press, 1982.

Bloch, R. Howard. *Medieval Misogyny and the Invention of Western Romantic Love*. Chicago: University of Chicago Press, 1992.

Bracton, Henry de. *De Legibus et Consuetudinibus Angliae*. Northford: Elliot's Books, 1942.

Brengle, R. L., ed. *Arthur King of Britain: History, Romance, Chronicle and Criticism*. New York: Appleton-Century-Crofts, 1964.

Brereton, Geoffrey, ed. and trans. *Froissart's Chronicles*. London: Penguin, 1978.

Brie, Friedrich W. D., ed. *The Middle English Prose Brut*. London: EETS, 1908.

Bromwich, Rachel, ed. and trans. *Armes Prydein*. Medieval and Modern Welsh Series, vol. 6, Dublin: Dublin Institute for Advanced Studies, 1982.

Bromwich, Rachel, ed. *Trioedd Ynys Prydein. The Welsh Triads*. Cardiff: University of Wales Press, 1961.

Bromwich, Rachel, with A. O. H. Jarman and Brynley F. Roberts, eds. *The Arthur of the Welsh: The Arthurian Legend in Medieval Welsh Literature*. Cardiff: University of Wales Press, 1991.

Bronfen, Elisabeth. *Over Her Dead Body: The Configurations of Femininity, Death, and the Aesthetic*. New York: Routledge, 1992.

Bruce, J. D. *The Evolution of Arthurian Romance*. Baltimore: Johns Hopkins University Press, 1928.

Bryan, Elizabeth J. *Collaborative Meaning in Medieval Scribal Culture: The Otho Laȝamon*. Ann Arbor: University of Michigan Press, 1999.

Bullock-Davies, Constance. *Professional Interpreters and the Matter of Britain*. Cardiff: University of Wales Press, 1966.

Burke, Peter, ed. *The Renaissance Sense of the Past*. New York: St Martin's, 1970.

Burns, E. Jane. "Refasioning Courtly Love: Lancelot as Ladies' Man or Lady/Man?" *Constructing Medieval Sexuality*. Ed. Karma Lochrie, Peggy McCracken, and James A. Schultz. Minneapolis: University of Minnesota Press, 1997. 111–34.

Burns, J. H., ed. *The Cambridge History of Medieval Political Thought, c. 350–1450*. Cambridge: Cambridge University Press, 1988.

Butler, Judith. *Gender Trouble: Feminism and the Subversion of Identity*. New York: Routledge, 1990.

———. *Bodies That Matter: On the Discursive Limits of "Sex."* New York: Routledge, 1993.

Carson, Angela. "Morgain la Fee as the Principle of Unity in *Gawain and the Green Knight.*" *Modern Language Quarterly* 23 (1962): 3–16.

Chambers, E. K. *Arthur of Britain*. London: Sidgwick and Jackson, 1927.

Chrimes, S. B., *English Constitutional Ideas in the Fifteenth Century*. Cambridge: Cambridge University Press, 1936.

Cohen, Jeffrey Jerome. "Decapitation and Coming of Age." *The Arthurian Yearbook, III*. Ed. Keith Busby. New York: Garland, 1993. 173–92.

——. "Midcolonial." *The Postcolonial Middle Ages*. Ed. Jeffrey Jerome Cohen. New York: St. Martin's Press, 2000. 1–17.

——. "Hybrids, Monsters, Borderlands: The Bodies of Gerald of Wales." *The Postcolonial Middle Ages*. Ed. Jeffrey Jerome Cohen. New York: St. Martin's Press, 2000. 85–104.

Coleman, Janet. *Ancient and Medieval Memories: Studies in the Reconstruction of the Past*. Cambridge: Cambridge University Press, 1992.

——. *English Literature in History, 1350–1400: Medieval Readers and Writers*. London: Hutchinson, 1983.

Copeland, Rita. *Rhetoric, Hermeneutics, and Translation in the Middle Ages: Academic Traditions and Vernacular Texts*. New York: Cambridge University Press, 1995.

——. "Rhetoric and Politics of the Literal Sense in Medieval Literary Theory: Aquinas, Wyclif, and the Lollards." *Rhetoric and Hermeneutics in Our Time: A Reader*. Ed. Walter Jost and Michael J. Hyde. New Haven: Yale University Press, 1997. 335–57.

Crane, Susan. *Insular Romance: Politics, Faith, and Culture in Anglo-Norman and Middle English Literature*. Berkeley: University of California Press, 1986.

Crick, Julia C. *The Historia regum Britanniae of Geoffrey of Monmouth: Dissemination and Reception in the Later Middle Ages*. Cambridge: D. S. Brewer, 1991.

Curley, Michael J. *Geoffrey of Monmouth*. New York: Twayne, 1994.

Dahood, Roger, ed. *The Avowing of King Arthur*. Garland Medieval Texts 10. New York: Garland, 1984.

Davies, R. R. *Conquest, Coexistence and Change: Wales, 1063–1415*. Oxford: Oxford University Press, 1987.

——. "Frontier Arrangements in Fragmented Societies: Ireland and Wales." *Medieval Frontier Societies*. Ed. Robert Bartlett and Angus MacKay. Oxford: Oxford University Press, 1992. 77–100.

Davis, Kathleen. "National Writing in the Ninth Century: A Reminder for Postcolonial Thinking About the Nation." *Journal of Medieval and Early Modern Studies* 28, no. 3 (Fall 1998): 611–37.

De Certeau, Michel. *The Writing of History*. New York: Columbia University Press, 1992.

De Lauretis, Teresa. *The Practice of Love: Lesbian Sexuality and Perverse Desire*. Bloomington: Indiana University Press, 1994.

——. "The Violence of Rhetoric: Considerations on Representation and Gender." *The Violence of Representation: Literature and the History of Violence*. Ed. Nancy Armstrong and Leonard Tennenhouse. New York: Routledge, 1989. 239–58.

De Rougemont, Denis. *Love in the Western World*. Trans. Montgomery Belgion. Princeton: Princeton University Press, 1983.

Dean, Christopher. *Arthur of England: English Attitudes to King Arthur and the Knights of the Round Table in the Middle Ages and the Renaissance*. Toronto: University of Toronto Press, 1987.

Deleuze, Gilles, and Felix Guattari. *A Thousand Plateaus: Capitalism and Schizophrenia*. Trans. Brian Massumi. Minneapolis: University of Minnesota Press, 1987.

———. *Anti-Oedipus: Capitalism and Schizophrenia*. Trans. Robert Hurley. Minneapolis: University of Minnesota Press, 1983.

Denholm-Young, N., ed. *Vita Edward Secundi*. London: Nelson, 1957.

Dinshaw, Carolyn. "A Kiss Is Just a Kiss: Heterosexuality and its Consolation in *Sir Gawain and the Green Knight*." *diacritics: a review of contemporary criticism* 24 (1994): 205–26.

Dumville, David. *Histories and Pseudo-Histories of the Insular Middle Ages*. Aldershot: Variorum, 1990.

——— "The Manuscripts of Geoffrey of Monmouth's *Historia Regum Britanniae*." *Arthurian Literature*, III, IV, V. Ed. Richard Barber. Woodbridge: Brewer, 1983–85. 113–28; 149–51; 164–71.

Dyboski, R, and Z. M. Arend, eds. *Knyghthode and Bataile: A XVth Century Verse Paraphrase of Falvius Vegetius Renatus' Treatise "De Re Militari."* Oxford: EETS, 1935.

Eckhardt, Caroline D. "Prophecy and Nostalgia: Arthurian Symbolism at the Close of the English Middle Ages." *The Arthurian Tradition*. Ed. Mary Flowers Braswell and John Bugge. Tuscaloosa: University of Alabama Press, 1988. 109–26.

———, ed. *Castleford's Chronicle or The Boke of Brut*. Oxford: Oxford University Press, 1996.

———. "The Figure of Merlin in Middle English Prophecies." *Comparative Studies in Merlin from the Vedas to C. G. Jung*. Ed. James Gollnick. Lewiston, N.Y.: Edwin Mellen Press, 1991. 21–39.

———, ed. *The Prophetia Merlini of Geoffrey of Monmouth: A Fifteenth-Century English Commentary*. Cambridge, Mass.: Medieval Academy of America, 1982.

Edwards, Robert R. *Ratio and Invention: A Study of Medieval Lyric and Narrative*. Nashville: Vanderbilt University Press, 1989.

Elliot, Ralph W. V. *The Gawain Country: Essays on the Topography of Middle English Alliterative Poetry*. Leeds: University of Leeds Press, 1984.

Erlanger, Phillipe. *Margaret of Anjou: Queen of England*. Trans. Edward Hyams. London: Elek Books, 1970.

Faral, Edmond. *La Légende Arthurienne, études et documents*. Paris: Champion, 1929.

Fernandez-Armesto, Felipe. *Before Columbus: Exploration and Colonization from the Mediterranean to the Atlantic, 1229–1492*. Philadelphia: University of Pennsylvania Press, 1987.

Field, P. J. C. *Romance and Chronicle*. London: Barre and Jenkins, 1971.

———. *The Life and Times of Sir Thomas Malory*. Cambridge: D. S. Brewer, 1993.

Field, Rosalind. "The Anglo-Norman Background to Alliterative Romance." *Middle English Alliterative Poetry*. Ed. David Lawton. Cambridge: Cambridge University Press, 1982. 54–69.

Finlayson, John. "Definitions of the Middle English Romance, Parts I and II," *Chaucer Review* 15 (1980): 44–62, 168–81.

Fisher, Sheila. "Taken Men and Token Women in *Sir Gawain and the Green Knight*." *Seeking the Woman in Late Medieval and Renaissance Writing*. Ed. Sheila Fisher and Janet Halley. Knoxville: University of Tennessee Press, 1989. 71–105.

Flenley, Ralph, ed. *Six Town Chronicles of England*. Oxford: Clarendon, 1911.

Foucault, Michel. *Power-Knowledge: Selected Interviews and Other Writings, 1972–1977*. New York: Pantheon Books, 5th ed., 1980.

Fradenburg, Louise Olga. *City, Marriage, Tournament: Arts of Rule in Late-Medieval Scotland*. Madison: University of Wisconsin Press, 1991.

———. "The Manciple's Servant Tongue: Politics and Poetry in *The Canterbury Tales*." *ELH* 52, no. 1 (1985): 85–118.

———. "The Wife of Bath's Passing Fancy." *Studies in the Age of Chaucer* 8 (1986): 31–58.

———. " 'Our owen wo to drynke': Loss, Gender and Chivalry in Troilus and Criseyde." *Chaucer's Troilus and Criseyde "Subgit to alle Poesye": Essays in Criticism*. Ed. R. A. Shoaf and Catherine S. Cox. Binghamton, N.Y.: Medieval and Renaissance Texts and Studies, 1992. 88–106.

———. "Sacrificial Desire in Chaucer's *Knight's Tale*." *Journal of Medieval and Early Modern Studies* (1996):47–75.

———. "Troubled Times: Margaret Tudor and the Historians." *The Thistle and the Rose: Essays on Late Medieval Scottish Culture*. Ed. Sally Mapstone and Juliette Wood. Edinburgh: Tuckwell, 1998. 38–58.

———. "Voice Memorial." *Exemplaria* 2, no. 1 (1990): 169–202.

Fradenburg, Louise Olga, ed. *Women and Sovereignty*. Cosmos 7. Edinburgh: Edinburgh University Press, 1992.

Fradenburg, Louise Olga, with Carla Freccero. "The Pleasures of History." *Premodern Sexualities. GLQ: A Journal of Lesbian and Gay Studies* 1, no. 4 (1995): 371–84.

Frame, Robin. *The Political Development of the British Isles, 1100–1400*. Oxford: Oxford University Press, 1990.

Freud, Sigmund. *The Ego and the Id*. Ed. James Strachey. New York: Norton, 1961.

———. *The Future of an Illusion*. Ed. James Strachey. New York: Norton, 1961.

———. *On Creativity and the Unconscious: Papers on the Psychology of Art, Literature, Love, Religion*. Ed. Benjamin Nelson. New York: Harper, 1958.

———. *Totem and Taboo*. Ed. James Strachey. London: Norton, 1961.

———. "The Uncanny." *On Creativity and the Unconscious: Papers on the Psychology of Art, Literature, Love, Religion*. Ed. Benjamin Nelson. New York: Harper, 1958. 122–61.

Fuss, Diana. *Identification Papers: Readings on Psychoanalytic Sexuality and Culture*. New York: Routledge, 1995.

Gairdner, James, ed. *Letter and Papers of Richard III and Henry VII*, Rolls Series (*Rerum Britannicarum Medii Ævi Scriptores,*), vol. 24, pt. 2. Weisbaden: 1861, Kraus reprint, 1965.

Galbraith, V. H. "Nationality and Language in Medieval England." *Transactions of the Royal Historical Society*, fourth series, XXIII. London: The Society, 1941.

Ganim, John. *Style and Consciousness in Middle English Narrative*. Princeton: Princeton University Press, 1983.

———. "Native Studies: Orientalism and Medievalism." *The Postcolonial Middle Ages*. Ed. Jeffrey Jerome Cohen. New York: St. Martin's Press, 2000. 123–34.

Gates, Jr., Henry Louis, ed. *Race, Writing and Difference*. Chicago: University of Chicago Press, 1986.

Gikandi, Simon. *Maps of Englishness: Writing Identity in the Culture of Colonialism*. New York: Columbia University Press, 1996.

Gillingham, John. *The Wars of the Roses: Peace and Conflict in Fifteenth-Century England*. London: Weidenfeld and Nicolson, 1981.

Giraldus Cambrensis. *Itinerarium Cambriae seu laboriosae Baldvini Cantuariensis Archiepiscopi per Walliam legationis accurata descriptio, auctore Silv. Giraldo Cambrense*. Ed. David Powell. London: Bulmer, 1806.

Given-Wilson, Chris, trans. and ed. *Chronicles of the Revolution, 1397–1400: The Reign of Richard II*. Manchester: Manchester University Press, 1993.

Goldberg, Jonathan. "The History that Will Be." *Premodern Sexualities*, Eds. Louise Fradenburg, Carla Freccero. *GLQ: A Journal of Lesbian and Gay Studies* 1, no. 4 (1995): 385–403.

Goldstein, R. James. *The Matter of Scotland: Historical Narrative in Medieval Scotland*. Lincoln: University of Nebraska Press, 1993.

Goodman, Anthony. *The Wars of the Roses: Military Activity and English Society, 1452–97*. London: Routledge, 1981.

———. *The New Monarchy, England, 1471–1534*. Oxford: Basil Blackwell, 1988.

Goux, Jean-Joseph. "The Phallus: Masculine Identity and the 'Exchange of Women.'" Trans. M. Amuchastegui et. al. *differences: A Journal of Feminist Cultural Studies* 4 (1992): 40–73.

Gower, John. *Confessio Amantis*. Ed. Russell Peck. Toronto: University of Toronto Press, 1981.

Gransden, Antonia. *Historical Writing in England, 550–1307*. 2 vols. Ithaca, N.Y.: Cornell University Press, 1974.

Griffiths, E. M. *Early Welsh Vaticination*. Cardiff: University of Wales Press, 1937.

Griffiths, Ralph A. *The Reign of Henry VI: The Exercise of Royal Authority, 1422–1461*. Berkeley: University of California Press, 1981.

———. "The Trial of Eleanor Cobham: An Episode in the Fall of Duke Humphrey of Gloucester." *King and Country: England and Wales in the Fifteenth Century*. London: Hambledon Press, 1991, 233–52.

Grigor, Francis, ed. *Sir John Fortescue's Commendation of the Laws of England*. London: Sweet and Maxwell, 1917.

Griscom, Acton, ed. *The Historia Regum Britanniae of Geoffrey of Monmouth*. London: Longmans, 1929.

Gruffydd, W. J. *Rhiannon: An Inquiry into the Origins of the First and Third Branches of the* Mabinogi. Cardiff: University of Wales Press, 1953.

Gutiérrez, Ramón. "The Erotic Zone: Sexual Transgression on the U.S.-Mexican Border." *Mapping Multiculturalism*. Ed. Avery F. Gordon and Christopher Newfield. Minneapolis: University of Minnesota Press, 1996. 253–62.

Haidu, Peter. "Romance: Idealistic Genre or Historical Text?" *The Craft of Fic-*

tion: Essays in Medieval Poetics. Ed. Leigh A. Arrathoon. Rochester, Michigan: Solaris, 1984. 1–46.

Halliwell, J. O., ed. *The Voiage and Travaile of Sir John Maundeville, Kt. Which treateth of the Way of Hierusalem; And of Marvayles of Inde, with Other Ilands and Contryes,* reprinted from the edition of 1725. London: Edward Lumley, 1839.

Hamel, Mary, ed. *Morte Arthure: A Critical Edition.* New York: Garland, 1984.

Hammer, Jacob. *Historia regum Britanniae. A variant version edited from manuscripts by Jacob Hammer.* Cambridge, Mass.: Medieval Academy of America, 1951.

Hanna, Ralph, ed. *The Awntyrs of Arthure at the Terne Wathelyn.* Manchester: Manchester University Press, 1974.

Hanning, Robert. *The Vision of History in Early Britain.* New York: Columbia University Press, 1966.

Hartung, A. E., ed. *The Manual of Writings in Middle English.* Vol. 8, *Chronicles and Other Historical Writing.* Ed. Edward Donald Kennedy. New Haven: Connecticut Academy of Arts and Sciences, 1989.

Haswell, Jock. *The Ardent Queen: Margaret of Anjou and the Lancastrian Heritage.* London: Peter Davies, 1976.

Hechter, Michael. *Internal Colonialism: The Celtic Fringe in British National Development 1536–1966.* Berkeley: University of California Press, 1975.

Helgerson, Richard. *Forms of Nationhood: The Elizabethan Writing of England.* Chicago: University of Chicago Press, 1992.

Heng, Geraldine. "Feminine Knots and the Other *Sir Gawain and the Green Knight.*" *PMLA* 106, no. 3 (1991): 500–514.

———. "Cannibalism, the First Crusade, and the Genesis of Medieval Romance." *differences: A Journal of Feminist Cultural Studies* 10, no. 1 (1998): 98–174.

———. "A Woman Wants: The Lady, *Gawain,* and the Forms of Seduction." *Yale Journal of Criticism* 5, no. 3 (1992): 101–34.

Higden, Ranulf. *Polychronicon: Middle English & Latin.* Trans. John Trevisa. London: Longman, 1886.

Hissiger, P. F., ed. *Le Morte Arthur: A Critical Edition.* Paris: Mouton, 1975.

Horrox, Rosemary. "Richard III and Allhallows Barking by the Tower." *The Ricardian* 5, no. 77 (1982): 38–40.

Ingham, Patricia Clare. "Homosociality and Creative Masculinity in the *Knight's Tale.*" *Masculinities in Chaucer: Approaches to Maleness in the Canterbury Tales and Troilus and Criseyde.* Ed. Peter G. Beidler. Cambridge: D. S. Brewer, 1998. 23–35.

———. "'In Contrayez Straunge': Colonial Relations, British Identity, and *Sir Gawain and the Green Knight.*" *New Medieval Literatures* 4 (2000), 61–93.

———. "Masculine Military Unions: Brotherhood and Rivalry *in The Avowing of King Arthur.*" *Arthuriana* 6, no. 4 (1996). 25–44.

———. "Marking Time: 'Branwen, Daughter of Llyr' and the Colonial Refrain." *The Postcolonial Middle Ages.* Ed. Jeffrey Jerome Cohen. New York: St. Martin's Press, 2000. 173–91.

Ingledew, Francis. "The Book of Troy and the Genealogical Construction of

History: The Case of Geoffrey of Monmouth's *Historia regum Britanniae*,"
Speculum 69, no. 3 (1994): 665–704.

Irigaray, Luce. *The Sex Which Is Not One*. Trans. Catherine Porter with Carolyn
Burke. Ithaca, N.Y.: Cornell University Press, 1985.

James, Mervyn. *English Politics and the Concept of Honour, 1485-1642*. Oxford: Past
and Present Society, 1978.

Jameson, Fredric. *The Political Unconscious: Narrative as a Socially Symbolic Act*.
Ithaca, N.Y.: Cornell University Press, 1981.

———. *Postmodernism or, The Cultural Logic of Late Capitalism*. Durham, N.C.:
Duke University Press, 1991.

———. "Imaginary and Symbolic in Lacan: Marxism, Psychoanalytic Criticism,
and the Problem of the Subject." *Literature and Psychoanalysis*. Ed. Shoshana
Felman. Baltimore: John Hopkins University Press, 1982.

———. "Magical Narratives: Romance as Genre." *New Literary History* 7 (1975):
135–63.

Jarman, A. O. H. "The Merlin Legend and Welsh." *The Arthur of the Welsh*. Ed.
Rachel Bromwich with A. O. H. Jarman and Brynley F. Roberts. Cardiff:
University of Wales Press, 1991.

Jennings, Margaret. "Heavens Defend Me From That Welsh Fairy: The Metamorphosis of Morgain la Fée in the Romances." *Court and Poet: Selected Proceedings
of the Third Congress of the International Courtly Literature Society*. Ed. Glyn S.
Burgess et al. Liverpool: Cairns, 1981. 197–205.

Jones, Ann Rosalind, and Peter Stallybrass. "Dismantling Irena: The Sexualizing
of Ireland in Early Modern England." *Nationalisms and Sexualities*. Ed. Parker
et al. New York: Routledge, 1992. 157–71.

Jones, Frances. *The Princes and Principality of Wales*. Cardiff: University of Wales
Press, 1969.

Jones, Gwyn. "Introduction." *Arthurian Chronicles: Wace and Layamon*. Trans.
Eugene Mason. Toronto: University of Toronto Press, 1996.

Jones, Gwyn, and Thomas Jones, eds. *The Mabinogion*. London: Everyman, 1979;
reprint. 1989.

Justice, Stephen. *Writing and Rebellion: England in 1381*. Berkeley: University of
California Press, 1994.

Kantorowicz, Ernst H. *The King's Two Bodies: A Study in Mediaeval Political Theology*. Princeton: Princeton University Press, 1957.

Keeler, Laura. *Geoffrey of Monmouth and the Late Latin Chronicles, 1300–1500*. Berkeley: University of California Press, 1946.

Keen, M. H. *England in the Later Middle Ages*. London: Methuen, 1973.

———. *English Society in the Later Middle Ages: 1348–1500*. London: Penguin, 1990.

Kelly, Kathleen Coyne. "Malory's Body Chivalric." *Arthuriana* 6, no. 4 (1996):
52–71.

Kennedy, Beverly. *Knighthood in the* Morte D'Arthur. London: D. S. Brewer, 1985.

Kingsford, Charles. *English Historical Literature in the Fifteenth Century*. Oxford:
Clarendon, 1913.

Knight, Stephen. *Arthurian Literature and Society*. London: Macmillian, 1983.

Kristeva, Julia. *Black Sun: Melancholia and Depression*. Trans. Leon S. Roudiez. New York: Columbia University Press, 1989.

———. *Strangers to Ourselves*. Trans. Leon S. Roudiez. New York: Columbia University Press, 1991.

Kruger, Stephen. "The Spectral Jew," *New Medieval Literatures* 2 (1998): 9–35.

Kuskin, William. "Caxton's Worthies Series: The Production of Literary Culture." *ELH* 66, no. 3 (1999): 511–51.

Lacan, Jacques. *Ecrits: A Selection*. Trans. Alan Sheridan. New York: Norton, 1982.

———. *Feminine Sexuality: Jacques Lacan and the École Freudienne*. Ed. Juliette Mitchell and Jacqueline Rose. New York: Norton, 1982.

Lander, J. R. *Conflict and Stability in Fifteenth-Century England*. 3rd ed. London: Hutchinson, 1977.

———. *Crown and Nobility, 1450–1509*. London: Edward Arnold, 1976.

Laqueur, Thomas. *Making Sex: Body and Gender from the Greeks to Freud*. Cambridge: Harvard University Press, 1990.

Lawton, David ed. *Middle English Alliterative Poetry*. Cambridge: Cambridge University Press, 1982.

———. "The Surveying Subject and the 'Whole World' of Belief: Three Case Studies," New Medieval Literatures 4 (2000) forthcoming.

Lloyd-Morgan, Ceridwen. "Continuity and Change in the Transmission of Arthurian Material: Later Medieval Wales and the Continent." *Actes du 14eme Congres International Arthurien*. (1984): 397–405.

Loades, D. M. *Politics and the Nation, 1450–1660*. Brighton: Harvester, 1974.

Loomis, Laura Hibbard. *Adventures in the Middle Ages*. New York: Burt Franklin, 1962.

Loomis, R. S. *Celtic Myth and Arthurian Romance*. New York: Columbia University Press, 1926.

———. *Wales and the Arthurian Legend*. Cardiff: University of Wales Press, 1956.

Lupton, Julia Reinhard. *Afterlives of the Saints: Hagiography, Typology, and Renaissance Literature*. Stanford, Calif.: Stanford University Press, 1996.

Lyle, Guy Fitch, and Stephen Orgel, eds. *Patronage in the Renaissance*. Princeton: Princeton University Press, 1981.

Malmesbury, William of. *Gesta Regum Anglorum. Rerum Britanicarum Medii Ævi Scriptores*, vol. 90, no. 1. Ed. William Stubbs. London, 1887, Kraus Reprint, 1964.

Mann, Jill. "'Taking the Adventure': Malory and the Suite du Merlin." *Aspects of Malory*. Ed. Toskiyuki Takamiya and Derek Brewer. Cambridge: D. S. Brewer, 1981. 71–91.

Marcuse, Herbert. "The Ideology of Death." *The Meaning of Death*. Ed. Herman Feifel. New York: McGraw-Hill, 1959. 64–76.

Matheson Lister. "Historical Prose." *Middle English Prose: A Critical Guide to Major Authors and Genres*. Ed. A. S. G. Edwards. New Brunswick, N.J.: Rutgers University Press, 1984. 209–48.

———. "King Arthur and the Medieval English Chronicles." *King Arthur Through the Ages*. Vol 1. Ed. Valerie Lagorio and Mildred Leake Day. New York: Garland, 1990. 248–74.

————. "Printer and Scribe: Caxton, the *Polychronicon*, and the *Brut.*" *Speculum* 60, no. 3 (1985): 593–614.

Matsuda, Takami. "The *Awntrys off Arthure* and the Arthurian History." *Poetica 19* (1984): 48–62.

Matthews, William. *The Tragedy of Arthur: A Study of the Alliterative Morte Arthure*. Berkeley: University of California Press, 1960.

Maynard, Mary, and Jalna Hanmer, eds. *Women, Violence and Social Control*. London: British Sociological Association, 1987; Humanities Press International Reprint, 1990.

McCarthy, Terence. *Reading the Morte Darthur*. Cambridge: Brewer, 1988.

McClintock Anne, Aamir Mufti, and Ella Shohat, eds. *Dangerous Liaisons: Gender, Nation and Postcolonial Perspectives*. Minneapolis: University of Minnesota Press, 1997.

Meale, Carol. "'The Hoole Book': Editing and the Creation of Meaning in Malory's Text." *A Companion to Malory*. Ed. Elizabeth Archibald and A. S. G. Edwards. Woodbridge, Suffolk: D. S. Brewer, 1996. 3–17.

Mills, Maldwyn, ed., "Introduction." *Yvain and Gawain, Sir Percyvell of Gales, The Anturs of Arthur*. London: J. M. Dent, 1992.

Mills, Maldwyn, Jennifer Fellows, and Carol Meale, eds. *Romance in Medieval England*. Cambridge: D. S. Brewer, 1991.

Moody, Patricia A. "The Childgered Arthur of *Sir Gawain and the Green Knight.*" *SMC* 8–9 (1976): 173–86.

Moon, Douglas. "The Role of Morgan la Fee in *Sir Gawain and the Green Knight.*" *Neuphilologische Mitteilungen* 67 (1966): 31–57.

Morse, Ruth. *Truth and Convention in the Middle Ages*. Cambridge: Cambridge University Press, 1990.

Nicholas, Sir N. H., and E. Tyrell, eds. *A Chronicle of London, from 1089 to 1483, written in the fifteenth century*. London: Longman, Rees, 1827.

Nicholls, Jonathan. *The Matter of Courtesy: Medieval Courtesy Books and the Gawain-Poet*. Woodbridge, Suffolk: D. S. Brewer, 1985.

Orgel, Stephen. *The Illusion of Power: Political Theater in the English Renaissance*. Berkeley: University of California Press, 1991.

Otter, Monika. "'Gaainable Tere': Symbolic Appropriation of Space and Time in Geoffrey of Monmouth and Vernacular Historical Writing." *Discovering New Worlds: Essays on Medieval Exploration and Imagination*. Ed. Scott D. Westrem. New York: Garland, 1991. 157–77.

————. *Inventiones: Fiction and Referentiality in Twelfth-Century English Historical Writing*. Chapel Hill, N.C.: University of North Carolina Press, 1996.

Parker, Andrew, with Mary Russo, Doris Sommer and Patricia Yaeger, eds. *Nationalisms and Sexualities*. New York: Routledge, 1992.

Parry, Benita. "Problems in Current Theories of Colonial Discourse." *The Post-Colonial Studies Reader*. Ed. Bill Ashcroft, Gareth Griffiths, and Helen Triffin. New York: Routledge, 1997. 36–44.

————. "Resistance Theory/ Theorising Resistance, or Two Cheers for Nativism." *Colonial Discourse/ Postcolonial Theory*. Ed. Francis Barker, Peter Hulme, and Margaret Iversen. Manchester: Manchester University Press, 1994. 172–96.

Partner, Nancy. *Serious Entertainments: The Writing of History in Twelfth-Century England*. Chicago: University of Chicago Press, 1977.

Partner, Peter. *The Murdered Magicians: The Templars and Their Myth*. Oxford: Oxford University Press, 1982.

Patterson, Lee. *Negotiating the Past: The Historical Understanding of Medieval History*. Madison: University of Wisconsin Press, 1987.

———. *Chaucer and the Subject of History*. Madison: University of Wisconsin Press, 1991.

———. "The Historiography of Romance and the Alliterative *Morte Arthure.*" *Journal of Medieval and Renaissance Studies* 13, no. 1 (1983): 1–32.

———. "Literary History." *Critical Terms for Literary Study*. Ed. Frank Lentricchia and Thomas McLaughlin. Chicago: University of Chicago Press, 1995.

Peck, Russell, ed. *John Gower's* Confessio Amantis. Toronto: University of Toronto Press, 1980.

Phillips, Helen. "Introduction." *The Awntyrs off Arthure at the Terne Wathelyne: Modern Spelling Edition*. Lancaster: University of Lancaster Press, 1988.

Pochoda, Elizabeth T. *Arthurian Propaganda*: Le Morte Darthur *as an Historical Ideal of Life*. Chapel Hill, N. C.: University of North Carolina Press, 1971.

Pollard, A. J. "Ideas, Principles and Politics." *The Wars of the Roses*. Ed. A. J. Pollard. New York: St. Martin's, 1995. 110–33.

Prakash, Gyan. "The Modern Nation's Return in the Archaic." *Critical Inquiry* 23, no. 3 (1997): 536–56.

Ramsey, Lee C. *Chivalric Romances: Popular Literature in Medieval England*. Bloomington: Indiana University Press, 1983.

Rees, David. *The Son of Prophecy: Henry Tudor's Road to Bosworth*. London: Black Raven Press, 1985.

Rees, William, ed. *Calendar of Ancient Petitions Relating to Wales*. History and Law Series, XXVIII. Cardiff: University of Wales Press, 1975.

Reynolds, Susan. *Kingdoms and Communities in Western Europe: 900–1300*. Oxford: Oxford University Press, 1997.

Rhys, John, and J. Gwenogvryn Evans, eds. *The Red Book of Hergest*. Oxford: Clarendon, 1887.

Richmond, Velma Bourgeois. *The Popularity of the Middle English Romance*. Bowling Green, Ohio: Bowling Green University Press, 1975.

Riddy, Felicity. *Sir Thomas Malory*. New York: E. J. Brill, 1987.

———. "Contextualizing Le Morte Darthur: Empire and Civil War." *A Companion to Malory*. Ed. Elizabeth Archibald and A. S. G. Edwards. Woodbridge, Suffolk: D. S. Brewer, 1996. 55–73.

Roberts, Brynley F. "The *Historia Regum Britanniae* in Wales." *Brut Y Brenhinedd*. Ed. Brynley F. Roberts. Dublin: Dublin Institute for Advanced Studies, 1984.

———. "Writing in Wales." *The Cambridge History of Medieval English Literature*. Ed. David Wallace. Cambridge: Cambridge University Press, 1999. 182–207.

———. "Geoffrey of Monmouth's *Historia Regum Britanniae* and *Brut Y Brenhinedd.*" *The Arthur of the Welsh*. Ed. Bromwich et al. Cardiff: University of Wales Press, 1991. 97–116.

Ross, C. D. *The Wars of the Roses: A Concise History*. London: Thames and Hudson, 1976.

Rubin, Gayle. "The Traffic in Women: Notes Toward a Political Economy of Sex." *Toward an Anthropology of Women*. Ed. Rayna Reiter. New York: Monthly Review Press, 1975. 157–210.

Sandquist, T. A. "The Holy Oil of St Thomas of Canterbury." *Essays in Medieval History Presented to Bertie Wilkinson*. Ed. T. A. Sandquist and M. R. Powicke. Toronto: University of Toronto Press, 1969.

Scarry, Elaine. *The Body in Pain: The Making and Unmaking of the World*. New York: Oxford University Press, 1985.

Scattergood, V. J. *Politics and Poetry in the Fifteenth Century: 1399–1485*. London: Blandford Press, 1971.

Scott, Joan W. "The Evidence of Experience." *Critical Inquiry* 17 (1991): 773–97.

Sedgwick, Eve K. *Between Men: English Literature and Male Homosocial Desire*. New York: Columbia University Press, 1985.

Shichtman, Martin, and James Carley, eds. *Culture and the King: The Social Implications of the Arthurian Legend*. Albany: State University of New York Press, 1994.

Shichtman, Martin, and Laurie Finke. "Profiting from the Past: History as Symbolic Capital in the *Historia regum Britanniae*." *Arthurian Literature XII*. Ed. James Carley and Felicity Riddy. London: D. S. Brewer, 1994. 1–35.

Simpson, James. "Ageism: Leland, Bale, and the Laborious Start of English Literary History, 1350–1550." *New Medieval Literatures* 1 (1997): 213–35.

Skidmore, Ian. *Owain Glyndwr*. Woodstock: Beekman Publishers, reprint, 1996.

Smallwood, T. M. "The Prophecy of the Six Kings." *Speculum* 60, no. 3 (1985): 571–92.

Smith, Barbara Herrnstein. "Belief and Resistance: A Symmetrical Account." *Critical Inquiry* 18 (1991): 125–39.

Southern, R. W. "Aspects of the European Tradition of Historical Writing: The History of Prophecy." *Transactions of the Royal Historical Society*, Fifth Series 22 (1972): 159–80.

Spearing, A. C. "The Gawain-poet's Sense of an Ending." *Readings in Medieval Poetry*. Cambridge: Cambridge University Press, 1987. 195–215.

———. *Medieval to Renaissance in English Poetry*. Cambridge: Cambridge University Press, 1985.

———. "Central and Displaced Sovereignty in Three Medieval Poems." *Review of English Studies* 33 (1982): 247–61.

———. "The *Awntyrs off Arthure*." *The Alliterative Tradition in the Fourteenth Century*. Ed. Bernard S. Levy and Paul E. Szarmach. Kent, Ohio: Kent State University Press, 1981. 183–202.

Spiegel, Gabrielle. *Romancing the Past*. Berkeley: University of California Press, 1995.

———. "History, Historicism, and the Social Logic of the Text in the Middle Ages." *Speculum*, 65, no. 1 (1990): 59–86.

Spisak, James, and William Matthews, eds. *Caxton's Malory: A New Edition of*

Sir Thomas Malory's Le Morte Darthur based on the Pierpont Morgan Copy of William Caxton's edition of 1485. Berkeley: University of California Press, 1983.

Stanbury, Sarah. *Seeing the Gawain-Poet: Description and the Act of Perception*. Philadelphia: University of Pennsylvania Press, 1991.

Stein, Robert M. "Making History English: Cultural Identity and Historical Explanation in William of Malmesbury and Laʒamon's *Brut.*" *Text and Territory*. Ed. Sylvia Tomasch and Sealy Gilles. Philadelphia: University of Pennsylvania Press, 1998. 97–115.

———. "The Trouble with Harold: The Ideological Context of the *Vita Haroldi.*" *New Medieval Literatures* 2 (1998): 181–204.

Stone, Brian. *King Arthur's Death: Morte Arthure, Le Morte Arthur*. London: Penguin Books, 1988.

Storey, R. L. *The End of the House of Lancaster*. London: Barrie and Rockliff, 1966.

———. "Lincolnshire and the Wars of the Roses." *Nottingham Medieval Studies* 14 (1970): 64–82.

Stowe, John. *Annales, or Generall Chronicle of England*. With continuation by Edmund Howes. London, 1631.

Strayer, Joseph. *On the Medieval Origins of the Modern State*. Princeton: Princeton University Press, 1970.

Strohm, Paul. *Hochon's Arrow: The Social Imagination of Fourteenth Century Texts*. Princeton: Princeton University Press, 1992.

———. "Middle English Narrative Genres." *Genre* 13 (1980): 379–88.

———. "The Origin and Meaning of Middle English Romance." *Genre* 10 (1977): 1–28.

Suleri, Sara. *The Rhetoric of English India*. Chicago: University of Chicago Press, 1992.

Summit, Jennifer. "William Caxton, Margaret Beaufort and the Romance of Female Patronage." *Women, the Book and the Worldly, vol. II*. Ed. Lesley Smith and Jane H. M. Taylor. Cambridge: D. S. Brewer, 1995. 151–65.

Sutton, Anne F. and P. W. Hammond, eds. *The Coronation of Richard III: The Extant Documents*. New York: St. Martin's, 1984.

Tatlock, J. S. P. *The Legendary History of Britain: Geoffrey of Monmouth's Historia regum Britanniae and its Early Vernacular Versions*. Berkeley: University of California Press, 1950.

Taussig, Michael. *Mimesis and Alterity: A Particular History of the Senses*. New York: Routledge, 1993.

Taylor, Rupert. *The Political Prophecy in England*. New York: Columbia University Press, 1911.

Theweleit, Klaus. *Male Fantasies, Vol I: Women, Floods, Bodies, History*. Minneapolis: University of Minnesota Press, 1987.

———. "The Politics of Orpheus: Between Women, Hades, Political Power and the Media." *New German Critique* 36 (1985): 133–56.

Thomas, A. H., and I. D. Thornley, eds. *The Great Chronicle of London*. London: George Jones, 1938.

Thompson, Edward Maunde, ed. and trans. *The Chronicle of Adam of Usk (A.D. 1377–1421)*. Felinfach: Llanerch Enterprises, 1990.

Thompson, Leonard. *The Political Mythology of Apartheid*. New Haven: Yale University Press, 1986.

Thomson, Derek S. *Branwen Uerch Lyr*, Medieval and Modern Welsh Series. Vol. II. Dublin: Dublin Institute of Advanced Studies, 1961.

Thomson, John A. F. *The Transformation of Medieval England: 1370–1529*. London: Longmans, 1983.

Thorpe, Lewis, ed. and trans. *History of the Kings of Britain*. London: Penguin, 1966. reprint. 1979.

———. *Gerald of Wales: The Journey through Wales and The Description of Wales*. London: Penguin, 1978.

Tipton, C. Leon, ed. *Nationalism in the Middle Ages*. New York: Holt, Rinehart & Winston, 1972.

Tolkien, J. R. R., and E. V. Gordon, eds. *Sir Gawain and the Green Knight*. 2nd ed. Ed. Norman Davis. Oxford: Clarendon, 1967.

Tomasch, Sylvia. "Judecca, Dante's Satan, and the Dis-placed Jew." *Text and Territory*. Ed. Sylvia Tomasch and Sealy Gilles. Philadelphia: University of Pennsylvania Press, 1998. 247–67.

Tomasch, Sylvia and Sealy Gilles, eds. *Text and Territory: Geographical Imagination in the European Middle Ages*. Philadelphia: University of Pennsylvania Press, 1998.

Turner, Victor. *The Ritual Process: Structure and Anti-Structure*. Ithaca N. Y.: Cornell University Press, 1977.

Turville-Petre, Thorlac. *England the Nation: Language, Literature, and National Identity, 1290–1340*. Oxford: Clarendon Press, 1996.

Tuve, Rosemond. *Allegorical Imagery: Some Medieval Books and Their Posterity*. Princeton: Princeton University Press, 1966.

Ullman, Walter. "Thomas Becket's Miraculous Oil." *Journal of Theological Studies* 8 (1957): 129–33.

Vickers, K. H. *Humphrey, Duke of Gloucester*. London: Constable, 1907.

Viswanathan, Gauri. "Raymond Williams and British Colonialism." *Cultural Materialism: On Raymond Williams*. Ed. Christopher Prendergast. Minneapolis: University of Minnesota Press, 1995. 188–210.

———. *Outside the Fold: Conversion, Modernity, and Belief*. Princeton: Princeton University Press, 1998.

Wack, Mary. *Lovesickness in the Middle Ages*. Philadelphia: University of Pennsylvania Press, 1990.

Walker, David. *Medieval Wales*. Cambridge: Cambridge University Press, 1990.

———. "Cultural Survival in an Age of Conquest." *Welsh Society and Nationhood*. Ed. R. R. Davies, et al. Cardiff: University of Wales Press, 1984. 35–50.

Wallace, David. *Chaucerian Polity: Absolutist Lineages and Associational Forms in England and Italy*. Stanford: Stanford University Press, 1997.

Wallace, David, ed. *The Cambridge History of Medieval English Literature*. Cambridge: Cambridge University Press, 1999.

Warner, Marina. *Alone of All Her Sex: The Myth and the Cult of the Virgin Mary*. New York: Vintage, 1983.

Warren, Michelle R. *History on the Edge: Excalibur and the Borders of Britain, 1100–1300*. Minneapolis: University of Minnesota Press, 2000.

Waswo, Richard. "The History that Literature Makes." *New Literary History* 19, no. 3 (1988): 541–64.

Watkin, Morgan. *La Civilisation Française dans les Mabinogion*. Paris: Didier, 1962.

Weston, Jessie L. *From Ritual to Romance*. Cambridge: Cambridge University Press, 1920.

Wheeler, Bonnie. "Romance and Parataxis and Malory: The Case of Sir Gawain's Reputation." *Arthurian Literature XII*. Ed. James Carley and Felicity Riddy. London: D. S. Brewer, 1994. 109–32.

White, Hayden. *The Content of the Form*. Baltimore: Johns Hopkins University Press, 1987.

———. "The Historical Text as Literary Artifact." *Clio* 3 (1974): 277–303, reprinted in *The Tropics of Discourse: Essays in Cultural Criticism*. Baltimore: Johns Hopkins University Press, 1978.

———. *Metahistory: The Historical Imagination in Nineteenth-Century Europe*. Baltimore: Johns Hopkins University Press, 1974.

Williams, Glanmor. "Prophecy, Poetry, and Politics in Medieval and Tudor Wales." *British Government and Administration: Studies Presented to S. B. Chrimes*. Ed. H. Hearder and H. R. Loyn. Cardiff: University of Wales Press, 1974.

Wood, Charles. "The First Two Queen Elizabeth, 1464–1503." *Women and Sovereignty*. Ed. Louise Fradenburg. Edinburgh: Edinburgh University Press, 1992. 121–31.

Wright, T., ed. *Political Poems and Songs, vol. II*. Rolls Series. *Rerum Britannicarum Medii Ævi Scriptores* vol. 14. London: 1859, Kraus Reprint, 1965.

Young, Robert. *Colonial Desire: Hybridity in Theory, Culture and Race*. New York: Routledge, 1995.

Žižek, Slavoj. "Eastern Europe's Republics of Gilead." *New Left Review* 183 (October 1990): 50–62.

———. *Looking Awry: An Introduction to Jacques Lacan Through Popular Culture*. Cambridge, Mass.: MIT Press, 1991.

———. *The Sublime Object of Ideology*. New York: Verso, 1989.

Zumthor, Paul. *Merlin le prophète: Un thème de la littérature polèmique de l'historiographie et des romans*. Lausanne: Imprimeries Reunies, 1943.

Index

Acknowledgments

A T the University of California at Santa Barbara, I had the careful guidance of Louise O. Fradenburg, Carol Braun Pasternack, Julie Carlson, and Richard Helgerson. The intellectual inspiration of Julee Raiskin and Richard Corum was also crucial in those days. I have enjoyed the counsel and encouragement of Kathleen Biddick, Jeffrey Jerome Cohen, Rita Copeland, Kathleen Davis, Tom Hahn, Ruth Mazo Karras, Peggy Knapp, Marshall Leicester, Elizabeth Scala, Larry Scanlon, Wendy Scase, Robert L. Stein, Sylvia Tomasch, Peter Travis, Gauri Viswanathan, Robert Young, and Michelle Warren. The generous and incisive readers' reports that David Lawton and Susan Crane provided for the University of Pennsylvania Press had the double effect of improving both the manuscript and my spirits immeasurably, for which I am most grateful. Portions of the manuscript were researched and written with the financial support of the Graduate Division, University of California, Santa Barbara, and the Paul Franz and Class of 1968 Junior Faculty Fellowships at Lehigh University. My colleagues at Lehigh have been both patient with my prose and generous with suggestions. I wish to thank Peter G. Beidler, Alex Doty, Mary Jo Haronian, Dawn Keetley, Rosemary Mundhenk, Barbara Pavlok, and most notably Scott Gordon, David Hawkes, and Barbara Traister. A special word must be reserved for my marvelous champion, Jan Fergus, who generously read everything more than once, offered suggestions, and cheered me on. Thanks also to research assistants Tracey Cummings, tireless in her attention to the details, and Miriamne Krummel, whose generous and speedy help came at just the right moment. I owe a debt to the excellent staffs of the Interlibrary Loan departments at both UC Santa Barbara and Lehigh University. Many thanks go as well to the University of Pennsylvania Press, most especially to humanities editor Jerome Singerman.

I wish to acknowledge colleagues from my Santa Barbara days. Rachel Adams, Rachel Borup, Jon Connolly, Parker Douglas, Rebecca Douglass,

Eileen Fung, Julia Garrett, Janice Grossman, Simon Hunt, Kathy Lavezzo, Shannon Miller, Nancy Plooster, Amy Rabbino, and Mark Schlenz may or may not recognize the ways that they helped the argument in this book. I continue to add to my debts from those days, thanks to continued friendship and counsel from the amazing Madelyn Detloff (who said exactly the right thing at precisely the right moment) and the compassionate Bettina Caluori.

My love and gratitude go to the friends and family who have helped me keep things in perspective: my sisters Mary Beth Ingham (ever helpful with Latin) and Sheila Waddington (hospitable and encouraging from Birmingham to Oxford and Aberwystwyth); the hilarious Waddingtons: Clare, Hugh, Katie, Anna, and Megan; my brother, Jerry (Nicholas) Ingham (giver of my first book on King Arthur); my silly sister, Corinne Dempsey; Nick, Jack, and Sam Dempsey Garigliano; Bettina, Paul, and Nava Caluori; John and Lois Moore; and Suzie Knapp. To Doug Moore whose contributions to this project, material and emotional, are too many to list, I remain grateful for his generosity, and for his unfailing belief that what I do matters. My parents did not live long enough to see this book, but my mother's passion for education and my father's creativity are, I hope, legible in its pages. The circumstances of their lives made college impossible for them; their sacrifices and commitments made that and so much more possible for me. I dedicate this book in their memory. But I also dedicate this book to my astonishing teacher, mentor, and friend Louise Fradenburg. Her inspiration, intellectual generosity, unflagging friendship, and ambitious imagination has helped me to believe in, and thus to reclaim, my own desires for medieval studies. Thanks to her I have been able to think the unthinkable, often in the details of this study but always in the very fact of its existence.